THE BODY
IN THE
RESERVOIR

The
BODY
in the Reservoir

MURDER & SENSATIONALISM
IN THE SOUTH

MICHAEL AYERS TROTTI

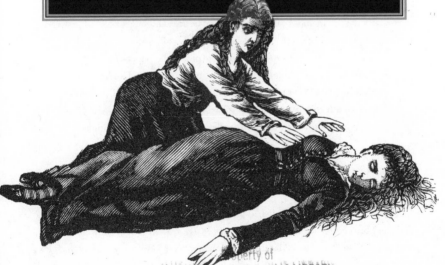

The University of North Carolina Press *Chapel Hill*

Set in Monticello and Smokler types

by Tseng Information Systems, Inc.

Manufactured in the United States of America

The paper in this book meets the guidelines for permanence and
durability of the Committee on Production Guidelines for Book Longevity
of the Council on Library Resources.

Library of Congress Cataloging-in-Publication Data

Trotti, Michael Ayers.

The body in the reservoir : murder and sensationalism in the South /
by Michael Ayers Trotti.

p. cm.

Includes bibliographical references and index.

ISBN 978-0-8078-3178-6 (cloth : alk. paper)

ISBN 978-0-8078-5842-4 (pbk. : alk. paper)

1. Sensationalism in journalism—Virginia—Richmond—History—
19th century. 2. Sensationalism in journalism—Virginia—Richmond—
History—20th century. 3. Murder—Press coverage—Virginia—Richmond
—History—19th century. 4. Murder—Press coverage—Virginia—
Richmond—History—20th century. I. Title.

PN4899.R54T76 2008

071.455'451—dc22   2007044720

Parts of chapter 4 were published in "Jim Crow Justice, the *Richmond Planet*,
and the Murder of Lucy Pollard," in *Murder on Trial, 1620-2002*, ed. Robert Asher,
Lawrence B. Goodheart, and Alan Rogers (Albany: State University of New York Press,
2005). Parts of chapter 5 were published in "Murder Made Real: The Visual Revolution
of the Halftone," *Virginia Magazine of History and Biography* III, no. 4 (2003):
379–410. Used with permission.

12 11 10 09 08   5 4 3 2 1

CONTENTS

FIGURES

ACKNOWLEDGMENTS

I have received scholarly, technical, financial, professional, and even emotional assistance at every turn in the road of this project. As much as it is my work, this book is also the product of the ferment I found among my colleagues in Chapel Hill and my colleagues in the Chapterhouse Beer and History writing group in Ithaca. The faults belong to me, but the book is much better than I could have made it due to the help I received from so many sources.

Fellowship support for this project came from the National Endowment for the Humanities (NEH), the Virginia Historical Society, the Mellon Foundation, Ithaca College (IC), and the history department and graduate school of the University of North Carolina at Chapel Hill. The State of North Carolina provided an institution of learning with tuition costs low enough to allow people without much in the way of means to receive a world-class education. The federal government helped with loan subsidies and Earned Income Tax Credits. Summer grant help from both Ithaca College and the NEH allowed me to utterly change and shift and revise the project into a book twice as meaningful as I first envisioned. These were significant financial contributions that all too often remain in the background. I thank everyone who made them available.

I have been blessed with a thoughtful, talented, and helpful array of friends, colleagues, and professors who inspired and pushed me. Jacquelyn Hall, Leon Fink, Peter Filene, and John Orth have helped me in more ways that I can count. They have read my work closely, offering advice on the project and on the profession. Leon Fink served as my advisor for a time, and Jacquelyn Hall became something like a second advisor and mentor to me. John Kasson was actively involved in my training from my first semester at Carolina, and he both inspired my work and helped to hone my skills in any number of ways. He was an ideal advisor. My debts to him and to these other Chapel Hill faculty are broad and deep. Thank you all.

The project has been transformed in the past few years; two writing groups and the support of the Ithaca College history department have been vital in that process. Thanks to the GTFTD writing group at Carolina: John Hepp, Robert Tinkler, Gary Frost, Stacy Braukman, Mike Ross, Tom

Devine, Gavin Campbell, Molly Rozum, Steven Niven, Jonathan Young, and Eric Combest. This group met regularly for several years, and at one point or another, they read most of the manuscript. In Ithaca, the IC history department has been supportive of my scholarship in every way. The Chapterhouse Beer and History writing group—Jefferson Cowie, Rob Vanderlan, Michael Smith, Aaron Sachs, Derek Chang, Adriane Lentz-Smith, Joel Dinerstein, Finis Dunaway, and Caroline Merithew—offers a scintillating mixture of good humor, good beer, and pointed, meaningful analysis. It is not an overstatement for me to say that without this group I would not have been able to write this book. Thank you; I'll start a tab.

The research for the project depended on a number of people who helped me gather together the primary materials so important to this study. The reference, interlibrary borrowing, and microfilm staffs at the University of North Carolina and the interlibrary borrowing personnel at Ithaca College have each facilitated my research. The librarians and archivists at the Virginia Historical Society, the Valentine Museum, and the Library of Virginia were all of tremendous help. Reviewers and editors at the *Virginia Magazine of History and Biography* (particularly Nelson Lankford) and at UNC Press (especially Chuck Grench, Katy O'Brien, Paul Betz, and Leslie Watkins) were very helpful as well. Daniel Cohen, in particular, put such tremendous energy into his review of the manuscript that it is now a much better book. Although my first glance at his nineteen-page, single-spaced review brought a gasp, I quickly realized what a precious gift I'd received. In the final stages of revision, Lauren Georger gave me an undergraduate history major's perspective on the entire book. Thank you all.

Life is much more than research and scholarship, even for a historian. Christine and I have been blessed with friends in both Chapel Hill and Ithaca who have helped sustain us. Jeff Cowie and Janis Whitlock, Robert Tinkler, and Rona Van Willigan all shared the house with us on McCauley Street in Chapel Hill. We have since found a wealth of friends who have made Ithaca home. My parents have provided tangible gifts that have eased the process of research, writing, and living throughout this project. Even more important, they have afforded meaningful support as my family. Thank you all for your love and friendship.

When I think of the sacrifices my wife has made as I have pursued this project, it becomes clear that despite all the help I have received from others, this work owes most—an incalculable debt—to her. If the subject matter of the book were anything other than murder, mayhem, and, in particular, wife killings, I would surely dedicate it to you, Christine. As it is, I think not. Poor taste. You have helped me through health problems, low points, successes, years of fatigue, and a stray panic attack or two. Or three. In the course of this project, you and I have shared the most amazing gifts we will ever know. Sophia Rose has screamed, smiled, toddled, walked, and danced around us, followed by Sam, who is now dancing around us himself, putting the book (and the rest of life) into perspective. Thank you for everything.

THE BODY
IN THE
RESERVOIR

INTRODUCTION

DISCOVERING THE BODY

An evil in this country is sensationalism.
We regret to say that in this country, from
long habit, the community of news-hunters and
sensation-followers is large. Anything subserves
the purpose of a sensation now, and the business
of agitating and cussing and discussing is exceedingly
active. Let us hope that in a year or two more,
our people will become less sensational and
volatile, and that they will settle down to more
solid reflections, more steady devotions to matters
vital to themselves and the Government.
It is time they had enough of sensation.

Richmond Dispatch, 27 August 1870

MYSTERY OF THE MORGUE!

REVELATIONS OF THE RESERVOIR!

From his nearby office, the keeper of the old reservoir walked briskly to its southeastern stairs, mounting the twenty-foot embankment that stood like a fort at the western edge of Richmond, Virginia. As on every other morning, Lysander Rose made a circuit of the reservoir from the top of the levee surrounding this artificial lake. He looked about as the gravel crunched beneath his feet, noting the height of the water, the dampness from last night's snow flurries, the clouds low over the city, and the disrepair of the forty-inch fence surrounding the large pool. He had worked here for years tending the reservoir and its grounds. But no other morning, no other spring, would be quite like this one for Mr. Rose or for the rest of Richmond.[1]

As he rounded the southern end of the reservoir, Rose noticed furrows marring the path, and beside them were a shoestring and a red glove. Looking over into the water, he saw what at first appeared to be a floating log or a piece of refuse. Or the flounce of a woman's dress and the leg of its wearer. Rose called to one of his laborers, and together they probed with a stick to be sure of what they had found. It was seven o'clock on the morning of 14 March 1885. It would be well past one o'clock on a Friday afternoon twenty-two months later before the horror, suspense, and fascination awakened by Lysander Rose's discovery began at last to subside.

When the coroner arrived, workmen roped and hauled the mud-covered body from the water. The coroner's investigation discovered only a few minor scrapes on her face and tears in her clothing. He found few signs of assault, chiefly a small bruise on her forehead. She had no skull fractures, and her lungs had some, but not an abundance, of frothy water, indicating drowning. But the major discovery was her pregnancy: she carried a male fetus in approximately the eighth month of gestation. The coroner thought the death a probable suicide.[2]

For two days the woman's body remained unnamed. Thousands paraded through the chapel of the almshouse to view the corpse and its clothing. "There was a large crowd in there," one local clerk said, "and I just passed right by and looked at it not two seconds hardly."[3] Two different women broke into tears, believing the body was that of a friend or relative. Each time, these leads lured the police to track down a surprised and living woman. "Yet Unknown—the Death of the Woman Found Floating in the Old Reservoir Growing More Mysterious" read one headline.[4]

But on 17 March, a young Richmond woman told the police that she recognized the deceased as a cousin, Fannie Lillian Madison. Originally from King William County to the east of Richmond, Madison had checked into the Exchange Hotel under the name Fannie Merton just days before Rose's grisly discovery. She was twenty-three years old and unmarried; she had worked as a teacher and governess in a distant western county for the last several months.

Other developments quickly superseded the coroner's first tentative conclusions. Reported one newspaper: "the deep imprints of a man's footsteps on the embankment, the broken shoe-string [evidently a man's] found on the gravel walk, and the indications of a contest shown in the tracks on the walk do not point to suicide."[5] Murder! Within two days of the body's identification, the Richmond police arrested Thomas Judson Cluverius for killing Lillian Madison. The accused was a recent graduate of Richmond College, a practicing lawyer in King and Queen County (adjacent to Madison's home county), and another of Lillian's cousins.

Thomas Cluverius was jailed, but no one saw the murder, if murder it was, nor could anyone definitively connect him to Madison near the time of her death. He protested his innocence; equally important, his family had the means to quickly hire the most prestigious lawyers to defend him. Yes, he was in Richmond on business that week, he said, but he had not seen his cousin Lillian, nor did he know she would be there. Evidence pointed toward Cluverius as the culprit but nothing unequivocal. A local youth found a watch key near the crime, and Cluverius was missing his. A torn note in the trash at the Exchange Hotel seemed to be to Miss "Merton" and in Cluverius's hand. The schedules of the cousins corresponded not just in mid-March, but also in a January visit to Richmond and in a stay at a relative's house the previous fall, around the time when Lillian conceived. Yet Cluverius disputed this all, and Lillian's own suicidal words in the last weeks of her life offered a very different story line.

There was room in this case for doubt, for troubling confusion. Did he do it? many in Richmond asked themselves in the coming months. Of course he did it, some thought, but was someone else involved? What was their story? Was the unborn baby his? Why did she walk with her murderer into such a secluded spot? Even if he did it, can he be convicted? His reputation raised further problems: he seemed like such an upstanding young man; perhaps he was telling the truth and some other fiend attacked poor Lillian. As the *Richmond Dispatch* wrote: "what all this means is not now known, and may never be."[6]

3

■

All Richmond seemed to be watching this story of murder unfold. In June 1885, Harry Calligan wrote in his diary that he "saw T. J. Cluverius the man that murder miss Madison the court will finish to day with the trial." Between 1883 and 1885, this young factory apprentice from Manchester, Richmond's sister city across the James River, opened his diary several times each week, noting in a few spare lines the weather and something about his activities and reading matter. As in so many diaries, little of wider social interest appeared in these pages, which typically traced the outlines of a life defined by family, work, and neighborhood. But on five different occasions in the spring of 1885, Calligan wrote about the murder of Lillian Madison, despite the fact that neither he nor any in his immediate circle were in any way connected to it. He also actively pursued the case, going to Richmond to see the prisoner and joining the audience at court, a jaunt that could take the better part of a day.[7]

Few crimes appear in anyone's diary. Many, especially violent crimes, receive press coverage, but it is usually fleeting: a flash of shock at the discovery of a street fight, a robbery gone awry, a lynching, or domestic abuse. The annual reports of the Richmond Police Department list 407 arrests for murder between 1874 and 1915.[8] Most murders began as domestic quarrels or drunken saloon brawls. Many occurred in public or before witnesses or at least with strong and incriminating evidence. Few murder defendants were of a class and standing to afford the best lawyers to safeguard their rights and prolong their trials. While the shock of violence might keep a murder story in the public eye for a time, the first bold headlines quickly diminished, and the story slipped into interior pages as the Richmond papers used more measured prose to describe the burial of the victim, the outcome of the trial, and the sentence. Harry Calligan would never have bothered to write about such crimes unless he knew the participants personally.

Most of the mundane murders in the city involved men killing other men, but even the murders of women generally prompted only moderate reporting. The death of Lillie Bennett, "a notorious white woman and denizen of Cash Corner," is representative of this most common sort of murder report. She died on 15 September 1877 from blows reportedly received from "a friend," a sailor named James Stevens. He was acquitted the next month due to the paucity of evidence to prove the charge; no one else was ever arrested. Similarly, on 16 March 1879, Angelo Baccigalupo stabbed his wife repeatedly and threw her into Richmond's Kanawha Canal. She survived, and he was apprehended as he fled the scene. Although the papers followed both of these incidents, they garnered only five and six stories, respectively, in the *Richmond Dispatch*.[9] Neither crime fully captivated either the editors of the Richmond papers or, apparently, the local population.

The cases of Bennett and Baccigalupo represent typical crime coverage in the late nineteenth and early twentieth centuries. They became "sensationalized" in the broad sense of the term, describing any sort of violence, danger, or crime earning public attention, but their sensation was both shallow and short-lived. "Sensational" in this book describes a more particular species of the lurid: that subset of violent crimes that struck a chord in the community, resonating strongly enough to maintain a passionate public interest for months. Many elements could lead to sensational treatment: the violation of blood ties (particularly women or children murdered by their protector), the accused being of the upper class, gaps in the evidence creating ambiguity or forestalling assurance, or the prospect of a legal battle between prominent, respected, and theatrical attorneys. Any element that added suspense, doubt, or horror to the case could add to its sensation. Such stories of murder evoked an emotional and visceral response from the community. They created a readership in the press and expressed themselves in crowded courtrooms. Each was "the crime of the century," a social drama that profoundly disturbed or harrowed the community. Newspaper circulations soared, and the public's attention was riveted.[10]

Not only in Harry Calligan's diary, but throughout Richmond's cultural life the Cluverius case spawned singular activity. In contrast to the straightforward story of the Bennett murder or the Baccigalupo attack, the *Richmond Dispatch* printed articles on the Cluverius case on 172 different days over two years. The *Dispatch* might have spoken out against sensationalism as "an evil in this country" fifteen years earlier, but it published furiously on the sensational case against Cluverius. On several occasions such stories filled the entire front page; their coverage in prose was also illustrated by thirty-five engravings. The murder garnered national attention, earning dozens of headlines in papers throughout the country and even overseas. In addition, *Frank Leslie's Illustrated Weekly* and the *National Police Gazette* printed brief notices and illustrations on the case.[11] Two "true crime" pamphlets, two melodramatic works of fiction, a poem, and a number of passages in later memoirs likewise reveled in this murder.[12] A merchant in Richmond became almost obsessed with it, filling pages of his diary—a much more elaborate tome than Harry Calligan's—with his thoughts on the case, which evolved from pity for the "unfortunate young man" to outrage at the "consummate hypocrite and liar" who was "as guilty as sin itself."[13] Dozens of Richmonders wrote inquiring and impassioned letters to the lawyers in the case, and others clipped the newspaper stories, pasting some into their scrapbooks as mementos of this event.[14] Richmond "emptied itself" at the scene of the crime, and thousands more flocked to the grave of the victim and to the courthouse where the trial took place.[15] Those connected to the case—lawyers, jury members, and witnesses—became celebrities, and the police received daily requests for "relics" from the possessions of the victim and the accused.[16] It was "one of the most remarkable [trials] in the annals of criminal jurisprudence," which became "the all-absorbing topic. Newspapers containing accounts of the affair are quickly seized and are eagerly read."[17]

■

The following pages explore a cultural history of dramatic murder cases in Richmond, Virginia, up to the Progressive Era. The Cluverius case is threaded through a number of chapters, illustrating the themes under consideration, but this story goes far beyond a single body in a reservoir to chart the wider terrain of sensationalism in the South over generations. Murder is the most common and universal form of horrifying violence, and sensational murders like the Cluverius case prompt a tremendous amount of "agitating, cussing, and discussing," as the *Dispatch* put it. This is a study of how dramatically different was the experience of crime sensations in different eras of the South, using murder cases as benchmarks in this evolution of sensationalism.

In the course of the nineteenth and early twentieth centuries, Richmond, the South, and the wider nation embraced modernity. Crucial to this modern sensibility was the prodigious growth of mass culture and its accelerating interest in lurid stories of crime and bloodshed. While Progressive Era reformers attempted to fashion a more orderly and civil society, mass culture provided a brazen counterpoint to this effort, reveling in the gruesome details of murderous disorder. Nowhere was that disorder more in evidence than in the South.

This book gets to the heart—or, perhaps, the vulnerable and shadowy underbelly—of the sensational as the South became modern. In terms of both technological change and style of covering sensations, the South mirrored in most (but not all) ways the elaboration of mass culture's sensationalism in the rest of the nation. In terms of race and gender, the South charted its own course. These continuities and discontinuities with national trends show the South putting the pieces of modernity and mass culture together in its own way, changing with the times but not following the trails laid out by the urban metropolitan pathbreakers to the North.

Few nationally focused works on either crime or culture engage substantially with the history of the South. In the nation's most violent region, the study of violence has long been of central interest, generally tending in the direction of studying lynching[18] or lynching in conjunction with other regionally distinctive forms of violence, like honor killings.[19] This rich material emphasizes the ways the South was exceptional, rarely placing the region within the wider framework of the nation or asking the sorts of questions historians of other regions were asking about violence and culture. A number of recent studies have expanded this literature of southern violence and culture, broadening the study of violence in the South to take a more inclusive view of race and gender in particular.[20] This study pursues many of the same issues as this literature—violence, lynching, race, gender, and southern culture. But it comes at those issues from a different direction, using the tools of the cultural historian to evaluate the changing nature of sensationalism over time.

Nationally, social historians dominate the scholarly study of crime. Their work examines various ways that crime and policing evolved over time: changes in crime trends,[21] the development of professional police forces,[22] the evolution of penal practices,[23] and much more. In general, social historians studying crime ignore sensationalized cases since they are each unique rather than representative of broader crime trends. To most social historians, the murder of Lillie Bennett or the attempted murder of Mrs. Baccigalupo would be of as much or greater interest as the Cluverius sensation, no matter how much attention society paid it.

As in social history, the tendency among historians in general has been to dismiss sensational stories like the Cluverius murder as either ephemera or examples of an enduring and ahistorical morbid curiosity—interesting, perhaps, but not important. A sensational case can provide a spicy demonstration of an era's cultural interests, perhaps, but it remains a tangent to the important streams of historical change. Several histories of Richmond, for instance, gesture to the Cluverius case but in a fleeting paragraph: "Perhaps the most sensational murder trial in Richmond's history occurred in the late 1880s, when Thomas J. Cluverius . . ."[24]

In contrast, in the last generation cultural historians have begun to explore the fertile relationships between violent crime and culture, finding in sensationalized cases a wealth of sources and historical questions of interest. These studies have taken three general forms, each tending to center on developments in the antebellum North: the transition from Puritan execution sermons to secular stories of crime,[25] the change in crime coverage with the advent of the penny press,[26] and the case study of an individual sensational murder.[27] All of these works pay close attention to narratives, the ways in which society makes sense of the awful crimes in its midst.

This range of scholarly effort amounts to a rediscovery of a body of evidence not only of crimes, but of the society and its cultural life. Historians have long emphasized the key political, intellectual, and literary markers of the nineteenth and early twentieth centuries. This was the age of national expansion, Jacksonian democracy, civil war, the Gilded Age, and progressivism; of the American Renaissance, American industry, and realism; of Thoreau, Poe, Whitman, James, Howells, Twain, and Crane. But it was also the age of the popular novel—*Charlotte Temple*, *Quaker City*, *Deadwood Dick*, and *Tarzan*—as well as the melodrama—*The Poor of New York*, *The Colleen Bawn*, and *Under the Gaslight*. It was the age of public executions turning private, of penny papers, of a growing, sensational mass culture. In popular culture, the undercurrents of sensation and violence were strong, and scholars have recently turned to explore this broad cultural terrain.

This growing body of scholarship has illuminated a number of historical transitions in the relationship between the South, violence, culture, and the nation. But it has also left a host of issues in the darkness. What changes took place in crime and culture in the decades after the mid-nineteenth century? Was the story of crime and sensationalism told differently in the South than in the North? Are African American sensations framed differently from those of whites that serve as the bases for previous work? What role does the radical change in the nature of images in the press play in the history of sensationalism and American culture?

■

The present work wrestles with these important questions. Richmond's historical record, in fact, reveals that a number of assumptions about the history of the press and the history of the South do not hold. Scholars of the North have found that the earliest sensational literature of crime appeared in the colonial era in the form of execution sermons.[28] Virginia had none, charting an entirely distinct early history of sensationalism. Other scholars have emphasized the importance of two nineteenth-century turning points in the history of the press: the revolution of the penny press in the 1830s and the yellow journalism of the 1890s.[29] Richmond experienced both of these developments, but neither was a dramatic moment of change. Instead, the role of the press and their exploration of sensations evolved gradually over the course of many generations. The importance of all three of these developments appears overstated when viewed from the perspective of the South.

Richmond's record likewise upsets casual assumptions about the history of the South. Given racist fears of black criminality and the upsurge of lynching, one might assume that the most sensationalized cases in the white press would be black-on-white attacks. Hardly; by far the most sensationalized murders involved prominent whites, usually killing their wives or lovers. Similarly, one might assume that blacks would sensationalize horrifying lynchings the most. No. The most sensationalized cases in the African American community were those in which black defendants were clearly innocent, raising the tantalizing possibility that the prejudiced white justice system might acquit. It would be natural to assume that the very devout South approached the issue of murder with a particularly acute moralism, editorializing on murders with hellfire and damnation. Instead, it had a strong penchant for realism, and its newspapers covered cases in a notably dispassionate manner. Since the Civil War was the singular discontinuity in the history of the South (and was rather important in the history of Richmond!), clearly it must be the great moment of transition in the history of the press and sensationalism as well. Not at all; while the Civil War and Reconstruction colored everything in the South between 1860 and the mid-1870s, the trends in the press and sensationalism follow a separate, evolutionary trajectory unconnected to the many important effects of that war.

Richmond, Virginia, provides an ideal setting for this investigation of crime, culture, and the South. It was not the typical American nineteenth-century town, if there were such a thing, but it was no less typical than any other city in the region or, for that matter, the nation. Of medium size (Richmond ranked between twentieth and fortieth in population among late-nineteenth-century American cities), Richmond longed to become the "first city" of the South, but it was also a city of the mid-Atlantic.[30] It boasted a range of industries (tobacco and flour among dozens of others), a high population density, and a variety of cultural institutions. Crucially, Richmond allows a comparison between the sensationalism of the white press and public and the framing of crime sensations and justice more generally within the black community (blacks representing between one-third and one-half of the city's population).

Richmond's sensational crime stories became more sensational as the nineteenth century progressed. The volume of print and other cultural productions centered on sensational crime increased along with, and even outpaced, the general expansion of mass culture, which came to dominate the American cultural landscape. But more important than their growing abundance was the fact that they became differently sensational. Stories of crime became more detailed and gory but also more matter-of-fact. What had been erratically covered in the press of the early nineteenth century was approached with a standardized, almost mechanical discipline in the early twentieth century. The ramifications of this shift were multifold and are the central concerns of this book: the penchant for melodrama at midcentury turning to a more distanced, professional objectivity; the move from public rituals of state punishment to private executions; the substitution of multitudes of detailed photographs for an (often) symbolically charged and (always) rare engraving; the reticence to discuss women involved in these cases transforming into a much more open discussion of sexuality and gendered misbehavior; and the shift from impassioned defense of black innocence within the African American community to a more muted and distant hope for eventual justice.

Whether sensational cases involved a celebrity knifing by a beloved football star, "forty whacks" with a bloodied ax, or a body found in Richmond's reservoir, their heady mixture of life and death, of mystery and vengeance, created a peculiar and telling cultural space in the early twenty-first century as it did in 1885 or before. If these cases were legal proceedings, they were also social and cultural events, endlessly discussed. Lawyers told stories intended to convince a jury, and reporters and editors fit the evidence into narratives as well.[31] These stories of murder and sensation reveal much—what story lines, motivations, and stereotypes were broadly convincing, for instance. They left behind a rich record of the ways people considered a range of issues important to their community: order, justice, crime, virtue, morality, and violence. Central to this book is an evaluation of the various stories deployed to make sense out of the violent crimes that occurred regularly in Richmond's history; of particular importance is how the nature of those stories changed over time. Throughout, race and gender are especially telling tools in evaluating the changing nature of sensationalism and southern culture.

Violent crime is enduring in its cultural appeal as prurient subject matter, but this does not imply that it is ahistorical. Contemporary America is saturated with images and stories of violence. Local newscasts feature an arrest or murder as the lead story virtually every evening, and crime thrillers are top moneymakers for book publishers as well as television and motion picture studios. In record numbers, American youth play video and

arcade games splashed with gore. By the 1990s, an average American child
entering the teen years had seen more than 8,000 murders and 100,000
other assorted acts of violence on television.[32] The American public has
developed a taste for tales of murder and mayhem, and our cultural media
are eager to sate this appetite. "Sensation" has started to lose its meaning
in this era of action, new-ness, and thrills covered by on-the-spot reporters
and around-the-clock news channels. Modern life is pervaded by sensation,
much of which is violent.

It was not always this way. In the colonial era, the press rarely addressed
crime at all. If communities surely discussed crime and violence, their press
seldom explored them, perceiving the role of a newspaper in narrow economic and political terms. It was in the nineteenth century that crimes of
violence became important stories in the popular culture of the South. A
growing, urbanizing, and more literate public provided opportunities for
papers to attract a broader readership. Technological advances facilitated
a growth in print media, and sensation suited well the needs of this more
popularly oriented press. But this growth was slow, evolutionary. As late
as 1846, a Richmond editor came close to apologizing for putting the prurient matter of a prominent murder trial before his readership, and then he
apparently tired of covering it. This was driven home when he failed even
to attend the culmination of the murderer's trial, publishing the verdict as
hearsay: "From the long continuance of this trial, and from its incidents
having occupied so much of the public attention, we had become so wearied
that we did not attend Monday night. . . ."[33]

In the 1885 Cluverius coverage, such a dismissive statement would seem
unimaginable, for newspapers had come to revel in the sensational, seeing
it as a great opportunity. By the 1910s, hundreds of newspaper stories with
accompanying photographs grew out of each sensational crime as murder
stories became staples of a mass culture continuing to grow. Papers would
proudly print their swelling circulation numbers, or stories about the number of reporters at the courthouse, or reports charting the number of times
their "extras" scooped the competition by being the first on the streets with
new information on a case. During one trial in 1911, the *Richmond Times-
Dispatch* printed so many pages of testimony each day that it felt the need to
also publish a summary "for busy readers" who "desire a brief account."

How different was sensationalism in different eras? Just one of those
brief summaries for busy readers in 1911 was far longer than the entire
press coverage of all but one crime in all of Virginia's history before 1800.
From almost nothing, sensational stories of crime became a commonplace

in the twentieth century, when a critic wrote that "the pages of even conservative newspapers have looked more like catalogues of crime, than like 'journals of civilization.'"[34] Mystery of the Morgue! Revelations of the Reservoir! This is the story of how Richmond's culture, and America's, became so sensationalized.

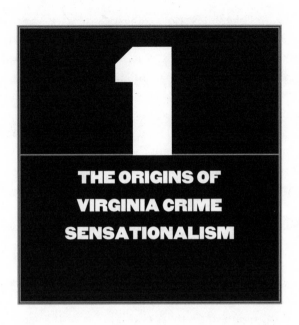

1

THE ORIGINS OF VIRGINIA CRIME SENSATIONALISM

I THANK GOD, THERE ARE NO FREE SCHOOLS NOR
PRINTING, AND I HOPE WE SHALL NOT HAVE THESE
HUNDRED YEARS; FOR LEARNING HAS BROUGHT DISOBEDIENCE,
AND HERESY, AND SECTS INTO THE WORLD, AND PRINTING
HAS DIVULGED THEM, AND LIBELS AGAINST THE BEST
GOVERNMENTS. GOD KEEP US FROM BOTH!

Virginia Governor William Berkeley, 1671

On 18 July 1766, "Dikephilos" (lover of justice) wrote a "candid narration" to the *Virginia Gazette*, which he hoped would "open the eyes of some well meaning men" to the murder of Robert Routlidge by John Chiswell in a Prince Edward County tavern the month before. The letter described how the two erstwhile friends exchanged insults while their acquaintances tried to separate them. Chiswell ordered his servant to retrieve his sword, but Routlidge, failing to back down, responded to Chiswell's taunts by dousing him with a glass of wine. Before friends could stop him, Chiswell ran Routlidge through, killing him instantly.

This narrative *was* eye-opening because the first reports of the conflict were much more friendly to Chiswell, saying that Routlidge advanced on Chiswell, who could not retreat and whose arms were pinned. According to the first reports, Routlidge skewered himself on Chiswell's sword.[1]

The local examiner's court decided that Routlidge, a wealthy merchant, had died by Chiswell's hand; the accused was refused bail and ordered to stand trial in the colony's general court for murder. Chiswell also had been prosperous until significant setbacks during the past decade had led him into dramatic financial difficulties. Both men's connections to the colony's gentry lent the murder a substantial audience among the *Gazette*'s readership.

As soon as local officials delivered the accused man to Williamsburg, three members of the general court—each of whom had business connections to Chiswell—allowed him bail. It was the suspicion that the ruling elites were allowing a murderer to go free that irked Dikephilos and others. A year after the contentious Stamp Act, the Virginia gentry were already in the midst of considerable turmoil and particularly sensitive to issues of justice, proportion, and favoritism. Bailing a prominent murderer appeared to be yet another affront to the body politic.[2]

Over the next three months, the *Virginia Gazette* published fifteen articles on the Chiswell case, some anonymous, others pseudonymous, still others penned above the names of some of the most prominent Virginians of the era, including the colony's most influential lawyer, George Wythe, and a leading member of the House of Burgesses, John Blair. In October, this flurry of activity ended when John Chiswell died of "nervous fits, owing to a constant uneasiness of mind"—probably suicide—shortly before he was to go to trial.[3]

In all, the *Virginia Gazette* printed slightly more than six pages on this case over the course of four and one-half months, or about one-quarter of a page in each issue. In volume, the coverage was significant, particularly for this era; in tone, it was moderate, even tentative. In fact, the "reporting" of this case consisted almost entirely of reprinted letters from readers: "To the Printer" they were titled. Far from investigating this crime, the newspaper publisher distanced himself from it.

In the two centuries from the founding of Virginia in 1607 to the end of the eighteenth century, this is the only case that could be called a crime sensation in Virginia's print media, and even this one probably stretches that category unduly, being largely centered on the politics of bail rather than the crime itself. Virginia had its share of crimes, and many Virginians must have become overwrought by some of them. But if they spoke to each other about their fears and concerns, their printers did not publish on them. Newspapers were for elites, and the weekly news was rarely local; real news came from elsewhere. The Routlidge-Chiswell case is the lone exception in an early history of Virginians—in print at least—minimizing the importance of crime. That neglect would change but not until the 1800s.

From these marginal beginnings, sensationalism in Virginia grew dramatically over the course of the nineteenth century. With the growth of a reading public, the elaboration of printing innovations, and changes in what was considered appropriate to publish, Virginians experienced a rising stream of print, including crime sensations. Editors extended their crime coverage but in ways that remained uneven and idiosyncratic, at times reveling in sensation while at other times avoiding it altogether. Of particular note are race and gender in this evolution of southern culture: Richmond editors were hesitant to write about either insurrection—as sensational a topic as the South would ever know—or crimes impugning the reputation of women. Starting with little coverage in the 1700s, Virginia papers developed crime sensations into an important part of the newspaper's function in the culture of nineteenth-century Virginia.

■

CRIME AND EARLY PRINTING IN VIRGINIA

Like most of the colonial world, Virginia in the seventeenth and eighteenth centuries lacked a vibrant tradition of publishing, despite being the first and, for almost two centuries, the most populous English North American colony and then state. Up to 1726, not a single printing establishment operated south of Pennsylvania. Of the original thirteen colonies, only three had printers in 1700, none of whom had yet printed an enduring newspaper. As the seventh of thirteen colonies to gain a printer, Virginia represented well the uninspiring history of colonial printing outside of Boston and Philadelphia.[4]

Governor William Berkeley hoped that Virginia would never have a press; later Virginia governors relented, seeing instead virtue in a press—at least one that they could control.[5] In 1730, William Parks, who four years before had established the first printing house in Maryland, opened a shop in Williamsburg, and in 1736, he began publishing a weekly newspaper, the *Virginia Gazette*.[6] After his death, two other printers successively retained a monopoly on the industry in Virginia.[7] Each of Virginia's colonial printers operated not only without competition, but also under the auspices of the colonial government, being dependent on printing official documents and decrees, work that could be quite lucrative and made up a large proportion of a printer's income. As Thomas Jefferson remarked, Virginia had one press with "the whole business of the government, and no competitor for public favor, [therefore] nothing disagreeable to the government could be got into it."[8]

Virginia's three colonial printers published a range of books, but none of them dealt with crime, much less crime sensations. In the entire colonial period, only one crime pamphlet even purported to concern Virginia, and it was published in London.[9] Similarly, the *Virginia Gazette* printed little of substance on crime, chiefly concerning itself with local advertising and reprints of colonial, British, and international news. This was in keeping with the norms for early American newspapers, which were relatively expensive and attuned to the interests of economic elites. Editorials were virtually nonexistent in the eighteenth-century Virginia press, and the local coverage was almost entirely advertisements, shipping arrivals, and legislative updates.[10] Most local news would have been fully aired by the time a weekly newspaper weighed in, but reports from Britain might be, well, "news."

When the *Virginia Gazette* mentioned crime, it tended to be terse, sometimes barely even informative: "John Emmet, from Berkeley, for bestiality, acquitted. Mary Howell, from Berkeley, for child murder, guilty. Death. Charles Tompkins, from Hanover, for theft, guilty. Burnt in the hand."[11] Sometimes even names were omitted from the lists: "At this General Court which ended yesterday, four persons received sentence of Death, viz. three men for Burglary and Felony, and one woman for the murder of her bastard child."[12] These brief notices appeared regularly, with the *Gazette* printing at least as many items on crime outside of Virginia as inside. On average, the paper made fleeting mention of at least one crime, trial, or punishment at least every two to three weeks and sometimes more often. Yet few of these items were longer than even two sentences.

This hesitant relationship between crime and publishing in early Virginia traces a course quite distinct from that of New England, the colo-

nies' first publishing center.[13] New England's unusually active (and devout) printers found an early audience for pamphlets of execution sermons
and the confessions of criminals. These stories culminated in the gallows
and a criminal's own warning to avoid his fate, all packaged with a fitting
sermon on the subject. Moralizing stories about what a slippery slope sin
could be, these cautionary tales also served as prurient and entertaining
reading matter.

Only New England witnessed the development of execution sermons;
Virginia printers never printed one.[14] Likewise, execution sermons were
not among the fare of the second largest printing center in early America,
Pennsylvania, where publishing, as in Virginia, was centered on government printing, almanacs, and newspapers as much as on religious works.[15]
Even in New England, execution sermons were tied to a particular era
of Puritan dominance. When the Puritan clergy lost their hold on public
discourse as America's most homogeneous region became more pluralistic,
execution sermons faded as well. By the nineteenth century, "such sermons
had indeed become little more than gratuitous vestiges of a disintegrating
literary regime." Execution sermons were unique in yet another way: New
England newspapers did not particularly spend any more time on crime
than did newspapers from other regions in the period.[16]

If Virginia presses did not follow the trends found in New England,
did the colony's readers nevertheless participate in this early print culture
about crime by purchasing and circulating books and pamphlets published
in New England? Little evidence remains of such trade: early Virginia
libraries contained few books published in the colonies at all and virtually
none from New England.[17] The economic patterns of colonial Virginia
worked against this possibility, for the economy of book sales ran with
tobacco to Britain; before 1736, Virginia had no intercolonial postal routes
at all. In that year, William Byrd sent a letter to a friend in Massachusetts,
and it first went to London![18] It was only in the second half of the century
that trade ties between Virginia and the other colonies/states developed to
a substantial degree.[19]

If the public forum of the press largely ignored the issue of crime in
colonial Virginia, it took a small step toward considering it more during the
turbulence of the revolutionary era. Growing discontent with the official
control of print motivated some Virginians to recruit a new printer in 1766,
part of a larger trend that led to the expansion of the ranks of printers in all
colonies during this decade. William Rind began publishing in that year,
offering his own almanac as well as a newspaper, which he also titled the
Virginia Gazette.[20]

The focus of newspapers remained squarely on economic and overseas news; therefore, crime coverage from 1766 to 1800 continued to be very minor. But two notable crimes earned mention in the papers of this era, if even these were rather brief flirtations with print sensationalism. The first was the 1766 Routlidge-Chiswell murder, which opened the chapter. This case was notable not only for generating a higher volume of print, but also for its focus on the decision to grant bail to Chiswell. Many of these letters to the newspaper failed to mention the sensational scene of the crime at all. Their responses seemed less an exploration of sensationalism and crime than an avoidance of them. Underscoring this is the fact that the competing Virginia newspaper, Rind's *Gazette*, avoided discussing the case at all.

This reticence to publish on crime sensations continued even as Virginia and its press expanded dramatically over the next two generations. Williamsburg was the site of all Virginia printing until 1780, when both the state government and its printers moved to the more secure and central site of Richmond to the west. Long presumed to be a logical site for a town because of the fall line's barrier to further upstream navigation, Richmond was formally laid out into plots in the 1730s and incorporated as a town of 250 people in 1742. The town remained small until it became the commonwealth's capital; by 1790 it had expanded to 3,761 inhabitants, a sevenfold increase in twenty years. By this time, printers were also operating in other Virginia towns: Charlottesville in 1781, Alexandria in 1782. Over the next decade, printing shops would open in another four towns and, in the 1790s, in a dozen others.[21]

In this steady growth of print, crime coverage remained in the background. In 1793 Richard Randolph, a prominent Virginian, was accused of infanticide, doing away with the evidence of his (supposedly) fathering a child by his sister-in-law. The *Virginia Gazette and General Advertiser* published an open letter from Randolph confronting this rumor, impugning the motives of those circulating it, and challenging them to take him to court. They did and lost. A relation of Randolph's then sent another letter to the newspaper and also published a broadside attempting to vindicate Richard and remedy the dishonor of the original charge.[22]

Merely a letter from Randolph and another from his relative? In a case concerning murder, very prominent Virginia families, and what must have been scandalous courtroom testimony, this story earned only this trifling (and sponsored) press coverage. Not once did the newspapers of the time print an original article on the trial, the decision, or the public interest in the case. Newspapers in eighteenth-century Virginia simply did not seek this fare. The role of the newspaper as purveyor of local news and crime sensations had not yet emerged.

Rumor and local gossip, however, clearly addressed the issue of crime more extensively, as the Randolph case attests. Little appeared in print, but rumors abounded: of how tender relations might be between Richard Randolph and Nancy Randolph, of how Nancy considered Richard's brother, Theodore (who died that year), as her husband although they were never wed, of Nancy growing larger in the belly, and, in late 1792, of bloodstained sheets, the purchase of "gum guaiacum" (an abortifacient), and screams in the night while on a visit to another's house. No infant was ever found, and Nancy refused to be examined by her aunt. There was plenty to talk about, and talk many did. Richard died four years later, some say due to poison, perhaps suicide. Nancy left Virginia and ultimately married the rich and powerful New Yorker Gouverneur Morris, although this story continued to follow her throughout her life.[23]

Twenty and forty years later, the rumors were renewed and spread further, but again, nothing appeared in print. John Randolph, Theodore and Richard's brother and a noted (and eccentric, some say mad) Virginia politician, raised the issue on an 1814 visit to the Morrises in New York, and again the accusations were raised when John Randolph died in the 1830s. John Randolph spread the rumors of infanticide among the Morris relatives (who were jealous of Nancy and the heir she gave Gouverneur Morris) and then blasted Nancy with a letter accusing her of poisoning Richard and perhaps working at that moment to kill Gouverneur Morris. She was a "vampire, that after sucking the best blood of my race, has flitted off to the north and struck its harpy fangs into an infirm old man." Her claims of intimacy with Richard's brother Theodore ("I was betrothed to him, and considered him my husband," she wrote) were laughable to him, since Theodore was at that point so sick that he was skin and bones, unable to walk; how could he be the father? Randolph goes so far as to charge her with "intimacy with one of the slaves."

Nancy replied to this letter with an even longer one of her own, countering his every charge and claiming that John himself had been her suitor and was trying to disparage others. His letter was "the suggestion of a disturbed fancy or the instigations of a malevolent heart." Written in 1814 and 1815, these letters were not published but were circulated widely. Nancy was afraid that Randolph's charges, if not confronted, would slander her reputation (and that of her son). This concern was intensified by the fact that Gouverneur Morris—her reputation's protector—was getting on in years. So she circulated both Randolph's letter and her own to dozens of friends and allies in New York, Washington (Dolley Madison and John Marshall received copies), and Virginia. "I am determined they shall appear in the neighborhood under your hand," she wrote in her letter to Randolph, "so that your character may be fully known and your signature forever hereafter be not only what it has been, the appendage of vainglorious boasting, but the designation of malicious baseness."[24] The letters must have been the subject of gossip up and down the east coast in 1815, and again after John's death, as his will was probated. In an ill-starred attempt to prove him insane (his last will benefited his slaves rather than his distant relations), relatives submitted the letters to the court, and copies of them thereafter circulated further.[25] But, again, nothing in print.

None of this apparently circulated in the open, but rather was a sort of underground Virginia gentry pornography. Surely many other crime stories circulated in the form of rumor and gossip. Neither in the 1790s when the supposed crime was committed, nor in the 1810s or 1830s when the rumors received fresh circulation did the press ever exploit this story. Only the two letters sponsored by Richard Randolph and his relative left a mark in Virginia newspapers. Given that John Randolph was a very public and vociferous Virginia politician, and considering that the press in the period was becoming increasingly and bitterly political, it seems quite notable that this "spicy correspondence" would be considered, as it must have been, out of bounds.

Why? Early newspapers had a much narrower mandate than later ones: much of life was "out of bounds" for early papers. The conception of a newspaper as a sort of public bulletin board, commenting on and updating the community on anything and everything of interest, was an invention of the nineteenth century. In this earlier era, newspapers tended to communicate a rather discrete set of what we would now call "news": events from far away (mostly political and economic and generally from Europe) and also local economic information, notifying merchants and planters of ship arrivals and advertising items for sale or those wanted for purchase. In this, Virginia papers conformed to the colonial norms. Throughout the colonies, editors were most eager to include news from overseas when they could get it (perhaps two to six months out-of-date) but published little on local matters. "There were too many spectators there to make it now a piece of public news," wrote the *New-England Courant* about an eclipse.[26] Most local news and rumor fell outside the purview of early, weekly newspapers.

20   It was not merely the newspapers that showed caution; similarly,

printers in the late eighteenth century continued to refrain from printing books, pamphlets, and broadsides on crime. In fact, the output of Virginia printers—who by the 1790s had grown to two dozen—was remarkably consistent with earlier fare: government publications, almanacs, newspapers, and a variety of other publications of local interest. The major change in this era was the rapid rise of publishing in the western part of the state, along with the equally rapid rise in the number of religious titles.[27] This demonstrates an enriched print culture but without a single crime publication.

A slave rebellion was categorically different from murder; one embodied the threat of an individual miscreant, whereas the other threatened social revolution. Despite this important distinction, an evaluation of Gabriel Prosser's plan for a slave rebellion further emphasizes the paucity of print in this era. The plan for central Virginia slaves to unite, arm themselves, and take Richmond was discovered in August of 1800; dozens of slaves were rounded up and tried, and twenty-seven of them were executed over the following three months.[28] Against the backdrop of the ongoing slave rebellion in Haiti, this discovery terrified white Virginians.

Yet no printer published a pamphlet or even a broadside on the conspiracy, and the *Virginia Argus* and the *Richmond Examiner* limited their printed coverage of the uprising chiefly to a number of letters from readers, as in previous cases. This included letters from white men rejecting rumors (and producing character witnesses) that they might have been involved in any way with the plotted insurrection, a governor's proclamation offering a reward for the discovery of the leaders of the rebellion, as well as a more substantive letter from a close observer of the trials of accused blacks. The unattributed, and apparently original, coverage in the *Argus* consisted of a single sentence notifying readers that Prosser was to be executed and two brief entries, including: "Ten of the Slaves concerned in the late insurrection, were executed on Friday last. Gabriel, and two of his accomplices, in this city; two near Four-mile creek; and five others near the Brook. Among the latter were Smith's George and Young's Gilbert. JACK BOWLER, alias JACK DITCHER, for whom a reward of three hundred dollars was offered by the Governor, is now confined in the Penitentiary. He surrendered himself to Gervas Storrs, Esq., one of the magistrates of Henrico county."[29] The *Examiner* had even less; it made no mention of Gabriel's arrest, his trial, or any of the hangings that followed the discovery of the plot. It is hardly possible to tell even what this case might be about from the spare and tangential pieces of evidence strewn occasionally in the *Examiner*.

This hesitancy to print was most striking when looking at the *Argus* issue by issue. The rebellion was discovered on 30 August; the next four issues of the biweekly *Argus* did not mention the plot, although the editor did find space for much else: a long discourse on Jefferson, an explosion at Nantes, France, the trial of Hadfield in London, the spread of yellow fever, and a piece on the conviction and execution of a slave for killing a white man (unrelated to Gabriel's plot). Even when the story was almost two weeks old, dozens of slaves had been rounded up, and a number of them were already in court, the *Argus* still refrained from printing a single story on the planned insurrection.

Even when the story was finally broached on the sixteenth of September, the *Argus* printed much longer stories on a battle in Europe, the murder of a young white woman in Henrico, and a Dublin story of a criminal on trial as well as the continued focus on political matters in the run-up to the contentious election of 1800. The local talk about this plot must have been substantial. But the editor did not conceive of the *Argus* as an appropriate conduit for this discussion, tapping into the public's interest and fear. Newspapers tended not to cater to this sort of material, but one letter to the *Norfolk Herald* argues that "a mistaken notion of prudence and policy" kept Richmond papers from printing the minutiae of the conspiracy. "Indeed, fear seems to have put an imprimateur [*sic*] on the press."[30]

In the two months they covered Gabriel's rebellion at all, Virginia editors dedicated far more space to political reporting and dispatches from Europe.[31] Perhaps fear of inspiring further violence influenced this quiet response to the threat of Gabriel's rebellion. But the Virginia press printed little on *any* crime. When a reader picked up a newspaper in this era, he or she must have had little expectation to receive information on local news of any sort, much less local issues of crime, even sensational ones. Exploring sensations was simply not what Virginia publishers did in this era. This would not be true much longer.

■

THE EVOLUTION OF PRINTING SENSATIONALISM IN ANTEBELLUM VIRGINIA

In the early nineteenth century, Virginia printers began to publish pamphlets and broadsides on criminal events; that was also when newspaper coverage of them started a long-term expansion. As in the rest of the nation, expanding cities and literacy rates coupled with innovations in printing played central roles in the development of sensationalism in the Virginia press. The history of Virginia print sensations yields little evidence of any one moment being the turning point, however. Instead, each decade of the nineteenth century witnessed an increasing interest in and production of crime sensations.

The earliest extant broadside of Virginia crime dates from 1805.[32] Framed by nine black coffins, this broadside describes how a man who "had always lived with them in a most affectionate manner" murdered his wife and eight of his nine children one night. Half of the page is a prose description of this grisly discovery; the bottom half is a poem exploring the most emotional sides of this horror. This crime likewise spawned the following year the earliest crime pamphlet published within the state.[33] Tense and dramatic, these documents clearly appealed to popular tastes, something new in Virginia history.

In 1816, Captain Thomas Wells shot and killed Judge Peter Randolph in the wake of a well-publicized conflict over politics and their personal reputations. Wells was tried for murder and acquitted, the court believing witnesses' reports that Randolph was advancing on Wells with a whip and a gun and therefore that Wells acted in self-defense. The conflict stemmed from personal correspondence between the two men that received widespread circulation when the *Virginia Argus* printed the exchange. As in the past, the newspaper appeared hesitant in its stand on the conflict, merely printing each man's letter to the other. A separate note comments on the publication and the newspaper's lack of prejudice, justifying it due to the (mistaken) assumption that "their difference evidently partakes more of the character of a popular, than of a private feud. Hence, the people at large have some interest in it; and both should be heard with equal candor and impartiality."[34]

When Wells went on trial for murder in August, however, the *Argus* never mentioned the case or its result. But another printer did, publishing a pamphlet by a "Member of the Bar of Nottoway County" titled *Report of the Trials of Capt. Thomas Wells.*[35] In ninety-four dense pages, the author paraphrased the testimony of all of the witnesses and presented extracts from the letters between the two men, the closing arguments in the trials, and the decisions. This was the most thorough treatment of any crime in Virginia history to this point. It is telling of the place of crime in the press, then, that newspapers did not cover the trial at all.

By the 1820s, the Virginia press was growing: newspaper circulations rose, and many more papers competed with one another than in the eighteenth century. They were printed on larger sheets and included more column inches of print. Whereas eighteenth-century papers were weeklies, now most papers were printed twice a week, and some were dailies.[36] With more frequent editions, more local fare would be "news" to newspaper readers. In addition, shifting demographics lured and pressured editors to appeal to a broader audience. Richmond had grown from a city of 3,761 in 1790 to 16,060 by 1830, a fourfold increase. The possibilities of such a readership would not be missed by antebellum editors.

At least as important were the growing numbers of readers and their growing purses, although firm numbers regarding literacy in this era are elusive. The American economy was growing as was the overall population, cities were experiencing their fastest growth in American history, and an increasingly large proportion of Americans—who had always been among the most literate in the world—were reading. By 1850, when the U.S. census first asked about literacy, 90 percent of American whites could read and write at least at a fundamental level.[37] Even if a much smaller proportion could read well enough to enjoy a newspaper in the 1820s, a trend toward rising literacy would nonetheless add weight to a growing population, growing disposable incomes, and growing concentration of that population in cities to provide an increasing incentive to add more popular fair to a newspaper's columns.

Despite this growth in both readership and newspapers themselves, Virginia papers retained much of the style of the eighteenth century: advertising, foreign news, and political updates from Washington and Richmond dominated their pages. Editors in Virginia continued to orient their fare toward the wealthy and toward business, a national trend in the press. Early national newspapers "were geared to the interests of economic and political elites," Daniel Cohen has written of the New England press. Crime in this era "tended to be treated, if at all, by little more than short, isolated paragraphs."[38]

So it was in 1820s' Virginia. In 1821, two itinerant thieves butchered a third in Norfolk, Virginia, apparently because of a rivalry over a Baltimore woman. Each accused the other of the deed, and both were convicted and executed. This case contained several thrilling elements—sex, rivalry, a gory murder, executions, and a criminal underworld—and spawned another true crime pamphlet published in the commonwealth.[39] Yet even in this case, Richmond's major newspaper of this era, the *Enquirer*, published only seven brief reprints from Norfolk papers on the murder, trial, and execution.[40] This coverage was much greater than the norm in previous eras, and the longest of these articles was almost a column and a half in length. Altogether the paper printed considerably less than a single page on this case, yet that was substantially more than the eighteenth-century norm.

In 1827, three Spanish pirates were convicted of murder and executed for their crime. The case was heard in a special federal court in Richmond before Chief Justice John Marshall. The press covered the case succinctly while it was at trial; the *Enquirer* even held off giving the details of the crime until the trials were over, apparently due to a particularly circumscribed idea of propriety: "When these trials shall be concluded we propose giving a statement of the principal facts disclosed. As the testimony in all the cases is the same, it would not be proper to make a further publication on the subject at present." The next issue of the *Enquirer* included a story on another pirate, Tardy, who had died, with the following issue filling a full page with the "tale of horror" on the high seas. In addition to the *Enquirer's* four stories on the case, a Richmond publisher also came out with a pamphlet.[41]

No crime sensation in Virginia earned the distinction of a printed pamphlet before 1806; between 1806 and 1830, seven cases did so. In content, these pamphlets feature the trial as the center of each story; most of each pamphlet concerns the paraphrased words of the witnesses and lawyers. Only one of them includes a sermon, and no others overly dwell on God's retribution upon the wicked or anything of the kind. They might mention a minister's words at the gallows and whether the accused confessed, but this tended to be merely a small part of a much larger narrative focused on the trials.[42]

In addition to this growing pamphlet literature, the political divisions of the second party system influenced the editorial outlook of Virginia newspapers. In this era, many Virginia papers were rabidly partisan sheets, leavening their news with an increasing number of editorials. In Richmond, the organ of the Jacksonian Democrats was the *Enquirer* (founded in 1804); the nascent Whig party started its own paper in 1824, aptly if unimaginatively naming it the *Richmond Whig*. As others have shown, editors gravitated toward political parties for a number of reasons: the parties needed vocal champions in the press, the reading public was increasingly divided by a number of issues, and—perhaps the most meaningful consideration—operating a newspaper was a very tenuous proposition financially. Political parties regularly donated to papers aligned with them, gave editors inside contacts and information, and awarded them printing contracts when in office. Such boons could spell the difference between bankruptcy and survival.[43]

This partisanship and the concomitant growth in editorializing had only a limited effect on the coverage of crime and sensations, however. In keeping with party ties, the press kept its attention on political matters. Nevertheless, this shift did mean that newspapers became more extravagant and evinced more personality as their editors increasingly stepped out from behind the printed (and, often, reprinted) news and letters from readers. Editors in the antebellum period were almost celebrities: part politicians, part literati, part entertainers, and, in Virginia at least, part marksmen. Wrote one Richmond editor bemoaning the changes in journalism: "neutrality in this country and in this age is an anomaly—it is a hybrid state of existence."[44] The high number of political appointments given to friendly editors, along with the high number of duels fought between rival editors, lend credence to this statement. In the most famous instance, Thomas Ritchie Jr., son and successor to his famous father as editor of the *Richmond Enquirer*, shot and killed John Hampden Pleasants, editor of the rival paper, the *Richmond Whig*. This 1846 duel arose from a particularly vituperative outburst of mutually insulting printed statements.[45]

If newspaper coverage of crime remained brief and somewhat erratic in the 1820s, at least papers consistently rendered the narratives of the murders—describing the act itself, the trial, and the executions. Even that sort of minimal coverage was generally lacking in Virginia papers before this time. This was a notable step up in coverage compared to printing mere letters from readers (or printing nothing), but it was merely the first step in sensationalizing crime.

The largest and most "successful" slave rebellion in the nation's history was the 1831 Southampton, Virginia, insurrection led by Nat Turner. Believing that God had chosen him to redeem his race and that a recent eclipse was his sign to begin, Turner joined with others in his neighborhood to slaughter all the whites they could find, starting with his own master's family. Ultimately, this group grew to several dozen participants (no one knows precisely how many), and over two days in August, they killed almost sixty whites before local militias dispersed and captured them (along with many innocent bystanders, a fact even contemporaries admitted freely). Whites killed in summary fashion an unknown number of (supposed) insurrectionists, making it quite difficult to say how many blacks died in the wake of this riot. Fifty were put on trial, nineteen were executed through legal means, but more than a hundred more blacks might have died extralegally during the backlash to the insurrection. Dozens more had their death sentences commuted to sale and transportation out of state.[46]

Nat Turner's rebellion was a turning point in southern history; a hardening of the defense of slavery was clear in the wake of the insurrection. This act of violence also yielded the most famous and reprinted—also one of the shortest and most peculiar—crime pamphlets in Virginia history. *The Confessions of Nat Turner*, transcribed (and/or invented) by a local white lawyer, Thomas Gray, is a spare twelve pages of text that starts with

Turner's version of his childhood and his belief that God ordained his actions. This narrative continues with a clearly articulated, coldly recalled blow-by-blow account of the murders. Gray portrays Turner as an insane fiend but also as a powerful man convinced of his place in God's plan.

The Confessions of Nat Turner is a conflicted document, published first in Baltimore (another testimony to Virginia's underdeveloped publishing institutions) within a month of Turner's discovery and a mere two weeks after his execution.[47] It was republished in Virginia a few months later; later editions had a one-paragraph treatment of Turner's execution at the end. The narrative is gory and matter-of-fact, and it demonstrates that Turner knew personally the families that the group attacked. For instance: "As I came round to the door I saw Will pulling Mrs. Whitehead out of the house, and at the step he nearly severed her head from her body, with his broad axe. Miss Margaret, when I discovered her, had concealed herself in the corner, formed by the projection of the cellar cap from the house; on my approach she fled, but was soon overtaken, and after repeated blows with a sword, I killed her by a blow on the head, with a fence rail."[48] In his introduction "To the Public," Thomas Gray editorialized mightily: "fanatic" "indiscriminate massacre," "fiendish band," "remorseless murderers." But the remainder of the document, which he claims to be straight from Nat Turner during three days of jailhouse interviews before his trial, Gray rendered dispassionately. There is little reason to question the Confessions at least in general as genuine; the narrative is in keeping with more abbreviated reports of Turner's beliefs printed in the newspapers as well as the brief record of the trial.[49] It is also important that no one at the time went out of their way to contradict Gray's narrative.[50] However, particularly given the loose journalistic standards of the day, we can assume that Gray reworded the tale and changed it in dozens of minor ways.

The Confessions dominates our understanding of Nat Turner and his rebellion.[51] Despite the importance of this event, there are few competing narratives, no published trial record, and certainly no unmediated records from blacks involved. Those African American insurrectionists who were not killed outright at capture were pushed through trials within weeks. Many were sold out of the state, and those who were executed died within a month of the insurrection. Nat Turner was the last captured, remaining hidden for ten weeks, until 30 October. He went to trial the following week and died on the gallows on 11 November, a mere thirteen days after capture.

Newspapers certainly covered the insurrection, and in greater abundance than any previous story of criminal activities, but, again, this is a peculiar moment and one quite different from even the most sensational murder stories. Given the distinctions between murder and insurrection, the contrast with Gabriel's rebellion and its coverage from thirty years before is particularly instructive. In 1831, the *Richmond Enquirer* conceived of its role quite differently from the one taken by newspapers a generation before. The *Enquirer* would be a conduit for accurate information and a corrective to the multiplicity of unfounded rumors in circulation: "So much curiosity has been excited in the State, and so much exaggeration will go abroad, that we have determined to devote a great portion of this day's paper to the late strange events in the county of Southampton.... We hope if they [the stories they reprint from other papers] have no other effect, they will be at least calculated to correct a thousand misrepresentations which are afloat."[52] The *Enquirer* went on to print much in the coming three months, including one story in almost every (semiweekly) edition from 26 August to 22 November. Most of the print coverage of the Turner insurrection was derived from other sources rather than the *Enquirer's* own reporting: twenty-two letters from individuals and twenty reprints from other papers. In fact, original reporting largely consisted of a paragraph inserted before a letter or reprinted article. Often these reprints were repetitive, giving not just one narrative of a development, but a multiplicity of them. For instance, the reporting in the first issue after the insurrection consisted of extracts from eight different letters received in the three days before publication, each of which gave its overlapping, sometimes contradictory narrative of the carnage. When Nat Turner was captured, the *Enquirer's* coverage consisted of reprints from three papers as well as three letters, most of which repeated the same information.[53]

Clearly the paper was attempting to put everything it could before the public—quite a different goal from the journalistic reticence to mention Gabriel's rebellion or any eighteenth-century crime. In this era before the railroad, telegraph, or penny press, putting everything before the public meant reprinting everything that came through the mail. The editor often spoke of having (or not having) "*authentic* accounts" of events, discussed how reports were "apt to be exaggerated," and yet rarely seemed to hold back from reporting a variety of rumors: that insurrectionists numbered up to four hundred, that the number of whites killed topped one hundred, or that the insurrection was led by three white and four black men, for instance.[54]

Like other murder narratives in this era, the *Enquirer's* coverage of the Southampton insurrection was much more descriptive and coherent than earlier efforts. If previous newspaper coverage of murders and even

Gabriel's insurrection had been piecemeal and incomplete (if covered at all), newspapers in 1831 strove to offer readers a comprehensible narrative of the Turner rebellion, updates of the latest facts available, and at least some understanding of the motive behind the attack.

But the editor was much more enthusiastic about printing some elements of the event than others. It was within the issue or two after two particular events—the realization of the extent of the butchery and the discovery of Turner—that the *Enquirer* published profusely and with multiple reports. Once the insurrectionists were captured, the paper covered the trials and executions but barely. After a long narrative of the progress of the murders, for instance, one article ended with this coverage of the trials: "Dispatches were received by the Governor last evening, stating that four of the prisoners had been tried and *condemned* on Wednesday and Thursday. Two of them were recommended for reprieve and transportation and two (Daniel and Moses) were ordered for *execution on Monday next.*"[55] Nat Turner's own trial and execution received just as scant coverage in the *Enquirer*: one spare paragraph on his trial and two similarly brief reports in successive editions concerning his execution. Of the trial, the paper's complete coverage was: "Nat Turner was tried at Jerusalem on Saturday last, and sentenced, of course, to be hung."[56] Considering that he represented the most terrifying threat in the experience of white Virginia, this brevity is quite noteworthy.

By 1831, the coverage of criminal matters and sensations in Virginia had grown substantially, but it also remained uneven. The bumper crop of crime sensations fifteen years later makes each of these trends still clearer. In 1846, two murders and the Ritchie-Pleasants duel each were prominent enough to warrant at least one published pamphlet. Importantly, three of the four pamphlets were printed outside of Virginia—a testimony to the continuing dominance of publishing in commercial centers (now New York and Philadelphia rather than London) over printing within the commonwealth.[57]

These three cases were prominent, yet their local coverage in print remained erratic. For example, one of the murder cases was that against William Dandridge Epes, charged with killing Francis Muir over a debt. Epes promptly hid the body then escaped to Texas, where he assumed several names, including, ironically, that of a Virginia judge. Neither at the time of the murder in 1846, nor in 1848 when Epes was finally apprehended, tried, and executed, did the Richmond press rise to the bait of this colorful crime. The most prominent paper of the time, the *Enquirer*, merely covered the trial of Epes by means of a few reprints from Petersburg papers. Even the most exciting moment in the case, Epes's execution three days before Christmas, warranted merely a single reprint published five days later.[58]

The Myers-Hoyt case of the same year gives even better evidence of how erratically crime sensations could be covered in this era. Virginia Myers had an affair with Marvin Hoyt, a reportedly handsome and dapper northern migrant to Richmond. Her adoring and intimate letters to him (and one from him to her) became public during the course of the trial. They discuss her marital problems, Mrs. Myers's despair, and her growing admiration, then love, then obsession for Hoyt. When the family of Mrs. Myers learned of these letters, Hoyt was given an ultimatum; he vowed not to see her again. When they were later seen together and other letters were discovered, Mr. Myers (and two others) burst in on Hoyt in his room, demanded he sign a paper agreeing to leave Richmond forever on forfeit of his life. When Hoyt refused, Mr. Myers leveled a pistol at Hoyt and shot him three times, one ball entering his brain. Hoyt lingered somehow for twelve days, and when conscious, he maintained his and Mrs. Myers's innocence. Mr. Myers, his brother, and a friend were all brought up on murder charges for Hoyt's death.

The *Richmond Whig* printed a synopsis of Mr. Myers's preliminary trial before the mayor's court. That coverage became expansive after the romantic letters between Virginia Myers and Hoyt were entered as evidence, but then the editor apparently tired of this activity. Following the letter-fueled binge of printing, the *Whig*'s coverage of this trial diminished to one- and two-sentence notices that the trial continued. For instance: "The Trial. The trial of the Messrs. Myers and Mr. Burr was resumed on yesterday at 11 o'clock. The whole day and a good portion of the night was consumed in receiving and discussing evidence adduced on behalf of the defense. The Court adjourned to 11 o'clock today."[59] To some extent, this was simply common practice: this was the second trial, the first, preliminary hearing having taken place the week before. Having covered the first trial with paraphrased testimony, newspapers in this era generally offered shorter coverage when that testimony was repeated. But the *Whig* did more than this (or less, rather), only reporting the trial's continuance in these notes, not even hinting at the course the trial was taking. Emphasizing this lack of commitment to covering this case, at the end of the trial the *Whig* editor concluded with this dismissive note, printed here in full: "Myers' Trial— From the long continuance of this trial, and from its incidents having occupied so much of the public attention, we had become so wearied that we did not attend Monday night. It will be sufficient to say that at a late hour, the

Examining Court pronounced in favor of the accused; the vote, we hear, standing five to two. The spectators are said to have evinced their acquiescence in the justice of the sentence with shouts of joy."[60]

The *Richmond Enquirer* was just as erratic. It published less than two columns of print (altogether) in the first eleven editions after the Myers murder, but then in one day of the preliminary trial—again when the letters were introduced—devoted a full page to testimony. After this paroxysm of coverage, it again printed only one column's worth of material on the rest of the two trials and Myers's acquittal. The *Enquirer* at least covered the acquittal, although its story was only four paragraphs (less than one-quarter of a column), merely stating that the attorneys gave their closing arguments and that the prisoners were discharged. "The announcement of this result was received with enthusiastic shouts of applause from a crowded Court room, which we cannot trust ourselves to describe."[61] A final letter from Virginia Myers to the public was reprinted in the *Enquirer* a few weeks after the trial. The *Enquirer* prefaced the letter with this editorial note: "We had hoped that our article of Friday last would have closed our columns to this most lamentable affair. We had hoped that all feeling would be permitted to subside, and that the subject in this community, would be permitted to die away."[62]

This coverage of murder cases in 1846 was much more thorough than that of any newspaper a century before or even a generation before. But it nevertheless remained derivative, minimalist, erratically pursued, and largely bereft of sensation. Where sensation intruded upon the business of Richmond's newspapers, it came with apologies and even annoyance. This might be interpreted as dissembling if the papers continued to publish scandalous matter. Like the introductions to contemporary romantic novels in which the author points to the moral lessons to be learned from all of the betrayals and scandals in the book, these comments might appear as fig leaves intended to give cover to editors reveling in the prurient. Yet the editors failed to revel.

The brevity of newspaper reports in the days before they apologized for continuing to print Myers material suggests that antebellum Virginia editors were legitimately sorry to have to work with such a story. They knew it was a story of interest—hence the publication of the letters—but they were not (yet) comfortable with the prospect of using this interest to increase their circulations. The Virginia editor's conception of a newspaper was changing, but slowly. Most still conceived of their paper's chief mission in the traditional terms of printing political and economic news and updates from overseas diplomacy and war. Not this.

The Myers case gives us a very interesting opportunity to evaluate the differences in coverage between North and South at this moment. The victim, Dudley Marvin Hoyt, was raised in Massachusetts before moving to Richmond in 1831, and northern papers took an interest in his death and the subsequent trial. The column inches devoted to the trials in the *Philadelphia Public Ledger* and the *New York Herald* were fewer than in the Richmond papers, yet their treatment of the scandalous letters was much larger. For the most part, the northern papers reprinted stories from Richmond papers. The *Herald's* coverage was rather matter of fact, printing the letters and the substance of developments without editorializing. In contrast, the *Public Ledger* was scathing in its denunciation of the events and what they considered a travesty of law:

> The conduct of all parties in this affair, excepting that of the Commonwealth's Attorney, Mr. Mayo, is exceedingly reprehensible, and that of the accused and their counsel fills us with unmitigated disgust. . . . But their guilt [Mrs. Myers and Hoyt], great though *hers* and enormous *his* be, does not mitigate our contempt for the thoroughly dastardly conduct of the husband in deliberately stealing into a chamber to shoot a man in bed, and in exposing, unnecessarily, his wife's love-letters. What ineffably pitiful conduct! But it is all according to *chivalry*! The *chivalry* that cowhides women with babies in their arms. *Chivalry*! Spirits of Godfrey and Richard and Bayard! Without fear and without reproach! What would *ye* have said of *such* chivalry? But the murderers will not be hanged. O no! *Chivalry* will not permit it.[63]

For its part, the *Richmond Enquirer* returned fire: "We would be callous to all feeling did we not throw back with scorn and contempt the taunts and sneers of those exquisite moralists of some of the Northern and Eastern cities. . . . When we wish moral lectures, we prefer the selection of our own teachers. We certainly shall not apply to those who defended the murder of a Heberton, who justified the burning of the Charlestown Convent, or who laughed at the murder of the Cigar Girl, &c., &c. We are much obliged to our friends of the North for their sympathy and advice, but we hope that they will hereafter withhold them until called for."[64]

In addition to the Philadelphia paper's excoriation of Virginia justice, both of the northern papers also demonstrated a greater willingness to explore the scandalous letters than did Richmond's press. The *Richmond Whig* and the *Richmond Enquirer* printed only the most important letters in the trial: the lone surviving letter from Hoyt to Mrs. Myers, for instance, as well as her letter prompting his reply.[65] Richmond papers also printed two other intercepted letters from a few months later—the discovery that directly led to the shooting—along with Mrs. Myers's last letter to Hoyt voicing her worry of what would happen. The only other letter that the Richmond papers published was one example (of many) of Mrs. Myers's effusive and loving letters to Hoyt ("I am your wife. Mine angel . . .") from the couple's happier moments.[66] Dozens of other existing letters were submitted into evidence (not all of which were read in court), but the Richmond press declined to print them.

Not so the press in the North. The *Herald* and *Public Ledger* published, generally, all of the letters that the Richmond papers did, but the *Herald* published an additional eighteen letters over two days of coverage. The *Public Ledger* published eight letters in full (only one of which Richmond papers published), with abstracts and quotations from an additional eleven. All of the papers—and even the pamphlet that includes a detailed appendix of all of their letters—left out a letter in which Mrs. Myers "hints at a subject, in connection with a consultation with Dr. Gray, of so dubious and delicate a nature as to make it unfit for publication."[67]

This regional difference in willingness to dwell on scandalous matters is intriguing. There are two possibilities for interpreting this: that distance allows for the acceptance of more off-color material or that northern and southern mores differed on the score of publicizing a woman's reputation. Distance had a clear impact on the coverage of sensations—more distant papers were more willing to print rumors, to stereotype, and to summarize. This alone might explain the difference. But southern editors also seemed less inclined to tread, in particular, on a woman's reputation, a subject that receives fuller consideration in the next chapter. In fact, the *Richmond Enquirer* decided not to publish what most narratives of this case considered to be the central exhibit—the first letter from Mrs. Myers that alerted her relatives to the romance. But this was such a notable absence that they remarked on it. "The first [letter submitted in court] which was supposed to have been the one to which Mr. Hoyt's, taken out of the office by Major Pollard, was an answer, was then shown to Maj. P. [Mrs. Myers' father], and he said it was not his daughter's handwriting. Therefore we have omitted the publication of it."[68] This would protect Mrs. Myers from the dishonor that might stem from a letter she might not have written. In fact, both Richmond papers at least express a hesitation in printing any of the letters. The *Whig* prefaced them with "We had determined as announced yesterday not to publish the correspondence in the case of the Messrs. Myers. Since, however, justice to ourselves and to the parties concerned requires that we publish a portion, we publish that found below as the most important."[69]

The Richmond papers were at least as terse when it came to other famous cases from around the nation. The 1836 murder of prostitute Helen Jewett in New York City, for instance, was one of the most sensationalized cases of the age. The *Richmond Enquirer*, however, printed merely a one-paragraph note alerting readers to this butchery, then a four-paragraph explanation of Richard Robinson's acquittal in the next issue—about one-half column of print altogether.[70] In contrast, New York papers printed a riot of coverage on the case.

The brief coverage of the Jewett case was quite different from the *Enquirer*'s coverage of another northern murder just fourteen years later. When John Webster was accused of killing George Parkman of Harvard in 1850—another case considered one of the most sensationalized of the century—the *Enquirer* printed a total of nine columns in four issues on the progress of the trial and the conviction and sentencing of Webster. The *Richmond Examiner* printed nineteen columns on this case in the two weeks it was at trial.[71] This shows how coverage of sensational crime was growing so quickly in the middle of the nineteenth century.

This difference in coverage also offers further evidence of a reticence on the part of southern papers to publish extensively on cases involving women. The Webster-Parkman murder was gory but also involved only males, unlike either the Myers-Hoyt case four years before or the Jewett murder before that. With the Myers-Hoyt case, Richmond newspapers were reluctant to publish Mrs. Myers's letters at all, published few of them, and came near to apologizing as well. Extant letters demonstrate that much more evidence was in circulation locally than appeared in the press about Virginia Myers and Dudley Marvin Hoyt. Some of these rumors merely added more emotional context to the revelations of infidelity, and others offer more particular evidence. "Her relations are afflicted almost to death, at the occurrence" wrote one Richmond woman to her son in Massachusetts. "It can be proven that every day for ten days that she went to a certain room at the Exchange to meet him, & they were lock'd up together for some time." At the end of the ordeal, this correspondent wrote: "poor Virginia, deservedly sunk to the lowest pitch of degradation. She has attempted to destroy herself by laudanum, but was prevented by her mother. I suppose no one can be more wretch'd."[72] As much as the Virginia press had expanded its coverage of crime sensations by the 1840s, they continued to refrain from pursuing material damaging to the reputation of women. Over the next several generations, that reticence too would erode.

By the 1850s, every Virginia newspaper was more concerned with crime coverage, a process accelerated by the founding of the *Richmond Dispatch*, Virginia's first penny paper.[73] New York was the birthplace of the penny press with the founding of Benjamin Day's *Sun* and James Gordon Bennett's *Herald* in the mid-1830s. These papers were inexpensive and not geared toward politics or economic elites, but rather to the masses and their interests, opening up a much broader market for newspapers. These penny papers and the dozens that followed in their wake—such as the *Richmond Dispatch* in 1850—gave their readers fiction, exposés, crime stories, and energetic and often controversial reading matter. Writers of crime pamphlets in this era, like those of the penny presses, "felt little of the modern journalist's compulsion for accuracy," as one scholar put it. "Fact and fiction blended blithely throughout the reporting."[74] The penny press covered crime much more voluminously than did earlier newspapers but not necessarily more accurately: they bandied the truth about, and a lively and spirited humbuggery prevailed.[75]

Within ten years of its founding, the *Dispatch* was the most popular daily in the city; in fact, it would continue to dominate Richmond's press from that time to the present. The growth of newspapers and their readership in the mid-nineteenth century and the relatively quick surge to dominance of Richmond's mass-market penny paper were founded on many factors: northern innovations in penny papers, printing inventions (the *Dispatch* proudly trumpeted each acquisition of new technology, such as a double-cylinder Hoe press in 1854), the introduction of telegraphy, and a growing, diversifying reading public. The most important differences between the *Dispatch* and the other dailies were its cost and its goal to remain nonpartisan, the two most essential components to the mass-market revolution in the press in this era. News of human interest, including news of the courts, challenged the previous era's emphases on economics, elites, and politics.

The *Dispatch* awarded crime a central place on its pages. Misdeeds from Richmond and from elsewhere in the commonwealth and the nation proved to be inexhaustible fodder for the mass-marketed *Dispatch*. The closer to Richmond the crime and/or the more horrible the misdeeds, the more the *Dispatch* would print. When two Richmond slaves murdered their owners in 1852, for example, the case received ample print coverage.[76] In 1846, the *Richmond Whig* apologized when it printed selections of Mrs. Myers's letters. The *Dispatch* would hardly have bothered to apologize, and the *Whig* and other papers quickly followed suit, giving crime and sensations a much more central role in the press.

The 12 April 1855 issue of the *Dispatch* is typical for a daily of this era. Each of its four pages had six columns, more than half of which comprised advertisements of various sorts. Most of the nine columns of news consisted of very short articles culled from around the locality, state, and nation. Many were political but even more were human-interest stories: fires, suicides, accidents, and crimes of various stripes. On the front page alone, this issue titled brief articles "Chloroform Thief Caught," "Outrage," "Sad Accident," "Suicide," "Murder at Philadelphia," "Woman Killed," and "Arrest of Bruisers." Another half-dozen such stories of crime and violence, including "Mobbing an Abolitionist," appeared on other pages. With the exception of three articles, none of which exceeded one-quarter of a column of print, each of these brevities was only a sentence or at most a short paragraph. Typical coverage of crime in this era involved not a substantive investigation, but rather a series of shock stories: headlines with little actual coverage. Every issue of the *Dispatch* had these sorts of brief stories, but only in the case of a local sensation would the editors print more substantive pieces on criminal matters.

At the same moment that penny papers emerged, so, too, did fictional stories of crime that appeared very much like the true crime pamphlets of the day. In the 1850s, two Virginia printers published the supposed confessions of criminals guilty of multiple murders. Henry Delter married and killed five wives in succession—each in a different manner and fully illustrated in the volume—before he took his own life out of belated remorse. In the other pamphlet, Mary Thorn was the indirect cause of her husband's death in Portsmouth, Virginia. But that was only the beginning of her career: she knifed a family in California who treated her badly, inherited and lost a fortune in Mexico, and finally killed another family in Norfolk by accidentally giving them an overdose of a sleeping concoction.[77] These fictional crime stories were not created in isolation; an important side of the development of mass culture in this period was the emergence of story papers: cheaply produced sheets reprinting works of literature or sensationalized stories of danger, crime, and romance. This was the precursor to the first surge of cheap paperbacks, dime novels, which began to appear in 1860. The sensationalism of crime stories both in the press and the wider publishing business had an important role in the cultivation and exploitation of a mass readership in the first half of the nineteenth century.[78]

In the 1860s, another branch of the mass-circulation revolution in print, the illustrated weekly, joined the *Dispatch* and other dailies. Combining the mass-market appeal of illustrations and stories with a fiery and partisan editor, the *Southern Opinion* (and its editor, Henry Rives Pollard) would each prove to be short-lived but fascinating attempts to engage the growing reading public. The paper was provocative, as the editor forcefully defended the cause of the Confederacy, preached white supremacy, lambasted Reconstruction, and frequently challenged the integrity of individuals in government. In 1869, Pollard stepped too far when he questioned the respectability of a local woman. Her brother returned from a trip to New York and proceeded to assassinate Pollard in the doorway of his office. The *Southern Opinion* failed a few months after Pollard's death, but it had provided a new, provocative, and visually engaging medium for a mass audience.[79]

These innovations in the press and in crime coverage emerged out of a rapidly changing city. Richmond had quickly grown to become the largest city in the fourth most populous state in the union. While dwarfed by the startling growth of a northern metropolis like New York, Richmond nevertheless grew quickly in the antebellum era, becoming the urban center of the state. From 1830 to 1860, Virginia's population stagnated as western migration countered any natural increase, growing only by 23 percent. Richmond's population, in contrast, grew nearly two and a half times larger in those years; since 1790, the city had grown by a factor of ten.[80] This larger and more concentrated population attracted all varieties of commercial and cultural entrepreneurs. With a theater, dozens of saloons, and hundreds of employers, Richmond offered an important concentration of readers for its many newspapers. In 1770, all of Virginia had only two papers; by the 1850s Richmond alone had four daily papers and even more weeklies and semiweeklies. Each was printed on a much larger sheet than newspapers in the nineteenth century, although they all remained in the one-sheet, four-page format.[81] The column inches generated by 1850s' Richmond newspapers alone, in other words, were something on the order of eighty times the amount of print generated weekly in all of Virginia in the revolutionary era.

The dry and spare reports from early-nineteenth-century courtrooms had been leavened with the extravagance of brash opinion by midcentury, and by the 1850s, all of Richmond's daily papers treated crime differently from how it had been covered in the 1830s or before. The *Dispatch* and the *Southern Opinion* were in the forefront of this change, but the other major dailies of the period, the *Whig* and the *Enquirer*, followed closely in their wake. Crime had become meaningful to Virginia's press and to Richmond's public culture.

A murder just after the Civil War demonstrates just how much the Virginia press had evolved in terms of crime sensations. In March 1867, a farmer found a young woman's body in the brush by one of his fields in Henrico County just southeast of Richmond. She had been shot in the head and had marks around her neck. No one recognized her, even after several days of extensive publicity. Oddly enough, no one appeared to be missing in either the county or city. The discovery of this body prompted a dozen stories in the *Richmond Dispatch* that March. If mystery sharpens the interest found in any story, such interest also requires clues to continue to grow and deepen. The body was soon buried, and although an investigation continued, nothing more was found. By April the story itself had died from lack of new evidence.[82]

But in June—three months after the body was buried—an Essex County man wrote to the Henrico Sheriff inquiring after his sister, Mary Emily Pitts Phillips, who was married to a local man, James Jeter Phillips. The sheriff confronted Phillips, who claimed that he had no wife. No one had seen him with this woman, no one in Richmond or Henrico knew of a wife, and no one saw who had killed the young woman. The embers of this story burst into flame with the revelation of letters between Phillips and these relatives of the deceased; for the next three years, the story would enter and leave the headlines many times. Phillips was given a preliminary trial before the Henrico County magistrates and was then arraigned twice before the county court, the first trial ending in a hung jury. In the second trial, Jeter Phillips was convicted and sentenced to hang; the case then proceeded through a series of appeals for the next two years.

The newspaper coverage of this case was extravagant; a local printer likewise capitalized on the interest in the case by publishing a pamphlet of court testimony.[83] The *Richmond Dispatch* printed 124 stories on the Phillips murder over the course of three years. The majority of these stories were as brief as reporting before that time often had been: merely updates of the progress of the case through the judicial system. Sometimes a sentence, sometimes a paragraph, most of these articles were less than half a column in length. For instance, during the two weeks when the case was before the Virginia Supreme Court of Appeals, the *Dispatch* barely listed the witnesses brought forth and gave no substance to the proceedings until the verdict was handed down.[84] When not at trial, stories tracing the progress of the Phillips case could be shorter still, amounting to one or two sentences. For example: "Jeter Phillips—This was the day fixed for the execution of this unfortunate man, but, having been respited, his unhappy existence will be prolonged until the 30th of next month."[85] The brevity of these updates is in keeping with earlier trends; the abundant number of them, however, is extraordinary.

If most stories were such updates of the tedious appeals process, dozens of other stories led readers through the facts of the case and through the testimony in court, witness by witness. Unlike earlier eras, some newspaper stories in this case were even overburdened with emotion and argument. Some editors phrased the issue in extreme terms: they considered Jeter to be a beast deserving of God's and society's swift vengeance. H. Rives Pollard of the *Southern Opinion* wrote that if the court of appeals were to overturn Phillips's conviction, "the greatest criminal of the age will go un-whipped of justice—saved by a technicality of law and a quibble of coun-sel!"[86] During its brief life, the weekly *Southern Opinion* ran eighteen stories on the Phillips case. Pollard warned against any legal maneuvering that might free Phillips and repeatedly charged that two members of the first jury, which could not agree on a verdict, had been bought by relatives of the accused.[87] Editor Pollard followed this charge by printing a number of intercepted letters from Phillips to his "sweethearts" in a Richmond brothel. This would be a damning contradiction of Jeter's otherwise ster-ling reputation, but the fact that no other papers followed this lead opens the possibility that this was a fabrication of the editor.[88]

These letters in the *Opinion* are of little consequence except that they demonstrate how elaborate narratives of crime and sensation had become. In fact, after Pollard's death, the *Southern Opinion* continued operation intermittently for another six months under a new editor, who printed sev-eral more articles on the Phillips case. These stories were just as opinion-ated and sensational but in the opposite direction! Now the editor claimed that the evidence of Phillips's guilt was questionable and that justice would be served only if his sentence of death were commuted.[89]

How different was sensationalism in the Virginia press by midcentury? Press coverage of the Phillips murder case resulted in ten times more stories than the antebellum norm, most continuing to be brief but others elaborating extensively on the presentation of such stories: full-fledged narratives and emotional editorializing. Far from being exasperated by the necessity of printing stories on such a case, Virginia's newspaper editors saw the crime as an opportunity to grab the interest of their readership.

Emphasizing this change, lawyers for Phillips's defense entered into a prolonged harangue against the press coverage during his 1867 preliminary trial. In an attempt to lure public opinion to their side, they argued that the Richmond press had reported every minute detail in the case, including a host of rumors that were without foundation. A daguerreotype found in Jeter's room, for instance, was of a relative of his, not of his supposed wife, as the papers erroneously reported. The press, they shouted in the courtroom, had convicted their client before he ever went to court.[90]

This sort of statement has been heard throughout the nation from this era to the present. What is important to note is that this is an argument *new* to this era. Lawyers would not have made this statement fifty years before, when newspaper coverage was so minimal. Such an argument simply would not have been plausible before the nineteenth-century press had elaborated on its coverage of criminal matters.[91]

■

A scholar researching crime in Virginia newspapers and pamphlets up to 1850 would hardly recognize the nature of crime sensationalism as rendered by scholars of New England publishing. Moving from a Puritan execution sermon tradition—which Virginia did not share—to a florid penny press sensationalism in the 1830s—which Virginia likewise did not experience in this era (but soon would)—the northern trends in sensationalism do not capture the nature of the southern experience. By 1850, however, this was changing, and northern and southern crime sensations began to look much more alike.

Southern sensations were still distinctive in terms of both race and gender, however. A reluctance to sully the character of women in Richmond's papers finds no parallel in the North. Likewise, this era shows Virginians to be both obsessed with black insurrection and pointedly unwilling to write very much about them. Richmond papers wrote so little on the 1800 planned insurrection by Gabriel that it can be difficult even to identify what this event was about. In 1831, they wrote much more, but even then the papers covered dozens of trials, murders, and executions with a bare sentence or two, even when it came to Nat Turner himself. The fact that he was captured, tried, and executed ("of course") within thirteen days demonstrates how abridged was any popular or official consideration of this crime. As much as blacks were kept illiterate due to southern laws forbidding the teaching of reading and writing, they were also made mute by a judicial process that shuffled them quickly off to sale in the west or to the gallows. Contributing to this effort was a press that abbreviated its coverage to the bare essentials when it came to insurrection.

There was no single moment when Virginia's press started to invest in sensationalized crime. Coverage of crimes was larger in the 1820s than at any previous time in Virginia's history, only to be superseded by coverage in each succeeding decade. Many of the attributes that scholars ascribe to the penny press "revolution" already appeared in Richmond before the city had a penny paper. And when penny papers arrived in the 1850s, they did not signal an end to this evolution of sensationalism, but rather an important new vehicle for the continual elaboration of these interests.

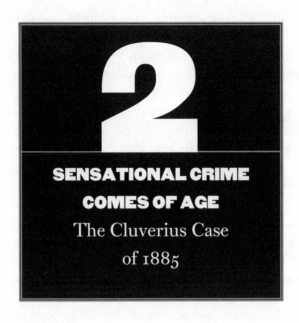

2

SENSATIONAL CRIME
COMES OF AGE
The Cluverius Case
of 1885

WE CONFESS THAT THE WIDESPREAD CURIOSITY WHICH HAS BEEN
MANIFESTED ABOUT THE MATTER HAS PAINED US. THE EYES AND EARS OF
THE CITY HAVE BEEN MORBIDLY GREEDY. . . . THE DEATH OF THIS GIRL IS
A PUBLIC EVENT, AND WE SYMPATHIZE WITH THE EAGERNESS TO RIP OFF
ITS MYSTERY AND PROBE TO ITS REAL EXPLANATION. THIS, HOWEVER, IS A
DIFFERENT THING FROM THAT GAPING AND RAVENOUS CURIOSITY WHICH
HAS BEEN SO RAMPANT IN THE CITY. RICHMOND HAS FAIRLY EMPTIED
ITSELF AT THE OLD RESERVOIR, THE SCENE OF THE TRAGEDY. MEN, WOMEN
AND CHILDREN HAVE STREAMED OUT IN A CEASELESS PROCESSION—ALL
STEADILY BENT ON THE POOR PLEASURE OF VIEWING THE SPOT WHERE
THE SAD YOUNG LIFE MET ITS LAST DISASTROUS STRUGGLE. THEN, TOO,
WHENEVER THE PRISONER—AS YET INNOCENT IN THE SIGHT OF THE LAW
AND ENTITLED TO THE CHARITY OF EVERY DOUBT—HAS BEEN BROUGHT
FORTH FROM HIS CELL, SURGING THRONGS HAVE HUNG UPON HIS PATH AND
SCRAMBLED FOR A SIGHT OF HIM. THE JAIL HAS BEEN INFESTED BY HORDES
OF LOUNGERS PRAYING FOR A PEEP AT THE PRISONER. WE WILL NOT SAY
THAT CURIOSITY IS A CRIME, BUT CURIOSITY ABOUT A CRIME IS
NOT BECOMING. IT IS A FEVERISH, ABNORMAL FEELING, WHICH, IF NOT
CHECKED, WILL LEAD TO SOMETHING WORSE. SELF-RESPECT SHOULD
FORTIFY US AGAINST YEARNING AFTER THE SENSATIONAL.

Richmond Religious Herald, 30 April 1885

Awakening this "feverish, abnormal feeling" in Richmond in the spring of 1885 was the discovery of Lillian Madison's body in the reservoir. Days later, Thomas Cluverius sat in jail, facing a capital charge for her murder. But the case against Cluverius rested upon circumstantial evidence, and many questioned whether he would be convicted. The indeterminacy of this evidence transfixed Richmond. Reverend William E. Hatcher, a local minister who spoke regularly with the accused, wrote that the murder was "the one absorbing topic in Richmond and many persons say that they cannot think or dream of anything else." This may be hyperbole, but newspapers likewise began to report not simply the developments in the crime investigation, but also the public's response to the case: describing the circulating rumors, for instance, or calculating the number of people viewing the body, the reservoir, and Madison's grave. The *State* claimed that the murder "is discussed at the clubs, on the streets, at the dinner-table, around the fireside and at business places, and is the all-absorbing topic."[1]

The *Whig* echoed this sentiment, adding a democratic flavor to the interest: "every word in reference to the case, and every suggestion as to the murderer and the cause is listened to with the greatest avidity, no matter from whom they come." Indeed, it seemed to affect all of Richmond. Crowds were described as black and white, male and female, and a variety of Richmonders wrote about the case in letters and diaries and cut out newspaper articles on the case for their scrapbooks. When asked in court why he had discussed openly a conversation with Cluverius, one witness replied commonsensically, "from the simple fact that everybody was discussing it and I discussed it with everybody else."[2]

Throughout May and into June 1885, Richmonders centered their attention on the makeshift courtroom of Richmond's hustings court where Cluverius was on trial for his life.[3] For almost a month, the lawyers, prisoner, judge, and a crowd of hundreds gathered to find a jury, introduce evidence, and to make the final appeals of the defense and prosecution to the jury. The Cluverius case of 1885 left behind it a rich vein of sources illuminating what occurred in the press, among the broader populace, and in the lives of the accused and the victim. This chapter explores the stories told about Lillian and Thomas alongside the broader historical record of them, drawing on court testimony, lawyers' arguments, and press reports as well as evidence from family letters and census records. It tells of the crime and the histories of the individuals but is chiefly concerned with stories: the ways in which Richmond's press, public, and lawyers turned, embellished, ignored, and shaped the histories of these people. Using the raw material of their own histories, Richmonders fashioned somewhat different stories of the couple, typecasting the stories of victim and defendant, woman and man. It is these distinctions—between history and story, fact and fiction—that reveal the community's concerns. Richmonders had an opportunity to write into the story of Lillian and Thomas something of their own hopes and fears, and the historical record gives us a chance to decipher that writing.

This case offers a telling example of the nature of sensationalism in the South in the late nineteenth century. No longer reticent to cover sensations, Virginia's press paralleled the national norms in print sensationalism, much to the evident distress of the editor of the *Religious Herald*, judging by the quotation that opens the chapter. The lone exception to Richmond's abundant sensationalism is an important one: southern chivalry apparently influenced editors to downplay anything negative about women brought up in the course of sensations, exhibiting a strong inclination to type them all as "true women." This era in the history of the Virginia press demonstrates particularly acute ties between its coverage of sensational crimes and the genre of melodrama popularized in so many forms in nineteenth-century America. During the last half of the century, the press covered sensations with abandon, yet editors clearly turned their coverage away from a strictly factual and dispassionate presentation to an emphasis on the most melodramatic elements. In the New South, murder sensations were now as marketable as in the urban, industrial North.

■

THE VICTIM AND THE ACCUSED

Fannie Lillian Madison lived a complex and checkered life; Thomas Cluverius was a cipher. Unmarried and pregnant, Madison had turned away from her parents and engaged in a variety of behaviors considered questionable for a young woman of her day. Practicing law and teaching Sunday school, Cluverius seemed too upstanding to possibly be a murderer. Most nineteenth-century crimes have left little behind beyond the public tales created about them. The rich evidence about Madison and Cluverius allows us to see just how great the distance could be between the narratives of crime and their realities.

Lillian Madison was born in King William County in the midst of the Civil War. Her father was in the Confederate army at her birth; her mother convalesced with relatives, with whom the family remained until her father returned. The eldest of eight children, Lillian grew up in a poor family that was unable to give her much of a step-up in life. The Madisons owned a farm of just over one hundred acres but could not afford to send Lillian to school for as long as she desired.[4] Her father wrote that "we have eight children to feed and clothe and send to school and otherwise provide for ... it seems to me that some people forget we have any children but Lilly."[5] The "some people" he referred to was Jane Tunstall, Lillian's great aunt, who was a well-to-do widow in the adjoining King and Queen County. According to census records, Tunstall's holdings amounted to nearly ten times the value of her poorer cousins' farm. Tunstall also had no children of her own on whom to bestow her largesse; she hoped to aid her young nieces and nephews instead, including both Thomas Cluverius and Lillian Madison.[6]

In her adolescence, Lillian found it difficult to live as she would like in her parents' home. Her family was riven with conflict, some of which had to do with her, though much of it did not. Lillian's parents and the Madison relations were on one side of this wider family conflict, and her maternal relations—Jane Tunstall chief among them—constituted the other. Among other issues,[7] the Madisons believed that Tunstall and other relations (like the Cluveriuses) were not simply disrespectful to them, but actively "poisoning the children" against them.[8]

Lillian Madison added several new twists to the family problems and became, for a time, one focus of the family's rancor. In the early 1880s, Tunstall paid for Lillian's board and expenses at Dr. Garlick's Bruington Academy in King and Queen County for one year. By that time, Lillian had already attended a free public school near her parents' home and another term at a school in King and Queen County, during which time she stayed in Mrs. Tunstall's home. The Madisons responded to this aid from Mrs. Tunstall with a mixture of humble appreciation and suspicion. Mrs. Tunstall wished to send Madison for another term at Garlick's academy, but her parents refused. A wider breach had opened between the two sides of the family, and the Madisons were not willing to have their daughter receive any further boons from Tunstall.[9]

Letters render other tantalizing hints regarding Lillian's place in the family conflict. In 1881, Thomas Cluverius's mother wrote that if Lillian visited "I will not ask her a question but do all I can to make her do wright [sic]."[10] A few months later, Beverly W. Cluverius (the accused murderer's father) wrote to Madison's mother that Lillian had stayed with them longer than planned "because I did not think it would look very well for her to be running off just because your Aunt Fannie was coming home."[11] Nothing in the extant historical record sheds light on these statements—what question Cluverius's mother will refrain from asking, how Lillian was doing wrong, or what would be unseemly about Lillian leaving the Cluverius's house at a certain time. In light of her later pregnancy, however, it is difficult not to read these letters as reflecting on her as a delinquent.

In the early 1880s, Lillian's mother and father forbade her from speaking to Tunstall and her own maternal grandparents; her parents also burned any letters found between them.[12] Both Lillian and Tunstall repeatedly broke that parental order.[13] Lillian's parents apparently wanted her to live a quiet, respectable life as a farmer's wife; Lillian appears to have drifted quickly away from her own family and toward the promise of a better—or at least different—life elsewhere. Although few documents survive recording her thoughts about her life and how it should develop, ample evidence suggests that she resented living on her parent's farm. Like many young women, she aspired to upward mobility, it seems clear. She found hope for a new destiny in the beneficence of Jane Tunstall. More immediately, she also appeared eager for excitement and attention. She seems to have been spirited and willful, perhaps to the point of being self-destructive.

Around 1880, a controversy concerning a well digger, G. Bailey Biggs, illustrates her impulsive character and ultimately prompted Lillian to leave her parents' home in the summer of 1884. The problem involved a number of "indiscreet" letters that passed between Lillian and Biggs and between her and three other local men. The neighborhood held Biggs in poor repute; Charles Madison described him as "a man of fine appearance, a little dandy looking fellow, about the kind of a man who would take the eye of any young girl just coming into her teens."[14] But he was also reckless and "disagreeable," quickly alienating the Madisons and their extended family. Biggs obtained letters between Lillian and the other men and proceeded to "make himself obnoxious" to the family, including writing anonymous letters to Mrs. Tunstall. One observer who read a few of Madison's letters said that they "amounted to nothing more than simply to demonstrate the fact that Miss Madison lived unpleasantly with her parents." But one letter did reveal Lillian's plan to meet and move in with one of the men when she came to visit the state fair in Richmond. The letter said that "once in Richmond, she never expected to return to her father's house."[15] The conflict with Biggs over these letters was resolved under the guidance of lawyers with the return of all letters between the two and each paying their own costs for the mediation. Biggs then left the county.

Lillian turned twenty-one in late June 1884, and within two weeks, she had burned the collection of letters surrendered by Biggs. Her parents were saving them "in case anybody in years to come should bring up this scrape, then [they] would have the letters to show the nature of it."[16] They were very angry that she had destroyed this protection of her character and their good name. They saw this act as reckless, willful, and self-destructive; they also must have seen her character as something that might easily be questioned, requiring this protection. On 8 July 1884, one week after she burned the letters from Biggs and two weeks after she attained her majority, Lillian left the home of her parents for good. She lived for the next several months in the household of her maternal grandfather.

Lillian could hardly wait to be free of her parents. In 1881, she wrote to Tunstall that her parents "have abused you & me for every thing that is unhuman. O! what a terror my life is. O! how I am struggling struggling with my poor weak self to night to keep my resolve. I have wept until tears are no relief and O! my sad suffering but I have Jesus to look to, he suffered too even death at the hands of merciless tormentors & of course he knows my suffering. It is my prayer to night that the sun of tomorrow may shine on me a corpse. O! if suicide were not a sin how soon the lingering spark of my life would vanish."[17] Tunstall's testimony in the trial revealed that Madison had long planned her escape from her parents as soon as she turned twenty-one, when, Tunstall believed, she had planned to move in with her. Mrs. Tunstall expressed fear of Lillian's self-destructive urges when she wrote to Mr. Madison in 1881 that Lillian's upbringing—"being shut out from all young society"—would be "the cause of throwing herself away, unless God restrains her by his powers."[18]

It is worth noting that all of this conflict occurred in the years and months *before* her most traumatic experience: pregnancy. When she learned of her condition, Madison left her home county. But instead of moving nearby to live with Tunstall, she took a position in the mountain county of Bath, far away from the family who would perceive her state most quickly. On 16 October 1884 she moved in with a local family there and taught their adopted son as well as a handful of other students in the community.[19]

If her flight was intended to forestall further conflict, it failed. Her parents were dismayed, and her move probably provoked nearly as much gossip as if she had stayed. In October of 1884, just as Lillian packed to leave King William County for good, Charles Madison wrote an extraordinarily frank and impassioned letter to the relative who planned to carry Lillian to Bath. In it, he demonstrated his concern about what this move appeared to imply: "I can not stand quietly by and see that performed which will certainly bring distress and grief without [my] giving any warning. . . . Have you not considered what the consequences may be? Don't you and your ma [Lillian's grandmother] know what reports will be raised? and what

[King] William [County] people will say is the matter with her? especially in her condition with her face all swolen [*sic*] and looking hit?"[20] This last line is intriguing, if vague. Was she abused, and was he concerned that a public outcry would arise against some sort of family violence against her? Or was she simply "swolen" from her pregnancy, and he was worried that neighbors would believe—rightly—that she carried a child out of wedlock? This is an interpretive conundrum, for only thin shreds of evidence reflect on this issue, and those shreds are not in agreement. Toward the end of this letter, Lillian's father implies knowledge of her pregnancy, or at least knowledge that she was sexually active. Likewise, he later testified in court that he had regarded Lillian and Cluverius as lovers by the summer of 1884.[21] Therefore, a fear of public knowledge of her condition might explain this comment.

But weighing in on the other side of the issue is a single reference in one letter to Lillian from Jane Tunstall, which implies much more than simply that she was "living unpleasantly with her parents." If this third-hand report from a questionable source were true, Lillian faced rather frightening violence from her own parents. According to Jane Tunstall, a young woman named Lizzie Brown had stayed with her for a time and, Tunstall believed, was jealous of the place Lillian held in Tunstall's life. Tunstall therefore discounted Brown's report, but she repeated it nonetheless to Lillian. After she left Tunstall's house, "Lizzie Brown wrote Nolie Bray word [that] your father and mother tied your hands behind you and whipped you nearly to death, and that they broke your trunk open and got your love-letters, and said you and Willie Cluverius were to be married as soon as you were of age, and much more."[22] This story is plausible in a number of regards, for we know that Lillian was sexually active by this time (hence the reference to enforced marriage), that she had love letters in her trunk, and that she had persistent conflict with her parents. But *Willie* Cluverius, Thomas's older brother? In addition, it seems important that Tunstall thought this might be a story manufactured by Lizzie Brown designed to disgrace Lillian. Ultimately, the record of Lillian's life only hints that she might have faced actual violence at the hands of her family. Like so much in the historical record, this question will remain unanswered.

Toward the end of his angry letter to John Walker, Charles Madison also reflected passionately on the previous years of feuding in the family:

> Several years ago some people who ought to have been myself and Lucy's [Lillian's mother] best friends became our *bitter* enemies. They took our oldest child for a tool to carry out their *Hell Blushing* schemes and from that day to this with my oldest child banded with them they have done

all that human brain could devise or Satan himself dictate to accomplish our ruin and what has been the result! Look around and see if the very ones who have been trying to sink us have not sunk lowest themselves and are still sinking every day. Well after all of Lillie's fine friends on her mother's side of the family have accomplished all of the Devil's work they can through her and sinn'd her name forever and reached the end of the rope they all at once got tired of her. She has served their purposes and now they want to get rid of her and instead of bonding together to take care of her after having ruined her they take her and shove her off on her relations on her Father's side of the family.[23]

This very rich and angry letter, written when Lillian was already pregnant and but five months before her death, underscores that Lillian was caught in the vortex of her family's bitter feud, and, even before her pregnancy, her character was blemished if not ruined. Certain loaded passages—"sinn'd her name forever," "having ruined her"—indicate knowledge of her loss of virginity—often considered a damning loss in the nineteenth century—at the hands of someone on the Tunstall side of the family. By the time this angry letter was written, however, Mr. Madison and his wayward daughter were thoroughly alienated. During her five months in Bath County, Lillian wrote to her mother but once, at Christmas, and to her father not at all.[24]

After becoming pregnant and leaving the county, Lillian found that her problems multiplied. In the weeks immediately before her death, several people in Bath County reported that she was often "blue" or "depressed";[25] some even heard her speak of suicide. A friend in her new home, for instance, testified in court that Madison had expressed the hope of her life ending in the month before she rode to Richmond. She reportedly burned most of her letters in the week before her last visit to Richmond, saying to a friend that she felt something horrible was about to happen and that she could not bear to have her mother read them. She recklessly crossed a thawing creek and when asked why she would do so dangerous a thing replied, "I don't care." On the train to Richmond in March, Madison voiced her hope that the engine would run off the tracks, killing her. She was speaking with a train porter, who hoped this was a joke, but he was not at all sure.[26] Two days later, she was pulled from the Richmond reservoir.

■

Like all "protagonists" in murder stories, Thomas Judson Cluverius was much more central than the victim to the public debate about the case. He was at the center of the legal as well as popular stories fashioned after the crime. Lawyers attempted to define his character—upstanding? malevolent?—and explore possible motives for the crime by pointing to his history. It was a very uneventful history, as it turns out, with the lone exception of his recent arrest for murder. Adding a tremendous amount of drama to his story, however, was the fact that his life was not yet over but was in jeopardy. Unlike Madison's, the final chapter of his life was yet unwritten, and therefore his whole story line was humming with contingency. Richmonders studied his expression while he was in the courtroom, his gait, his clothing—even reports of his digestion—for evidence of guilt or innocence. Likewise they studied his family, his history, for clues to his character. This might be the key, they apparently thought, that would help explain his seemingly inexplicable crime.

The sensational criminal flew in the face of this effort at articulation. An upstanding man like Cluverius was at the heart of the white middle- and upper-class society in the late nineteenth century. This was no outsider charged with horrible crimes: an African American, a foreigner, or a madman who could be distanced from white, middle-class normalcy with little intellectual effort. Cluverius was one of their own: white, educated, and esteemed. Society wrestled with the question of his guilt but also with ways to distinguish him from the law-abiding community. If *this* man was a monster, how could they discriminate between the monster and themselves?

In the diary of one Richmonder, Charles Wallace, we can see the range of responses possible to such an accused murderer. Early on, Wallace treated Cluverius as a pitiful fool and a depraved sinner worthy of our prayers: "Everybody's pity goes out to the poor Maiden who is supposed to have been seduced and afterward killed by Cluverius. I saw Cluverius friday last as he walked from the court to his carriage between two policemen. I was deeply touched by the sight of him, and had I been called to judge him then, would have given him a charitable judgment. Poor man! I pity him as I do his dead sweetheart. I pity him even though he killed her. The greater the depravity, the greater my pity."[27] Even after his conviction, Cluverius remained a sad figure to Wallace, one hounded by a mob that seemed as terrible as the murder itself: "Thank God that I still feel a profound sympathy for this brutal and ignorant criminal. How many of those who thirst for the blood of the felon call themselves Christians! 'Thou shalt not kill' means [to them] they shall not kill me, but thou shall kill him."[28]

A year and a half later, however, the diarist characterized Cluverius with the most dangerous and evil words at his disposal. No longer pitiable, Cluverius appeared to embody a threat to all of society: "No more awful scoundrel can have lived than Cluverius. He seemed to be what he was not, a christian and gentleman. It is this seeming like the gold plate upon coin that passes with the ignorant world for genuine metal. So you seem to be, so you seem to pray, so you seem to abstain from vicious excess. So you hide from curious eyes your manifold sins. . . . He had the head of a fiend and the smile of an angel. He was eaten up with lust."[29] A lustful fiend, a pitiful sinner, a mob ready to do violence in retribution. An accused murderer such as Cluverius provoked a range of responses from the community around him and even from a single individual.

Thomas Judson Cluverius was born near Beulahville in King William County to the east of Richmond on 10 August 1861. By 1880, the Cluverius family had moved to King and Queen County, also in the same part of the state. In that year, Thomas's father rented forty acres of land and actively farmed ten of them. Despite its small size, the farm provided the family with potatoes, chickens, hogs, corn, oats, wheat, peaches, and timber. They had the help of one teenage farmhand, and they produced enough to have a small surplus for sale. The Cluverius family was not blessed with bounty, but they apparently had a sufficiency, particularly given the moderate size of the family. Unlike the Madisons, with eight children, the Cluverius family numbered just four: parents and two sons. According to Thomas: "far from being in affluence, we had all the necessaries and comforts and many of the luxuries of life."[30]

Those luxuries came not only from having a small family, but also from the beneficence of a wealthy relative. Thomas and his older brother William went to live with Jane Tunstall, their childless aunt, in 1876. In August of that year, Jane's husband died, leaving her in a comfortable position from his years as a successful local merchant. Except for periods boarding at school, Thomas lived with his aunt near Little Plymouth, King and Queen County, until his arrest in 1885. William likewise lived with Tunstall for the rest of his adolescence and into adulthood; in fact, Jane Tunstall bequeathed her house and lands to William at her death in 1892. In effect, Tunstall treated William and Thomas as her own sons.[31]

As a youth, Thomas was first taught by his relatives, and then for short durations he attended a number of small schools in his neighborhood in King William County. After his move to King and Queen County, Thomas studied at Dr. Bland's Locust Academy for two years (one of the schools Lillian Madison also briefly attended). He then boarded for two years at the Aberdeen Academy of J. C. Council. This was a more rigorous school, the previous programs having been rudimentary and piecemeal, typical attributes of Virginia country schools in the 1870s. With continued financial help from his aunt, Thomas took a course in law at Richmond College (now the University of Richmond) beginning in September 1880. He graduated with a bachelor of law degree in June 1882. His stay at the college was neither so distinguished nor so dishonorable as to warrant more than a spare mention in the school's records. According to his own memory, "I cannot claim that I was specially studious, but I had to work pretty hard to get my diploma."[32] Later testimony at trial revealed acquaintances there who held him in high regard.[33] Yet a Richmond prostitute reported that he had learned his way around the city well enough to find at least one of the city's brothels as well.[34]

Nevertheless, he was considered an upstanding young man by virtually all who knew him, a measure, perhaps, of the range of behaviors acceptable to young men of the time. After graduating, he returned to King and Queen County and began his practice, traveling monthly to the courts in his and the surrounding counties. He taught Sunday school at Olivet Baptist Church in his neighborhood. At the time of his arrest, in fact, he was assistant superintendent of this Sunday school. According to a number of neighbors and schoolmates, he gave no evidence of reckless habits or intemperance; several testified that they had not seen him so much as take a drink. "I look upon him, gentlemen of the jury," said one associate in words little stronger than those of a half-dozen other character witnesses, "as one of the most correct, straightforward and Christian young men of my whole acquaintance."[35]

In July and again in August of 1884, Cluverius visited overnight at the house of his cousin, John Walker. This was the house Lillian Madison had recently moved into when she left her parents after reaching the age of majority. While there, Lillian and Thomas "used to go out every evening, look at the flowers and walk around there . . . they seemed right smartly attached to each other" but gave no evidence of having more than a cousinly fondness, according to Walker.[36] The two cousins were both in Richmond on 6 January 1885, and one hotel maid remembered that Lillian did not sleep in her bed that night.[37] And again, in March of 1885, the two would arrive in Richmond at the same time. Only Lillian's father testified that he suspected them of being intimate; otherwise, no one even noticed these overlapping stays in Richmond until after Madison's death.[38]

Cluverius was engaged at the time of Lillian Madison's death in 1885. Little was made of the woman he was to have wed. It is difficult to interpret this silence: it could simply be the reticence of society to publicize a young woman's private connections, or it may be that the engagement was not serious. It was apparently not widely known, for Charles Madison, among others, testified that he had not heard of Cluverius's fiancée.[39] Nolie Bray was the young woman's name, and she had been acquainted with both Cluverius and Lillian Madison for some time. During the trial, Nolie Bray simply submitted a brief "agreed statement" in which she stated that they had been engaged for the two years before his arrest, "with one intermission about eighteen months ago." Bray continued that Lillian Madison had mentioned this engagement in more than one of her letters to Miss Bray, so she was sure she knew of the connection.[40]

Without his arrest for murder, Cluverius's life would hardly have attracted notice. It was the stark contrast between his normal, middle-class young life and the horror of a brutal murder of a pregnant cousin that made his story so anguishing and riveting to all of Richmond. If it was agreed that Cluverius was a well-respected member of the community, much was left in contention about his character, his morality, and several particular moments of his recent history. In addition, much could be read into this agreed history: piety or deception, a wronged innocent or a confidence man pretending to be of good standing.

■

THE STORY TOLD

When Lillian Madison was discovered in Richmond's reservoir in March of 1885, the *Richmond Whig* subtitled its article "A New Colleen Bawn."[41] Dion Boucicault was one of the most widely known and prolific of the nineteenth-century melodramatic playwrights, and *The Colleen Bawn* (Gaelic for "fair-haired girl") was among his most popular.[42] Set in Boucicault's native Ireland, the play was named for a poor, lovely, and virtuous young lass who was secretly in love with and even married to an impoverished aristocrat. This young man, in turn, was under pressure to marry into a wealthy family in order to keep his family land from falling into the hands of evil creditors. Typical of the genre, this melodrama took many twists and turns as innumerable revelations were uncovered about the interconnected principal characters. These included misdirected—and therefore misconstrued—notes between lovers and a cloak found in the lake misinterpreted as a sign that the Colleen Bawn had committed suicide. In the climactic "sensation scene," the Colleen Bawn was thrown off a rock into a lake by a cruel and misguided henchman of her aristocratic husband. She was saved by a watchful admirer, and it was revealed finally that her husband loved her and did not instruct his servant to kill her. On the final page, all of the deeply felt loves that had been hidden were revealed, the evil characters were likewise exposed, a pair of happy weddings were proposed, and the impoverished aristocrats saved their land by other means than a distasteful marriage. Melodrama, indeed.

The *Whig* drew a superficial parallel between the sensation scene of the Boucicault play and the drowning of Madison in the Richmond reservoir. But the paper might as well have conjured it as a representation of how male and female figures appeared generally in both popular literature and crime sensations in the nineteenth century. The conventions of the melodrama, along with the strictures defining respectable manhood and womanhood more generally, provide a frame of reference for understanding the popular perception of these stories of violence. The Colleen Bawn was a static character, a foil and an inspiration to the other characters. She was beauty, she was virtue, she was a true woman, but she was not in control of her destiny, much less a character with any complications or even facets. Similarly, the Richmond press and public delved very little into the history or place of women victims.

Likewise, Cluverius embodied the classic melodramatic villain. The action in *The Colleen Bawn* centered on the male characters: the villainous creditor, the misguided henchman, the secret husband, and the admirer-savior (a role originally played by Boucicault himself). In stark contrast to the victim's passivity, the aristocratic husband was in turmoil, and the evil creditor was meddling actively in the affairs of the entire cast. Was the husband truly in love with her ("I have neither slept nor waked—I have but one thought, one feeling; my love for her, wild and maddened")? Or was he an erratic lover or even an evil, loveless man who would kill her to better his prospects ("the villain—the monster! He sent her to heaven because he wanted her to blot out with her tears the record of his iniquity")?[43] The narrative power of this story arose largely from the conflict within this male character.

Much of the debate over the Cluverius case occurred in just such terms. It reflected elements of not only Boucicault's *Colleen Bawn*, but also a host of popular literary forms in the nineteenth century. The darkness of this tale was like gothic novels, and the mysterious and haunting questions about circumstantial evidence compared to detective stories pioneered by Edgar Allan Poe (who was raised in Richmond, incidentally) and institutionalized in popular dime novels. The tendency toward the "melodramatic mode" was common to all of these popular forms, a "mode of excess" in which "nothing is *under*stood, all is *over*stated."[44]

Fiction writers blurred the distinction between popular literary forms and true crime narratives by using true crimes as models for their plots.

Susanna Rowson's early novel *Charlotte Temple* (1794) was reportedly based on a true story, the sad tale of a woman seduced, brought to America, and abandoned to die, pregnant and penniless.[45] Another early historical romance, Hannah Webster Foster's *The Coquette* (1797), was founded on the recent reports of Elizabeth Whitman's death. Some of the most famous nineteenth-century murders have inspired fiction. The 1841 murder of Mary Rogers in New York was fictionalized by a number of authors, most famously in Poe's "The Murder of Marie Roget."[46]

Not only did book and pamphlet publishers produce fiction linked to true crimes, but the same newspapers that pursued true crime stories also printed countless pieces of crime fiction. The stories "Wanted—a Clue" and "The Murdered Cashier—Strongest Circumstantial Evidence of Guilt" each appeared in the *Richmond Dispatch* during its coverage of the Cluverius case, for example.[47] Likewise, other papers in Richmond printed "How I Became a Murderer," "The Detective's Story," and "A Murderer's Story," among dozens of others.[48]

If true crimes influenced writers of fiction, at least as often the inspiration flowed in the other direction. Journalists, publishers, lawyers, and spectators regularly employed motifs and stereotypes readily available— and, importantly, readily recognizable—from popular culture. At times, the connection was quite direct. In 1885, Lillian Madison left behind her a copy of a periodical containing a love story called "The Gilded Sin." Marked in the margins of this volume were—purportedly—Lillian's own responses to a tale of romance and woe, which the *Richmond Dispatch* promptly made into a story of their own. "Alas! a mistake," she wrote of one character's deception; "true, true," she marked as another character declared death better than abandonment by a lover; and at the end, when all mistaken notions were put to rest and two marriages were proposed, "Truth is Mighty."[49] Here, sentimental literature and the victim's response to it actually intrude upon a real murder case.[50]

In more substantial ways melodrama helped to shape the nature of the Cluverius case as well. Lillian Madison's history provided the possibility of creating a more complex characterization than that afforded by melodramatic stereotypes. Here was a young woman caught in tidal forces, torn between factions in her family, between the farm and education, between poverty and plenty, between "purity" and "knowledge." Like Eliza Wharton in the early American novel *The Coquette* and like so many young women who turned against their parents and the rigid role designed for them, Lillian "naively sought to exercise her freedom only to find out that she had none."[51] She was the tortured center of conflicts that interest historians as well as watchful neighbors: sex and violence, strife and betrayal, modern life and the protection of family. This has many of the ingredients of a great tale, investing with even more pathos her life and death and opening up a range of rich and disturbing issues to mull over. Who might have saved her? What did she lack at home? What place should women have on the farm or in the city? These questions are embedded in Lillian's life and death, deepening the crime to reflect more broadly on the city, society, and the lives of everyone.

Or, rather, such questions *would have* raised such issues if the story of Madison's life were told as I have rendered it above. It was not. Most of her history outlined in the section above is culled from extant letters in the family that were never made public. Major parts of Lillian's history never appeared in court or in print, others appeared in the trial but not in the more public treatment of the case, and still more appeared in both but were mentioned only in passing. In this way, the public history of the murder edited the victim's life, trimming away and brushing over unwanted twists, turns, and complications in order to render a compelling and powerful— but different—tale.[52]

In court and even more in the press, "Lillian Madison" appeared as an abstraction of her history. The family conflict that surrounded Madison hardly entered the courtroom. The issue of conflict in general arose during the questioning of several members of the family, but each deflected such questions, and the lawyers rarely pressed. Except for several letters directly to or from Lillian, little of the correspondence cited above entered the trial transcript.[53] Only a little more of Lillian's wayward or delinquent behavior surfaced there. The prosecuting attorneys in the case had an obviously compelling reason to avoid delving deeply into these matters: it helped them not at all to sully the reputation of the victim.

The defense, however, might have gained a considerable advantage by attempting to characterize Lillian as depraved or unstable rather than as a betrayed woman. Juries rarely convicted when the victim was a prostitute or otherwise considered corrupt.[54] On only one occasion (in a month-long trial), however, did the defense pursue a witness in an attempt to sully Lillian's character. When questioning John Walker, Lillian's uncle, the defense called the victim "a fugitive" and probed into the issue of Biggs and his letters and into a picnic she attended in the autumn before her death (where she might have had a rendezvous with a suitor). Walker was not very helpful, however, giving only the broad outlines of the Biggs matter and forcefully testifying to his longstanding belief that Madison engaged in no improprieties whatsoever.[55] Other than this one instance, the defense downplayed any evidence of Lillian's missteps. Perhaps they simply calculated that such an aggressive defense would alienate the jury and public further.[56]

The defense team did bring before the court's attention—and, through the papers, the public's attention—Lillian's suicidal words as well as two other men who had written amorous letters to Madison in her last years. Emmet Williams, of Bath County, stated that he and Lillian had exchanged something like ten letters on each side "of a loving nature" between December 1884 and her death in March. They had no engagement of marriage, according to Williams, nor any intention of such. He only met her in October of that year, and he believed the letters to be "in fun." Similarly, Carey Madison, a distant relation, admitted that he had been a suitor of Lillian's from the spring of 1884 to her death. They also had written ten or so letters apiece, and in one, of 12 September 1884, she expressed her love for him and her wish only to be with him. He claimed there was no engagement and that no other letters expressed this love.[57]

Most important here, the defense attorneys as well as the prosecution downplayed even this evidence that others were romantically interested in Lillian. The defense, for instance, never quoted letters from the two men courting her. In fact, the debate over the Carey Madison evidence illustrated the terrific reticence on the part of the legal counsel on both sides to broach the subject. The prosecution implied that the defense was slandering "this girl who is dead" for the sake of their client, and the defense responded that "nobody could be more averse to making these letters public than ourselves" and that they simply had a duty to bring the subject into the case. They finally agreed to introduce the issue in a guarded and even tangential way: terse written statements from each man, with neither testifying and with no letters presented as evidence. In a case that filled 2,314 pages (plus closing arguments) of the transcript with every conceivable minor point of law, evidence, and interpretation, the story of these men who were competing for Lillian's affections received but eleven pages: a one-page statement from each man and a nine-page legal debate about the introduction of the Carey Madison evidence. Only once did a defense lawyer refer to this line of discussion in the closing arguments, using it as evidence that Lillian had not given her heart to Cluverius.[58] The defense also declined to press the issue of her earlier inappropriate connection to Biggs, who likewise never took the stand in the case. They mentioned only that she had family "difficulties," and one attorney stated: "what [troubles] they were I care not to know."[59] With a man's life on the line, this reticence seems extraordinary.

The most damning pieces of evidence of Lillian's wayward behavior to arise at trial were tied directly to Cluverius. Police discovered a sexually explicit poem, "On the Delaware," at the bottom of her clothes chest, for instance. Written in Cluverius's hand, the four-page poem described explicit sexual encounters, arguing for women to explore their sensuality instead of satisfying themselves with the life of quiet respectability. More important than this poem, hundreds of pages of the trial transcript—more than one day of the trial—concerned a weekend in late August of 1884 when both Madison and Cluverius were staying in the house of their uncle. Witnesses testified to the dates the two were there, the layout of the house, and the plausibility of Cluverius quietly stealing out of his room to meet Lillian in her room at the other end of the house. John Walker testified, for instance, that Cluverius claimed to be discomfited in his bowels one night and had to go to the outhouse. Walker wakened as Cluverius left their shared room but fell back asleep and could not be sure when he returned. The lawyers led the jury and the public through terribly intimate details of family life in a way that would soil Madison's reputation as well as that of Cluverius.[60] But even in the context of this important issue in the trial, the question was always could *he* have done this thing? This left Lillian as the passive victim, perhaps in love with Cluverius but certainly not culpable for the transgression that possibly occurred that night.[61]

The newspapers reported almost everything from the trial in some fashion. By 1885, Richmond publishers printed thirty-five daily, semiweekly, weekly, and monthly periodicals. Together, the city's three English-language dailies reached estimated circulations of more than fourteen thousand, perhaps nearing the number of households in the city now populated by about seventy thousand. The dailies all remained four-page papers; the dramatic increase in volume would arise in the coming generation but not yet. Expansion of the Richmond press in the late nineteenth century was in circulations rather than column inches.[62]

If the papers mentioned most aspects of the case, tender matters were quickly passed over and ultimately blanketed by the abundance of other testimony, not to mention the occasional generic printed statements of pity, horror, and hope for her rest in heaven. For instance, nothing in print ever explained or gave definition to the "foul poem" in her trunk: it was merely mentioned in general terms and passed over.[63] More importantly, rarely was anything stated that was unfavorable to her character, even when considering her leaving home, burning the Biggs letters, writing amorous letters to other men, or her headstrong manner in general. Nevertheless, the press response to Lillian's complex life was itself complex, a mixture of frank, if fleeting, coverage and melodramatic typecasting.

In the absence of any evidence—indeed, in the face of contrary evidence—the press and public regularly emphasized (or imagined) Lillian's feminine virtues, refracting attention away from her faults and toward the guilt of her murderer. The most common coverage of Lillian's history and character was simply to render some of the facts of her story very briefly, missing all the complications. For instance, a week after the discovery of the body, the *Richmond Dispatch* outlined her history in three paragraphs—schooling, Bath County, and then murder. The article made no mention of her family problems, pregnancy, or suicidal unhappiness. The story here was simply of a young woman starting out in life who then was found dead.[64]

On several occasions, however, the press would flesh out this skeleton of a tale with more editorial flourish, leaving an interesting body of sources that reveal the sort of story they *wished* to give to the facts of her life: "From the best evidence attainable, it is safe to assert that Miss Madison was brought up with the strictest regard to the proprieties of life. Her father is a typical Virginia farmer, with plain, unassuming manners and an honest bearing. In her father's quiet home, away from the tempestuous strife of the world, tasting only of the joy that such a quiet home yielded, Lillian Madison grew toward womanhood. She saw in her early life the harvest and the springtime, and watched the seasons come and go, while health, not paint, caused her cheeks to be touched with bloom."[65] The *Dispatch* continued by describing her in school, where she was a "model girl," "pointed to as the example," after which she "returned to her father's home and began to look out on life's prospects just as any young girl freed from the cares of the schoolroom would be apt to do. Actuated by a desire to do something for herself, [she] succeeded in getting a position as a private teacher. But before this, a dark shadow had been thrown across her young life, and it grew darker and darker, until it finally culminated in the dread tragedy at the Old reservoir."

Even when a later retelling cast a darker shadow across her history, the narrative did not sully her character. After painting another glowing review of Lillian's upbringing and education, the article dwelt on her last months of misery, adopting the melodramatic style of contemporary sentimental fiction:

A good while before Xmas she must have known she was not only a ruined woman, but it was only a question of a few months more before she would be shamed before the world; when, perhaps, she would be disowned by her relations; when good Mrs. Dickerson [employer in Bath] would refuse to know her any longer; when the girls with whom she had gone to school with, would mention her name with contempt . . . Day and night Lillian must have been haunted with the shadow of coming evil. She was living a double life. She had been reared in good society; she had had excellent educational advantages; she had been thrown with ambitious girls at Bruington. She was sentimental, and no doubt had romantic plans, and now she was to be an outcast.[66]

In other instances, the press highlighted the gothic elements of the tale, an effect that similarly emphasized the tragic web ensnaring her. In one article, the *Dispatch* wrote of the "poor girl" whose only hope lies in "the guardian angel that watches over the poor weak female," for instance.[67] Lillian "had a presentiment of coming evil," the paper continued, which was fulfilled as she approached the reservoir.

It was that dreary and lonely place, after dark, when the tombstones gleam in the moonshine and show their snowy outlines in the dark shade of the trees in Hollywood Cemetery. The grounds around the small-pox hospital and the cemetery present a picture more lonesome and dreary than can be seen anywhere around the city. It is a place where dark deeds could be executed so secretly that no breath of blame would ever be thought to touch the perpetrator.

The small-pox hospital buildings are old, tumbled-down-looking structures, with window-panes broken and gone, and the sashes left grinning with jagged pieces of glass that look like serpent's teeth. A few shade trees scattered about add to the gloomy look of the place, and the old buildings suggest the abode of haunts. Just where the planks are torn from the high fence around the reservoir is the grave-yard.[68]

And yet, this sentimental story was not the only frame given to Lillian's life and death, particularly as time went on. From the distance of two years of reflection, a review of the case in the *Dispatch* mentioned many more of Lillian's problems, integrating them more fully into the story. The paper mentioned the Biggs conflict and her estrangement from the family, for instance, if only in three sentences. The opportunity for a rendezvous at the Walker home received more than a paragraph, and her suicidal words filled yet another paragraph.[69] If the most common treatment was to muffle the discordant notes of her history, the broader coverage included occasional references to many of her various problems.

On the whole, however, Lillian and her history were *under*stated aspects of this otherwise *over*played sensational murder case. Lillian Madison embodied a range of attributes irreconcilable with "true womanhood," as historians have termed the narrow domestic role allowed nineteenth-century women. But the public narrative demanded of her a different, more circumscribed role. It is as if the real story of her life merely slipped out from behind the edges—and often failed to do so—of the more prominent props that society, reporters, and lawyers placed in view. In this way, the editors, lawyers, and public could call Madison "innocent" despite her violation of the taboo of premarital sex and despite her hoarding a pornographic poem in her clothes trunk. She was an "angel" despite turning away from her parents and willfully abandoning their home and their guidance. To Charles Wallace, a Richmond liquor merchant, amateur geologist, and writer, Madison was a "dead sweetheart" and "poor maiden." To an anonymous woman of Richmond, she was "gentle and lovely in her nature. Having no evil in her nature she was not prepared to suspect him. Her love for him was not sin, it was a God given instinct."[70] She was a fallen woman, but the public worked hard to find an agonizing beauty in her fall. No insouciant "woman about town" or "painted woman" to them, she was rather the sort of beset heroine—a Charlotte Temple or Colleen Bawn—that they wished they might have saved from the torments that finally befell her.

The lawyers, editors, and readers of Richmond did not invent a new Lillian Madison to play this role of fallen heroine. Rather, they edited and pared down the rough edges of the real one, selectively reconnecting parts of her sad story to make a simpler tale. The narrative required merely that she be acted upon; the rest of her history was chaff. Or was it? The stories that appeared in public—in the press, at the trial, and in pamphlets—simplified their treatment of the victim. But what of the elusive reader response? If publishers proved uninterested in her real story, does that mean that the public was likewise uninterested, that her rich and troubled history was disregarded by all? I suspect that the inhibition against dwelling on the faults of the victim found its strongest examples in the most public venues where these stories appeared. When papers printed spare accounts of the foul poem, or the Biggs matter, or the night in August at the Walker home, the readers may well have filled in the gaps with their imaginations. Their private thoughts, casual conversations, and rumors must have explored a much broader terrain than what the public stories chose to emphasize, just as they did with the scandalous material circulating in the 1793 Randolph infanticide rumors. But of rumors circulating about the Cluverius case, the historical record is silent.

Melodramatic typecasting flourished in the stories of the Cluverius murder but was not unique to it. Few facts at all remain of the history of another victim, Mary Pitts Phillips, murdered outside of Richmond by her husband Jeter in 1867. She was as an "angel" of few contours who served as the counterpoint to the horror that was the focus of most of the attention. The press never bothered to investigate Mary's history, leaving the awful revelation of her hidden marriage to Jeter Phillips as the singular and defining moment in her life's story. In the introduction to the printed pamphlet on the case, the author mentions her but once: "the wife of his bosom, whom he had lured by insidious wiles from the security of her happy country home to die by his treacherous hands." In the rest of this volume, she appeared only in the context of her appearance: "plainly dressed," for instance, or a "country looking woman."[71]

This was no aberration on the part of the pamphleteer; every newspaper story followed this pattern in the Phillips case. Mary was of "fair character and the member of a Christian church," wrote the *Daily Enquirer and Examiner*, a "simple country woman who had probably never traveled further than Richmond in her life."[72] One Richmond paper underlined her position in her family by sketching the scene as they were informed of Mary's death: "The mother . . . burst forth into lamentations which became heart-rending, when the officers, with the greatest delicacy, informed her of the facts of the case. The whole family joined in her grief; and even the officers, accustomed to scenes of suffering, could not restrain tears which flowed in sympathy with the distress of a heart-broken family . . . 'poor Em' was universally esteemed and beloved as a lady, intelligent, refined, affectionate, and fully endowed with all the graces which should adorn a woman."[73]

Even the three trials of Phillips did not illuminate her life in any greater detail.[74] If she was mentioned—and that was rare—it was within one of two frames. The first would be the context of the murder scene and the state of her body. These accounts did not dwell on the ghastly facts of her wounds, but nevertheless this image was central to the victim's characterization.[75] The second was simply an aside, as in the pamphlet on the case, bowing to her role as the "simple country woman." "She was a willing servant," one article paraphrased from the closing arguments of the prosecution. The attorney continued: "Not a syllable of hers had been adduced to prove that she was not his affectionate wife. The last words she was heard to speak were, 'There's Jeter, now,' as she caught the sound of the footsteps for which she had been listening with woman's expectancy. The accused was her protector, to him she looked up with all a woman's confidence and love, for him and with him, she left her mother's home and he was the controller of her actions."[76] In his oration handing down a sentence of death after the second jury had found Phillips guilty, Judge Christian described the victim as "a weak, defenseless woman, carried or enticed into a lonely wood, where no cry for help could be heard, and there stricken down, beaten and the life crushed from the feeble form by that hand which should only have been raised to shield and guard it from harm."[77] Every word pointed solidly in the direction of her inherently good and true nature; nothing complicated this simplistic view of her life and character.

Only in this manner of characterizing the female victim does Richmond's sensationalism diverge from the national norms. In volume, tone, reliance on testimony, and heightened emotionalism and melodrama, the Phillips and Cluverius cases share much with those arising from murders around the country. Stereotypes abounded in the North just as in Richmond: villains as murderous fiends or rogue tricksters, victims as poor unfortunates ("frail flawed female undone by sex") or siren/predators (a style not found in Virginia pamphlets).[78] Daniel Cohen described the style of nineteenth-century crime literature as "legal romanticism," indicating both the new emphasis on trials in the pamphlets and the impact of novels and romantic literature on the framing of crime stories both in the courtroom and in print. Several nineteenth-century lawyers used language in the same ways as sentimental fiction: Rufus Choate, for instance, "argued his case as though writing a 'romantic poem,' portraying his client as the 'hero of the narrative' and treating the jury like the 'reader of romance.'"[79] Postbellum Virginia experienced crime sensations in just these ways.

But in the North, the press was also willing to cast aspersions on the female victim or at least to provide prurient details that might sully reputations. In 1846, northern papers were much more inclined to publish the scandalous letters in Richmond's Myers-Hoyt murder case. In 1836, the life of New York prostitute Helen Jewett was much more prominent in the stories of her murder than was the history of her male murderer who was standing trial.[80] Karen Halttunen investigated a number of antebellum cases that hinge in part on the character of the female victims. How important did she find this trend? "Men who killed chaste women were typically found guilty of their crimes. Men who killed the victims of their seduction were frequently convicted. But men who killed prostitutes were acquitted."[81] At least by the 1830s in the North, stories of crime included much more forthright material on sexuality and women violating society's standards.

But Richmond's southern sensibilities revolted at such treatment of women. In 1793, the press published virtually nothing at all on the Randolph infanticide charge. In 1846, Richmond's newspapers minimized what they printed about Mrs. Myers's affair. In 1867 and 1885, they stereotyped the victims as true women and avoided emphasizing anything else—like Indiana Turner (Jeter's "other woman") or Lillian Madison's checkered history—that would muddy the waters. In Richmond, even wayward women were treated better than that.

■

Not so the accused men. The story of the accused occupied much more space in the public forum of the press. Cluverius's defense did not have much to add to the story of his life outlined above. In the view of his lawyers, he was a well-bred, well-educated, good-natured, and respected member of the community who was suddenly arrested for erroneous reasons and placed in the vortex of rabidly prejudiced public opinion. Poor Lillian Madison tragically took her own life, just as the coroner originally thought and just as she hinted to several people in the days before her death.

Virginia law did not allow Cluverius to take the stand (he and his lawyers later claimed they would have desired this option), and the defense rarely presented evidence except to deny or confront individual charges and evidence of the prosecution. The exception was their brief effort to introduce the evidence of Madison's suicidal words and her amorous letters to others. Their overall argument, of course, was that nothing occurred involving their client, and therefore any evidence the prosecution claimed to have was false or misleading. Legally, they needed to do no more than create reasonable doubt that Cluverius had killed Madison. This was a simple story that did not involve much elaborate investigation of his history and character, for both were already perceived by most acquaintances as good.

Yet such a strategy was hardly enough. Charles Wallace wrote that the defense "must get some honest man or woman to testify that Cluverius was where he says he was, at the Dime Museum from 8 til 11 of the night of the 13th March. Unless they do this, their client goes to the wall. Good character for him & bad character for her go for nothing. He may appear a saint and she a devil. If the saint kill the devil, the law ill know the reason why."[82] This is overstatement if it applied to the law in general, for many cases in this era were greatly influenced by the reputation, standing, and character of the victim and the defendant. The problem was that the defense was reticent or unable to attack Lillian's character, and the prosecution raised many issues that conflicted with Cluverius's claim of innocence.

65

The prosecution presented evidence that Cluverius had not lived the virtuous life to which many testified. Mary Curtis admitted that she not only saw Cluverius and Lillian together in a bedroom at the back of a downtown cigar store on the day of the murder, but also that she had entertained him privately at least six times in 1883 when she worked as a prostitute. She said that he "used to come there off and on frequently and visit the house; and I have heard Miss Lizzie Banks [the proprietor] say he used to come there before I ever went there."[83] This sort of evidence opened the door to the accusation that Cluverius was a confidence man skillfully insinuating himself into polite society. Yet, given the questionable reputation for veracity of "wretched women" from the "purlieus and the sewers" (as a defense attorney characterized them), this blow to Cluverius's reputation was still not fatal.[84]

More damning, the events leading up to the crime all seemed to point in the direction of his duplicity. This was where his defense needed to do more to undermine the prosecution but failed. Letters between Madison and Cluverius implied that they were close, and the "foul poem" reportedly written in his hand (his counsel denied it vehemently) seemed to point to a sexual relationship.[85] The fact of her pregnancy and of their staying under the same roof at approximately the right time for her to conceive raised the issue that he might be tied to her more closely than by cousinly affinity and more closely perhaps than he cared to be. Add to this the fact that they each visited Richmond on the same days in January as well as March of 1885, raising the possibility of further rendezvous. Finally, several Richmonders testified to seeing them walking together at various points in Richmond on the day of the killing.[86]

The prosecution connected these disparate pieces of circumstantial evidence by arguing that Cluverius was a monster. He had used Lillian Madison and thrown her away when it became clear that she would be a weight on his future prospects and that he could expect to marry better. To the prosecution, and ultimately to most in the wider public, Cluverius was the worst sort of fiend: an evil presence, deftly masked to walk among innocents. In the florid prose of the prosecuting attorney, Charles Meredith:

> I believe that in that summer time [of 1884] the open doors of that old home remonstrated against so revolting a violation of the laws of hospitality, and would to God that the presence of that crippled paralytic grandfather could have silently appealed to [Cluverius] with effect to spare him in his old age the pollution of his hearthstone and the disgrace of his favorite grandchild. . . .

He took his cousin, cold blooded, with no intention of ever redeeming her character, with no intention, as some men have done, of making reparation to that woman and taking her as the wife of his bosom. But with deliberate intention, regardless of the home of his uncle, regardless of all associations of his childhood, he takes her, in cold blood, without anything ever to redeem her, and makes her an incipient whore.[87]

Meredith continued his energetic attack on the accused murderer by comparing his character unfavorably against the lowest women of the night in Richmond. He ended his closing argument with a description of his character and motive: "If anybody has done dishonor to the name of Virginia, it is those who suggest the existence of such an awful monster amongst the people, it is those who suggest that the people of Virginia have sunk so low that the mere gratification of lust seems to be the only desire of their hearts, and men nor women treat not as an object of scorn him who ruthlessly destroys the virtue of his cousin. The love of wealth, the cover of comfort, the love of gratification, all called him; and his life up to this period shows that his life has been one of self gratification, even to the injury of his cousin."[88]

This treatment of Cluverius is again in line with other sensations. In the 1867 Jeter Phillips case, the prosecution presented the accused as a fiend, and they had plenty of evidence to draw from, including his own incriminating letters sent to the victim's family. Newspapers followed suit. Upon the discovery of Jeter Phillips's connection to the murdered body found in the woods, the editor of the *Enquirer* painted a dramatic scene of the crime: "the blood of the murdered victim seems like that of Abel, to cry from the ground to Heaven for vengeance upon the murderer. The slight clues which have so often led to the detection of the shedder of human blood seem sometimes to be almost miraculous, and might almost lead one to imagine that the finger of offended Deity visibly pointed out the brutal assassin."[89] H. Rives Pollard, editor of the *Southern Opinion*, framed the murder within an extraordinarily poetic, emotional, and romantic tale. After a lengthy, melodramatic description of twilight on a wintry February day and what happy families might be enjoying, he continued: "It was twilight here in the lonely woods of Drinker's farm, where stiff, stark, and cold, lay a poor young woman. Life's warm blood had ceased to flow in her veins, and the warmth of life had been frozen out by the clammy iciness of death. . . . Here she struggled, here she died, with a pleading face upturned to Heaven, and to her murderer, and in the agony of a cruel, brutal death, clutching the leaves and soft earth around her between her fingers."[90] Pollard, even more than the norm in this era of overflowing prose, invested the murder of Mary Phillips with emotion and extravagance.

Unlike Pollard, some in the public found enough holes in the circumstances against Jeter to admit doubt, and these doubts seemed to rise as time went on. Jeter's family, especially his father, earned a great deal of respect in the community, a fact that served to militate against his guilt, as did Jeter's wartime record. As might be expected, Phillips's attorneys emphasized their client's good character. During his trial, they mentioned his service to Virginia as a protector of southern womanhood, for instance, and stressed the fact that "not a solitary stain" had appeared on either his own character or that of his family. Other witnesses corroborated the opinion that in Henrico and wherever he had lived, he was considered to have "as good a character as any man in the country."[91] His own bearing also aided his cause: "the man bore himself so calmly, protested his innocence so stoutly, and his defense was conducted with such masterly ability, that public opinion was much divided, and the deep interest excited by the trials kept the community in a ferment of controversy," so much so that "nearly every family in the city was divided in opinion."[92] Wrote one editor: "There is something in that open countenance and clear blue eye that repels suspicion and rebukes calumny. It tells us of the gallant soldier who did a patriot's duty to his country without fear and without reproach, and of the meritorious young man who had not one bad habit and a thousand virtues."[93]

With both Phillips and Cluverius, many observers apparently felt stuck between the hard evidence and the difficulty of imagining *this* man capable of committing *this* deed. This was the central narrative tension in melodrama: the tortured questions surrounding the male actors in the dramas. This point was underscored by melodramatic fictions that appeared in the wake of both the Cluverius and the Phillips murders. Two years after Lillian Madison's murder, in 1887, a Richmond printer published a fictionalized reworking of the Cluverius case. In *Lillian's Marriage and Murder*, Lillian met a wealthy and solicitous young man while at a religious camp meeting in the country near her home in the summer of 1884 (an actual event mentioned at the trial). This young man convinced her to marry him, they lived together briefly, she became pregnant, and he left her, showing his true nature. In this story, Cluverius serves merely as Lillian's upstanding, cousinly confidante who was unfortunate enough to bear a striking resemblance (mistaken identity is a worn trope in nineteenth-century melodrama) to her ill-chosen husband. After many twists in the story, Lillian found herself on the streets of Richmond late on 13 March 1885 and was mugged by a brutish rogue who accidentally killed her and threw her into the nearby reservoir in an attempt to hide the body. The narrator of the story then described the improbable series of events leading him to the deathbed confessions of two different people who gave him this "true" history of the crime. Armed with the truth, the narrator raced from New York to Richmond to stop the impending judicial murder of the innocent Cluverius.[94]

In this retelling, both Thomas and Lillian were innocents, and the villains were created from whole cloth. As in other melodramas, this one was full of revelations, disguises revealed, and other emotional twists of plot. It is possible that the author consciously deepened the parallels between this story of Madison and the *Colleen Bawn*. Not only did Lillian Madison die in water, but in this retelling of the tale—as in Boucicault's play—she was attacked by a rogue, married secretly into an aristocratic family, dying words implicated the culprit, and a savior attempted to ride to the rescue of the mistakenly accused criminal.

The following year, the Cluverius case received national attention as a New York dime novel publisher, Norman L. Munro, printed its own fictionalized version of the "reservoir mystery." Mistaken identities again peppered this tale, but in this case it was mistaken victims. Lillian looked much like another woman who was the target of murder that fateful evening in March 1885. The famed (fictional) Richmond detective in the story—"Old Man Bruce"—was able to piece all of the puzzle together in this convoluted, awkward story that again vindicated the convicted Cluverius.[95]

The 1867 Jeter Phillips murder case also earned a fictionalized re-creation. In 1868, W. C. Elam, a Virginia editor, embroidered the story and changed the names of the participants; for instance, he made the romance intersectional by having the Confederate soldier "John Randall" crawl away from the fighting at Gettysburg to a house where he was nursed back to health by the kind, young, Pennsylvanian "Mary Ordolf." But virtually every element of the Phillips case remained in this version, if not quite presented accurately: his return after the war, their marriage, his leaving for business reasons, her disappearance after she finally goes with him, the unknown body found, letters disclosing their relationship, and his conviction. Elam then created a fictitious ending to the drama—at the time of publication, Jeter was still in jail appealing his case. Elam resolves the case by revealing that John Randall was innocent, dying on the gallows to protect another from prosecution, as he felt was his duty. "Indiana

Randall," his cousin and previously his fiancée, had killed Mary in a fit of insane jealousy. In a pathetic coda, Indiana, driven insane by the imminent hanging of her lover, ran away from her family. In the moments after John Randall died, she slipped onto the gallows and somehow managed to hang herself beside him.[96]

Gothic and sentimental novels, adventure stories, historical romances, melodramas, and fictional tales of crime, corruption, and detection were all nineteenth-century developments emerging alongside the penny press and the sensational treatment of true crime stories. Each of these genres was exciting, emotional, and gripping, and most of them involved lurid or horrifying scenes and themes; "good and evil battle toward inevitable conclusions in a narrative freighted with symbolism and exaggeration."[97] These popular fictions were abundantly available in the mid-nineteenth century, and their narrative style became a broadly shared part of American culture. Wrote one critic of this growth in 1855: "A few years since, every new publication was transformed into a 'sensation book'; and the nation seemed for a time, in danger of becoming a land of novelists. To be a successful 'disher-up' of absurd probabilities was one of the primal talents of profitable speculation. Book-making became contagious. One successful production—such as Uncle Tom, the Lamplighter, or Ida May—called into existence from ten to forty trashy and stupid imitations of it. They were all puffed, and, probably, all sold."[98] Harry Calligan, a young factory worker who followed the 1885 Cluverius case closely, was among those who bought these sensation books. He joked in his diary that "I am goin[g] to stop reading novel[s]—when they stop making them."[99]

The Colleen Bawn and the fictionalized stories of the Phillips and Cluverius cases show how closely sensational crimes were intertwined with melodrama in the mid- to late nineteenth century. The melodramatic mode provided a comprehensible form, characters, and plot for complex and violent events. A poem written by "a Richmond Lady" at the time of the Cluverius trial emphasizes these connections. Described as "a poem sad and serious, / of Lillian and Cluverius," "Cousin Tommie!" paints a picture of a "poor, soiled dove" willing to follow "a viper" "whereso'er he led" until he laughingly kills her and throws her in the water.[100] The heightened response of Richmonders to the crimes was closely akin to the "aesthetics of astonishment" at the heart of melodrama's hyperbole.[101] Jeter and Thomas became "vipers" in the eyes of many just as Mary and Lillian became "poor soiled doves." In this way, the lawyers, press, and public read them into the roles that came so readily to hand.

DOUBT

The drama of sensationalism derived from conflict, particularly the conflicting possibilities opened by ambiguity, mystery, and horror. Circumstantial evidence is not definitive; to some, it was unconvincing. Can we execute a man on the basis of a watch key, a torn note, and a few witnesses that saw him with the victim earlier in the day? The contest of famous lawyers created another layer of ambiguity and curiosity: would the expensive attorneys of the accused find a way to acquit him? In the late nineteenth century in particular, these enduring issues were joined by a range of questions surrounding the competency of the police and the judicial system.

Together, these dynamics, along with the horror that the violence inspired, created a peculiar cultural experience which anthropologist Victor Turner termed "social drama." A social drama breaks through the everyday pattern of normal social order, upsetting the community enough to raise the threat of crisis. During social dramas, writes Turner, "a group's emotional climate is full of thunder and lightning and choppy air currents! What has happened is that a public breach has occurred in the normal working of society, ranging from some grave transgression of the code of manners to an act of violence, a beating, even a homicide." Social dramas like sensational crimes can create a meaningful limbo-space full of doubt, emotion, and (melo)drama.[102] The Cluverius case offered several layers of such doubt.

The case against Cluverius admitted doubt in part because of the perceived problems in the judicial system itself: even if he was guilty, would the courts be able to convict, particularly on circumstantial evidence and in the face of well-funded and prominent lawyers? The lawyers in sensational cases were usually among the most prominent in the region, and such a closely watched trial tended to make them even more well known. Of the attorneys representing Cluverius, W. W. Crump had already served briefly as a judge in Richmond, and he was considered one of the venerable leaders of the Virginia bar. His son, Benjamin T. Crump, joined him in defending Cluverius and later served as a city alderman, state legislator, and circuit court judge. Cluverius's two other lawyers, A. B. Evans and Henry Robinson Pollard, also had distinguished careers: Evans as a district court judge and Pollard as Richmond's city attorney and member of the legislature. As for the prosecuting attorneys, Charles Meredith served as the Richmond city attorney for thirteen years after the Cluverius case (until defeated by Pollard), and he and several of the other lawyers in the case participated in the Virginia Constitutional Convention of 1902. William Roane Aylett, the other prosecuting attorney, served seventeen years as the commonwealth's attorney for King William County.[103]

The lawyers were well aware of the stage they occupied, and their oratory could rise to great heights during the closing arguments of a sensational trial. This could involve an invocation of the grace of God and the machinations of hell as well as hours of more mundane evaluation of the evidence. As he took center stage on the last day of the Cluverius's trial, the chief prosecuting attorney, Charles V. Meredith, began by thanking the jury for its service to the state and then moved to refute some of the claims made by the defense in their closing arguments the previous day. For the next four hours, Meredith led the jury and the public through each piece of evidence in the case, in turns describing minutely and accusing with passion. He praised the composure of the young black boy who saw Lillian and Cluverius together and faced the cross-examination of the defense team with poise, and he reiterated the importance of the wounds on Lillian's face, the watch key, the torn note, the foul poem, and almost every other shred of evidence in the case. He also pilloried the accused man, saying more than once that there was "no name save 'fiend'" for him. There might not have been human witnesses, Meredith said at one point, but heaven would not let him go unpunished: "God was watching the murder."[104] It was late in the afternoon when he finished his speech, which filled 198 pages of the court stenographer's transcript. The following day, all the Richmond newspapers printed significant excerpts from Meredith's speech, acknowledged to be among the best in recent memory.[105]

In the theater of the courtroom, the contest between prominent lawyers added an important layer of drama to any sensationalized case. But even more substantial doubts arose from cases decided on circumstantial evidence. The combination of evidence forcefully presented against Cluverius was not conclusive to some. It asked witnesses to remember events from months and years before, and many of the witnesses were of questionable standing. Some were prostitutes, others were African Americans, and both groups were viewed with terrific prejudice despite the fact that they were not on trial themselves.

Murder cases worthy of sensationalized treatment tend to lack direct evidence; it is the nature of the criminal to seek the dark, the secluded, to "perform his nefarious deeds in secrecy, and where no eyewitnesses are present to behold him," as one nineteenth-century scholar phrased it.[106] In law, circumstantial evidence was both commonplace and unproblematic. Nineteenth-century legal authorities agreed that such evidence was governed by the same rules as direct evidence and that the jury should weigh all such evidence with an open mind.[107]

But various writers warned against the possible misuse of circumstantial (or "indirect") evidence, particularly in cases that aroused a lot of passion, as in the case of murder. S. March Phillips, a prominent early theorist of Anglo-American evidence, stated simply the problems of circumstantial evidence in relation to heinous crimes: "circumstantial evidence ought to be acted on with great caution especially where an anxiety is naturally felt for the detection of great crimes: this anxiety often leads witnesses to mistake or exaggerate facts, and juries to draw rash inferences. Not infrequently a presumption is formed from circumstances which would not have been noticed as a grounds of crimination, but for the accusation itself;— such are the conduct, demeanor, and expressions of a suspected person, when scrutinized by those who suspect him."[108] The larger threat was that jurors would discount any sort of circumstantial evidence: "there is a superstition with regard to circumstantial evidence which often prevents conscientious jurors from rendering convictions in cases in which justice demands such convictions."[109] In 1885, Charles Wallace questioned the evidence arrayed against Cluverius: "Let some respectable man testify that he sat with Tommie at the Dime Museum from 8 to 11 pm of Friday evening, and all the circumstances of the prosecution will go for nothing. Circumstances are only good as corroborative, good only against conflicting circumstances or doubtful testimonies."[110] One of the Cluverius jury was discharged when it was revealed that he had said "the evidence published was *nothing but circumstantial evidence*." When his inquisitor replied that men had been hanged on such evidence, the juror continued: "Well, [I] *would not hang any man on circumstantial evidence*."[111]

The press regularly introduced a steady drumbeat of stories about innocents accused of crimes, sometimes going to their deaths, more often cleared before that. In 1867, the *Dispatch* printed the story "How an Innocent Man was Convicted and Hung."[112] While Cluverius was in the city jail waiting for the Virginia Supreme Court to hear his appeal, the *Dispatch* printed a story about a false accusation of murder against a miner in Colorado that had recently come to light. Two weeks after the discovery of Lillian and the arrest of Cluverius, it printed a long front-page story on circumstantial evidence in general, using the example of another case decided in Virginia in 1849. In that instance, the jury convicted, the judge called for a new trial, but a mob first took the prisoner from jail and lynched him.[113]

Doubts arose out of circumstantial evidence; similarly, the unprofessional nature of the police raised questions as to whether Cluverius might be convicted. The first city watch in Richmond was instituted in the wake of the Revolution in 1782, but it took fifty years more for the city to build its first jail. In the 1850s, the six policemen of the city did little crime-prevention work, did not carry guns, did not wear uniforms, and did not work at night. The separate night watch, composed of forty men, was supposed to police the city after dusk. The first detective bureau was formed briefly during the Civil War by the military command but was disbanded within six months after facing stiff criticism for being a band of "plug uglies."[114]

In the late nineteenth century, police procedures improved, if slowly. By the 1880s, the force numbered one hundred officers and patrolmen armed now with pistols as well as clubs. But problems remained; the police regularly dismissed patrolmen for various infractions, especially for being drunk on their beats.[115] In addition to perceived and actual unprofessional behavior, procedures in general were neither uniform nor clear-cut. Until 1884, the police had the arduous and unrelated assignment of lighting and extinguishing the city's streetlamps. This menial task hampered their policing abilities by distracting patrolmen on the beat at certain well-known hours, allowing criminals free rein at dusk.[116] As late as 1875, the police lacked even a clear standard for uniforms, an omission that affected discipline, according to the chief.[117] In arrests, the police regularly misused their power. Fully 638 of the 711 arrests made in one month of 1888 were dismissed, leading one paper to claim that the practice of promoting policemen based on arrest rates was perverting justice and inflating the number of spurious arrests.[118]

A private detective, John Wren, played a particularly prominent role in collecting evidence for the Cluverius conviction. Wren had been a city detective until the city completely disbanded the detective branch in 1874 due to wholesale improprieties, including collusion with gamblers. John Wren was tried but not convicted in a case stemming from that conflict; he was also tried for shooting a man and on three different occasions for allowing a criminal—a contact of his—to go free.[119] In the late nineteenth century, detectives were chiefly concerned with recovering stolen property, for which they received the incentive of rewards for returning articles to their rightful owners.[120] To do their work well, detectives cultivated connections with many in the underworld, connections that seemed at best questionable to others outside their profession. John Wren, detectives in general, and even the police department as a whole had a seedy reputation at this time.[121]

The Richmond police force did not have so bad a reputation as Wren, and many editorials praised various aspects of Richmond's justice machinery even as others criticized them. But something of the criminals that the police dealt with rubbed off on their own reputations. Attracted to the force from the ranks of the city's poor and provided with little training, salary, equipment, or respect, the Richmond police were protectors of the city's peace, but they also were seen as cut from the same cloth as the criminals they opposed.

The strength of defense lawyers, weaknesses of circumstantial evidence, and questions about police abilities all added to the doubt in sensational cases like Cluverius's. But the most pervasive doubts about Virginia's system of justice centered on the jury trial. Wrote the *Enquirer* in 1871: the police "do their duty yet it amounts to so little when the offenders are so lightly dealt with by the courts."[122] The heart of the problem was the uncertainty of jury trials, due in part to the nature of juries and in part to the tendency of Virginia appellate courts to grant new trials to criminals based on the slightest of errors, often leading to eventual acquittal. In 1900, one attorney writing for the *Virginia Law Register* promoted reforms: "We hear a great deal of complaint about the uncertainty of the criminal law, and we must admit, whether we like to do so or not, that there is among our people a prevailing distrust of the certainty of punishing crime. Even among the legal profession this same feeling exists. . . . The public do not hesitate to say, that if a prisoner has sufficient counsel and the means to continue litigation from court to court, he will probably wear the case out by delay, and finally, though quietly, escape justice."[123] As distressing as this concern about technicalities was the common complaint that the jurors were not well versed in the law and therefore not worthy stewards of it. Many critics found it telling that criminals reportedly preferred jury trials to those before a judge.[124] The process of jury selection was itself designed to eliminate all who knew anything about the situation, leading to a more ignorant jury, said critics.[125] They too often balked at conviction in capital cases where it would be appropriate. In fact, some juries made entirely illogical verdicts, even those not brought forth in the indictments.[126] Often the jury was sufficiently unsure of guilt to feel queasy about sentencing someone to die but sure enough of guilt to assign him the highest penalty allowable to a lesser charge. As one lawyer at the time put it: "the jury in this case, as juries frequently do, resolved itself into a legislative body or a board of pardon, instead of exercising its legal function and regarding its sworn duty to ascertain a fact."[127]

This predisposition to leniency in juries was evident even in the absence of bribery, intimidation, or less obvious forms of persuasion that many believed to be common, particularly when the case involved a prominent, popular, or wealthy defendant. One antebellum murder trial from a rural Virginia county ended with a jury acquitting a local man of the crime. "If the whole truth could come out that from the corruption that I seen in this trial of the case," wrote a local man, "that there was no honor due to Dave [the accused] or any of his friends." Only after he committed another murder, this correspondent noted, did Dave's friends abandon him to the courts.[128]

If such questions arose concerning the normal functioning of Virginia's legal system, how then could it cope with the mystery and indeterminacy inherent in sensational murders? Each such case was balanced between assurance of guilt and questions of doubt; each of the accused had the best counsel the region had to offer. If anyone could get them off, their lawyers could. These crimes began with mysteries of bodies and identities, riddles that quickly melded into a richer concoction concerning guilt, motives, law, and social order. All of which was leavened with another layer of anxiety: that the police and courts would fail to discover the truth in these most horrifying of crimes.

The public probed for answers and assurances in the face of conflicting evidence. As much as they looked to the physical evidence in the case to give them the answers, Richmonders obsessed over the accused man himself as well. Looking at the prisoner became a sport in Richmond in the spring of 1885. Crowds gathered everywhere that the police escorted Cluverius. They looked at his face, his lips, his eyes, his bearing, his clothing, his posture, his breathing, his gait, his habits. They read the newspapers for hints of new leads, and the press rewarded them with more print on this case than any crime in Virginia history to this point: articles in 172 different editions of the *Richmond Dispatch*. The public watched Cluverius closely in the courtroom and later spoke of his demeanor, particularly noting his coolness, although they might be conflicted about what that meant. Others were eager to become witnesses, to do more than simply observe; one paper even reported attempts to go to the jail to "wring admissions from the prisoner."[129]

As much as any murder in this era, the case against Cluverius admitted doubt. Charles Wallace confided to his diary that "All think him guilty, though many think the evidence will be lacking in fullness and power to convict."[130] Others were more doubtful still. William Hatcher, the spiritual advisor for the accused, wrote to his son: "The case is extremely perplexing to me. It has crushed me into a painful depression. At one moment, I fear that he is guilty and will die with a lie on his lips; the next, I think that he may be innocent and I fear that it will be a judicial murder" if he was hanged.[131] Perhaps those who saw him in town were mistaken? Perhaps a link in the chain of circumstantial evidence was faulty? Perhaps he was less like Judas than like Jesus, the innocent about to be sacrificed? Said one of his counsel: "Since the day that the maddened mob cried, 'Crucify Him! Crucify Him!' no reliance is to be placed upon the demands of the impassioned mob."[132]

■

What made the Cluverius case so wrenching to Richmonders—it remains the most sensationalized case in the city's history—was this mystery, the sense that perhaps they never found out just what happened to Lillian Madison and just what role Cluverius played in the murder. The public and the press explored this crime in all the same sorts of ways that northern papers and publics did in the mid- to late nineteenth century, with the important exception that they refrained from drawing Lillian's character into question. She would be a beset victim, not a delinquent. With exorbitant amounts of ink, testimony, banner headlines, and occasional heightened, melodramatic prose, Richmond's papers found the Cluverius murder case to be as interesting and attractive a subject for newspaper sales as any murder splashed across the front pages of metropolitan papers in the northeast.

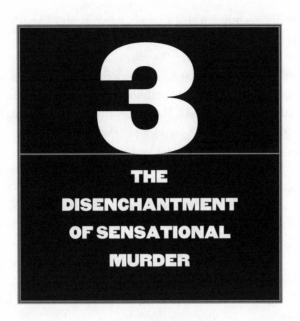

3

THE DISENCHANTMENT OF SENSATIONAL MURDER

Somehow the facts have been overdone, or they have been too redly painted in the press. The pictures that accompany them have added to the weariness. It used not to be so. The time was when a horror of any sort, physical or moral, had its specific physiognomy, its peculiar temperament, which one remembered for days, weeks, even years.

Harper's Monthly Magazine, October 1913

It was a very hot evening on 18 July 1911, when Henry Clay Beattie Jr., his wife Louise, and their infant son visited Louise's aunt and uncle just to the south of Richmond. After dinner, the couple left their five-week-old baby in the care of their relatives and went for a cooling drive west on Midlothian Turnpike into the country. About an hour later, their car screamed into the driveway and skidded to a halt, Henry yelling for help. Henry's face was cut and bleeding, and Louise lay in a pool of blood in the front seat, her face blown apart by a gunshot blast.[1]

The family called for a doctor and the police as Henry reported what had happened, first to the family, then, repeatedly, to the police. On their way home, a tall white man with a bushy beard had stopped them on the road, accusing them of trying to run him down. The grizzled man then leveled a shotgun at Louise and fired. Henry leapt toward him, struggling to wrest the gun away, and received a blow from the barrel of the gun in the process. The man ran into the woods by the side of the road and was gone. Henry found that Louise was severely injured; he raced back to the house to get help. By the time he skidded to a stop, she was dead.

That night and the next morning, the police and neighbors searched for the gun, for the man, and for further signs of the crime. Bloodhounds were unable to find a trail, and the police began to question Henry's story. Within three days, he was arrested for murdering his wife and was called before the coroner's inquiry.

The case quickly became a sensation on the order of the Cluverius murder before it. But this was a different era, and the Beattie murder fostered its own variety of sensationalism. Between the Civil War and the Progressive Era, public narratives of crime became more detailed, exhaustive, reasoned, and objective, mirroring a shift in cultural mentality from Victorian to modern. As the pamphlet on the "Great Beattie Case" emphasized, the Beattie sensation coverage would be rife with "special photographs" and "special reports," which would be "complete, fully detailed and concise," rendering as much as possible the "whole history of the crime." It seemed that Richmond might drown in the coverage.[2]

In the late nineteenth and early twentieth centuries, America became a modern nation, larger, more standardized, and bureaucratic. If these trends affected every corner of the nation, no region was more transformed than the South. In this era, the foundations for a modern mixed economy were formed in the South, the white population began to think of itself again as American, and every New South city aspired to become the next Birmingham or Atlanta, burgeoning with commerce and industry. Every modernizing trend in the nation accelerated in the South in the fifty years after the

Civil War, even as the region wrestled with persistent poverty, low prices in agriculture, and periodic depressions.

The powerful engines of growth in the rising population, in the surging economy, and in urbanization had tremendous cultural consequences operating within them. "The reality of the twentieth century is not the reality of the nineteenth century, not at all," to borrow a phrase from Gertrude Stein.[3] A part of that new reality was a dominant mass culture that emphasized sensation seemingly in all forms. The breadth and depth of the newspaper coverage of stories of sensational violence expanded, but other broad trends in American culture also affected the framing of the sensational: the emergence of realism in its many forms, the rise and professionalization of the social sciences, and the advent of muckraking and yellow journalism.

These trends gave more attention to sensation than ever before but also explored them with a different style. If Jeter Phillips and Thomas Cluverius were fiends in the minds of most Richmonders, the 1911 wife killer Henry Clay Beattie was not. As one New York editor wrote of the treatment of the Beattie case, "the human interest of the criminal" now outweighed all other factors, including the moral outrage that he believed the crime warranted.[4]

The Phillips, Cluverius, and Beattie cases shared much; after all, they were all murders, and many similarities in the coverage connect all three: ample coverage and a focus on the trials, for instance. But in several important ways, the press treatment and the reaction of Richmonders to a wife killer in 1911 was decidedly different from their responses to the murderers in either 1867 or 1885. Most obvious was the utter torrent of print greeting the 1911 murder; the volume of print in sensational cases had grown for decades, and this trend continued into the twentieth century. But more had changed. Melodramatic stereotypes—so familiar to nineteenth-century murder narratives—were less central and stark, though they never went away. And scandalous details of the cases—only hinted at in earlier years with broad brushstrokes—came to the fore, many of them boldly stated in print.

The nineteenth-century turn toward elaboration and abundant detail affected the evolution of sensationalism in the press into the twentieth century. By 1911, this amounted to a change in what was considered good taste to mention in public, a shift in the frame given to disturbing breaches in social order. The Victorian style of melodramatic sensationalism faded as the new century approached, even if it never went away. Instead, it was increasingly submerged beneath a rising tide of mass culture's voluminous, detailed treatment.

Sensational crime remained sensational, but what that meant had changed. The crowds watched, but they saw with different eyes; the papers trumpeted the Beattie case more than ever before, but with different emphases. Like all commodities in this age, sensational crimes became a bit more commonplace. They were recognized as a regular part of the culture, expected, a part of modern life's background. It would not be long before an editor would write that "a nationally famous trial for homicide is no longer a startling interruption in a more lethargic train of thought. It has become an institution, as periodic in its public appearances and reappearances as the cycle of the seasons."[5]

■

THE DEATH OF LOUISE BEATTIE

Louise Wellford Owen was born in 1890 in Manchester, Richmond's sister city to the south of the James River.[6] The Owens' household was large: five children, and the parents of the father lived with Mr. and Mrs. Owen in 1900. By 1910, the grandparents had died, and the Owens had taken in two boarders. Mr. Owen worked for a local lumber company as bookkeeper, a white-collar position. Other signs confirm the family as part of the growing middle class: they rented their home and took in boarders, which implies some financial need, yet were able to keep their children in school at least until their middle teens.[7] In May of 1910, Louise's parents moved to Dover, Delaware, where her father worked for the Dover Lumber and Milling Company. Louise did not join them, however, for by this time she was engaged to Henry Clay Beattie Jr. That summer, the two were married, and they moved into the household of Henry's father in Manchester.

Henry Beattie Jr. was born to a wealthy family in 1885, also in Manchester. His father, Henry Beattie Sr., was a prosperous dry goods merchant in that city. The elder Beattie owned this thriving business just at the moment when such establishments expanded to become the department stores that dominated retail sales for the next half century.[8] The family owned a large house on Porter Street near the Presbyterian church where Henry Sr. served as elder. The Beatties had a daughter and two sons, including Henry Jr. In addition, their household included widowed sisters of Mr. and Mrs. Beattie, a nephew, and two live-in servants. Henry Beattie Sr. was a prominent figure in the city, serving not only as one of its leading merchants, but also for a time as a councilman for Manchester. The elder Beattie also regularly balanced the books of his church down the street, and he was treasurer for one of the city's daily papers, the *Richmond Virginian.*[9]

Henry Clay Beattie Jr. went to school until eighteen, approximately when his mother died. He thereafter joined his father at the department store, beginning as a clerk in the gentlemen's furnishings department. By 1911, he ran that section of the store as well as the shoe department. Young Henry Jr. was but twenty-six and in charge of almost half of his father's thriving establishment.[10]

Raised in a family of means, Beattie Jr. made a name for himself quite early. Unfortunately for the family, his notoriety came not as much from his emerging business acumen as from his reckless habits. He reportedly entangled himself with several young women in his teens and twenties. His was of one of the most prominent families of Manchester, and yet he was intimately familiar with such plebeian and risqué slices of life as ragtime, automobile races, baseball games, and Richmond's houses of ill fame.[11]

One of his affairs became a central element in every story spun from the murder trial. When Henry met Beulah Binford, a "woman about town," she was but thirteen, although as Beattie stressed in court, "no one in the world would have taken her to be a girl of thirteen years, with the reputation she had." In August of 1907, when they began their relationship, she seemed a caricature of society's fears regarding the "new woman": she was already "running with men" as a prostitute and had apparently contracted a venereal disease. The two rented a room at May Stuart's brothel regularly over the course of several months, and they took rides in his Buick out into the secluded countryside. In September of 1908, Beattie paid Beulah's tuition to St. Mary's Academy in Alexandria, Virginia. Beulah's family was ready to send her to a house of correction but were persuaded by family friends that this school would be more suitable. Beulah only stayed a month, however, before she was expelled, apparently for becoming involved with local boys. She returned to Richmond, became reacquainted with several men, including Beattie, and became pregnant at the age of sixteen.[12]

Beulah Binford had been "going with several men" and did not know who the father of her child was. Probably due to the fact that the Beatties had more standing and money than others, she accused Henry of paternity. Beulah's mother wrote to Beattie asking for money, and ultimately lawyers settled the problem quietly. Henry paid her a certain undisclosed amount for the birth. In return, Beulah left town and renounced any further obligation to him, giving birth to the baby, whom she named Henry Clay Binford, in Raleigh, North Carolina.[13] With her departure from Richmond, Beulah Binford seemed permanently out of Henry's life.

Henry's father pressured him to settle down, start a family, and move from this wild youth to a more stable and respectable lifestyle. The wedding of Henry to Louise Owen in Manchester on 24 August 1910 received ample coverage in the local press as one of the social events of the summer. Reports from after the murder added (perhaps apocryphally) that a veiled and unknown woman had stood at the back of the church during the ceremony, causing much gossip. Nevertheless, Beattie's carousing days seemed over: Beulah was out of the picture, the newlyweds conceived a child, and most reports of their marriage claimed that they both were happy. Beattie family members uniformly described their relationship as loving, as did a number of friends of Henry. The two kissed each other as Henry left and came back from work each day, they all reported. Several friends of Louise living nearby in Manchester likewise testified that they seemed perfectly happy and that they never saw anything to the contrary.[14]

Matrimony slowed Beattie's playboy lifestyle but only temporarily. Before the birth of his legitimate son, Beattie again encountered Beulah Binford. Their first meeting, in April of 1911, might have been accidental: according to Beulah and Henry, he went to Norfolk to see a baseball game, and they stumbled on one another there. The two also agreed that Henry had no interest in her and that she was pursuing him. Beulah told him, for instance, that she was returning to Richmond, and Henry replied firmly that she should stay away. But Beulah and Henry were apparently downplaying their involvement, at least according to their acquaintances. Henry's companion on this Norfolk excursion reported that Henry became interested in the idea of a trip only after he had received a letter from Beulah. Likewise, this and another of the couple's acquaintances in Norfolk testified that Henry and Beulah took rides together and went to "disreputable places" and led a "dissipated life," much as they had done three years before in Richmond.[15]

Within a month, Beulah had returned to Richmond. May Stuart, the madam of a brothel in Richmond's red-light district, remembered seeing the two together at her house four times between May and July 1911. Indeed, Beattie admitted in court to seeing Beulah once or twice a week since she returned to Richmond. Beulah first lived with her disapproving sister but soon began arrangements for her own apartment. A letter submitted as evidence in court showed that Beattie helped buy furniture for her new abode. Despite the protestations of both Beulah and Henry that he was devoted to his wife, uninterested in Beulah, and knew that she kept company with other men, plenty of evidence shows a renewed and intimate acquaintance.[16]

84   It is difficult to piece together just what happened in the first three

weeks of July 1911. Later reports in newspapers hinted that Henry's father learned of the resumed liaisons with Binford and threatened his son with the withdrawal of financial support if they continued. The elder Beattie denied this claim vehemently, saying that he knew all along of the problems caused by Binford and that he never threatened his son. Other reports indicated that Louise was unhappy and that their marriage was near collapse. Perhaps she was infected with a venereal disease; she was at least aware that her husband was so afflicted. Louise's mother, Mrs. Owen, who had stayed with her in the Beattie household since before the baby was born, said that in the last months she "did not seem to be very happy. She looked sad and had frequent crying spells." Mrs. Owen also testified that Louise had shown her Henry's underwear with blood on it. A local pharmacist recalled that he "gave him medicine intended for venereal disease. As to whether he had it or not, I don't know, but he said he did." Further testimony from a doctor revealed that Beulah had to be treated several times for a medical condition sensitive enough not to be named directly. Since another doctor verified that Henry had gonorrhea, we can assume this was the affliction.[17] While friends and family said the couple was happy, other evidence showed their marriage to be troubled and perhaps disgraced.

And then came the events of 18 July, with screeching tires, a pool of blood, and a very questionable story from Henry about a roadside shooting and struggle with a bearded man who left no trail. At the coroner's inquiry, Beattie's cousin took the stand and confessed to purchasing a gun for Beattie just weeks before. As if the case needed more drama, while on the stand, Paul Beattie had a seizure, requiring him to leave the courtroom and receive medical attention. After further salacious revelations from Beulah Binford, the inquiry found enough evidence to send Beattie to trial.

Within one month, Henry Beattie sat in the Chesterfield County Courthouse, a small building now swamped with reporters and curious Richmonders, facing a capital charge for shooting his young wife.[18] The nineteen-day trial featured the erection of new buildings and stalls "that would rival an Arizona boomtown" around the courthouse green by local farmers to take advantage of the crowds and a riot of press coverage from Richmond papers and from those around the nation.[19] Western Union broke transmission records from its newly erected courtside office, filing almost a million words over the coming three weeks. The public interest rose to a crescendo when the accused man himself took the stand in his defense. After heroic and prolonged closing arguments, the jury pronounced Beattie guilty of the murder. The judge sentenced him to death, and his

85

lawyers promptly appealed, citing seventeen separate exceptions to the proceedings as bases for overturning the conviction.

■

THE STORY TOLD

In most ways, the story of the Beattie murder parallels the sensational stories of crime like the Cluverius case from the late nineteenth century. Almost as much as Mary Phillips and Lillian Madison, Louise was marginalized in the story of this crime. A pamphlet appeared shortly after the trial that hardly mentioned her. In fact, the wordy cover did not even hint that a wife was involved in the crime, although the equally verbose title page at least made reference to the "trusting wife's sufferings and death." In the rest of the 128-page pamphlet, Louise appeared roughly a dozen times, the majority of which were descriptions of her death or the state of her body.[20] Newspapers treated Louise Beattie in a similarly abrupt manner, despite the growth of coverage. In those few moments when Louise was mentioned, it was usually in soft, muted passages about her trusting nature and sad end. An editorial printed in the *Richmond Times-Dispatch* in the week after the murder contrasted their wedding day the summer before with the day's news that Henry was charged with the crime. Yet, even in this rare story purporting to develop the two sides of her life and death, Louise appears as a character in the background. Although the case was embraced as a "tragedy which has shocked this community as it was never shocked before," public attention remained focused on the accused murderer and his "iron nerve," just as in the Phillips and Cluverius cases long before.[21]

Similarly, some of the press treatment of Henry Beattie—but only some—paralleled the caricatures of Phillips and Cluverius decades before, including an obsession with the way the murderer looked and acted. Moreover, heightened prose on occasion castigated him as a murderous fiend in comparison to Louise's innocence. The closing arguments of the prosecuting attorney, L. O. Wendenburg, provided the trial's most hyperbolic moments, including this passage:

When the silence of that fatal night was broken by the screams of that poor, defenseless woman, as she realized that the man who had sworn to protect her was a fiend incarnate, and he silenced that scream with the report of that death-dealing gun, God frowned and the law shuddered. . . . This is the greatest crime and the worst under the roof of heaven. This young man, gentlemen, has bound a band of blood around his name so that generations will slowly go by it until it is blotted out from memory. The dark and bloody annals of the past have nothing to equal this crime. . . .

They tell you to let him go free. Let him go free! I tell you that every unpunished murder takes away something from the security of every one of our lives. Every unpunished murder of a wife takes away something from the security of every woman's life and adds terror to our homes. You let this man go free and I say to the State of Virginia, 'Go to the grave of Cluverius! Go to the grave of the wife-murderer McCue! Go to the grave of wife murderer Jeter Phillips! Take up their bodies and apologize to them for the way you have treated them, and put a black band around the escutcheon of Virginia and wear it until eternity.'[22]

Following Wendenburg's lead, an editorial of the same day read: "The public is familiar with the facts of the case—the brutal atrocity of the deed, the deliberate preparations for the murder, the flimsiness of the story told by the man of how his wife came to her death, the dissolute life of the defendant, his utter lack of human feeling throughout his imprisonment . . . and now the degenerate creature awaits the execution of the just sentence of the law."[23] Likewise, the *Religious Herald*, a weekly most likely to uphold the torch of Victorian morals, issued an editorial that harkened back to those of the nineteenth century: "He is a brute to begin with, and he is a brute to end with. Such a man is not to be judged by the ordinary standards that prevail among civilized people. His perverted moral nature, his brutalized instincts account in all such cases for the fact that he is the least interested apparently of all who hear and witness the trial."[24]

Like the charges against Cluverius, the case against Beattie was based upon circumstantial evidence. Public distrust of this sort of evidence persisted, raising questions once more as to whether this young, wealthy man who hired very able lawyers would be convicted. Muckraking journalist Adon Yoder wrote in his weekly that the Beattie case stood on shaky evidence: "Now you and I after the newspaper trial of the man may easily be persuaded that he is the guilty party, but that rightfully don't satisfy the law. . . . With evidence so far adduced I believe H. C. Beattie, Jr. guilty of the murder of his wife but with such evidence only I'd be a fool to convict on the present warrant. Belief is built on uncertain, hasty, inaccurate newspaper reports. Proof is another thing and should be at the mouth of two or more witnesses."[25]

All of these elements show a basic continuity between late-nineteenth-century murder and the coverage afforded the Beattie case, demonstrating how enduring have been the typologies of the criminal kind. From the emergence of crime sensations in the nineteenth century to the present, we can find similarities in these stories: elements of melodrama, of stereotyping, of reticence in disclosing some particularly distasteful and complicating facts, of enduring public interest.

As important as these continuities were, however, there were significant differences as well, and even the continuities were more difficult to find in the Beattie case than in those of a generation or two before. If the subject and characters of the story were largely the same, the context was not. As with many historic changes, the impact of melodrama never definitively ended, but rather it was challenged by other, competing developments, and its influence in the broader narrative dwindled.

The melodramatic treatment of sensations was by 1911 awash beneath a rising tide of cultural production that created a complicated, visual, descriptive, and three-dimensional story line. Realistic, detailed description and viewpoints from a variety of supposedly objective sources—trial testimony, eyewitness accounts, personal interviews, and photographs—overwhelmed the editorial content, shifting the public's experience of sensations and their place in cultural life. Few of these elements were new to this era—testimony and detailed description in particular can be found in coverage even in the antebellum era—but their use had been transformed. What had been erratically pursued in the nineteenth century would be systematically exploited on a daily basis in the twentieth. As *Harper's* complained in the quotation that opened the chapter, coverage was now so "overdone" as to lead to "weariness. It used not to be so."[26]

The 26 August 1911 edition of the *Richmond Times-Dispatch* provides a representative example of sensationalism in this era. This twelve-page edition, published during Beattie's trial, includes nineteen columns of material on the trial, fully 22 percent of the newspaper's print space. Of the sixteen images printed in this edition, nine of them illustrate the Beattie story. The front page includes a different headline for each of its seven columns, with the one column for the Beattie case illustrated with six images that dominate the page above the fold, along with the page-wide headline "Tide Turns against Beattie." The murder coverage fills pages six and seven and a portion of page nine. While this paper has many ads and covers sports, society, other crimes, and politics, Beattie coverage dominates the issue, so much so that it is offered in three layers. Most succinct is the Associated Press synopsis of developments in the previous day's testimony, totaling about one column of print. Color commentary is provided by a reporter's firsthand accounts of the courthouse crowds and the major developments along with the public response to them. This is the layer that often continues to offer melodramatic treatment of the case. Finally, most of pages six, seven, and nine is made up of straight testimony—columns and columns of questions and answers. Much of this testimony is verbatim, although the paper edits some passages and leaves some out. What is most notable is that these large chunks of testimony are presented without editorial commentary.

In 1846, the *Richmond Whig* came close to apologizing when it printed one day's flurry of raw material in the form of love letters between Mrs. Myers and Mr. Hoyt. In 1885, the *Dispatch* was much more thorough (as well as unapologetic) in printing testimony in the Cluverius trial. But it was often paraphrased, and plenty of short updates and editorializing continued to color the Cluverius coverage. In 1911, a reader has to look more closely to find editorial commentary amid the sea of print on the Beattie case; and the reader will utterly fail to find anything brief.

The philandering of the accused in the Beattie and Jeter Phillips (1867) cases provides a striking example of this elaboration of reporting of violence and crime. Like Henry Beattie, Jeter Phillips had strayed from his wife, but little was made of the matter. He simply, in the words of a number of witnesses, "acted the part of a single man." He was connected to one local woman in particular, but any reference to this romance remained tangential and largely implied. Two stories in a single paper discussed his visits to a certain bawdy house in Richmond but nothing more.[27] Deeming it inappropriate for the newspaper audience, editors refrained from probing the issue. Instead, they kept to the safer generalized terms of beast and fiend, terms that masked the particular faults at the same moment that they condemned in strong terms.

In contrast, the Beattie case primarily centered on the marital difficulties of the couple and Henry's adultery. "The woman in the case"—a phrase that recurred regularly (including on the cover of the pamphlet)—was not the victim of the crime, about whom the papers wrote little. Instead it was Beulah Binford, the teenage lover of Henry Beattie. In every popular treatment of the Beattie murder, in fact, the extramarital liaisons between Henry and Beulah formed the broader context for the story of the murder. The *Richmond Times-Dispatch* published so much about this relationship—including a series of four front-page photographs of a smiling Beulah Binford—that it was criticized for purveying trash. The editors felt it necessary to defend themselves in an editorial about how they were reporting "the crime not the woman."[28] They also refrained thereafter from publishing any more photos of Beulah.

The extent to which reporting in the Beattie case exceeded the more staid standards of the past can be gauged by the federal charges facing two Richmond papers for sending "unfit matter" through the mail. This material consisted of an interview with Beulah Binford in one case and the testimony of Louise's mother in the other. Binford's interview, published in the *News Leader*, traced her history, how Beattie was "only one of many whom she has 'liked,'" and how she did not love any of them. She "tried to be good, but it was no use," so she returned to her "old life" (prostitution). "Why not?" she asked—a rather bold question in 1911. Not only did this article fail to criticize her choices—this was presented as a straight interview—it began with a description of her looks in a prurient style that might have come from a pulp novel: "Barring a certain too obtrusive sensuousness, this child woman—she is 17 years old today—is strikingly pretty. And she is altogether half girl, half woman. Her figure, her face, her complexion and her hair—masses of yellow—all are girlish. But her eyes are hard and her mouth—a full sensual mouth it is—has the cynical twist of a woman who has seen, and seen too much. She is rather slight of stature, but her figure is beautifully rounded."[29]

This sort of coverage raised the eyebrows of a variety of defenders of nineteenth-century decorum. Complained the conservative *Religious Herald* about the general coverage of Binford: "The public has been informed repeatedly of all the disgusting details of her bad life. Upon her every appearance, we have been told what sort of hat she wore, her dress has been described in detail, her bearing, every word she uttered. Interviews with her have been printed again and again. The toilet articles in her cell, the items of food in her breakfast—surely nothing surpassing what we have had in Richmond could be found in the *New York Journal* or the *Cincinnati Enquirer*."[30]

This is different from the critique in 1885 over the volume of print and public interest in general. With the Cluverius case, conservative social critics had little to complain about in terms of personal, sexual, and prurient material appearing in the press because Richmond newspapers either did not print off-color material or only hinted at it. And they printed very little that might reflect poorly upon womanhood. The most adamant critic, the editor of the *Religious Herald*, admitted that "Our city papers have evinced admirable delicacy in the publications they have made concerning the tragedy. . . . as a rule their reports have been so scrupulously clean that they could have been read in a mixed company without embarrassment." What was disgusting to the editor of this publication in 1885 was the general "gaping and ravenous curiosity which has been so rampant in this country."[31]

By 1911, gaping curiosity and torrents of print were the norm, commonplace. Critics focused their attention on what was new and most disturbing. Only when particularly questionable material of a sexual nature arose was there an outcry and a lingering reticence in the press to present the details. When Louise's mother testified that her daughter showed her evidence of Henry's venereal disease—bloodied underpants—the *Times-Dispatch* described the testimony with euphemism: "exhibits which contained the reasons for her daughter's sorrow." Likewise when Beulah Binford's mother described her daughter's lifestyle, the paper simply wrote "most of the evidence it is deemed best not to print."[32] The *Evening Journal* and some other papers were more explicit, printing Mrs. Owen's testimony that her daughter had shown her Beattie's undergarments stained on front and back.[33] Although the pamphlet on the case failed to say "gonorrhea," it came close: "Beattie had contracted a serious physical ailment by his wrong doing, which he had in turn communicated to his wife."[34]

When Beattie himself was questioned closely about his relations with Beulah, the *Times-Dispatch* ignored how the prosecution pressed him on what was statutory rape, itself a capital offense, fixing instead on more generic lines in the testimony: her "representing herself to be much older" and not being "able to break loose from her."[35] Beattie's brother testified that Henry "came to me and said, 'Don't you know that damned girl is back in Richmond again?'" and the *Times Dispatch* printed the line, inserting "d——d" in place of the curse. In this age of ragtime, naturalism, and Margaret Sanger's crusade for legal birth control, it was even becoming acceptable to discuss these private issues (at least to some extent). We know little of Nolie Bray (Cluverius's fiancée) and Indiana Turner (Jeter's love interest), but the Beattie murder was thoroughly bound up with all sorts of prurient details of Henry's misbehavior, with Beulah Binford playing a central role. The struggle between those who wanted to see and hear everything to do with sensations and those who wanted strict propriety in the press continued, but the battlefield had moved away from general prurience to a specific hesitancy concerning sexuality.

One moment during the trial reveals how reticence could still be found in the courtroom as well, albeit a very contested reticence. Just as in nineteenth-century cases, when the courtroom was cleared during the reading of the "foul poem" reportedly penned by Cluverius to Madison, the judge in the Beattie case asked the women in attendance to leave for the closing arguments. With lawyers planning to lead the jury through all sorts of off-color evidence, the judge—who had hinted several times earlier in the trial, to no avail, that women should consider leaving the courtroom—ordered them out, and the bailiff helped them to comply. When several returned after lunch, the judge ordered them out again. Crowds, including women, nevertheless gathered at the open windows of the courtroom and listened in all the same: "There seems no way to get rid of them" sighed a local reporter. The judge's words were particularly telling, for he "warned them that argument over evidence even newspapers refused to print was about to begin."[36] Even newspapers. . . . It was now commonplace to have papers printing thoroughly on a case, even including off-color material.

From marital unhappiness to gonorrhea to prostitution to evidence of Beattie's fast life to police testimony of the blood and gore of the murder scene, newspapers in the early twentieth century printed a broad range of salacious and scarlet material. By this era, the Richmond press published as much prurient matter as any paper in the nation; the lingering southern reticence about womanhood had faded to inconsequence in terms of sensational coverage. The Richmond papers remained hesitant to publish stories explicitly describing sexual matters, but the new, active brand of journalism in this era even made inroads into covering such issues as divorce and paternity cases, prostitution, and sexual hygiene.[37]

The Richmond press printed thousands of words each day, drowning the case in its particulars and painting a picture of a troubled modern marriage. Louise Beattie married not so much a melodramatic and stylized monster, something outside of normal life, unexpected, or unbelievable, but rather a tangible and particular character, a wealthy delinquent. Henry Beattie was a misguided youth who with his background might have thought himself invulnerable, who chased skirts, and who did not value what he had. Louise was sweet and innocent in this story; in that way, she reprised Lillian Madison's role from twenty-five years before. But the script of the drama had been rewritten, for the context that invested her story with meaning had shifted considerably away from melodrama. This did not go unnoticed at the time. The *Nation* criticized this tendency in the press in general and in the Beattie case in particular, noting that "the newspapers which have been spreading the details of this case before the public have been telling of all sorts of 'sympathy' and 'interest' in this brutal and cowardly murderer." The writer of this piece apparently believed that modern newspaper coverage could use a little more of the fiery condemnation of earlier days: "no sooner does a case figure conspicuously in the newspapers than the monstrousness of the crime is lost sight of."[38]

This factual, dispassionate, and verbose style undercut the sharp polarization of good and evil in the story line of Louise Beattie's murder, lowering the pedestal on which the victim was raised and filling in the fiery pit into which the accused was thrown. It brought to light all manner of marital difficulties that muddied the image of the Beatties' relationship, mitigating and complicating the impact of his betrayal. The Beattie murder was freighted with different assumptions and fears from those in the 1885 Cluverius case. The stories of that earlier sensation included much testimony (albeit heavily edited or paraphrased), but they also demonstrated a clear sense of individual right and wrong: Cluverius had betrayed his family, his cousin, and his community. A beast had entered the fold. The Beattie case described instead a bad and vicious element emerging from *within* society. Beulah Binford was no trickster but, rather, a bad type found in Richmond and elsewhere; Henry was less a confidence man than an amoral youth without scruples. Both murder stories typecast the crimes and criminals but according to different registers: melodramatic versus sociological, romantic versus realistic.

The response of Richmond muckraking journalist Adon Yoder illustrates this point most overtly. In his interpretation of the Beattie crime, Yoder was less interested in the person who pulled the trigger on Midlothian Turnpike than in the wider context. In his view, the assignation houses of Richmond and the "coalition of crime and politics" that allowed them to flourish were the real culprits. Young Beattie and his even younger paramour engaged in their trysts in just such a house. According to Yoder, this was where Henry degenerated into a murderous lout. He began one article with a series of steps leading from the murder to the city government:

> Back of murder was adultery,
> Back of adultery was greed,
> Back of greed was crooked politics.
> In place, back of Midlothian Turnpike [the murder site] was West Main Street, [commercial district]
> Beyond West Main Street was Mayo Street, [the red-light district]
> Beyond Mayo Street was City Hall.
> In person, back of H. C. Beattie was Beulah Binford,

Back of Beulah Binford was May Stuart [a local Madam],
Back of May Stuart was Chris Manning [current police commissioner]
and the police board.[39]

If the city were kept as clean as it should be, Yoder wrote in this and other articles, such tragedies would have no soil from which to spring.[40]

Yoder's view was extreme, but it found milder echoes in other publications. The preface of the Beattie pamphlet set the context not as an individual act of brutal duplicity, but as a sign of the times: "Truly a pathetic picture of twentieth century civilization and enlightenment, a sad commentary on the wild passions of the day, and a pitiable condition of human affairs."[41] Even the *Religious Herald* reflected upon more than the culpability of the accused alone, printing an editorial ("Automobiles and the Devil") on the dangers of modern automobiles and how they provide opportunities for good but also for bad.[42] More than one paper connected the crime to a recent *Collier's* story comparing murder rates in Europe (Germany: five per million population; Italy, "the land of the stiletto": fifteen per million) to those in the United States: seventy murders per million population.[43] More generally, the extensive coverage of Henry's "fast life" blurred the blame for the crime, indicting to a certain extent the loose lifestyles of all young men: their ragtime music, fast cars, drinking, carousing. Even when the stories did not indict the wider community overtly for the murder, the prominence of his "fast life" in the story of this murder drew attention to the perhaps unwitting complicity of modern society.

No single or simple development in the South or in American life in general adequately explains these changes in the place of violent sensations in twentieth-century American culture. In superficial ways, seemingly little had changed: sensational crime stories continued to center around trials, murderers, victims, lawyers, evidence, and questions of guilt. But the freight carried by these crimes of violence shifted due to the evolution of an entire cultural mentality: sensationalism became a part of the stock and trade of journalism rather than an exceptional moment. In short, sensations of violence became, more or less, commonplace.

In the process, it became rare to find any lingering inclination to print brief and blunt updates on developments. The coverage was so rife with details and particulars of every description that it threatened to lose the thread of what developments occurred in the Beattie case. Newspapers delved deeply into evoking the scene and into relating every moment, large and small: descriptions of the courtroom, the traffic congestion around the courthouse, what the principle witnesses and the accused wore, their moods, and their health. Large swaths of testimony were virtually tangents from the main line of argument, but the papers covered these witnesses with photographs, headlines, and vast chunks of undigested testimony nonetheless.[44]

Sensations of violence became commonplace in the South? The land of evangelical Christianity and romantic tales of the past? In the late nineteenth and early twentieth centuries, evangelical Christianity began to dominate the region, making war on drink, Darwinism, and other signs of modernism. At the same time, Thomas Nelson Page and others rigorously romanticized the South's past, turning the antebellum world into an idyllic dreamworld (for whites). This context makes it even more curious and notable that southern journalism in this era approached crime sensations with less moralistic, melodramatic, and romantic content and with greater objectivity and forthright prurience.

This increasing coverage of crime and violence would be easy to explain if it occurred in a moment of increasing criminal activity. Instead, it occurred in an era in which violence and crime trends decreased in America. From the mid-nineteenth century into the 1930s, the nation experienced a steady decline in the rates for homicides as well as for general disorder. Far from experiencing a crime wave, America was becoming a more orderly society, even as it was becoming an urban and industrial nation. "We have waves of news, and we think we are having waves of crime," said one New York crime commissioner in the 1920s.[45]

■

A MORE RATIONAL WORLD . . . OF DISORDER

By the 1910s, Richmond's newspapers were larger, giving them more space in which to explore sensations; their reading public was likewise much larger and from more diverse backgrounds. Professionalization of the press and the police drained sensational stories of some of their idiosyncrasies and ambiguity. The emerging social sciences looked at crime in a more concerted and less emotional and moralistic fashion, and the cultural movement of realism likewise affected crime reporting by emphasizing the importance of discussing and investigating even the darker sides of society. The rising importance of mass culture overall bypassed the Victorian style of stressing self-improvement and edification in leisure time, moving toward a modern style of fun and interest in morally neutral subjects.

Each of these developments heralded important individual shifts in American society and culture; each also contributed to the development of a new cultural mentality in twentieth-century America. Together, these developments influenced editors to approach crime as a profitable and un-exceptional avenue to pursue, a normal if horrible side of the human experience. This was no less true in the South; in this era and with these sets of changes, the region was in keeping with national trends.

Editors printed abundantly on crime sensations like the Beattie case in part because the nation was awash in abundance in general. In the late Victorian era, America grew in abundance in every way, growing larger, wealthier, and better educated. This provided the material foundation for an explosion in the cultural life of the nation, including the newspapers hawking sensations. Between 1860 and 1910, the U.S. population tripled (from 31 million to 92 million). Virginia's population increased by a smaller margin (69 percent), albeit its urban communities grew fourfold (411 percent). Despite the burning of its business district in 1865, Richmond quickly rebuilt, expanding from 37,910 inhabitants in 1860 to 127,628 by 1910.[46]

The economy grew more sharply still—if unevenly in boom-and-bust cycles—during this age of industrial revolution. It is a testimony to the scope of economic growth that, despite such a swelling of population, real income per capita in the United States more than doubled in the half century after the war.[47] Richmond never became the first city of the New South, as many boosters had hoped in the wake of the Civil War, but it nevertheless succeeded in growing at a prodigious pace. Its tobacco, iron, and flour industries continued to prosper, as did a host of smaller businesses. According to census records, the value of Richmond's manufactured products in 1910 was four times what it was in 1860, and manufacturing firms employed more than twice as many people.[48]

The readership of print media expanded at least as rapidly as this growth in population and wealth. Nationally, illiteracy fell from an 1870 mark of 20 percent to 7.7 percent in 1910.[49] Much of this progress was due to the expansion of public school systems in the late nineteenth century South, particularly schools for African Americans. Virginia, for example, fell short of the national average, but was making even faster progress, moving from 40 percent illiteracy in 1880 down to 15.2 percent in 1910. In that year, Richmond's public was more literate still (8.2 percent illiteracy), nearing the national average.[50]

This multilayered growth in the size, wealth, and literacy of American society provided the foundation for a tremendous expansion in American cultural life, including the press. This growth appeared both in rising circulations and in the development of larger newspaper editions. By 1911, the combined circulation figure for Richmond's three English-language

dailies—61,987—was more than four times the figure at the time of the
Cluverius murder just twenty-five years before. And, in the midst of exploring a particular sensation, circulation numbers skyrocketed. The *Richmond
Evening Journal* trumpeted its circulation figures during the Beattie case,
announcing that the paid circulation on 24 November 1911 was 64,210,
almost four times its daily averages. "For weeks past," wrote the sensation-
weary editor of the *Religious Herald*, "we have heard from 10 in the morning on until we closed our desk for the day the shrill cries of the newsboys,
rising above all the strident noises of the street, as 'Extra!' after 'Extra!'
poured from the presses."[51]

Not only were more copies printed, but the size of papers expanded as
well. Typesetting had long been the most intransigent bottleneck prevent-
ing newspapers from growing larger; in 1880, typesetters were still setting
type by hand as in the 1700s. Along with cheap paper, the invention of the
linotype—a mechanized means of setting type for presses—promoted the
rapid growth of newspaper editions after 1880. The typewriter, in use in
the 1870s and ubiquitous by 1900, likewise facilitated the expansion and
ease of office work of all sorts, including the press. Throughout the nation,
the number of pages in daily newspapers grew steadily over the coming
decades.

All Richmond papers had been four pages up to this time: one sheet
printed on both sides and folded once. The *Richmond Dispatch*, with the
city's largest circulation, grew to six to eight pages in 1895. Its successor,
the *Richmond Times-Dispatch*, grew to ten to sixteen pages for weekday
editions in the 1910s.[52] Starting on 3 February 1903, the *Times-Dispatch* in-
augurated a Sunday edition (it previously had published six days a week),
which by the 1910s could be up to forty-six pages long. By the time of
the Beattie murder, the *Times-Dispatch* printed—every week—at least
four times the pages it had printed just twenty years before, and it circulated about three times as many copies of those pages. Newspapers from
throughout the nation experienced a parallel growth: a quadrupling of the
size of papers was the norm between the 1890s and 1920s.[53]

In the midst of this abundance, press coverage of crime sensations rose
markedly in the late nineteenth and early twentieth centuries in both numbers of articles and pages devoted to them. Although important developments, neither the increase in the number of articles nor their expanding
lengths is very surprising given the dramatic enlargement of the overall
size of papers in this era. In total numbers, sensational crime articles almost
doubled between the Phillips case in 1867 and the Beattie case of 1911. The
Beattie coverage was even more dense than these numbers imply due to

the fact that the judicial system in Virginia increasingly sped such cases through the court system. A ratio of articles to days the case was in play demonstrates the growing density of print devoted to these sensational cases: the Beattie case received almost five times the number of stories per day as did the Cluverius case just a generation before.[54]

This rise in quantity of coverage is further emphasized by the fact that these growing numbers of stories were also longer. The average article concerning the Cluverius case was at least twice the length of the average Phillips story; likewise, the Beattie coverage at least doubled again the average length of a Cluverius article. This further change can be ascribed to the quadrupling of the size of newspapers as well as a continuation of the late-nineteenth-century trend toward involved, thorough, and even repetitive description.[55] Even during the peak moments of coverage, the Beattie case was much more densely covered in terms of both the number of stories produced and their lengths. Testimony during the trial, for instance, which had been heavily paraphrased, summarized, and edited in the nineteenth century, regularly appeared in large, verbatim chunks during the Beattie trial.[56]

So great was the volume of print in the *Times-Dispatch* during the Beattie trial that the paper also printed the Associated Press wire reports as a summary of each day's events "for busy readers" who "desire a brief account." Richmond was not alone; between 1899 and 1923, the amount of newspaper space nationally that was devoted to crime grew by 58 percent, far outpacing the growth of general news (1 percent), political news (1 percent), business news (4 percent), foreign news (9 percent), sports (47 percent), and even advertisements (47 percent).[57] Violent sensations across the nation—the Lizzie Borden case in Massachusetts in 1892, the Harry Thaw murder in New York City in 1906, and the Leo Frank case in Atlanta in 1913, for instance—all testify to this rising volume of print. During each of these trials, local newspapers were virtually overcome with coverage, printing numerous stories filling multiple pages of each edition. The *Boston Globe* filled something like one-fifth of its total print space with news of the trial of Lizzie Borden in 1893, including several pages every day of verbatim testimony. During Harry Thaw's trial for the murder of architect Stanford White, the first three pages of every edition of the *New York World* was filled with the story.[58]

In an age when everything seemed to be growing quickly, sensations grew at least as fast. This is true not only in newspaper stories in Richmond or national papers, but also in the size and number of pamphlets and paperbacks printed on sensations. The average length of murder narratives increased by 30 percent between the antebellum era and the early twentieth century. In addition, a murder at midcentury would prompt a single publisher to print a volume, whereas those at the turn of the century found competing publishers exploiting the market.[59]

More than the size of newspapers and pamphlets changed in this era; the nature of journalism was changing as well. Despite the influence of the penny press on the mid-nineteenth-century United States, a more staid, partisan press continued to dominate the field for another two generations.[60] In 1880 two-thirds of American newspapers continued to be tied overtly to a political party, but a focus on politics was on the wane as news and local coverage waxed.[61] Virginia papers clearly took part in this national trend: a politically competitive Richmond press had persisted into the 1880s, when the major non-Democratic paper passed from the scene.[62] After 1890, a general Democratic consensus among the white-owned and -operated papers was threatened only slightly by the populist movement of the decade and never seriously challenged thereafter. Because every paper toed the same party line, political coverage lost some of its intensity and perhaps some of its column inches.

In place of the politically centered newspapers arose the "new journalism" in the late nineteenth century, making the field more a profession and less a haphazard undertaking. In the process, general news—including crime and sensation—displaced political news as the central feature of papers. Even as production of crime sensations expanded, the urban newspaper and book publishing businesses grew from idiosyncratic, editor-dominated firms of the mid-nineteenth century to corporations in the early twentieth century. More than ever, the press was enmeshed within a bureaucratic system, one that became increasingly professional and standardized. This is particularly true when considering the broad impact of news-gathering associations on the press in the period. The first press association appeared in the 1840s (with the advent of the telegraph), but news sharing underwent a number of metamorphoses before the Associated Press became dominant late in the century, with the United Press as its main challenger after 1907. These associations allowed for news to be transmitted more cheaply and effectively to papers around the country (and the world), but it also affected the style of reporting. Pitching to an audience of hundreds of different editors, wire reports increasingly centered on the facts, presenting them without value judgments. In addition, syndication of features, comics, and interviews became the norm at the turn of the century, interconnecting newspapers and standardizing much of their fare. In its extreme form—the use of "ready-prints" or boilerplate in the nation's rural weeklies—syndication imposed something close to uniformity on thousands of smaller papers.[63]

With newspapers incorporated and tied together into a national network more than ever before, the ripples of any one sensation spread much further than in the nineteenth century. Richmond papers offered brief daily updates during New York's famous trials of Stanford White's murderer, Harry Thaw, in 1907 and 1908, as they also did when Leo Frank went on trial in Atlanta in 1913 for the murder of young Mary Phagan. In turn, the *New York Times* printed stories on the Beattie murder in sixty-two different editions. If these tended to be rather small stories compared to the volume of Beattie-related print rolling off the Richmond presses, the *Times* nevertheless reported the murder on the front page twenty-four times and printed six editorials on various sides of the Beattie case.[64] Wrote an editor of the *New York Times*: "The Beattie case furnishes a very striking illustration of how small a place the world has become. . . . [Now] human interests have broadened, and the public concern no longer fails, even if the scene of action is laid a long way off, so long as the story is a good one. Through the newspapers the world is rapidly becoming just a big neighborhood with every community touching elbows."[65] Not only did Western Union set up a temporary office one hundred feet from the Chesterfield Court House during the Beattie trial, that office "broke records", sending 50,000 words along the nation's wires each day. Of course, this record telegraph volume was, in turn, the subject of yet another story for publication in the Richmond papers.[66]

The twentieth-century press, wrote one observer in the 1920s, was "less the personal product of an editor-owner and more the product of an efficient machine."[67] So was its treatment of crime. Newspapers professionalized their procedures by expanding the roles played by the reporters and by inventing the interview and making it central to modern journalism. Up to the 1860s, the interview was unknown, a style of writing not yet invented. The press covered many individuals, to be sure, but such articles consisted of either speeches printed verbatim or the description of a narrator. Beginning in the 1870s, newspapers began experimenting with the interview format, and by the 1910s, the interview "was the central act of the journalist."[68] Speeches were now "covered," with the story as much on the setting, the audience, and the context of the event as on the words themselves. The interview changed the flavor of news coverage by putting the reader closer to the action — hearing as if firsthand the story of the news. The goal was to give the facts in a dramatic form, like "a participant who spits on his hands, rolls up his sleeves, and jumps into the fight."[69]

Nowhere was this active style clearer than in the variety of muckraking journalists who appeared on the national scene at this time. "Facts, facts piled up to the point of dry certitude, was what the American people needed and wanted" in the first decades of the 1900s, according to the muckraking reporter Ray Stannard Baker. He explained that the public had tired of hearing only accusations and charges and so "eagerly read the long and sometimes complicated and serious articles we wrote. Month after month they would swallow dissertations of ten or twelve thousand words without even blinking—and ask for more."[70] Convinced they were scientifically analyzing the facts of social problems, the new journalists raked muck from throughout the nation into public view.

These muckraking reporters were known by name, a distinction few of their colleagues from a generation before enjoyed. Like the interview, reporting as a profession was invented in America in the wake of the Civil War, particularly developing in the 1880s and 1890s. Once a position with no formal training and paid by the column-inch, by the turn of the century, the job of reporter was typically salaried and increasingly was filled by college graduates. No reporters had their names printed with their stories in the 1885 Cluverius case (or any preceding it), for instance, whereas several did in the 1911 Beattie coverage.[71] In addition, some nationally known reporters, most notably Dorothy Dix, covered the Beattie trial, and were, in turn, the subject of Richmond area newspaper stories.[72] As with the interview, developments in reporting also brought the reader closer to the action by making eyewitness accounts and on-the-spot stories more common in the press.[73]

During the course of the late nineteenth century, newspapers became larger but also more adept at discovering information and more innovative in the forms given that information. They provided more details and did so in an increasingly value-neutral style. One study of both local and wire reports found that only one-third of all stories from 1865 to 1874 were "objective" (centered on factual reporting and avoiding personal values), a proportion that rose to one-half between 1885 and 1894. But this style of reporting became dominant in the twentieth century: two-thirds of all stories surveyed between 1905 and 1914 were "objective," and that proportion rose further to four-fifths in the decade 1925–34.[74] Charging by the word and demanding speed as much as literary merit, telegraphy itself imposed a premium on concise, to-the-point writing devoid of flowery language. The dynamic of news sharing (through syndication and press associations) likewise pressured writers to seek moderation and common ground and to avoid both idiosyncratic asides and value statements that could alienate a diverse readership. The overwhelming torrent of Beattie coverage reflected this trend toward value-neutral reporting.[75]

These multifarious changes in the nature of the press might be considered sufficient context to explain the differences in the nature of crime sensations in the early twentieth century. But other changes in society—in culture, social sciences, and policing—likewise nudged these narratives of murder toward a more objective style.

Muckraking journalists were inspired in part by the growing influence of both the social sciences and the literary movement of realism. History, economics, political science, and sociology each became organized disciplines in this era, taking as their model the natural sciences with their extraordinary growth, dynamism, and, most important, goal of objectivity. Wrote one historian of the American social sciences: "The mainstream social science that took shape in the United States from 1890 to 1920 was anxious to recreate the historical world in accord with the demands of scientific prediction and control."[76] On the local level, numerous social uplift groups initiated studies of Richmond's social conditions, gathering data to better understand social issues like the underclass, housing, and sanitation.[77] In the Progressive Era, academics and social reform groups around the nation studied society and social ills as never before.

This scientific approach to human interaction dramatically affected perceptions of crime and the criminal. The emerging authority of the social sciences turned attention toward a number of faults and failings in modern society, with the understanding that these, too, were natural phenomena worthy of close study. Italian criminologist Cesare Lombroso believed in a "criminal type," an inborn predilection to crime that might be predicted with the proper measurements of physical attributes. Lombroso taught that criminals, like children or "inferior" races, were by nature hedonistic, cruel, and uncivilized. Indeed, they represented primitive reversions to an earlier race of humankind or even to animals: the criminal "reproduces in civilised times characteristics, not only of primitive savages, but of still lower types as far back as the carnivora."[78] This new perspective, broadly influential in American criminology around the turn of the century, turned from a moral view of the criminal to a (putatively) scientific perspective.

Yet the Lombrosian idea of regressive criminals faced stiff opposition from competing scientific views of the criminal after the turn of the century. "Modern science has any number of names to describe a nature like Beattie's," wrote the *Nation*. "He may be a defective, or a victim of neurosis, or a reversion to type."[79] Among these "any number" of perspectives, sociology in particular tended to view crime more as a *social* problem than a moral or individual failing. Émile Durkheim, a major figure in this change, argued strongly against the prevailing focus on the individual miscreant. He believed that crime was a normal element of all societies and that it was a social phenomenon rather than simply the actions of aberrant individuals. In fact, he considered crime to be necessary—a society without any crime would continue to police itself by developing new infractions. This development in the social sciences not only sanctioned a more thorough exploration of crimes and crime sensations, it also fostered an understanding that crime was a constituent part of the human condition.[80]

At the same time that the emerging social sciences amended the context for any understanding of crime sensations, the cultural movement of realism pushed in the same direction: "The world has grown tired of preachers and sermons; to-day it asks for facts. It has grown tired of fairies and angels, and asks for flesh and blood. It looks on life as it exists to-day—both its beauty and its horror, its joy and its sorrow. It wishes to see all; not only the prince and the millionaire, but the laborer and the beggar, the master and the slave. We see the beautiful and the ugly, and know what the world is and what it ought to be."[81] Realism as a cultural movement had its fullest impact on American life and culture at the end of the nineteenth century. Rejecting both the classicism and romanticism that preceded them, realism and naturalism turned attention away from the ideal and toward the commonplace, often taking as their subjects nature, the middle and lower classes, and aspects of human experience previously ignored or downplayed. The method of capturing this subject matter also differed from previous movements, being more detached, objective, detailed, and often pessimistic.[82] From the beginning, realism and naturalism were slandered by critics for being consumed by animal passions, sex, and the exploitation of base instincts; in short, it was seen as overly sensational and coarse. A naturalistic candor has become commonplace in American culture and literature, but the frank tone and sexual content of Theodore Dreiser's *Sister Carrie* (1900), for instance, was shocking in its time. Realists pushed for greater objectivity, seeing passions, instincts, and flaws as natural and describing them without moral judgments.[83] In place of archetypes and excess, these writers developed social types; in place of heroes and antiheroes, they created everyday characters with rich mixtures of positive and negative attributes.[84]

In essence, both realism and the emerging social sciences legitimized serious study of "low" subjects—including crime and violence—both artistically and sociologically. The moral perspective that such attention was simply pandering to base instincts was fading; increasingly, discussing crime at length was seen as portraying the dark, but also the real and vital underside of life itself.

In the same generations, a more efficient and professional system of justice drained stories of violent crime of one source of their mystery and indeterminacy, again making them more commonplace. From the antebellum period through the end of the century, a variety of critics believed the Richmond police and courts needed reform. By 1910, the judicial system had been streamlined, and the press in the state was crowing about its achievements. Henry Beattie was arrested but a few days after killing his wife. He faced a preliminary trial within a week, a circuit court trial one month later, and the state supreme court decided not to hear his case six weeks after that. In all, the Beattie case went through the court system of Virginia in only four months.[85] The wheels of Virginia justice were turning more quickly in the early twentieth century, and the public faith in their courts seemed to grow apace.

If the courts were more prompt, an equally dramatic change took place in the Richmond police at the turn of the century. No new policemen were added to the force from 1888 to 1906; thereafter, the force grew as steadily as the city. The city police department introduced a signal system (1904), bicycles (1905), a target range (1905), motorized patrol wagons (1907), and motorcycles (1908). In addition, they reintroduced a detective force (by 1898), they adopted the Bertillon system of identifying criminals in 1900, and in 1913 they began to fingerprint offenders. These efforts are all in keeping with national trends in the professionalization of the police.[86] If one mystery in cases centered on whether the city's police and judicial systems would be competent to investigate and prosecute high-profile crimes, those issues were mitigated by the 1910s.

Fewer doubts about the courts and the police helped to ease some of the mystery in cases sensationalized in the press, making its stories more about "facts piled up to the point of dry certitude." But the subject of this new journalism was much more: it also entertained more than ever. The accelerating growth of mass culture at the turn of the century—like all these other factors—pushed toward exploring sensational material more thoroughly as it transformed the cultural landscape on the broadest scale. Twentieth-century mass culture lacked the moralizing and highbrow perspective of both Victorian culture and artistic movements like realism; instead, it was about fun. Modern mass culture geared its fare to the largest swath of the population, the middle and working classes. In essence, it was "more vigorous, exuberant, daring, sensual, uninhibited, and irreverent" than ever before. In other words, it was more sensational.[87] At least as much as realism, the social sciences, population growth, or literacy, the development of a fast-flowing current in American popular culture oriented toward the middle and lower classes changed the context for the production of culture altogether, including the context for sensational crimes.

Trends in popular literature demonstrate this shift. One scholar has found a notable change in the values considered meaningful in American best sellers between 1850 and 1920. At midcentury, a novel's successful and lauded characters, both male and female, were most often considered pious, pure, and selfless.[88] Best sellers, then, paralleled the "Christian earnestness" of melodrama. In the early twentieth century, however, these values lost ground. The proportion of female characters styled as pious in the best sellers, for instance, decreased from 70 percent to 30 percent (male—50 percent to 25 percent). The popular novels in the age of ragtime centered on individualism, self-reliance, and personal strength and power. Rarely did these novels explicitly embrace the "new woman," the "new man," or realism; more often they turned away from modernity toward settings in myth or history. Even so, popular fiction's new interest in assertive individualism demonstrated a turn toward the more active and vital lifestyle of the era. As unrealistic, even regressive, as was the character Tarzan, for instance, he also represented an aggressive, self-reliant personality that was a response to the modern condition.[89]

In the press, this growing interest in active, value-neutral entertainment found expression in the stories of sex, crime, and social conflict in the yellow journalism of the period. Strongest in New York and other major metropolitan centers, this style gave birth to headlines like "Baptized in Blood" in Joseph Pulitzer's *New York World* and "Startling Confession of a Wholesale Murderer Who Begs to Be Hanged" in William Randolph Hearst's *New York Journal.*[90] Perhaps most telling, the defining moment in the history of the yellow press was a war.[91] These papers also championed workers and the disadvantaged against the might of the monopolies and aristocrats. Pointed, mass-oriented, entertaining sheets, the yellow press could be inventive and innovative but also shamelessly self-promotional and superficial.

Like much of the nation, Richmond experienced this popularization but in a moderated form. The city's papers rarely engaged in the pranks, fakery, and bad taste that gave the yellow press such a poor reputation, nor did they often champion crusades like those waged by muckrakers. Richmond had but one muckraking Progressive Era journalist: Adon Yoder, an iconoclast publisher of a small weekly magazine called the *Idea*. Unafraid to name names and decry the corruption of officials—the mayor and police chief were his favorite targets—Yoder frequently defended himself against charges of libel and was driven out of the business in 1911 after only four years of publishing. Circulation figures are not available, but it can be safely assumed from Yoder's own statements that the *Idea* never became a driving force in Richmond's reading public but was rather a gadfly annoying the powerful for a brief time from the margins of the Richmond press.[92]

Yet a subtler version of muckraking and yellow journalism—bereft of most of the stunts, crusades, and gaudy self-promotion—became a part of mainstream newspaper reporting everywhere, including Virginia. This might be called "ochre" journalism, a yellowish turn toward entertainment, local news, crime, and detailed coverage. As newspapers grew in size, their political coverage did not keep pace; instead, papers in Richmond and elsewhere increasingly added features to their pages—women's page, sports coverage, comics, photographs, human interest stories, fiction, and movie and theater reviews. According to a nationwide study, true yellow journalism was practiced in only about one-third of the papers in the largest cities and for only about a decade. By 1910, few remained. Much more enduring were more moderate changes in style and an emphasis on entertainment.[93]

Each paper in America tacked its own course through these conflicting winds: detailed, objective reporting, on the one hand, and engaging, more prurient sensationalism, on the other hand.[94] Overall, there was a trend toward an uneasy combination of the two: exciting, topical, alluring reading matter to draw the burgeoning masses coupled with the efficiency of a professional staff. The culmination was often the dispassionate and value-neutral presentation of sensational material: banner headlines implying sex or scandal followed by columns of (at least tacitly) nonjudgmental interviews or court documents or reporters' eyewitness accounts.[95]

■

The rising volume of exhaustive attention given crime sensations in the twentieth century amazed and disgusted those raised on nineteenth-century standards. Wrote the *Century Magazine* just two months before the Beattie crime took place:

> Many have been the mornings in recent months when the pages of even conservative newspapers have looked more like catalogues of crime, than like "journals of civilization." . . . ordinary killings and poisonings,

"black hand" stealings and explosions, strike outrages, public defalcations, and plain burglaries, are set forth with an exhaustiveness stimulating those inclined to follow criminal example, and terrifying to those fearful of becoming future victims. It is plain that the average sensational editor handles a topic of that sort with a determination to surpass his rival's "duty to publicity," by making the most of its possibilities as salable news. No matter if premature publicity will baffle so-called "justice"; the public shall know all of the hideous reality, and more than all of the imaginary direfulness, even if civilization must thereby perish lingeringly on the altar of journalistic commerce.[96]

Another editor believed that so many articles described in such minute detail the crimes being committed that he titled his own article on the phenomenon "Lessons in Crime Fifty Cents per Month."[97] Some thrilled to read everything they could about these murders; others were revolted by the spectacle of such attention, particularly when public discussion approached sexual matters. Both responses emphasized the scope of the change: sensations had become prominent elements of modern life in the South as well as the rest of the nation.

The coming century would slake the public thirst for lurid and salacious tales like no period before. New media would allow for faster dissemination of sensational news as motion pictures, radio, television, the Internet, and video games increasingly broadened the range of ways an interested public could satisfy its obsessions with shocking stories and horrifying violence. If crime sensations first became a part of the South's culture in the nineteenth century, they grew to become a central constituent element of that culture in the twentieth.

True crime sensations continued to retain much of the romanticism and melodrama of the nineteenth century, exploring moments of heightened emotionalism, gestures to sin and God and fiends and angels. In other fields, like genre fiction and motion pictures, melodrama continued to flourish, in some cases to predominate. And elements of what was so striking in the Beattie coverage—trial testimony, for instance, and abundant coverage— certainly appeared in the nineteenth century, even in the antebellum era, if in smaller doses. This was no wholesale cultural revolution in sensationalism at the turn of the twentieth century but, rather, a continuation of the ongoing, long-term evolution of culture and cultural forms.

If not a revolution, melodrama had become just one layer of crime sensations drowning in close and detailed description. By diffusing the focus of attention away from moral abstractions and toward society and social types, crime sensations—like realism, naturalism, and the emerging social sciences—moved toward the ordinary, toward considering it the darker side of normal life. The deluge of details had become more than a momentary, notable aberration from the norm, a few days of excitement, an erratic or idiosyncratic mix of details and brief updates, as in the nineteenth century. In the twentieth century, a murder sensation became "an institution, as periodic in its public appearances and reappearances as the cycle of the seasons," covered by newspapers in systematic, persistent, and regularized ways.[98] This amounts to the disenchantment of sensations, making them more worldly, more sociological, more *a part of* society rather than *a breach in* society.

A development at the end of Henry Beattie's trial emphasizes just how different American culture had become in the twentieth century. Free to leave Richmond after Beattie's trial, Beulah Binford took a train north to New York City. A theatrical producer convinced her to capitalize on her substantial notoriety by contracting to appear on the stage.[99] City after city banned her from performing, an action that brought her further publicity. She was barred from performing in New York as well, but within a month she appeared in a small part in an off-Broadway theater and made a short film describing her sad life story. In the twentieth century, the press treated criminals in such a morally muted and complex manner that the consort of a convicted murderer could misread her infamy as fame and agree with a promoter that she might succeed on the stage and in film.[100]

In the eighteenth-century South, crime was hardly covered by newspapers at all. By the mid-nineteenth century, crime sensations received front-page coverage but in an irregular and limited manner—often brief updates or, when more extensively covered, explorations via the tropes of melodrama. The influence of realism coupled with the rise of the social sciences opened the door to greater exploration of violence in the twentieth century. A growing cultural abundance widened and deepened the possibilities for this exploration. The emerging "ochre" press supplied the means of fulfilling this possibility by delving into the graphic material of murder sensations.

This added up to a cultural matrix in which sensational crime played a particularly important role. It provided a gathering spot for two central threads of the cultural change: a realistic treatment (via trials and testimony) of lurid material (murder). By the first few decades of the twentieth century, Richmonders were reading a new sort of newspaper, one more standardized, thorough, entertaining, even thrilling and certainly much more verbose. Importantly, it was also one that explored sensations—of crime and violence as well as other sensations—much more than ever before. If a central element of modern life is increasing rationality and a search for order, it is also an increasing obsession with the ghastly possibilities of disorder.

4

AFRICAN AMERICAN
SENSATIONS

Jim Crow Justice and
the *Richmond Planet*

THUS GREW UP A DOUBLE SYSTEM OF JUSTICE . . .

W. E. B. Du Bois, *Souls of Black Folk* (1903)

On 14 June 1895, an aging white farmer, Edward Pollard, returned from his fields to find the body of his wife, Lucy, outside their home in Lunenburg County, Virginia, southwest of Richmond. She had been hewn repeatedly with an ax, and more than eight hundred dollars was missing from the Pollard home. Found with two twenty-dollar bills, a black man from North Carolina, Solomon Marable, was charged with the crime, and he confessed to his involvement as an accessory. He implicated three local black women, Mary Abernathy and Pokey and Mary Barnes, as the actual murderers. "Feelings were high" in Lunenburg and the surrounding counties, and lynchings appeared imminent. The local sheriff spirited the four defendants out of the neighborhood, assigning a deputy to guide them on a trek on foot through the night to the Petersburg jail to the northeast.[1]

In the following eighteen months, this case would become a sensation in Virginia's African-American community and, to a lesser extent, among whites. Solomon Marable would be tried twice, convicted both times, and hanged for his part in the crime. This part of the story was expected by most observers. Pokey and the two Marys—who came to be known collectively as the Lunenburg women—had a much more interesting, complex, and telling path to tread.

The saga of the Lunenburg women provides a sort of best-case scenario for blacks facing southern justice in the Jim Crow era. They resided in Virginia rather than the still-more-prejudicial deep South. Lunenburg County was 60 percent black, and in 1895 this population was not yet fully humbled by disfranchisement.[2] Indeed, black as well as white citizens sat on their juries in the first series of trials. The defendants were women, and what chivalry whites could muster for black womanhood therefore softened the hardest edges of Virginia's judicial system. The case attracted enough attention that prominent white lawyers helped to protect the rights of the accused. And the case against them stood chiefly upon the weak evidence of an accusation from a black man who was himself accused of the crime. It is a measure of southern racism that—despite these mitigating circumstances—the Lunenburg women were repeatedly convicted in the Virginia courts. It was only a series of unusual actions by both blacks and whites that saved the women from the gallows.

This story of sensation, crime, and justice vividly demonstrates how different African American sensations were from those in the white press and public. Because blacks had a very different relationship to the government, the police, and the entire system of jurisprudence in Virginia, the cases most sensationalized in the black press and community were quite distinct from the patterns of interest and public obsession so evident in white culture. Just as Du Bois found a double system of justice, so did Jim Crow spawn a double cultural system of sensationalizing crime. Black sensations were simply unlike the white sensations outlined in previous chapters; this chapter, therefore, must have a similarly distinct tone and focus.

From 1880 to 1920, African Americans in the South experienced not only segregation and disfranchisement, but also a surge in lynching, whites rioting against their neighborhoods, and milder forms of intimidation. White crimes against the race were so common as to be a steady drumbeat in the black press for decades. But their ubiquity also meant that individual crimes against blacks rarely became notable sensations in the African American press; they were simply too commonplace. Prosecutions of black criminals in white courts were likewise everyday occurrences. In place of these sorts of stories, the most haunting cases in the black community involved strong evidence of the innocence of black defendants, as with the Lunenburg case. Such cases raised a larger question: would prejudicial white courts be able to acquit? In a sense, the greatest crime for African Americans at the turn of the century was no single case but, rather, the condition of justice itself. This makes for a very different variety of sensationalism.

The Lunenburg murder case becomes most telling within the wider context of justice, race, and African American culture in Virginia, particularly in light of the perspective of one of the South's most prominent black editor-activists. John Mitchell, editor of an African American weekly, the *Richmond Planet*, covered the case closely, and his newspaper provides a rare source within the historical record of lynching: a southern black condemnation of southern white injustice.[3]

Who was this unusual editor? John R. Mitchell Jr. was born near Richmond in the midst of the Civil War. In his childhood, Mitchell obtained the sort of education that had been denied most African Americans, graduating with distinction from Richmond's Colored Normal school in 1881. For the next two years, he taught in Fredericksburg, then briefly in Richmond, where he began his newspaper career as a weekly reporter for the African American *New York Globe*.[4] In 1884, he took over the editorial post at the newly founded *Richmond Planet* and remained in that position for the next forty-five years. Little in John Mitchell's early history marked him as a radical. But in the 1880s and 1890s, he was as strident and vocal in opposition to lynching and white supremacy as any editor in the nation. According to the *Colored American Magazine* in 1902, Mitchell had "the reputation of being the bravest Afro-American editor in the country," in large part due to his "uncompromising war on lynching and all other forms of lawlessness."[5]

The *Richmond Planet*'s John Mitchell evolved from a sensational "fighting editor" in the 1890s into more of a black businessman in the 1910s. His distinctive path allows us to chart the ebbs and flows of African American sensationalism amid the wider currents churning through the South's black communities. Mitchell lies in between the poles of W. E. B. Du Bois's assertive philosophy and Booker T. Washington's quieter path to raise the race, and Mitchell's years editing the *Planet* (1884–1929) nicely coincide with the pinnacle of the black press's influence. Mitchell could be aggressive, but he could also counsel caution, emphasizing business development and social peace. Mitchell confronted tidal forces: black people's postslavery yearning for equality clashing with a repressive, white-run South tending toward the retrograde. He was what some whites called a "new issue Negro," born to freedom's first generation. Unlike many other vocal defenders of his race in the era, however, he never moved North. His struggle would be to find a place for himself and his people within this white-dominated New South.

Mitchell's *Richmond Planet* from 1890 into the 1910s demonstrates the importance of race in understanding how crime was sensationalized.[6] More importantly, it requires a shift in our understanding of what sensational crime *is*. Like his white counterparts, editor John Mitchell fashioned crimes into social dramas, turning the events to mold them into a certain recognizable shape with recognizable characters. But Mitchell's stories carried a different freight; crime sensationalism had a distinct meaning—a different nature and function—within the black community. These stories awoke passions but, set as they were within the context of a persistently racist system of justice, often outrage as much as horror. The heroes and villains of these dramas were typecast but not so clearly from literary and cultural genres in vogue. Rather they were cast in roles representing the forces at battle in the black community: the rule of law, the prejudiced mobs and officials, the innocent victim, the protecting arms of the black community. Much more than the white sensations, those trumpeted in the African American press were overtly political, speaking to the place and predicament faced by the entire black community.

In the 1890s, editor John Mitchell discussed crime, violence, and justice in many ways. The moments of the most heightened and sensational rhetoric occurred when circumstances convincingly argued for the innocence of black defendants. These victims, along with the active public (and

Mitchell himself, of course) were the heroes, fending off a system of white justice that was patently and persistently unjust. One such moment, when the injustice of the system stood out with the deepest contrast, deserves a closer look.

■

THE LUNENBURG WOMEN

Solomon Marable, Mary Abernathy, Pokey Barnes, and Mary Barnes returned to Lunenburg County three weeks after Lucy Pollard's 1895 murder to face trials in the county court. So intense was the feeling against the prisoners that the sheriff asked for state militia to protect them upon their return to the county and during their trial. The governor ordered two companies, approximately eighty men, to guard the prisoners around the clock. Three days into the trials, the commanding officer perceived that a mob might attempt to take the prisoners despite these troops. Writing that he could "not with safety perform the duty required of me with the number of men now under my command," the major in charge asked for reinforcements of "one company of not less than thirty men with 2,000 rounds of ammunition. Matters are becoming complicated," he explained.[7] The complication was the local concern that the women might be acquitted, whereupon the county's whites would probably lynch them.[8] But with 120 armed militiamen encamped on the courthouse green, the threat of lynching was over.

This caution on the part of officials was probably due in good measure to the events in Roanoke two years before. In 1893, a black man, identified only by his "slouch hat," was imprisoned in that city for attacking and robbing a white woman. But before he could stand trial, a mob of thousands attacked the jail, someone fired a gun, and in the ensuing melee, eight men died. The prisoner was spirited out of town, but then, inexplicably, the officers returned and handed him over to the crowd, who promptly hanged him, then burned his body to char. These events horrified Virginia—particularly the loss of white lives in the gunfight. When elected the next year, Governor Charles T. O'Ferrall made a concerted effort to stifle any further mob violence in the state. Lunenburg's angry crowds seemed to threaten this resolution, and the state responded in strength.[9]

Lynching was the first challenge that accused blacks faced as they ran the gauntlet of southern justice: the possibility that whites might completely abrogate the rights of black Americans by violently pulling them outside the ambit of the judicial process. Every year, dozens of cases never made it to trial because the defendants were brutally murdered by mobs.[10]

In the thirty years between 1890 and 1920, nearly seven African Americans were lynched in America every month; the 1890s averaged the lynching of more than two blacks every week. Lynching was never as prominent in Virginia as in the deep South, but it followed the same pattern: twenty-seven lynchings in the 1890s, falling to thirteen and then three over the following two decades.[11]

If many stories of black defendants ended early with the rope, Solomon Marable, Mary Abernathy, and Pokey Barnes withstood this threat of lynching, thanks to the militia. But that was only the first challenge confronting them; they all still faced the charge of first-degree murder, a capital offense.[12] The defendants had no money to hire lawyers; common custom was for the court to appoint an attorney to such cases. When pressed by the judge, J. B. Bell, a local lawyer present in the courtroom, "respectfully declined on the ground that he could not spare the time."[13] A former judge in the county, William Perry, submitted a motion for a change of venue on behalf of Mary Abernathy, stating that the local population was so prejudiced against all the accused women that the defendant feared for her life and did not believe she could get a fair trial. When that motion was denied, he retired from the case. No other lawyer agreed to take these defendants, and under Virginia law, the judge could not compel one to serve.[14] In the words of the Supreme Court of Appeals of Virginia: "If a prisoner is unable to employ counsel, the court may appoint some one to defend him, and it is a duty which counsel owes to his profession, to the court engaged in the trial, to the administration of justice, and to humanity, not to withhold his aid, nor spare his best efforts in the defense . . . But we cannot presume that the trial court denied the prisoner her right to have counsel, or failed if she were unable to employ counsel, to assign some one to aid her in her defense."[15]

Until the U.S. Supreme Court's decision in *Gideon v. Wainwright* (372 U.S. 335 [1963]), state constitutional safeguards of the right to counsel were not interpreted to mean that a state or municipality had to secure counsel for indigent defendants. Without this protection, neither Solomon Marable nor the women accused by him had much of a chance to avoid conviction. Each defendant testified on his or her own behalf, and Pokey Barnes in particular attempted to bring witnesses and cross-examine those brought against her. But to no avail.

In succession, each defendant was tried without counsel, convicted, and sentenced to death. The three capital cases, along with the trial of Pokey Barnes's mother for second-degree murder, were completed in the space of seven days. This included one court day cut short to allow the women to attempt to find attorneys and another day spent trying to find a witness who could not be located.

Solomon Marable's trial took less that two days, and on the strength of his confession as well as the money found in his possession, the jury deliberated only nine minutes before convicting him of first-degree murder. But little more than Marable's accusation implicated the women.[16] Their juries took much more time, and two hours into deliberations in Mary Abernathy's trial, her jury reported that they could not agree. They were sent back to continue their discussions and continued to deliberate into the following morning. This was precisely the moment when the threat of lynching arose and new troops were called for. The following morning, the jury found Mary guilty. Likewise, Pokey Barnes's jury could not agree when they first deliberated late into the evening and returned a guilty verdict the following day. The juries struggled more with the two women's cases but ultimately found against them both. Again concerned for their safety after the convictions, the authorities removed the prisoners from the county once more, this time sending them back with the militia to Richmond.[17]

In the midst of these trials, Solomon Marable changed his story, then switched back, then reversed himself once again. He first said that he had been drafted by the local women simply to hold Mrs. Pollard while they robbed her house. The women then slew her with the ax, much to his horror, and paid him off with the two twenty-dollar bills. It was this story that sent the Lunenburg women toward the gallows.[18]

But even early reports spoke of contradictions and changes in his story that drew Marable's accusations into question. During Mary Abernathy's trial, in fact, he made a number of conflicting statements and admitted to lying in court during his own trial.[19] Then, during the course of the trial against Pokey Barnes, Frank Cunningham, the captain of one of the militia companies, took Marable aside and assured him that, despite what he might have been told, the soldiers would not allow any lynch mob to take him, something Marable seemed to hold "in very great terror." He would hang for his crime, admitted Cunningham, and nothing would change that. But if Marable had any hope of avoiding eternal damnation, he continued, then he must tell the truth and go to his death without innocent blood on his hands. Marable then changed his statement, saying that a white man he had never seen before compelled him to grab Mrs. Pollard and then this man, whom he later identified as David Thompson, killed her. Marable made this admission to several parties and again in the trial of Barnes. But during this testimony, a confusing series of events occurred. A juror passed a note to the judge informing him that a white man in the audience was attempting to tamper with the witness, having winked and nodded at Marable. The judge cleared the courtroom, but Marable was apparently unnerved by the incident: he recanted his story of the white man and returned to his accusation of the women. After the convictions and the removal of the prisoners to Richmond, Marable again said that the women were innocent and that a white man had done the deed and told him that if they were caught, he should implicate these women. After this series of oscillations in his charges, most observers concluded simply that Marable was, in the words of the *Richmond Times*, "a colossal liar" and his testimony worthless.[20] Nevertheless, that testimony convicted three women.

A month after the murder, the three blacks faced the imminent threat of the scaffold; their hangings were scheduled for late September. For most cases against poor blacks, that would be the end of the story: only their executions awaited them. In fact, the *Richmond Dispatch* made just such a prediction for the Lunenburg women. After charting the path of possible appeals, the *Dispatch* ended with realism: "It is, of course, quite unlikely that we shall see these cases take such a course: it would cost a great deal of money, and the accused are penniless."[21] So ended virtually all cases against poor blacks in the South in this era.

But the vacillating testimony of Marable raised a host of questions in the minds of many observers. The militiamen returned to their homes telling stories of untrustworthy testimony and witness tampering. Many of them felt that the lack of counsel for the defendants, coupled with widespread intimidation and inflamed passions that required the militia to be there, meant that these women were unfairly condemned.[22] Three white lawyers—paid for by John Mitchell and by donations from around the state and nation—agreed to help the Lunenburg women. If the first fortuitous action on behalf of the Lunenburg convicts was the strong action of the governor to stave off the threat of lynching, this support from the community and from prominent white lawyers was the second exceptional moment in the case.

These lawyers were among the most respected white attorneys in the commonwealth. George D. Wise was the commonwealth's attorney for the city of Richmond from 1870 to 1880, whereupon he served Richmond in the House of Representatives until 1895. Henry W. Flournoy was a judge in the city of Danville, also serving several terms as secretary of the commonwealth as well as having a private practice. Captain A. B. Guigon, the youngest of the three, was the son of a long-serving and respected Richmond judge and an attorney mostly in private practice, although from time to time he also served as acting attorney for the commonwealth in Richmond.[23]

These lawyers earned the defendants a hearing before the state supreme court of appeals in November of 1895. Virginia's highest tribunal ordered new trials for both women and for Solomon Marable as well, thus ending their first stay on death row. But the court did not overturn their convictions on the basis of any weakness in the cases against them. "The granting of a new trial by the Supreme Court of Appeals was an act of justice which will be readily recognized by right thinking people everywhere," the *Planet* crowed. But it added more ominously, "And yet the result of this prolonged contention was achieved upon technical grounds alone."[24] The records of the first trials of Barnes, Abernathy, and Marable did not show that their juries were committed to the care of the sheriff and thereby insulated from popular sentiment while sitting in judgment on these cases. The sheriff may or may not have adequately sequestered the jury; but in any event, the record of the case was at fault for not noting the fact, and that was enough for the supreme court to overturn their convictions. What is most surprising here is not this decision—appeals were regularly decided on procedural grounds—but that such a case against poor blacks ever made it to the state's highest court.[25]

The second set of trials began in March 1896 and ended in a telling split decision. A change of venue to neighboring Prince Edward County should have helped the defense by avoiding the passions of the excited Lunenburg population. As expected, Solomon Marable was again convicted, and he was executed in July of that year. The more engrossing and indeterminate part of the Lunenburg story involved the women. John Mitchell's hyperbole that "they cannot be legally convicted" was echoed in a more moderate tone by much of the white press.[26] The *Richmond Times*, for instance, editorialized that these women "have had no trial, and that if they are to be judicially murdered under the present programme, the life of none of us is safe."[27] Nevertheless, these women had been convicted and sentenced to die the summer before.

In April of 1896, the Prince Edward court retried Mary Abernathy for the murder of Lucy Pollard. With a formidable defense team in place, the case took more than a week, longer than all four of the first Lunenburg trials together. Also promising, the jury deliberated for some time before returning a verdict. But despite the weakness of the evidence against her, the jury again found her guilty of first-degree murder and sentenced her to the gallows for the second time. In fact, the jury's verdict was unanimous on the first ballot.[28] "This is no surprise to us," wrote Mitchell in the next issue of the *Planet*. "When we learned that there had been no difficulty experienced in selecting a jury, and this too in a county where the people had been as much wrought up over the atrocious murder of Mrs. Lucy Jane Pollard as they were in Lunenburg county, we were confident as to what it meant. We knew so far as the jury was concerned that Mary Abernathy's fate was sealed."[29]

The verdict in the first trial cannot be surprising: without counsel and with feelings high in Lunenburg, Abernathy's conviction was almost assured. But this second trial is particularly telling—here there was a change in venue, a strong defense team, public criticism of the earlier testimony and verdict, and a period of time elapsing that might cool heads. But the Prince Edward County jury was at least as forceful in its guilty verdict as the Lunenburg court had been.

Was justice in Virginia this prejudiced? John Mitchell thought so, and most blacks in the South would have joined in his pessimism. From the police to the gallows, the system of justice in the South was perceived by African Americans with a jaundiced eye. The racist behavior of Richmond police had abraded the city's black community for some time. In 1867, the arrest of a drunken and disorderly black man in Richmond prompted several dozen neighbors to surround the officers and pelt them with brickbats and loose cobbles from the road. This conflict escalated to gunfire before reinforcements held off the mob.[30] This skirmish—along with countless other conflicts, mobs, and riots[31]—confirms that, from the earliest moments of postwar Richmond, African Americans were thoroughly suspicious of the white institutions responsible for dispensing justice.

African American Richmonders had much reason to be suspicious of the police, for racial prejudice is clearly evident in the historical record.[32] On a number of occasions, officers shot blacks on the street with little provocation.[33] The police routinely and prejudicially arrested blacks for little cause, often "on suspicion." In an unusually frank assessment in 1874, Richmond's mayor decried the "flagrant outrage" that was common practice up to that time of the police "arresting whole companies of colored people on general warrants," thereby making all of them pay for court costs.[34]

In addition, the law itself allowed room for prejudice to flourish. In the antebellum period, slaves had been punished with harsh, often corporal measures. Offenses classed as capital crimes were much more numerous for them, including not just violent crimes, but also those against property as well. Even free blacks faced harsher penalties when the crime involved assault on whites.[35] After the Civil War, overtly race-specific laws became unconstitutional, and Virginia revised its criminal statutes to comply. But the resulting criminal code reflected a continuing desire to differentiate in the law. The harsh penalties against slaves were not abandoned after the war; rather, the commonwealth combined the white and black codes, widening a jury's options in regard to punishment for a number of crimes. Before the war, slaves faced death or transportation out of the state for burglary, for example, while whites faced a prison term. Beginning in 1866, anyone "guilty of burglary shall be punished with death, or in the discretion of the jury, by confinement in the penitentiary for not less than five nor more than eighteen years."[36] In all, three capital crimes—rape, robbery, and burglary—were grafted from the slave codes onto the new "colorblind" Virginia legal code. Whites and blacks faced the same laws in the same courts before the same judges. But if the laws themselves were evenhanded, they also allowed juries to make as many distinctions—now informal rather than statutory—in their verdicts as before the war. And, as the *Planet* emphasized, they regularly made those distinctions.

In the context of routine discrimination, it is not surprising that white juries provoked a good deal of contempt in the black community. Occasionally, judges in late-nineteenth-century Virginia allowed blacks to sit on juries, but it was rare enough to be noted by the press as an unusual sight.[37] A visitor to Virginia in 1879 noted with shock "that blacks are here systematically excluded from the juries. This seems to be avowed, the excuse being, 'they have got votes, and we cannot give them everything.' In the United States Courts black are put on the juries, but not in the Virginian Courts."[38] By 1901, "a negro juryman is seldom seen in Virginia. . . . [Judges] have been deciding almost unanimously for several years that he has no place in the box."[39]

How could Virginia exclude blacks from the jury box? In 1880, the U.S. Supreme Court affirmed that the Fourteenth Amendment to the Constitution and other federal legislation outlawed any and all official state action to discriminate against blacks in selecting jury pools and juries.[40] West Virginia, for example, passed a law specifically excluding blacks from juries, and the Supreme Court ruled it unconstitutional. In the same session, however, the Court vitiated this ruling by making it clear that it was limited to overtly racist statutes and actions of state officers. In other words, the Supreme Court banned discrimination in form but not in practice. In *Virginia v. Rives*, the court decided that an all-white jury, grand jury, or even the wider jury pool did not, in itself, constitute evidence of discrimination.[41] A mixed jury was not, they held, essential to justice. A lily-white jury would constitute a violation of federal guarantees of equal protection only if it could be proven that a court *intentionally* excluded blacks; otherwise, the assumption would be that it was a fair selection. Since intention rarely can be proven, that was a high bar indeed. This set of decisions in 1880 prohibited statutory discrimination but gave ample room for racial prejudice to flourish informally in the practice of selecting juries. In effect, these decisions helped to bar blacks from juries a generation before disfranchisement erected yet another barrier, for jurors in Virginia were drawn from eligible voters.[42]

Facing white juries, black defendants had little chance, even if other elements in the judicial system operated fairly. On more than one occasion the *Planet* praised judges and Virginia's higher courts, saying that they adhered to the letter of the law as they should. Mitchell likewise applauded more than one governor for being "as generous as he is in the granting of pardons." In contrast, such articles typically continued, cases in lower courts, those before magistrates, and those given over to juries regularly rendered "remarkable evidence of [their] prejudiced character." In 1899, the paper prefaced the story of a jury's harsh decision by saying "we have never seen injustice of some of the decisions of juries more impressively emphasized, and the kindheartedness of the judge more strikingly shown" than when a judge personally appealed to the governor to commute the jury's outrageous sentence.[43]

Interestingly, the Lunenburg juries (the first trials) each included blacks. Mary Abernathy had four black and eight white jurors, while both Solomon Marable and Pokey Barnes had ten white and two black jurors. The presence of these black jurors surely helped the cause of the defendants, and one rumor hinted that at least one of the black jurors delayed a decision by holding out (briefly) for acquittal. But given the racial climate in Southside Virginia, an African American juror would be signing his own death warrant by disagreeing with the white majority in a case of black-on-white murder. Importantly, no blacks served on any of the second set of trials in Prince Edward County.[44]

If white juries were of particular concern, the *Richmond Planet* in the 1890s repeatedly emphasized the lack of fairness in the judicial system overall. Mitchell illustrated this injustice most effectively with well-chosen comparisons of white and black treatment. On dozens of occasions, Mitchell's editorials and features described how a black infraction drew the penalty of years in prison or even death while a white man might be fined lightly for serious offenses. Beginning with the guarantee of equal protection in the Fourteenth Amendment, one such story, titled "No Justice in Virginia," described a white man's ten-dollar fine for killing a black man, contrasting it to the death penalty rendered a black man for committing highway robbery.[45] Mitchell regularly pointed out the disparity between the penalty of death typically imposed on black murderers and the acquittals granted to white lynchers. In 1899, the *Planet* greeted with banner headlines "A New Departure in Virginia Criminal Justice" when six white men were convicted of second-degree murder for lynching.[46] Yet, such a laudatory (and sarcastic) headline merely drew into deeper contrast the dozens of cases each year of white assaults on blacks that went lightly punished if at all, particularly since these convicted lynchers had killed not a black man, but a white man who was "a discharged lunatic and almost an idiot."

Lynching, then, was a horror, but it was only the most blatant, violent, and extralegal wrong in a system of justice that persistently discriminated against blacks. The Constitution and the laws of the nation provided certain protections for all its citizens, and Mitchell's *Planet*, along with the broader black community, protested loudly when those protections were so regularly violated—by the police, the courts, and juries as well as lynch mobs. Their activism on behalf of the Lunenburg women was merely one part of a broader effort to achieve justice for African Americans in Virginia. Here was a case against black women that was so clearly unfair, where the injustice was so blatant, that perhaps, for once, blacks might achieve the justice they sought.

After Mary Abernathy's second conviction—this time by a Prince Edward County jury—the court turned to the case against Pokey Barnes. She had a stronger alibi than Abernathy, leaving only a brief window of opportunity for her to have participated in the supposed conspiracy to murder Mrs. Pollard. On the fifth day of her trial, when the prosecution's testimony was completed, the commonwealth's attorney for Prince Edward County, Asa Watkins, surprised everyone. He submitted a motion of nolle prosequi, dropping the charges against Barnes. Watkins explained that the evidence failed to incriminate her: "Now that all the evidence in the possession of the Commonwealth has been given in, I cannot believe that it is sufficient to justify the jury in bringing in a verdict of guilty. This murder has been fixed upon two persons, but so far, in my opinion, there has been nothing adduced to connect this prisoner with these persons, nor have there been any evidences of a conspiracy between the prisoner and those persons."[47] Freed immediately, Pokey Barnes quickly left the county for Richmond and a celebratory tour of Virginia's black churches. It is telling that she first returned to jail until her train arrived, and when on the train, her father hid her for fear that whites might yet accost them.[48]

Of the prosecuting lawyers, the commonwealth's attorney was alone in his assessment of the weakness of the case against Barnes. As the attorney in charge of the case, Watkins had the authority to submit this motion, and he was careful to say that he had "reached this conclusion without consultation with any one," apparently inoculating his two fellow prosecuting attorneys from any popular backlash against the decision. One of the other attorneys, Judge Mann, while bowing to Watkins's authority, added that "as far as I am concerned, I wish to state that I believe as firmly in the guilt of Pokey Barnes as I do in my own existence."[49] It was yet another exceptional moment in their cases, particularly since the other attorneys were willing to continue the case and conviction by the jury appeared possible if not probable, given the previous verdicts.

Mary Abernathy's lawyers again appealed, and after she spent several more months on death row, the circuit court set aside her conviction in September 1896 as contrary to the evidence. Lawyers in this era regularly filed exceptions on the grounds that the verdict was contrary to the evidence—a sort of formulaic objection. But rarely did an appeals court judge remand a case to a court on those grounds. Again, this is an unusual action in favor of the defendant. Rather than attempting to prosecute her again on the same evidence, the commonwealth once more dropped the charges, and Mary was free. Barnes and Abernathy had spent eleven and fifteen months in jail, respectively, but at last they gained their liberty.

What of Mary Barnes, mother of Pokey, who was convicted of being an accessory to the crime? She served eighteen months of her ten-year sentence in the penitentiary before being freed in January 1897. In this case, it was the governor, presented with a petition for her pardon, who freed her. In his pardon, Governor O'Ferrall wrote that Solomon Marable's testimony, which was "the only testimony against her," was "absolutely unworthy of belief." He continued in a manner that surely gratified the black community. "The life or liberty of a citizen, however humble, is too sacred in the eyes of the law or of civilized man to be taken upon the testimony alone of a self-convicted perjurer and murderer. . . . Every mandate of justice and dictate of conscience require that the prisoner be restored to her liberty."[50]

■

JOHN MITCHELL AND BLACK SOLIDARITY
AGAINST INJUSTICE

Late-nineteenth-century African Americans were understandably obsessed with the issues of crime and justice in the white-controlled world about them. "The most talked about subject of the period was clearly violence," according to one national study of the black press. "Blacks did not take it without struggle. As much militancy as has been seen in black papers could be seen in some of the papers publishing toward the end of the century."[51] The *Richmond Planet* provides an example of this militancy as editor John Mitchell Jr. made violence and justice the central themes of his columns.

If the Lunenburg case was the most sensational of the era in Virginia's black community, it was not alone. It became so important to black Virginians, in fact, because the issue of justice was such a raw and painful wound. Mitchell's voice throughout the Lunenburg case allows us to see the injustice of the system in stark relief against the nation's purported ideal of fairness.

Each year, dozens of stories in the *Planet* simply described the brutal injustice of whites, ending with a final sentence stating only "Lynch Law Must Go!" "the case speaks for itself," or "no comment is necessary."[52] The *Planet* first reported the Lunenburg murder in just this way. It was almost a commonplace: yet another crime, yet another black man to be hanged in Virginia. Only when Marable renounced his confession implicating Abernathy and Barnes and the women were nevertheless convicted did the *Planet*'s coverage burst from this flat and cynical frame. The accounts of the militiamen returning from the trial gave even more support for the women. With this growing likelihood of their innocence, the Lunenburg case became a cause célèbre for the paper and the black community.[53]

For a year and a half, this case simmered on the pages of the *Planet*, with John Mitchell leading the charge to fund prominent white lawyers in an effort to save the women. Richmond's black paper described and illustrated every aspect of the Lunenburg case: the crime, the women and their pasts and families, their jail cells, the lawyers, courts, and public opinion. Between June 1895 and January 1897, the *Richmond Planet* published more than 120 articles or editorials on the case.[54] It became a staple of the front page, completely filling it almost a dozen times. But it was not just the *Planet* immersing itself in the Lunenburg case: in a precursor to NAACP-style action of the 1920s and 1930s, hundreds of individuals and groups contributed thousands of dollars to support hiring the white lawyers.[55]

Throughout this sensation, the *Richmond Planet* emphasized the obvious innocence of the women. They were of good character and family, the paper argued (with mixed evidence to draw upon). They had no convincing motive and nothing to tie them to the crime but a false accusation later recanted. Mitchell did not investigate the women or mention anything that might sully their reputations but rather invested them with the typecast roles of embattled heroines. Just as white papers turned murder victims into virtuous female stereotypes, so did Mitchell turn the Lunenburg women into paragons. Photographs of Mary Abernathy show her with her baby, born in jail, while other articles set the convicted women within the context of their families bemoaning their absence. "No one who has gazed upon the open countenance of poor Mary Abernathy and [the] mirth-loving face of Pokey Barnes," wrote Mitchell, "will doubt the innocence of these two people."[56] In turn, Mitchell castigated the whites of Lunenburg, officials and citizenry, for their prejudice and malevolence. Their conviction was "one of the most flagrant outrages perpetrated upon human beings," he avowed. "Most of the people in Lunenburg County were grievously in error when in their blind fury they condemned" the prisoners to death. The whites were overcome by the "evil propensities" of prejudice and race hatred.[57] There was little distance or objectivity in these stories; in keeping with bold late-nineteenth-century journalistic standards, these *Planet* articles were passionate, emotional, active, and sometimes shrill.

Convicted a number of times, Mary and Pokey were saved from the gallows by the pressure of the black community and the actions of a number of white officials. John Mitchell, of course, was central to this effort, a driving force in the crusade to save the innocent women.[58] But even Mitchell admitted that others had aided the prisoners. The sheriff, the governor, the militia, the wider populace funding lawyers, and the higher courts all contributed to the protection of these women. Without each of these actors, according to the *Planet*, a single spurious charge by Marable might have led to the execution of these innocent women. That is how close they came—and how close all African Americans were to injustice in the courts of Virginia. The Lunenburg case was "an object lesson never to be forgotten," wrote Mitchell after Mary Abernathy was freed. He envisioned it as an example of "the relentlessness of prejudice" and "everlasting aggression of our people" as well as "the most phenomenal effort ever made for the saving of human lives."[59]

But what a sour object lesson it was. If accused of a violent crime, blacks in Virginia might be lynched. If they avoided lynching, they might face a court without the means to protect themselves. Even if they were somehow able to hire lawyers, they might still be convicted by white-dominated juries and hanged despite insubstantial evidence.

Sadly, the Lunenburg case was not the only sensation of black innocence in this era; this dynamic recurred on a number of occasions. In July of 1893, for instance, a black man from Nansemond County, near Norfolk, was accused of burning a white neighbor's house and poisoning his horses. A white mob abducted, shot, and hanged Isaac Jenkins, leaving him for dead.

None of his several wounds, however, was life threatening, and the noose was improperly tied, slipping off as he struggled.[60] In covering this case, Mitchell leads the reader to marvel at Jenkins's luck to have survived the ordeal. But as important as his survival was the active nature of the whole incident: his efforts to save himself but also the vigorous efforts on the part of Mitchell and the wider African American community to aid him. Even in this successful case, his lynchers were never prosecuted, and Jenkins endured three jury trials, almost a year in jail, and permanent effects from the many wounds he received.[61]

This activism on the part of Mitchell culminated in a call for African Americans to defend themselves with violent force when necessary. If the ballot, the courts, and the Constitution could not guarantee the protection of home and family, then bullets would prove necessary.[62] John Mitchell and the black community in Richmond concluded that Virginia's judicial and law enforcement systems were enemies as often as defenders of their safety and well-being. After listing two dismissed cases of white-on-black murder in one of many editorials titled "No Justice for the Negro," Mitchell declared, "It is far better to hang for the killing of one of these worthless creatures than to be ourselves ushered to our Maker unprepared. We are sick at heart over the butchery of our people. Self-defense should be our watchword, and when this is heralded from one section of the country to the other, these murders will cease, and not until then."[63] If a lynch mob approached, Mitchell thought, the best remedy "is a 16-shot Winchester rifle in the hands of a Negro who has nerve enough to pull the trigger."[64] It was this sort of talk that earned Mitchell the title of Richmond's "fiery" editor: "We are in favor of [a hardworking black man] firing upon all intruders and law-breakers who would despoil his home, and we earnestly beseech our leading men to preach the dawn of the new day, and bring about a realization of our fondest hopes. . . . Colored men, buy shot-guns, purchase rifles. Use them with discretion, fire them with wisdom; but let every charge find a resting place in the bosom of some would-be murderer who regards neither God nor Mammon, and are anxious to shed human blood and to sacrifice innocent victims. Lynch law must go!"[65]

John Mitchell even acted out this assertive philosophy when a black man was lynched in Charlotte County in 1886. Mitchell argued that the lynchers deserved to die. After receiving an unsigned letter the next week stating that "if you poke that infernal head of yours in this county long enough for us to do it we will hang you higher than he was hung," Mitchell published the letter and his defiant response. Armed with two Smith and Wesson revolvers, he then traveled to the county. Detained briefly in jail but otherwise unharmed, this "fighting editor" from Richmond lived to tell of this moment of bravado.[66]

Mitchell never called for an uprising, noting that all the force of white America, state and federal, would crush any such effort.[67] Rather he wrote that blacks must protect themselves when threatened, concluding that reasonable whites would concur with this sound American philosophy. It was an argument not for lawlessness, but rather for upbraiding whites for *their* lawlessness and urging them to live up to the standard of justice that the law had enshrined. Radical only in the context of the era's racism, this philosophy was the natural conclusion of his broad-based indictment of southern justice.

A small number of articles in the 1890s described just such moments of active resistance when bullets were used. These columns portrayed their black protagonists as neither brutes nor passive victims to be added to the litany of martyrs of vicious white violence. Instead, the accused blacks were strong and in control. "A Colored Man's Nerve, Died but Carries Two White Men with Him," read one headline.[68] Apparently in the midst of an argument over pay, this black man talked back to the white man, who responded by clubbing him on the head for his insolence. What made this story unusual was the fact that this beaten black man had a gun, and he used it with effect. A second white man—who did not even see or know about the original conflict, according to the witness—then rushed into the fray. Both men fired; both died. In this case, the framing of this letter to the *Planet* emphasized not the horror of violence, but rather the nerve of the black man to stand up against not one but two whites who threatened him: "He defends himself against threats to take his life because he demanded his whole pay."[69]

What of cases where active black protagonists were clearly violating the law? In this the *Planet* is much more difficult to parse, in part because it rarely reported stories of black crime at all. Occasionally, it introduced a black criminal in an ambivalent way that did not overtly praise him but that might lead the reader to do so. For instance, a brief story taken from an Alabama paper received the headline "His Deadly Aim—A Colored Man's Unerring Rifle Killed the Sheriff—Not Yet Captured."[70] Like the headline, the entire article was full of ambiguity: he was a criminal, but the harshest language used against "Railroad Bill" was that he was "notorious," a man whose "record for the year is a bad one." Even these words could be interpreted as implying a nod and a wink. The central point of the article was how powerful and dangerous a man he was, not his crimes: "Several

128

hundred men are scouring the swamp to-day. The outlaw will probably never be taken alive." This article appeared in the first week of Railroad Bill's fame: he foiled the authorities and robbed freight trains until he was shot down a year later. But his legend continued to grow until he became a part of the black folk pantheon of "bad men," each interpreted in much the same way as in this early *Planet* article: censure for their bad deeds mixed with a healthy dose of admiration.[71]

Even a reported massacre by Native Americans received this ambiguous treatment. Significantly, the Seminoles were responding to the lynching of two Indians by local whites. Titled "The Indian's Revenge," the article described how twenty-five whites were reported killed in this "avenging" raid. The *Planet* did censure this action, but the bulk of the article simply described the events and the horrible lynching that prompted this violent response. Given that this was a mass murder, the story had little of the moral indignation that the *Planet* managed for other crimes.[72] This revenge upon lynchers, as with the black desperado above, shows how the *Planet*—and surely the wider African American community—found appealing these accounts of countervailing tendencies in the late nineteenth century. They longed for instances when the victim won and when the real culprit in their lives—a system of justice that was not just—received some semblance of retribution or at least was denied its prey.

In 1895, Mitchell summed up his philosophy of race and justice: "We maintain that every official in this state is in honor bound to recognize the civil and political equality of all men before the law. In dealing with a white man and a colored one they must treat the two just as they would two white men or two colored ones when the aforesaid gentlemen come to them with conflicting interests. . . . We aver that severity in dealing with a Negro and leaning [leniency?] in dealing with a white man is in direct antagonism with the oath of office and in violation of the guarantees of the Bill of Rights of Virginia."[73]

It is this strong language that has earned John Mitchell a place in history. At the time and since, observers have held him up as a model of brave, unyielding defiance of white domination. "His forte is to battle against the outrages perpetrated upon his people in the South," according to I. Garland Penn in his 1891 volume, *Afro-American Editors*. This sentiment was confirmed by the *New York World*, which called Mitchell "one of the most daring and vigorous Negro editors," particularly notable to the writer since Mitchell lived in the South. With even more heightened prose, Mitchell was described in William Simmons's 1887 collection of biographies, *Men of Mark*, as "a man who would walk into the jaws of death to serve his race ... the gamest negro editor on the continent—a man of grit and iron nerve."[74]

If in the 1890s John Mitchell couched his fight for black rights and for justice in clear, bold terms, the world around Mitchell was changing. In the same year that Richmond's African American community reveled in the successful freeing of Mary Abernathy and Pokey Barnes from the grip of white injustice, the U.S. Supreme Court upheld the constitutionality of separate-but-equal accommodations for blacks and whites in Louisiana railcars.[75] Not wishing to legislate social mores, the Court opened the door for states throughout the South to tighten their grip on their black populations. The turn of the century would witness a precipitous step for the worse for African Americans in the South, a development that had a telling impact on African American communities, their press, and its frame for crime, violence, and justice.

■

"SHALL THE WHEELS OF RACE AGITATION BE STOPPED?"

In May of 1914, a young white woman in Henrico County, Fannie Chenault, accused John Clements, a local black man, of accosting her on the way home from work. She said that he pulled her off the road and into the woods, hit, strangled, and raped her, keeping her there for three hours before he left and she made her way home.

At first glance, this crime seems yet another of the dozens of stories each year that ended in a mob, a rope, and a black man's death. But several elements of her story raised questions among listeners both white and black. Clements had an alibi, albeit not an unimpeachable one. But more than this, Chenault's own behavior made many doubt the story. Defying expectations, she went to church the morning after the assault. Moreover, it appeared inconceivable to many that a white woman could be assaulted by a black man, held for three hours not far from a populated area, engage in conversation some of that time, and never cry out for help or attempt to flee. Most importantly, Chenault previously identified another black man—one who bore no resemblance to Clements—as the attacker.[76]

Instead of affirming the black race's inherent criminality, this case brought the reputation of a young white woman into serious doubt. One of the magistrates who first heard the case believed the evidence against Clements to be so thin that the case should be dismissed.[77] It was not.

130 At trial, Clements's defense lawyers declined to present witnesses or put

Clements on the stand, believing that the prosecution had failed to make its case.[78] Even so, would a court be able to overcome its racial biases to render the verdict that justice demanded? As in Lunenburg County, this was again the central question in the case. Reports in the *Richmond Times-Dispatch* ranged from describing the case against Clements as "unusually strong" to voicing its support for his acquittal. Again, like the cases in the 1890s, the decision was a close call: the jury twice announced it was deadlocked, despite the widespread belief in both white and black communities that there was little evidence to support a conviction. Finally, after eighteen hours of deliberation, the jury delivered a verdict of not guilty, and Clements was freed.[79]

Despite these similarities to earlier sensations of black innocence, the *Planet* characterized the 1914 Chenault-Clements case in a notably mild-mannered tone.[80] In 1914, with a black man facing a capital charge on seemingly spurious grounds, the *Planet* had nothing of the rancor it expressed a generation earlier. The paper criticized a few facets of the case—most notably how one black suspect was shot by a police officer when resisting arrest. This man soon died, and Miss Chenault confirmed that he was not the guilty party. Yet this killing of an innocent black man was but a side issue even in the *Planet*, touched upon in several editorials but never becoming the chief concern. Mitchell asked why the police were arming men who could do this, and he wondered whether this shooting should be considered murder and prosecuted as such. Yet he also called it merely a "blunder" and said that he was not asking for punishment of the officer, that public contempt would be punishment enough. This is a mild rebuke for shooting down an innocent man, and editor Mitchell was critical of nothing else in the case.[81]

Instead, the *Planet* demonstrated a thorough revolution in the tone and texture of its coverage of this case of black innocence. Mitchell penned muted editorials, as when he summed up the case early on: "This is one time where we can trust the better class of white people hereabouts and we indulge in the thought that a jury and a judge will be all that is necessary to give to John Clements the freedom for which he craves."[82] In perhaps the most telling change of all, the *Planet* did not even report the 1914 John Clements case itself. Mitchell published a handful of editorials on various sides of the case—censuring the police for shooting the black suspect, for instance, and praising the courts and jury for absolving Clements. But the *Planet's* actual reports of the crime and trial were mere reprints from the white daily papers.[83] Far from providing black Richmond with an alternative voice about crime and injustice, Mitchell did not even send a reporter to cover the trial. In fact, he reprinted so much from the *News Leader* that the competing *Evening Journal* attempted to use this fact in its competitive war for white readership. Mitchell felt compelled to pen an editorial showing how an image of Fannie Chenault in the *Planet* had come from the pages of the *Journal*; this sort of warfare, he continued, only distracted from the central point that a man's life was in jeopardy in this case.[84]

After Clements won his case, Mitchell praised those who helped secure his defense, just as he did in the Jenkins and Lunenburg cases. But this time his praise went almost exclusively to whites: to the Henrico jury, to an anonymous Henrico white man who reportedly bankrolled the defense lawyers, and to the Rev. Charles Hannigan, who helped the prisoner in various ways during his incarceration. This was not a story of black activism wresting justice from prejudiced Virginia courts; it was a story of "kind hearted whites" ensuring that justice was done in their neighborhood. Mitchell thought that this decision should give "the average colored man of respectability hope." But he phrased that hope in a peculiarly distant and downtrodden manner: "Some day conditions will improve and some day all of us shall receive our reward. In His own time, our God will pity us and as a race, with His own lily-white hand, wipe all of the tears from our eyes."[85] Far from making an energetic demand for justice and rights of citizenship for his people, Mitchell in 1914 saw those goals as a hazy vision in the distance. They remained his destination but no longer seemed within reach. To receive justice, blacks could not force the issue; it would take the help of a lily-white hand.

What happened to the John Mitchell who had strapped guns to his belt, swaggering through rural Virginia, challenging lynchers, and demonstrating his commitment to self-defense? By the 1910s, the *Richmond Planet* was a mass-market paper, full of images, advertisements, and reprinted reporting as well as fiction. In place of screaming headlines and forceful editorials, the *Planet* framed injustice within a more muted context. The editor of the *Cleveland Gazette* pointed in the right direction when he wrote that Mitchell "seems to have grown very pessimistic in recent years." Said another editor: this "is not the John Mitchell of ten years ago."[86]

The nature of sensational coverage of violence had changed at least as dramatically in the *Richmond Planet* and other black papers of the South as it had in the white press. All the factors pursued in the previous chapters—professionalization, realism, and new journalistic standards—also influenced this new tone in the *Richmond Planet*. The paper bought new, faster presses, doubled in size, and was tied into the host of changes that made for a modern newspaper business, including syndicated columns and stories that could fill several pages of print. Added to this evolving professional context was an even more proximate cause for a shift in the *Planet*'s coverage of violence: whites dominated Virginia and the South in a new way in the twentieth century.

By 1900, conservative Democratic forces throughout the South were calling for constitutional conventions to introduce formal voting restrictions for African Americans at the same time that new laws were passed segregating the races in transportation, residences, and social spaces.[87] The threat of lynching persisted, and the equally dangerous spectacle of race riots erupted in a number of southern cities and towns. Since the Civil War, African Americans had never enjoyed the full panoply of rights guaranteed to whites, but at the turn of the century, they faced a deteriorating rather than an improving situation. Wrote John Mitchell in 1908, "There is no use denying the fact that the revulsion of feeling against us is manifesting itself all over the country."[88]

In the face of a worsening situation, John Mitchell turned from boldly forcing the issue of the rights of the entire race and from decrying the injustices of Virginia law to representing the concerns of good, upstanding African Americans and furthering connections with the respectable classes of whites. The "fiery" editor of the 1890s became a black businessman in the 1900s. In the 1890s, Mitchell sounded like the antithesis of Booker T. Washington and his brand of racial harmony and accommodation. But the editor of the *Planet* founded a bank in Richmond in 1902, and by 1910, he often sounded like a Tuskegee man himself: "Colored men should be respectful in their demands. We can secure the support of the conservative contingent of the white folks by a discreet management of our cause, and will lose if we go beyond the bounds of reason."[89] Mitchell's solution to the "revulsion of feeling" against blacks was mild mannered: "Each man, woman, and child can most surely counteract its effect by being on their good behaviors."[90] Talk of bullets, of defense, of equality, or even of justice seemed more hopeless and self-defeating than at any time since the Civil War.

Mitchell's change of tack makes sense only in the context of the strong winds blowing against African Americans at this moment: the repeated failures of black pressure to stem the tide of white racism. Some Virginia blacks—Mitchell believed this effort futile—sought to challenge disfranchisement in Virginia legally, but the federal courts dismissed their lawsuits.[91] Mitchell himself had been very active in Richmond and Republican party politics in the 1880s and 1890s, but political activism also bore little fruit. The city council largely ignored its black representatives and then defeated them through outright fraud; by the late 1890s, even the Virginia Republican party began drawing the "color line." By the time disfranchisement statutes took effect in 1902, John Mitchell already perceived that politics in Virginia would offer no help to African Americans. With typical sarcasm a few years earlier, he wrote that he would like to see "any method of [political] robbery that can beat that which is in vogue at present."[92]

As if to emphasize the futility of political activism, the federal government, which had already absolved itself from any post-Reconstruction obligation to protect blacks, gave a firm sign in 1906 that it could be as prejudicial as any other white, official institution. In that year, black soldiers were blamed for inciting racial violence in Brownsville, Texas. African Americans watched, horrified, as the Republican administration of President Theodore Roosevelt decided to discharge three companies of black troops without a trial, an act that blacks considered as unjust and racist as any perfunctory condemnation by a white southern jury. John Mitchell fumed: "President Roosevelt has left the bench as a judge to accept service as a prosecutor. He has stabbed Justice and slaughtered Mercy. . . . In his furious state, the distinguished occupant of the White House seems to lose sight of the fact that it is this very species of indignation [against the supposed crimes of the black troops] which when aroused in the breast of the average Southerner converts him into the devote[e] of the lynching habit. He forgets that a charge by order, a trial by order, a conviction by order and a punishment by order is no less a form of lynching than is the usual practice of that method of punishment."[93]

When both politics and the courts failed to protect black rights, John Mitchell and other leaders in the community tried another peaceful but assertive tactic later deployed by the post–World War II civil rights movement: a boycott of Richmond's newly segregated streetcars. In 1904, the state legislature passed a statute that did not mandate but "authorized and empowered" railroads and other transit companies to segregate their cars and coaches.[94] In April, Richmond's Virginia Passenger and Power Company became the first to take advantage of the new law. In response, many prominent black citizens—editor John Mitchell among them—called for a boycott of the streetcars. Throughout the summer and into the fall, the *Richmond Planet* reported how black Richmond was wearing out its shoe leather rather than support the law by riding the cars. But the company never rescinded its decision, and in 1906 the legislature changed the wording of the statute: all transportation companies were now "required and directed" to provide segregated cars on all of the commonwealth's conveyances.[95]

The black community failed in its attempt to end streetcar segregation, an effort representative of the broader failure of protest in the South in this era. In the face of black opposition, Jim Crow laws like the streetcar ordinance in Richmond were far from wounded; rather, they were strengthened. At the same time, disfranchisement reduced what little influence blacks wielded in politics both directly (through the vote) and indirectly (as the Republican party increasingly ignored them). Lynching continued to be pervasive throughout the South, and added to this threat was the equally fearful specter of race riots that regularly broke out at the turn of the century: in Wilmington, North Carolina, in 1898, for instance, or the even more infamous riot in 1906 Atlanta.[96] In the 1890s and into the 1900s, Mitchell and middle-class blacks attempted to fight the system of segregation, disfranchisement, and judicial racism. Even when the black community was able to mobilize against its deteriorating situation, their efforts met with defeat.

In the face of this pervasive and deepening prejudice—violent and political, local and national—Mitchell's strategy for racial progress changed course. Much of his attention in the early twentieth century turned toward developing the black business community and the slowly growing ranks of its middle class. Racial uplift, which comprised a collection of efforts—self-help, thrift, respectability, temperance, and the accumulation of wealth—outpaced militancy among middle-class blacks in the South like editor Mitchell.[97]

In 1904, Mitchell gave what might be considered an announcement of this shift when he rose from the audience to give an impromptu speech before the American Bankers Association national meeting in New York. Responding courteously and obliquely to the racist remarks of a white Georgia delegate the previous day, he traced the economic advancement of southern blacks, and he averred that there was no racial clash between the "best elements" of each race. Receiving "applause that followed almost every period," he continued lightheartedly by saying that blacks in the South "had tried religion first, but we had found we weren't ready for heaven. Then we had tried politics, but after thirty years you drew us out of that. Now we have tried finance and business. Here we expect no discrimination. A man is judged by his worth. . . . we have found that the way for us to reach success and respect is through finance."[98] In the *Planet* that year, Mitchell sounded a similar note: "this is the beginning of an age of conservatism, which means the sacrificing of principle temporarily."[99]

Finance and business became the central interests of John Mitchell in the early twentieth century, and he was not alone. If a majority of Richmond's African Americans remained laborers and domestic servants, a growing number nevertheless rose to become clerks, skilled workers, and owners of substantial businesses. By 1900, the black community in Richmond numbered over 32,000, amounting to 38 percent of the city's population. This sizable community supported Mitchell's *Planet*, a number of large and prosperous churches, dozens of stores, four banks, ten attorneys, eleven doctors, two photographers, and more than one hundred other small businesses. Segregation had tremendous and obvious costs for the black community, but it also fostered a market and opportunities for a growing black middle class. As a bank president, the only black member of the American Bankers Association, a former city councilman, an official in two fraternal organizations, a middle-aged homeowner, and a publisher of Richmond's black newspaper, John Mitchell belonged to this class, and he oriented the *Planet* particularly toward its concerns.[100]

John Mitchell did more than turn to racial uplift; he also changed the pitch of his coverage of violence and injustice in the *Richmond Planet* from a militant, impassioned, and sensationalistic intensity to a more distanced, impersonal, even sociological tone. Editorials and stories against injustice never left the *Planet*, however, and occasional articles were invested with the flaming rhetoric common to the 1890s, particularly regarding lynching. A bold front-page story in 1904 titled "Mrs. Larremore's Heroic Defense" described a Texas lynch mob that killed a man but whose wife came to his defense armed with a rifle; another described the "Horrible Massacre" of a 1910 race riot.[101] A front-page cartoon illustrated the hypocrisy of banning Jack Johnson boxing movies while allowing violent lynchings to continue.[102] Editorials against lynching also continued, if less frequently. They could be quite assertive: Mitchell again praised a black man in Georgia for defending himself well against lynchers.[103] Other crime stories likewise still received coverage: the murder of a black woman by a white man, a police officer's shooting of a black man for denouncing the brutal arrest of another, or the beating of an elderly black man by a white watchman.[104] Mitchell could still be outspoken about such issues, demonstrated by his rage over the treatment of black troops in the 1906 Brownsville incident mentioned above.

The *Planet* continued to discuss crime and violence; however, it did so through lone stories that were rarely followed up and were crowded out by other print matter. After the turn of the century, the *Planet*, more often than centering on justice, filled its columns with less controversial matters: cultural events, advertising, fiction, and news of local black schools and businesses. A sampling from 1897 reveals an average of slightly more than one editorial, three brief reports, and one long story on crime and justice for each four-page issue of the *Planet*. These averages drop sharply in a similar sample for 1913: the number of short articles on crime and justice remained the same (three per issue), but editorials and longer stories fell by more than 65 percent. Even more dramatic was the change in the content of the front page: fourteen long articles on crime filled the front pages in the sample from 1897, but only one did so in 1913. Gone too was the weekly graphic of hanging men with its accompanying list of every lynching for that year. Moreover, this drop in gross numbers of stories was in spite of the doubling of the size of the *Planet* to eight pages. Clearly the paper had shifted its priorities, for stories of injustice fell in proportion to total print space by more than 70 percent.[105] Editor Mitchell was no longer a crusader.

Nor was the *Planet* alone in this shift from crusades to moderation; there is a parallel change in the tone of the black press regionally. Between 1897 and 1913, one of the most prominent black newspapers in the North, the *Cleveland Gazette*, decreased its coverage of crime and violence by one third.[106] But in general, northern papers demonstrate a mixture of trends. A sampling of the *New York Age* in 1913 show that paper printed many articles and editorial on crime and violence, for instance.[107] In 1905, the *Chicago Defender* began publishing, and by the 1910s, it was the most assertive and influential black American newspaper agitating against lynching and segregation. In 1910, under the editorship of W. E. B. Du Bois, the NAACP began publishing the *Crisis* out of New York. It is by focusing on these northern papers and magazines that some scholars can speak of a trend away from accommodation and toward more radical precursors of the civil rights movement in the early twentieth century.[108]

Not so for the black papers of the South. Along with Mitchell's *Planet*, one of the region's most vocal and aggressive black newspapers was the *Voice of the Negro*, published by Max Barber in Atlanta from 1904 to 1906. After the 1906 Atlanta riot, Barber's life was in danger, and he was forced to flee to the North; his *Voice* was quieted soon thereafter. Likewise, W. E. B. Du Bois soon moved permanently out of the South, while other confrontational editors, such as Jesse Duke in Alabama, Alex Manly in North Carolina, and Ida B. Wells in Tennessee, fled under threat of mob violence.[109] Assertive black voices were simply endangered in the South.

Black editors who remained in the region tended to adopt a less confrontational editorial stance. Like the *Richmond Planet*, the *Savannah Tribune* demonstrated a dramatic shift away from coverage of violence. Between 1897 and 1913, the *Tribune* decreased its coverage of crime and violence by around 70 percent.[110] Both the *Richmond Planet* and the *Savannah Tribune* doubled in size in the early twentieth century, more often including reprints from other papers, syndicated columns, fiction, and articles less connected to the direct experience of blacks in their communities.[111] Both also show a massive erosion of coverage of crime and violence in the early twentieth century even in the face of their growing volume of print space.

It is important to add that the coverage of violence that continued in southern black papers was written more as if in passing and was less loaded in tone. When the *Planet* published an assertive editorial in the twentieth century, it printed one rather than a series of them. The precipitous decline in the two most elaborate and opinionated categories of print—editorials and long articles—is in keeping with larger trends. In the antebellum period and continuing into the late nineteenth century, black papers were rich in what historians of journalism call "expression" categories of print—editorials, letters, interpretation, and opinion. These papers were often on crusades; they were tied to and involved in their communities, rarely very successful commercially but ideologically influential. By the early twentieth century, print space reserved for expression categories had declined significantly, while two categories rose to ever greater prominence: news and advertising. Missionary zeal and the ties to the community declined as the papers became more financially stable, prominent, and commercially oriented.[112]

This muting trend plays out in particular examples from the *Planet*. In 1907, a white jury fined a white man $25 for selling liquor to a minor, then fined a black man $100 for the same offense. Noting the discrepancy, the judge reversed this second judgment and called for a new trial. The *Planet* still covered such a case, but instead of a sarcastic headline, such as "First Case on Record Here," the story was titled simply "A Just Judge." Instead of loaded and passionate editorial comment, this story was told dispassionately, the most colorful phrase used being "a remarkable scene."[113] In another example, one 1914 editorial in the *Planet* advocated shooting lynchers, a sentiment less often voiced in these years than in the 1890s. Importantly, this piece was centered on a *Times-Dispatch* editorial voicing admiration for a *white* woman who shot at and scared off a group of "white-cappers," as KKK-style vigilantes were sometimes called. It was, therefore, in congruence with rather than in the face of white opinion, and Mitchell ended the editorial emphasizing this point: "When the good white people and the good colored people decide upon a definite line of action, many of the present abuses will disappear like frost before the sun." Even when addressing injustice in the early twentieth century, the *Planet* was less confrontational.[114]

This softer coverage in the *Planet* was at least as evident in those moments when the white community became fixated on a crime sensation. When Samuel McCue murdered his wife in Charlottesville in 1905, Mitchell printed nothing on the case until McCue's execution, when he ran a spare two inches of type stating that McCue was hanged and printing the brief confession. Here is a famous, bloody white crime, and Mitchell declined to editorialize in any fashion.[115]

When Henry Beattie murdered his wife in 1911, Mitchell printed dozens of pages on the story—from the crime through the courts and to the electric chair. During the trial, this amounted to several pages of material in each issue. In fact, throughout September he continued to print testimony and closing arguments in his weekly editions in order to complete the trial narrative even though the case was decided on 8 September. Clearly he—and presumably his readership—was interested in this case, and at first glance this appears to continue the trend of pointing up white crime in contrast to the stereotypes of black crime—except that this was not his tack. As in the Clements case of 1914, every single story on the Beattie murder was a reprint from the white dailies. John Mitchell simply passed along to black Richmond the narrative that whites created of this crime. Mitchell also declined to editorialize. In the only editorial he printed, written after Beattie's execution, Mitchell starts by saying that the murder "shows that crime is not confined to any one race or to the ignorant and the vicious." But the rest of the nine-paragraph editorial discussed other issues—the relief of having a confession, Beattie's pampered upbringing, the creditable action of everyone in the justice system. In fact, Mitchell spent more ink discussing black weakness than pursuing how this brutal murder showed that whites were as corrupt as blacks. Blacks "prefer to imitate" whites of "high social standing" and therefore "the follies and foibles of the colored folk are intensified by the actions of white people of the Beattie type."[116]

At times, Mitchell actually spoke out against *black* crime as ably as the white *Richmond Times-Dispatch*, albeit making a strict distinction between "irresponsible thugs" and African American gentlemen and ladies. "These Negro criminals are an incubus upon our prosperity and a dangling weight to the neck of all our fondest hopes," he wrote in 1909.[117] He continued in stark contrast to his tone in the 1890s, when Mitchell would have countered the story of a black rapist with a story of a white rapist. Instead: "We should not forget that there is a duty devolving upon each and every colored person in this city, to the end that some steps be taken, not only to purge the city of the Negro criminals, but to bring up this crowd of roving, dissolute boys and girls in the paths of rectitude and reclaim them from the dens of vice and crime in which they are now located."[118]

Six years later, Mitchell was even more forceful in this call: "There is no longer any question as to the necessity for action on the part of the reputable, law-abiding, God-fearing colored people of the Southland in particular, and the United States in general with a view to restraining and putting out of business the lawless elements amongst us, who are persistently bringing the race into ill repute."[119] Quite clearly, the *Planet* would now choose its fights much more carefully: "All the white folks have to do is to punish the lawless Negroes. They have all of the offices and all of the governmental machinery for so doing. When they come grabbing up the law-abiding ones though and begin meting punishment, there's where our voices will be heard in protest."[120]

"Reputable, law-abiding, God-fearing colored people" were the backbone of the *Planet's* circulation and its targeted audience. Mitchell was now a voice for a certain class of blacks, and he joined with whites in chastising offenders of both races—a clear, conservative stance for a paper serving any race. The *Planet* was in favor of and supported the "good class of whites" in the city: the judges, the wealthy, and the educated. Mitchell believed that well-bred white Virginians could be counted on to be fair. The most profound threat in the eyes of editor Mitchell was a mob—the lower-class whites whose unreasoning hatred threatened all blacks regardless of their standing, prosperity, reputation, or law-abiding character. In 1898, a mob killed many blacks and burned the local black newspaper in Wilmington, North Carolina. In 1906, racial tensions exploded in Atlanta, resulting in many deaths and the destruction of a host of black businesses. More locally, a small town on the eastern shore of Virginia, Onancock, experienced its own race riot in 1907, complete with the utter destruction and abandonment of the property of black businessmen there. Despite the fact that many middle-class and upper-class whites led or participated in these mobs, Mitchell perceived the greatest danger arising from the lower class.[121]

In this context, editor Mitchell's condemnation of the lawless elements of his own race—along with that element among whites—takes on a greater relevance. In essence, he and a host of other middle-class blacks during this "nadir" of African American history were circling the wagons around their hard-fought gains.[122] From their perspective, the black middle class was the hope and the way to the future for the race, and they could not risk losing everything to the violent mobs of white rabble. In 1909, the

Richmond police searched for the black rapist of a white woman. "Such happenings as these furnish the lawless, hoodlum white elements with the excuse for summary action," Mitchell wrote. He added his relief and gratitude that the white papers and law enforcement officials had declined to tar the entire race in regard to this 1909 case, an action that reflected well on their "good grace and kindness of heart." Even more telling, perhaps, was this passage: "The prompt manner in which the officers of the law have acted and the discountenancing of all talk of summary vengeance will commend itself to good citizens everywhere and cause persons of both races who own real estate and who have capital invested in this community to feel secure."[123] The early twentieth century—after disfranchisement, after riots throughout the South—presented a different reality for blacks, and the *Richmond Planet* along with most other black papers in the South recognized this difference.

So when John Clements was accused of rape in 1914, Mitchell used the occasion to render his more general philosophy of crime and race. And what a different philosophy it was from his editorials of the 1890s: "Colored folks hereabouts have absolutely no sympathy for any man, be he black or white, who assaults a woman, and less, if such a thing be possible for a colored man, who assaults a white woman. When a colored man is guilty of criminally assaulting a white woman, colored men are as forward as white ones in aiding in putting him in the electric chair."[124]

Booker T. Washington could not have said it better himself. In an 1899 "Letter to the Southern People," Washington wrote "that no one guilty of rape can find sympathy or shelter with us, and that none will be more active in bringing to justice, through the proper authorities, those guilty of crime. Let the criminal and vicious elements of the race have at all times our most severe condemnation. Let a strict line be drawn between the virtuous and the criminal."[125] Far from issuing a message of protest against Virginia injustice, the *Richmond Planet* framed the story of John Clements's trial as validation of a Washingtonesque interracial understanding about the necessity of convicting sexual criminals.

■

Quite naturally, Richmond blacks presumed and expected injustice in Virginia courts, a conclusion that colored all crime stories, sensational or mundane. In a sense, the persistent racism in the administration of justice polluted the cultural waters, making innocence rather than guilt the sensational story. Not only did professionalization, new technologies, and new journalistic styles lure the black press away from their nineteenth-century style of crusades, but disfranchisement, Jim Crow, and racial violence also persuaded them that militancy yielded few results. Unlike the white culture's sensationalized stories of crime, African American sensations were intimately bound up in this reality of violence, discrimination, and loss of political rights.

Evaluating sensations in the South's black communities demonstrates that sensationalism itself—what cases were deemed worthy of sensational treatment as well as the content invested in those cases—was much more complex than if this study considered only white crime sensations. This is the most profound way that a study of the South shifts our understanding of culture, crime, and sensationalism. The impact of race and racial politics was felt in every side of life, not just in social but in cultural realms, not just legally but in every way. The sensationalism in the African American community does not merely elaborate on or parallel the model of white sensationalism. It is in many ways its opposite: in place of probably guilty prominent whites getting convicted, blacks were most interested in probably innocent blacks striving for acquittal.

The shift in African American sensations at the turn of the twentieth century is much more complex than a simple retreat from militant race pride to accommodation or even defeatism. It is important to stress that this shift was piecemeal and incomplete—the *Richmond Planet* continued to speak out against injustice and particularly against lynching throughout the early twentieth century. If this coverage was more muted in tone and more rare in its appearance, it was nevertheless still an element of the *Planet*'s reporting. In addition, some "conservative" dimensions of its coverage were evident in the 1890s on occasion: praising white judges and the governor (as in the Lunenburg case), for instance, or speaking in terms of the "respectable" class of blacks. If such sentiments became more common and central to the *Planet* after the turn of the century, their presence before that time nonetheless warns against any simplistic argument for a wholesale declension.[126]

Mitchell's change in tone is best perceived as a thorough shift in tactics and emphases. Most American blacks were surely neither strict accommodationists nor aggressive militants. Like the protagonist in Ralph Ellison's *Invisible Man*, African Americans inherited a mixed and conflicted perspective concerning their place in the modern South. In that novel, the main character's grandfather seemed the quintessential accommodationist ("the meekest of men"), but his disturbing deathbed instructions leave the matter infinitely more complex: "our life is a war. . . . Live with your head in the lion's mouth. I want you to overcome 'em with yeses, undermine 'em with grins, agree 'em to death and destruction, let 'em swoller you till they vomit or bust wide open. . . . Learn it to the younguns."[127] Without coming to the conclusion that blacks could successfully "agree" white supremacy "to death and destruction," Marcus Garvey (whom Mitchell admired in the 1920s), Malcolm X, and many other future black activists would demonstrate the radical potential inherent in economic advancement. They would, in fact, agree that many aspects of the racial uplift philosophy—its stress on self-help, thrift, respectability, and generally building the black community and black businesses—were necessary prerequisites for a successful future for the race. This was a shift in tactics, then, but one that retained a potential for racial progress.

For his part, editor John Mitchell always had a concern for issues of injustice *and* issues of respectability for African Americans of his class. In the 1890s, Mitchell had the sense that justice was within reach, that the nation *could* treat its black citizens with fairness and give them their due. That belief was broken at the turn of the century. "We submit," wrote a dispirited Mitchell in 1901, "because we are powerless to do otherwise."[128] By the 1910s, a concern for justice and rights was not erased, but it was now in the background, with the foreground occupied by a more conservative vision of how to raise the race—through economic development. "When we are strong enough financially," wrote Mitchell, "we will go back and win all we lost politically."[129]

That vision included creating a modern, commercially oriented newspaper, one as professional, objective, informative, and technologically sophisticated as the white newspapers of the era. In this, Mitchell largely succeeded. Indeed, the *Planet* was unusually long-lived among black newspapers, publishing under his leadership from 1884 past his death in 1929. In 1938, the *Planet* merged with the larger *Baltimore Afro-American*, which distributed a Richmond edition until dwindling subscriptions forced it to fold in 1996.

The turn in Mitchell's treatment of sensationalism, and in southern black activism overall, evolved over the course of a decade of disappointments and defeats. But the year 1902 best marks the moment when editor Mitchell's priorities began to shift. In that year, Mitchell wrote a manifesto, published in the national *Colored American Magazine*, charging black America to arms, literally and figuratively, in defense of their rights.[130] Yet Mitchell hauntingly titled the piece "Shall the Wheels of Race Agitation Be Stopped?" hinting at the turmoil roiling through southern black communities as well as the white opposition they faced. Mitchell casts himself as the hero—a crusader against lynching, saving the Lunenburg women and other victims of injustice. He calls for agitation, for manliness, for meeting lynching parties with rifles, and he celebrates heroes who have done just that and have paid with their lives, naming Robert Charles of New Orleans in particular. Adopting a rhythm in his prose like that of a minister preaching to his flock, Mitchell returns throughout the essay to the refrain: "shall the wheels of race agitation be stopped?" Never, he says.

But 1902 is also the year that Virginia disfranchised its black population as well as the year that Mitchell became a banker. The modern reader is struck as much by the asking—nine times in all—as by Mitchell's forceful answer to this question. By 1902, it had become a question, an issue for southern blacks that required a forceful answer. The very existence of his article emphasizes how strong other responses to this question were becoming. One passage in particular is haunting as it reflects the contradictions of its author: "We must agitate until the country comes to know that the slave and the slavish Negro is a thing of the past." But instead of continuing with an image of bold, powerful, and free African Americans, Mitchell finished the sentence with a rather meek portrait of his hopes: "and that there now stands forth the polite, affable, progressive business citizen of color who is ready to take his place in the economic equation of the New World."

In another generation, a great migration, a great depression, and the experience of fighting a world war against racist foes would again shift the ground under the issue of race in America. But at the turn of the twentieth century, the generation who built the black communities that would nurture those later developments would have to forego immediate gain for a more distant goal. Facing a "revulsion of feeling against us," Mitchell advised a "discreet management of our cause," but he continued to look toward the future when "some day conditions will improve and some day all of us shall receive our reward." In the mean time? Editor Mitchell and his generation invested in their communities and bided their time, awaiting the next turn in their fortunes. They had some time to wait.

John Mitchell Jr. died two months after the stock market crash that signaled the beginning of America's Great Depression.[131] It is fitting to note that 1929 also witnessed the birth of a leader who would become the most famous African American in our history. An Atlanta minister's son born that year would grow to become the resonant voice of a movement to free his people from the confines of racist segregation and disfranchisement— the very bonds that John Mitchell had witnessed the white South erecting a lifetime before.

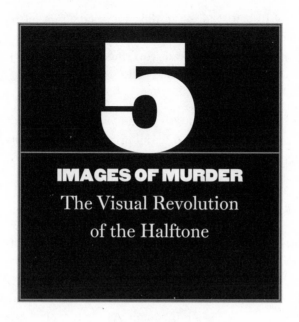

IMAGES OF MURDER
The Visual Revolution
of the Halftone

Not only has [photography] vastly extended the gamut
of our visual knowledge, but through its reproduction in the
printing press, it has effected a very complete revolution in the
ways we use our eyes and, especially, in the kinds of things our
minds permit our eyes to tell us.
It has taken a hundred years of slow progress in
the technology to produce this result, which, except for the
flurry of excitement that accompanied the first announcements
of Talbot and Daguerre, has come into being by such gradual steps
that few people are very much aware of it. We take its results so
much for granted that we never think of the situation
before there was photography.

William M. Ivins Jr., *Prints and Visual Communication* (1953)

The murder of Lillian Madison in 1885 spawned dozens of engravings in the regional press and drew crowds to the courtrooms, jail, and police station. Everyone was interested in discovering what a criminal like Thomas Cluverius looked like. This included police officers:

Q: What business carried you to the Third Police Station?

A: I heard the prisoner had arrived and of course I wanted to see him. I think every officer should see all prisoners charged with so grave an offense.

Q: Did you go there to see him for the purpose of examining him?

A: No, sir, I did not. I had the curiosity the same as everybody else to see a man charged with such an offense.[1]

Richmonders also yearned to hear a confession, to see Cluverius "crack." This close scrutiny, then, was an effort to probe for guilt written on his body, for physical signs that would betray his practiced calm. And every perceived or imagined slip was taken as proof, as in this diary entry written during the Cluverius trial: "When a box containing the cast off clothes of Lillian was brought into court, and there opened, it is said the prisoner evinced some feeling—his colore [sic] came and went like quick blushes upon an innocent cheek. . . . But the newspapers are silent concerning it."[2]

For his part, Thomas Cluverius argued that the public had misinterpreted his own behavior and that this mistaken indifference was a factor in his conviction. In his autobiography, Cluverius voices an acute awareness of the attention given his appearance and his conscious effort to project a certain image: "I knew that hundreds of hostile eyes were watching every movement and every expression. If I had smiled they would have interpreted it as a sign of the most cruel and wicked indifference to the sorrowful details of Lillian Madison's death. On the other hand if I had wept they would have published to the world that I was suffering the pangs of remorse. I knew all this, and so I sought to be calm and unmoved. How far I succeeded is not for me to say; I need only add that the quiet demeanor which I sought to maintain was all in due time used as an argument to establish my guilt. Such was the public sentiment which I had to meet."[3]

New to the nineteenth century was the ability of the public to view a criminal not just in person, but also through illustrations. Public demand fostered dozens of engravings in the regional press picturing Lillian Madison, Cluverius, the reservoir, pieces of evidence, lawyers, the jury, and more. (See figures 1 through 5.) At least one enterprising huckster hawked photographs of Madison and Cluverius on Richmond streets. Other photographs, found in Madison's trunk, became evidence in the trial.

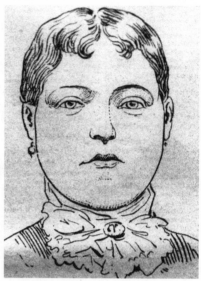

FIGURES 1 AND 2.

*Typical of nineteenth-century illustrations, engravings like
these of accused murderer Thomas Cluverius and his murdered cousin,
Lillian Madison, were expensive to produce and tended, therefore, to be small
and simple. Rarely seen in the Virginia press before 1870, they became more
common with technological innovations in the last quarter of the century.*
Richmond Dispatch, *31 March 1885.*

FIGURE 3.

These portraits of Cluverius and Madison were more refined renderings of the poses in figures 1 and 2. The last half of the nineteenth century saw the elaboration of the skilled work of engravers as well as the development of new technologies to better approach the realism of the photograph. It was now possible to develop a photographic image on a plate, thereby serving as a guide for the engravers. These illustrations were probably produced by this process.

Richmond Dispatch, *12 May 1885.*

FIGURES 4 AND 5.

Photographs of Cluverius and Madison. Photography blossomed in the late nineteenth century, affecting the style of illustrations rendered in the previous figures. Soon the invention of the crossline screen would allow for a direct mechanical reproduction of photographs into a form printable with text on the huge and fast rotary presses used by newspapers and magazines throughout the nation. By the turn of the century, wood and metal engraving was virtually defunct as an occupation, as publishing turned to Frederick Ives's halftone photomechanical process. Commonwealth v. Cluverius, *Richmond Hustings Court Records, June 1885, Library of Virginia Archives, Richmond. Courtesy of the Library of Virginia.*

The prominence of images in this case does not surprise an observer from the early twenty-first century, when Americans are surrounded by photographs and video clips of crime and violence on television newscasts and dramas, films, video and computer games, and magazine and newspaper coverage of local and national crimes. To the modern eye, the most notable feature of the Cluverius images is their simplicity, the primitive style of the engravings. Such an observation seems merely common sense: images gradually gained in sophistication as the society itself advanced.

In fact, there is much more to this development. These images of the 1885 Cluverius murder stand in the midst of a sea change in America's print media in the late nineteenth century. Abundant and widely circulated in this 1885 case, images in sensational crime stories—or any other stories in print for that matter—had been rare in the antebellum period and almost nonexistent before. The images in the Cluverius case were also much more elaborate than antebellum engravings: simple illustrations, typical of mid-century, gave way to more detailed and proportional styles, such as those rendered here. Yet the illustrations in the 1885 Cluverius case were trifles compared to those of a mere generation later. More images appeared in a single week of the 1911 Henry Beattie murder trial coverage than during the entire twenty-two months of the Cluverius sensation. The contrast with earlier murders is even more stark: images from *one day's* reporting of the Beattie trial outnumbered the total of all images arising from any single murder case in all of Virginia's history up to the Civil War. Moreover, in the twentieth century, crime sensations spawned images of transformed quality: halftones—a mechanical means of reproducing photographs for printing presses—had displaced engravings in America's print media.

This cultural change affected the nation as a whole—North and South, white and black—and it affected all regions at roughly the same time. This chapter, therefore, sets the experience of Virginia sensations more within a national context than a regional one. In fact, it would not be exaggeration to call this a visual revolution in American mass culture. Historians of photography and the graphic arts view this as an important, even transforming, moment in American cultural history,[4] but historians in general have been less apt to perceive the implications of this change. Most historical work on crime and on cultural sensations, for instance, include images but chiefly as illustration—to give a feel for the documents—rather than as an engaged subject of study.

Images in print deserve more than this. The issue is not merely that new technologies were developed, although they were. Nor is it simply that images became more elaborate and sophisticated, although they did.

At least as important, the perceived cultural meaning of visual images changed in a way that prefigured the direction taken by mass culture in the twentieth century. Visual images *meant* something different in the twentieth century than they did in the antebellum era. Just as the stories told of murder sensations were freighted with different meanings, halftones conveyed a different sort of information than engravings and held a new place in American culture, which was itself becoming more visually oriented overall.[5]

Images of criminals in sensations—which could picture shady and monstrous figures earlier in the nineteenth century—became mimetic in the twentieth century. The character of murder illustrations evolved from an attempt to capture the essence of the crime and criminal—what we might call moral realism—to an effort to render an accurate representation of the criminal's appearance—photographic realism. Equally important, the sheer number of illustrations printed in the press expanded enormously, changing the experience of sensations in the new century. Between the Civil War and the age of ragtime, what Americans saw in the course of a sensational case evolved, as did the meanings they ascribed to these images. And they saw more than ever before.

■

NINETEENTH-CENTURY IMAGES OF CRIME

By the turn of the twentieth century, photography provided the basis for recording images in the media. But before the Civil War and for decades thereafter, engravings dominated the field of printed illustrations for sensations as well as book and newspaper publishing more generally. These engravings had quite a range of quality and style: some rough and simplistic, others more refined; some representational, others more fictive and even symbolic. These images often expressed more than a visual likeness, investing the frame with much of the criminal events and their resulting emotions. These images illustrated not just the appearance of the culprit, but often his character and his particular misdeeds as well.

These simple engravings of crime stories were themselves a recent innovation. Colonial-era crime pamphlets in the North typically had as their only image—if any image at all—a generic representation of a coffin or a man hanging from the gallows.[6] Similarly, eighteenth-century newspapers like the *Virginia Gazette* used only stock woodcuts in their layouts, such as a caricatured figure for a notice of a runaway slave.[7] Except for such figures, the press in the eighteenth and early nineteenth centuries used no illustrations at all; they simply did not provide this sort of visual information.

Engraving was skilled work, and publishers in this era typically had little capital for such an investment.

In the late eighteenth and early nineteenth centuries, engravings became more common in pamphlet and book publishing, and at midcentury, illustrated national periodicals, such as *Harper's Weekly* and *Frank Leslie's Illustrated Magazine*, depended on them. Antebellum illustrations tended to be simple and often were inaccurate or stereotyped even as the press used them more. Wrote one Virginia critic of the illustration-laden *Harper's Weekly*, a "morbid curiosity now demands the likenesses of police officers as well as Presidents." But, the critic continued, *Harper's* delivers "such palpable humbugs" as the portrait of a senator, which was unrecognizable "but for the name under it" or an image of a steamboat that looks like "every other Western steamboat that ever was built and every other representation of a Western steamboat which has ever been made. What do the readers of *Harper* want with a picture of that or any other steamboat?"[8] Still quite rare, engravings at midcentury were of erratic quality, and even the best tended to be simple, small, and rough renderings.

Unlike earlier generic images, engravings of sensational cases in the nineteenth century were tailored to individual crimes. This was a major step toward realistic depiction: replacing categorical images with particularized ones.[9] Instead of a coffin or a noose, these engravings might depict the murder scene, the victim's prostrate body, the murderer fleeing, or simply a bust of the accused murderer. For instance, the only existing print of William Dandridge Epes, who murdered Francis Adolphus Muir south of Richmond in 1846 before fleeing to Texas, is from the pamphlet of his case.[10] (See figure 6.) This engraving demonstrates the simplicity common to images of the era; it is merely a bust in stark white and black. If most antebellum images remained quite simple, they also displayed a new effort to tie the images more directly to the crime at hand. This was not just any man or a stereotyped criminal, it was meant to be an image of William Epes in particular.

This attempt to capture the looks of individuals marks a significant shift in the orientation of the graphic arts as it relates to mass publications, one that parallels both the growing volume of prose reporting and its first halting steps toward "objectivity." Among images in the antebellum period were some "palpable humbugs," stick figures, and stock characters. But the desire of the press to offer—and the public's "morbid curiosity that demands"—visual information geared to a particular event marks an important turn in American cultural history.[11]

The simplicity of antebellum engravings had much to do with the pro-

WILLIAM DANDRIDGE EPES.

FIGURE 6.

Even straightforward portraits of antebellum criminals could be laced with emotion. Here Epes appears fully capable of the murder charged to him. Frontispiece of Trial of William Dandridge Epes for the Murder of Francis Adolphus Muir *(Petersburg, Va.: J. M. H. Brunet, 1849).*

cess. Woodcuts and metal engravings were expensive and time-consuming luxuries at midcentury. Reflected one newspaperman in 1895: "Twenty years ago, if we wanted to print a portrait of any distinguished man, Senator Hill or Mr. Cleveland, for instance, why, we had first to get a photograph, then we had to get a draughtsman, then a wood engraver, and after the engraving was cut in the wood we had to have a stereotype made of it before we could print it. It was a very expensive operation. I should think, to make a good and adequately extensive portrait of Mr. Cleveland, after the old fashion, would cost forty or fifty dollars."[12] By implication, not all images in print were either "good" or "adequately extensive."

If this were the whole story, then conventional wisdom would suffice to explain changes in images: their simplicity early in the nineteenth century was due to their expense and to artistic limitations, both of which changed over time allowing more and better images—ones more closely tied to reality—to emerge. Antebellum images served the same function as later ones, if this logic prevailed, and what evolved was the technical ability to live up to the ideal of verisimilitude in engravings. Indeed, many antebellum images attempted to present as accurate an image as possible. On the surface, written evidence seems to reinforce this idea that engravings *were* attempts to create lifelike visuals in the antebellum period. Many engravings were printed with the caption "from a daguerreotype," "from a miniature portrait," or "from life" to emphasize that the engraver was working from a dependable source rather than from his imagination.[13] If many of these engravings have elements of caricature, we could ascribe that to the technique—the limitations of engraving for the press in the antebellum period.

But that does not obviate the fact that many of these images *were* caricatures—simple figures that hold tenuous connections to the appearance of their purported subjects. Moreover, why would publishers feel compelled to say that an image was "from a daguerreotype" unless the common wisdom was to question the accuracy of engravings? The frequent use of this phrase actually implies its reverse—that typical engravings in the press were considered to be of questionable authenticity. These images required the support of defensive captions to bolster their claim as accurate representations of their subjects.

In addition, a significant proportion of antebellum images were not merely rough, they were pointedly stylized, emotional, and stereotyped.[14] At midcentury, engravings were carved freehand, meaning that a multitude of artistic decisions mediated the representation of the person or scene at issue. Adorned with a single image on its title page, an 1821 pamphlet detailed the trial of two rogues, Garcia and Castillano, for murdering and dismembering their erstwhile compatriot, Peter Lagoardette, in Norfolk, Virginia.[15] (See figure 7.) Every element central to the story is in the frame: not only the principal actors, but the weapons, the bucket and fireplace in which body parts were found, and the chest with clothing that led to the arrest of the perpetrators. But this is more than a simple engraving giving visual representation to elements of the crime scene. In this image, the culprits stand over the mutilated body with knives still drawn and bloody, their faces etched with anger or simple malevolence. This was not an attempt at dispassionate (or objective or realistic) reporting, but rather a forceful attempt to capture the passions, to evoke the moment of violence.

Even the less active engraving of William Epes shown in figure 6 might imply something more than simply an effort to capture the looks of a murderer. The artist did not picture the murder scene but nevertheless suggested something more subtle than the criminal's superficial appearance. Epes is not pictured as an evil character, exactly, but he has a troubling visage: stern and cross, with wrinkled brow, creases around his mouth, and shadows across his face. Epes is clearly disturbed in this image, perhaps angry, perhaps mentally unbalanced. His appearance might imply a capacity for violent action, even if the engraving does not show him actively committing a crime.

Coarse engravings likewise illustrated the publications arising from several of the most studied nineteenth-century murders across the nation. Like the Epes engraving, many antebellum images captured the accused criminals in relatively dispassionate poses.[16] But many others are notably stereotyped and stylized. An 1836 pamphlet on the murder of a young New York prostitute, Helen Jewett, for instance, was accompanied by a woodcut of a bare-breasted figure—almost a stick figure in its lack of sophistication—lying across a bed.[17] A fictive re-creation of the death of New York "cigar girl" Mary Rogers in 1841 included an engraving of crude figures of a man strangling a woman in a secluded glade.[18] Another publication on that case recycled an image of a *different* New York "cigar girl" from an earlier story that had nothing to do with Mary Rogers, demonstrating how uneven was the development of illustrations particular to the event at hand.[19] Almost half of the antebellum images published in Karen Halttunen's nicely illustrated study of murder pamphlets, *Murder Most Foul*, were re-creations of the moment of action in the crimes. Others were portraits and other scenes, some rather rough and others more representational.[20]

As in Richmond, daily papers throughout the nation at midcentury

AN
ACCOUNT
OF THE
APPREHENSION, TRIAL, CONVICTION, AND CONDEMNATION
OF
MANUEL PHILIP GARCIA *marked* I
AND
JOSE DEMAS GARCIA CASTILLANO, *do.* II

Who were executed on Friday the 1st of June, 1821, in the rear of
the town of Portsmouth, in Virginia, for a most horrid
murder and butchery, committed on

PETER LAGOARDETTE,

IN THE BOROUGH OF NORFOLK ON THE 20th OF MARCH PRECEDING.

TOGETHER WITH AN

APPENDIX,
CONTAINING THEIR CONFESSIONS, &c.

Norfolk.
PUBLISHED BY C. HALL,
And sold by most of the Booksellers in the United States.
June, 1821.

FIGURE 7.

*An example of the emotional and stereotypical images common in antebellum
engravings—the moment of action. Note the expressions on the murderers'
faces. Title page of* An Account of the Apprehension, Trial, Conviction, and
Condemnation of Manuel Philip Garcia and Jose Demas Garcia Castillano
(Norfolk: C. Hall, 1821).

found images too costly to use often. The largest dailies in northeastern cities began to use them around midcentury in association with sensations, but, again, they were still simple images and rare. The *National Police Gazette*, a weekly, regularly included illustrations, but they remained rude engravings, especially in its early years. In 1845, for example, the *Gazette* printed a woodcut of Albert Tirrell murdering Maria Bickford in the famous somnambulism murder case.[21] (See figure 8.) Like many from this era, this illustration shows the moment of action: a woman hanging over the edge of a bed with a shadowy man bearing down on her throat. Connections to melodrama are clear in this and many other images from this era: the dark villain overpowering the helpless victim, whose alabaster breast and throat appear so vulnerable to his razor. In fact, these true crime reports could include as many active and melodramatic images as adorned fictional crime pamphlets of the era. (See figure 9.)

The darkness of the villain and the whiteness of the victim in the Tirrell-Bickford case as shown in figure 8 raises the issue of race in midcentury typecasting. If few illustrations of sensational white crime arose in this era in Virginia, none were drawn of blacks. Crimes that involved blacks were less sensational, due to the widespread "commonsense" belief among whites in the innate barbarity of African Americans. Even in the case of the Nat Turner slave insurrection, newspapers and pamphlets included no images at all. Likewise, images produced by African Americans were rare, and Virginia had no black newspaper until well after the Civil War. The few images of African Americans in the broader white culture conformed to well-known stereotypes of minstrel shows: exaggerated features, informal poses, and insulting and comic contexts. More even than with white criminals, images of blacks (whether criminals or not!) were pushed toward demeaning stereotypes in the nineteenth century. When shown a realistic portrayal of Hiram Revels, the first black U.S. senator, Frederick Douglass responded by saying that "we colored men so often see ourselves described and painted as monkeys, that we think it a great piece of good fortune to find an exception to the general rule."[22]

Whether of white or black subjects, melodramatic and stereotyped images were in keeping with several broad trends in nineteenth-century American cultural and intellectual life. The era's sciences of phrenology and physiognomy argued that character could be perceived from a person's physical attributes—the contours of the skull and one's general appearance, respectively. (See figure 10.) This transparency of character was a safeguard for social order according to some in the mid-nineteenth century, "insuring that men shall ultimately be known for what they are. In

FIGURE 8.

Engravings in the early to mid-nineteenth century were rare, expensive, and tended to invest much of the excitement and the action of the crime into the frame of the image. Mirroring contemporary melodramatic typecasting, the dark villain in this image, the purportedly sleepwalking Albert Tirrell, attacks the vulnerable, alabaster victim, Maria Bickford, National Police Gazette, *13 December 1845, 129.*

This enraged me, and without a thought I raised a chair to strike her. She told me to do the worst I could do. Not knowing what I was about, I let the unwieldy weapon fall on her head.

FIGURE 9.

In an inexplicable rage, Henry Delter smashes the skull of his first wife, starting him on the path of murder, mayhem, and, ultimately, suicide. In the antebellum period, fictional works like this one could mirror true crime pamphlets and their images in both form and content. The two genres borrowed much from each other; in fact, many such fictions were inspired by actual crimes. Awful Disclosures! or, Narrative and Confession of Henry Delter, the Murderer of His Five Wives!! *(Richmond: Barclay and Co., 1851), 13.*

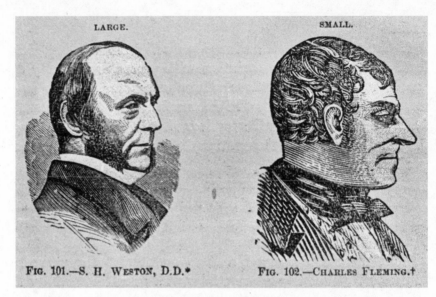

LARGE.   SMALL.

FIG. 101.—S. H. WESTON, D.D.*   FIG. 102.—CHARLES FLEMING.†

FIGURE 10.

An example of how closely appearance was tied to personality in nineteenth-century physiognomy, these engravings compare the relative abundance and deficit of benevolence in the visages of an Episcopal clergyman and a man whose "cruelty almost exceeded belief." From Samuel R. Wells, How to Read Character: A New Illustrated Handbook of Phrenology and Physiognomy *(New York: Samuel R. Wells, 1869), 84.*

vain do the profligate, the base, the wicked, and the selfish mimic those outward indications which pertain naturally to the pure, the good, and the generous. The inward unworthiness, despite all effort, *will* glare through the fleshly mask."[23] Melodramas and sentimental novels—tremendously popular throughout the nineteenth century—shared these concerns relating appearance to character. Melodrama particularly made physically manifest the character of individuals, embodied in stereotypes of innocence (the pure, beset heroine) and savagery (the caped, mustachioed villain). The process of revealing true virtue and villainy was therefore a central concern in melodrama.[24]

Given this broad midcentury scientific and cultural context, appearance was anything but superficial. "Surely the soul shows its features in the face," glowed one photographer considering the potential of his medium. "Outward expression is the revelation of inward feeling."[25] But it was more: a revelation also of society's prejudices. Appearances and expression were biological attributes, in this view, but such beliefs were also openly ethnocentric and racist: the physical features most lauded were those most pronounced in northern European physiognomy. This sheds a harsher light on nineteenth-century popular and scientific beliefs in character expressing itself through the features. Not only was such an idea revealing, it also formed a pillar supporting the daunting edifice of white supremacy.

The typing of criminals in illustrations finds a telling example in the 1867 murder case against Jeter Phillips. As with antebellum murders, no photographs of either Jeter or his victim exist. Richmond's daily papers printed no images associated with this case at all—illustrations remained quite expensive and exceptional. The *Southern Opinion*, a local illustrated weekly, printed an image of Phillips, however, and a closely related engraving of Jeter Phillips served as the frontispiece in the pamphlet on the case.[26] (See figure 11.) It pictures Phillips with hollow, dark eyes, sunken cheeks, and an open mouth drawn down in a grimace. Except that he lacked fangs, this image might serve as a plausible representation of a vampire. This sketch allowed for no double readings, no ambiguity in the character it claimed to represent. The image of Phillips can be seen to invest the face of the accused with the crime itself, figuratively etching the violence onto his body. It is as if the engraver caught Jeter unaware, reflecting on his evil heart or scheming to commit some new crime. His "inward unworthiness," to employ the general comments of a contemporary, glared "through the fleshly mask."[27]

This engraving becomes particularly meaningful when contrasted against the prose descriptions of his looks. The *Southern Opinion* juxta-

JAMES JETER PHILLIPS.

FIGURE II.

As late as the 1860s and 1870s, engravings might type their subjects even when prose descriptions rendered a very different judgment. Frontispiece of J. Wall Turner's The Drinker's Farm Tragedy: Trial and Conviction of James Jeter Phillips for the Murder of His Wife *(Richmond: V. L. Fore, 1868).*

posed its version of this caricatured image with the following attempt to depict his features in words:

> The science of physiognomy is at fault when the facial features and cranium development of James Jeter Phillips are examined for those physical evidences which declare the murderer and the "bold, bad man." The head of Phillips is fully, but not inordinately developed; neither does it lack any of the features that indicate the presence of all the humanizing and controlling traits of character found in the best of young men. Of medium stature—about five feet six inches—rather stout, regular featured, fair complexioned, light hair and light mustache, one can look straight into the pupils of his blue eyes and see himself daguerreotyped there without detecting a quiver of the optic nerve.[28]

Another Richmond paper agreed for the most part, writing that one "could discern nothing in his features or appearance consistent with the perpetration of so brutal a crime. Tall and rather slender with an oval face and features inclining to be regular, his nose is small and well cut, his eyes dark blue, his forehead good and shaded by heavy masses of dark hair, it is only in the rather heavy lower jaw that a physiognomist would detect firmness, perhaps cruelty."[29] Both of these passages describe the looks of the prisoner, demonstrating the desire to paint a thorough picture of the accused, if only in words, in an era when technology did not allow the easy reproduction of images. They also exemplify the imprecision of such descriptions: was he tall and slender with masses of dark hair, or was he of medium stature, stout, with light hair?

Leaving behind the contradictory elements of these descriptions—which alone implies that one or both editors were playing fast and loose with the story (as many nineteenth-century editors did)—let us assume that they sought to be realistic, detailed, and objective. These prose descriptions, then, are further examples of the public's desire to see. Why, then, use such an image to go along with this text? Why, indeed, are there so many antebellum images that are caricatures, stereotypes, and fictive re-creations of the moment-of-action?

It would be interesting to know whether a reader in 1868 would notice the contradiction between this ghastly image and the *Southern Opinion* likening Phillips to the "best of young men." The fact that such simple and almost allegorical images were commonplace in the mid-nineteenth century hints that perhaps no contradiction existed at this time: images were not understood to be "realistic" in the sense that we are conditioned to understand the term. The engraving of Phillips, like so many other images from midcentury and before, sought to give physical expression to a criminal nature, a visual analog of the typecast fiends peopling the popular melodramas of the day. Images in this period carried a very different symbolic freight than do illustrations in our own day; they performed different "work" for a publisher.

Plenty of images from this period were representational: attempts to render a good likeness of people associated with sensations. But many engravings from this era communicated more. Rare and expensive, these mid-nineteenth-century illustrations often employed a sort of shorthand, a synopsis of the entire crime boiled down to one image. This should not be considered "unrealistic" in this era, but rather an attempt to express much more than the surface reality of events. The act of violence, anger, pain, jealousy, insanity, or sexual overtones (as applicable) each might find its way into the single moment purportedly captured in the image. In a sense, these engravings illustrated a romantic truth or even a moral realism, an attempt to display the character and not simply the form of the malefactors.

■

HALFTONE SENSATIONS

In the decades after the Civil War—the same era when realism, sociology, and the professionalization of journalism altered the broader cultural context for sensational crime reporting (chapter 3)—this connection between simple, melodramatic typecasting and the images of crime dissolved. Instead, in the late nineteenth century, illustrations of criminals moved progressively closer to emulating photographs. At midcentury, this process had already begun: many published engravings were representational, and many others were cloaked in the legitimacy of the photograph with captions reading "from a daguerreotype." At the end of the century, the advent of the halftone process completed this transition by transforming the entire economy of image production in publishing.

Louis Jacques Mandé Daguerre announced the invention of his photographic process in 1839, and within months, thousands of entrepreneurs around the world were inspired to set up shop as daguerreotypists.[30] Further innovations led to the collodion or wet-plate process in 1851, ushering in the second generation of photographers. Unlike daguerreotypes, each a unique print on a polished metal plate, the collodion process yielded a negative which could then be used to make multiple prints on paper. In its first twenty years, photography showed itself to be a phenomenon with far-ranging cultural impact, from portraiture and landscapes to the stereograph and the cheap and popular tintype. What had been unknown in 1838 were produced in the millions each year of the 1850s.[31]

Photography was a revelation to nineteenth-century Americans, but it was not, of course, the mirror to nature that its earliest proponents presumed. It was a tool in the hands of subjective actors; photographs could be manipulated during and after exposure. Recent scholars have stressed this human element in photography: as a historical document, a photograph must be interpreted like a written source or any other evidence. Scenes can be composed rather than simply discovered; the camera leaves out of its view more than it captures; images can be manipulated in the darkroom. Like engravings, photographs are artifacts that carry symbolic content.[32]

In fact, criminal photography provides a peculiar and interesting example of photographic manipulation. The British photographer Francis Galton tried to use photography as a tool to uncover a range of fundamental human types. Beginning in the 1870s, Galton published a lengthy series of "composite" photographs, developing as many as thirty portraits—of criminals, or Jews, or consumptives, or other presumed "types"—as a single print. The resulting image, he thought, would cancel out idiosyncratic elements, leaving only the common and fundamental elements of the type. This "composite portraiture" produced fuzzy images of dubious utility, but the practice remained a popular fad throughout the last quarter of the nineteenth century.[33]

If photographers could manipulate, to most of the public and to the photojournalists engaged in documenting sensations, the photograph was nevertheless the most mimetic likeness ever created, capturing visual images with accuracy previously unimaginable. Photographs seemed essentially different from engravings: objective, an unmediated communication, a transparent medium. Many nineteenth-century writers ascribed the artistry of a photograph to nature itself: these images were "painted by Nature's self with a minuteness of detail, which the pencil of light in her hands alone can trace . . . *they cannot be called copies of Nature, but portions of Nature herself.*"[34] Our rhetoric still echoes this perspective: we "take" a photograph rather than "make" one.

As revolutionary as photography was, it had little direct effect on crime sensations or publishing in general in its first decades. The press and publishing houses continued to rely on engravings; none of the various means of reproducing photographs could be adapted to the high speeds and curved printing surfaces of commercial presses.[35] The nineteenth century witnessed a cascading series of innovations in the press—the replacement of flat-bed, hand-powered presses with faster, steam-powered multiple-cylinder presses along with the expansion of print due to the availability of cheap wood pulp paper—yielding a dizzying array of print media.[36] But not in photographs. Both technological and artistic[37] barriers kept photographs from feasibly entering newspapers and magazines. The chief problem was that photographs, like life, include an almost infinite range of grays, a tonal scale absent in the white-black dichotomy of ink printing, where any space not blackened with ink appears entirely white. Thus it was impossible to transfer photographic images directly to a form that could be integrated into newspapers.

Between the 1850s and the 1890s, a series of innovations produced an increasing volume of illustrations in the press with a growing approximation to photographic quality well before halftone technology fully mechanized the process. Early in the period, photos served as models for engravers who worked freehand ("from a daguerreotype"). By the 1860s, photographs began to be developed directly onto surfaces for the engravers to follow more mechanically. The images of Lillian Madison and Thomas Cluverius in figures 1 through 3 probably were made using this technique.[38] The increased ease and accuracy of these prints inspired the press to use them more often.

With more print space to fill—due to the growing size of virtually all newspapers and magazines in the late nineteenth and early twentieth centuries—publishers readily demanded escalating numbers of these increasingly cost-effective images. Weekly papers and magazines exploited these developments most and first. The first daily paper to attempt regular illustrations was the New York *Daily Graphic* in 1873, and an 1880 census report stated that illustrations were popular among the "class periodicals"; thereafter, they became more common everywhere.[39] One of the most famous photographers of the era, Henry Peach Robinson, wrote that "Illustration used to be employed to 'embellish' and help the author; now the author, instead of being embellished, goes in palous [sic] fear of being abolished, for few have time to read, and it is as much as he who runs—to catch a train—can do to look at the pictures."[40]

Not only was illustration on the rise in the late nineteenth century, further innovations led to a third generation of photography, one that had a more direct impact on sensationalism. In 1871, Robert Leach Maddox invented a means of using gelatin in place of the wet collodion for negatives. Perfected in the ensuing decade, the dry-plate process, as it came to be known, had all the virtues of collodion prints—sharp detail and reproducibility—with the added and important benefits of speeding exposure times and disassociating the process of taking photographs from the process of developing them. Unlike the cumbersome wet-plate system, negatives with a stable emulsion could be stored, exposed, and stored further until it was convenient to develop the images. The basis upon which all subsequent photographic innovations rested, the dry-plate process increased the speed and flexibility of photography.[41] In the next generation, George Eastman's consumer-friendly Kodak cameras further expanded the reach of photography.

But the growth in press illustrations was neither uniform nor quick: the *Daily Graphic* limped along for less than a generation under a variety of owners before failing in 1889, and engravings remained the standard for another decade. Some illustrations in the 1885 Cluverius case were rather sophisticated engravings (as shown in figures 1 through 3), but others were freehand drawings and diagrams in keeping with the more primitive style in vogue at midcentury.[42] (See figure 12.) The late nineteenth century saw a movement in the press toward photorealism in illustrations, with visual accuracy trumping emotionalism. But this was an uneven development, a half-measure.

In the 1890s, new technologies more thoroughly revolutionized images in the press. The adaptation of halftone engravings—an invention of the 1870s—to the large and fast presses used by almost all American newspapers meant that photographs could be incorporated into text with comparative ease and economy. The breakthrough in creating a tonal scale including grays (halftones) was the development of an image through glass etched with a screen. This "crossline screen" broke the image into tiny units that would be either entirely white or black (suitable for ink printing), and the density of those dots would create a close approximation to a range of grays. (See figure 13.) The New York *Daily Graphic* printed the first halftone illustration in 1880, but more than a decade passed before commercially feasible halftone screens were on the market.[43]

At the turn of the century, the appearance of the print media across the country radically changed: halftones supplanted engravings in the magazine industry, and engravings were increasingly challenged in the newspaper market as well. At the same moment when linotype machines allowed for a dramatic expansion of prose in daily papers, the halftone provided less expensive visuals for a publishing industry growing by leaps and bounds. Wrote Frederick Ives, the inventor of the crossline screen: "In the early days of halftone, one wood engraver said that he wanted to murder me for virtually destroying the industry which he had chosen for his life occupation. . . . Not only is almost all of the illustrating in books

undertook to persuade Mr. Joel. He to prove an *alibi.* They stand

The Prisoner at the Fence.
(*Evidence of His Father Describing How Prisoner Slipped and Struck His Hand Against a Rail.*)

FIGURE 12.

Although many images from the Cluverius case of 1885 show a growing sophistication, others, like this one, were in keeping with the more primitive style of midcentury engravings. Richmond Dispatch, *31 May 1885.*

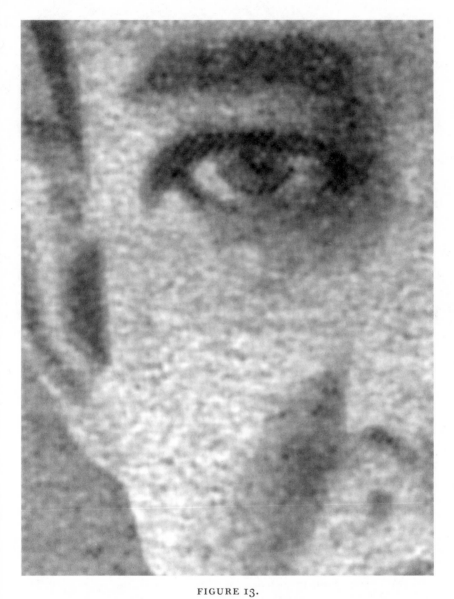

FIGURE 13.

A close-up view of a halftone image of Henry Clay Beattie Jr., reproduced from A Full and Complete History of the Beattie case, Most Highly Sensational Tragedy of the Century . . . *(Baltimore, Md.: Phoenix Publishing Co., 1911). Courtesy of the Virginia Historical Society.*

and magazines now done by 'process,' but there are probably a thousand illustrations used now where there was only one when wood engraving was the only method of production."[44]

After the introduction of halftone, the illustration of African Americans becomes an interestingly complex issue. Of course, halftone photographs of blacks represent a parallel shift away from stereotypes and toward "straight" representations—a similar move toward realism as with white subjects. In addition, black newspaper publishers adopted halftone technology as quickly as did whites, and papers like the *Richmond Planet* became as illustration-filled as the *Richmond Times-Dispatch*. According to one study of black newspapers from around the nation, the increase in illustrations was the most notable change in the African American press as a whole in the late nineteenth century. The first black paper to market itself as an illustrated weekly, the Indianapolis *Freeman*, appeared in 1889, and it became one of the most popular black periodicals of the era.[45]

At the same time, harsh racism persisted throughout this period and continued to color the presentation of African Americans in the press, as elsewhere. This "nadir" in African American history saw repeated race riots, Jim Crow laws, and the creation of the tremendously popular, racist, and stereotype-laden movie *The Birth of a Nation*. Even in the face of realism, photography, and more nuanced theories in sociology and criminology, the strict stereotypes of race and inferiority retained their places and in some ways were even further elaborated. Yet images of blacks as savages and fiends were more rare than those of a lighter, comic vein. As in minstrelsy, blacks were portrayed more often in early-twentieth-century images "as irresponsible, non-threatening, slightly exotic buffoons with a childish fondness for aping whites." These dismissive and demeaning stereotypes only began to erode, if ever so slowly, in the 1920s and after.[46]

As a consequence of this halftone technology, popular coverage of crime sensations in the early twentieth century was saturated with visual data. Weeklies adopted this technology first, often by the mid-1890s. The African American weekly the *Richmond Planet* included halftone photographs in its coverage of the 1895 Lunenburg murder case, several years before the white daily *Dispatch* invested in this technology. In its eighteen months of Lunenburg coverage, the *Planet* published forty-one engravings and seventy-six halftones, as many images as might be expected in white papers.[47]

In 1911, the local white papers were filled with photographs of everything having to do with the Beattie case. These halftones included images of the murder scene, the accused murderer's home, the judge, jury, jailer, courthouse, witnesses—there were 114 to choose from—and the victim. (See figure 14.) In 1867, the *Richmond Dispatch* printed no images of the Phillips case, and in 1885, it published around thirty-five engravings related to the Cluverius murder.[48] In 1911, the *Richmond Times-Dispatch* printed 174 halftones, almost as many images as articles on the Beattie murder.[49] A similar trend can be found in extant Virginia pamphlets and paperbacks on sensational trials. Among nineteenth-century pamphlets, half contained one or two images, and half had none at all, but in the early twentieth century, such publications averaged one engraving or diagram and eighteen halftone photographs.[50]

Newspapers in 1911 photographed everything in the Beattie case, but most of all they printed photo after photo of Henry Beattie and "the other woman" in the sensation: young and pretty Beulah Binford. (See figures 15 and 16.) In fact, so many halftones of Beulah appeared after the story broke that the *Times-Dispatch* was roundly criticized for making this dissolute "woman about town" into a public figure.[51] Cues to an evil character on the part of the accused murderer and his consort are entirely absent in these photographs. Often framed in decorative designs, the photographs show Henry and Beulah as pleasant young people—smiling, bright eyed, and well groomed.

Accurate these images certainly are, but they also are deafeningly mute concerning the issue that brought Henry and Beulah to public notice. Nothing in these images distinguishes these young people jailed for a murder from images of debutantes and their beaus on the social pages. This is not merely true in this one case. When Harry Thaw, the jealous husband of Evelyn Nesbit, killed architect Stanford White in New York in 1906, the press erupted with images, as in the Beattie case. Desiring to present views from inside the courtroom (where cameras were not allowed), the *New York World* published 106 engravings during Thaw's trial, along with 113 halftones of other scenes and people.[52] Similarly, when Leo Frank went on trial for the murder of Mary Phagan in 1913, the *Atlanta Constitution* published 48 engravings along with 160 halftones.[53] These halftones tended to be "straight" photographs, devoid of stereotypes or overt editorial comment. That does not mean, of course, that the halftones were without a context or that some were not augmented. On rare occasions, for instance, images combined engraved scenes with halftones to communicate more of the story line. But the context was as often as not irrelevant to the subject (and to the modern eye, bizarre and jarring): images of accused murderers framed

FIGURE 14.

With the introduction of the halftone print at century's end, the press was
transformed into a much more visually rich medium. In its coverage of the
1911 Beattie murder, the Richmond Times-Dispatch *printed 174 photographs;*
during the trial, it averaged six halftones each day. These included photographs
of everything to do with the case, often a half-dozen clustered together
in this sort of eye-catching, ornamented visual collage.
Richmond Times-Dispatch, *25 August 1911.*

FIGURE 15.

Halftones not only made images in the press more numerous, they also communicated a significantly different sort of visual information than in nineteenth-century engravings. Rather than typing him as an evil criminal, photographs of accused murderer Henry Beattie instead provoked the thought in Richmond's public that "some terrible blunder had been made, somehow, somewhere." No longer emotional or symbolic stereotypes, halftone prints were "realistic" in a different way, picturing the accused man in a lifelike and accurate manner. Richmond Times-Dispatch, 6 August 1911.

in engraved filigree (some designs even more ornate than in figure 14, for instance). Like in the Beattie case, little is evoked by these images except the outward appearances of the subjects.[54]

This trend toward the "straight" presentation of early-twentieth-century criminals is strong, but it is not without other currents. In the wake of the Leopold and Loeb murder case in 1924 Chicago, for instance, many believed there must be something "wrong" with these young men from prominent families to have kidnapped and murdered a boy, a crime with possible sexual overtones. This led to a series of stories on their characters, including some images parsing their looks. Reminiscent of nineteenth-century practitioners of physiognomy, various experts measured, X-rayed, and evaluated the brains, faces, and features of the accused. Yet even in this case, such treatment was rare: out of 266 halftones published in the *Chicago Herald and Examiner*, for example, only on five occasions (sixteen images total) were the photographs presented in this way. The other 250 halftones printed in the paper were presented—like those in the Leo Frank, Harry Thaw, and Henry Beattie cases—as straight photographs.[55] So, even when twentieth-century culture explored this sort of context for images of criminals, it appears as a "vestigial" or atrophied cultural form, one overtaken by other developments rather than the main thrust of the visual story line.

At the same time that the halftone transformed visual images in the press, other shifts in American intellectual life reinforced this change. The sciences of phrenology and physiognomy were largely displaced by sociology and psychology, fields that undercut the perceived direct connection between character and appearance. American culture in the late nineteenth century also began to turn from romantic or melodramatic typologies toward an understanding of the world through social types and realism. The late-nineteenth-century professionalization of journalism similarly strived for dispassionate observation. Mirroring changes in sociology, muckrakers and social activists increasingly turned from innate and inward explanations of deviance to environmental influences: the city, poverty, and the alienation they fostered. Each of these complex movements in science and society nudged Americans away from the nineteenth-century penchant for reading character into the faces of criminals. To adopt the terminology of Warren Susman, American culture was turning from an inward, moral understanding of people, "character," to a new social and individualistic perception, "personality."[56]

It was not that the whole culture turned from melodrama—far from it. The early twentieth century saw the phenomenal popularity of the novel

Tarzan of the Apes (1914) and other melodramatic and stereotyped-laden fictional genres, *Birth of a Nation* (1915) and other melodramatic films, and would soon include popular radio soap operas and melodramatic mystery serials. Twentieth-century culture is pervaded by melodrama, from newspaper tabloids to story papers, from comic books to romance novels. This context of melodrama's persistence in some arenas makes it still more interesting that, in contrast, images in crime sensations increasingly conformed to the goal of objectivity that professional reporting lauded as its chief virtue.

Against the backdrop of this overall evolution of American thought, this twentieth-century explosion of visual material in the press—most of it mechanically reproduced halftones—created a very different set of visual standards than those of the nineteenth century. When the *Richmond Times-Dispatch* printed an engraving of Henry Beattie at the end of his trial in 1911 (the only engraving it printed), it did so for *stylistic* reasons, to offer a refreshing visual contrast to what had become the norm. This image was not defensively captioned with a phrase reaching for authority (as in the common nineteenth-century caption: "from a daguerreotype"). Instead, it had a title emphasizing its distinction from photography, perhaps stressing as well the newspaper's pride in offering something more than its normal fare: "Pen Sketch of Beattie."[57] An engraving was now considered art rather than an approximation of a photograph.

One particular moment in the case against Henry Beattie demonstrates the implications of the change in the style of images with the introduction of the halftone, particularly when contrasted with the image of Jeter Phillips from 1867. Shortly after Beattie's arrest, the *Richmond Times-Dispatch* printed the photographs in figure 15. Dressed in coat and tie, Beattie had a pleasant expression, and a slight smile crossed his face. The next day, an article charted the public response to these photographs: "The comment was general that he did not have the look of a man guilty of so brutal a crime. . . . His eyes are sharp and clear and penetrating, and people said that his appearance was in his favor even if the evidence was all against him." The article ended with the statement: "It is ridiculous, of course, to assume that a little thing like a photograph would upset a chain of circumstantial evidence well nigh complete, and no such inference is to be drawn from what is printed here. But the fact remains that Richmond people felt yesterday as if some terrible blunder had been made—somehow, somewhere."[58]

This comment speaks directly to the change in the cultural role played by images, a change much more subtle and far-reaching than simply the introduction of the technologically sophisticated halftone. Often in the nineteenth century (although certainly not with every image), a criminal's presumed character had been fashioned into the engravings made of him, images that were notably emotional and active. Knowing that they would only print one or two images, publishers and illustrators often "telescoped the action for enhanced dramatic effect," using the shorthand of an engraving to get at the crime's essence, if possible.[59]

But the flood of halftones at the turn of the century altered the visual story line, trading the emotionalism possible in engravings for the detail and accuracy of halftones. A photograph is a very different visual document than an engraving, each having different limitations and potentials. Taken well after a crime, a photo freezes an instant, flattening one moment as seen from one perspective. As such, photographs could not capture the "moment of action" in the same way that engravings might—the gun firing, blood dripping from the knife, murderers grimacing villainously. At the very least, exceptional synchronicity would be required for the shutter of a camera to catch such a thing. In addition, most states did not allow cameras inside the courtroom. The public wanted views of the trial, but the camera was stymied in this attempt, relegated to showing witnesses, the accused, and his family entering the courthouse, or the accused at the jail, or important figures in a trial on a break resting on the courthouse green.

Even if a cameraman did catch an image of a murder as it was happening, halftones of gore would have been culturally unacceptable, at least in the popular press. Such images would be too realistic and lurid: what had been acceptable as symbols—blood dripping from knives, renderings of murder scenes—became too disturbing in a lifelike halftone. So often considered as "truth" in black and white, these photographs were in a sense too powerful a cultural form for gore to be acceptable. Halftones were very lifelike *but muted* snapshots, not of the crime but, rather, of the personalities involved. Photography offered abundant and accurate visual information but with new and distinct limitations framing its consumption.

The glaring exception to these new limits of prurient visual matter in the age of the photograph is telling. In this period, images of lynchings became more common in the South, although it is very difficult to discern just how widely they were circulated and how accepted they were. Some pictured the crowd; some, simply the corpse, hanging, shot, burned, and/or mutilated. These ghastly photographs circulated around the region as tokens of white supremacy that could be bought and sold, if usually under the counter and often expressly against the law. In that way, they appear to be a sort of underground pornography of white power and authority.

They rarely if ever appeared in the white press, and they had the fascinating unintended consequence of offering a wealth of harrowing visual data for lynching opponents to exploit. As Grace Elizabeth Hale notes, these images demonstrate how the modern technology of photography could be wed to brutality, allowing a much more permanent, graphic, and widely disseminated "proof" of the awful power of white supremacy.[60] Just how much did race matter in American culture in this period? In no other context were photographs this gruesome in public circulation.

Quite in contrast to these lynching photographs and also quite in contrast to images from a half-century before, the manner in which newspapers presented halftones of violent crimes in the twentieth century gave criminals no trace of stereotyping and little emotional charge. To paraphrase Estelle Jussim, a historian of the graphic arts, American culture in the mid-nineteenth century valued symbolic representations in illustration, but this emphasis shifted in the last years of the century. By the 1890s, according to Jussim, "the screened process halftone or the photogravure reproducing photography was accepted as equivalent to seeing the originals. . . . It was not viewed as a message about reality, but as reality itself, somehow magically compressed and flattened onto the printed page, but, nevertheless, equivalent to, rather than symbolic of, three-dimensional reality."[61]

In this way, the disparity between the Beattie halftone photographs and the earlier engravings represents much more than a growing technological sophistication. It also describes a change in how the visual image was understood, what an illustration meant to readers and publishers. This change reveals a deeper shift in the cultural context that invests images with meaning. Jeter Phillips was a good-looking man whose features did not seem to fit the expectation of what a criminal was supposed to look like: he was likened to "the best of young men." Yet the image publishers chose to print (the one in figure 11) was nothing like this description; it was a symbolic embodiment of a fiend, a "message about" criminality rather than a strict visual representation. In contrast, halftone images of Henry Beattie were commonly presumed to be, in a visual and physical sense at least, *him*. Compared to mid-nineteenth-century engravings, the message embedded in halftones was attenuated, reduced to detailed observation: "this is what Henry Beattie looked like yesterday at the courthouse."

■

Photography had not existed in 1838; by the turn of the twentieth century it had changed the way people viewed the world: "through its reproduction in the printing press," wrote noted critic William Ivins in the passage that opened this chapter, photography "has effected a very complete revolution in the ways we use our eyes and, especially, in the kinds of things our minds permit our eyes to tell us."[62] Photography has often been cited as an inspiration for the broader turn in American thought and culture toward realistic depictions of life in the second half of the nineteenth century.[63] Whether or not photography helped to cause these changes, the detail and immediacy of the photograph clearly embody this important transition in American culture. The power and importance of the medium, then and now, lie in just this accuracy, this realism: an effect so powerful as to obscure the photographer's artifice. Roland Barthes overstated the case, but not by much, when he wrote that "the Photograph is never anything but an antiphon of 'Look,' 'See,' 'Here it is.'"[64]

The steadily expanding influence of photography on American cultural life during the nineteenth century and the revolution of the halftone process provided a preview of what was to come in the twentieth century. American culture was becoming more visual in more ways than merely in the press. After his trial, Henry Beattie's "other woman," Beulah Binford (shown in figure 16) moved to New York City to appear onstage. She also made at least one short movie telling the sad story of her eventful life to the age of seventeen. Just six years after the "invention" of the nickelodeon, movie houses still typically showed a series of one-reel films of brief vignettes designed to distract and entertain for a few moments at a time. Topical stories of crime, like the Beattie case, as well as other newsworthy current events provided fodder for this new visual medium that would become one of the dominant forms of popular culture in the twentieth century. Binford's film was shown in New York and other cities, despite the widespread censure of this undertaking that seemed to reward a prostitute for her misdeeds.[65]

Motion pictures, slide exhibitions,[66] theatrical engagements, halftone photographs—in many related ways, sensations (and American culture more generally) became more visually saturated in the twentieth century. Mass culture had grown from nineteenth-century prose and theater to become a much broader current within American life. In the process, images became more important than ever: not merely embellishment, they were a mainstay of modern mass culture.

The growth of photography could be told as a story of inventors and innovations, but such a story would miss the cultural imperatives that fueled this search for new technologies. Early on, the American public wanted both to see the criminals and to read all about them. The drive to invent the half-measures of the late nineteenth century was predicated upon the widespread and growing public interest in viewing illustrations closer to life. The rising tide of mass culture lifted the place of images

FIGURE 16.

The young "woman about town" who figured in the Beattie case was also a prime subject for photographers and appeared often enough on the pages of the Times-Dispatch to prompt some readers to complain. After Henry's trial, Beulah Binford went to New York City in an attempt to capitalize on her notoriety onstage and in motion pictures. The movies were a new medium, demonstrating yet another way that American culture became increasingly visual in the twentieth century. Richmond Times-Dispatch, *8 August 1911.*

with it; it was the driving force inspiring the technological inventions that yielded the halftone. The development of halftone prints was therefore the culmination not only of a series of technological innovations, but also of a deeper cultural current pushing for a visual, photographic realism. Drained of much of the emotion and symbolism of so many nineteenth-century engravings, the tiny black-and-white dots of the halftone arranged themselves into a new sort of visual grammar at the turn of the century, rewriting what an image in print could mean.

6

THE PUBLIC SUSPENSE IS OVER

WE WERE INTERESTED IN OBSERVING THE STATE OF THE PUBLIC
MIND ON THE MORNING OF THE [1911 BEATTIE] EXECUTION AND IN
CONTRASTING IT WITH THE CONDITIONS WHICH PREVAILED ON THE
MEMORABLE DAY IN JANUARY, 1887, WHEN ANOTHER NOTED MURDERER
[CLUVERIUS] PAID THE PENALTY OF HIS CRIME. ON THAT DAY THE HILLS
OVERLOOKING THE JAIL WERE BLACK WITH A DENSE AND MOTLEY THRONG,
EAGER TO GET A GLIMPSE OF THE CONDEMNED MAN AS HE PASSED OVER
THE OPEN BRIDGE FROM THE PORTION OF THE CITY JAIL IN WHICH HE WAS
CONFINED TO THAT WHICH GAVE IMMEDIATELY ON THE YARD WHERE THE
SCAFFOLD STOOD. THAT WAS ALL THEY COULD SEE, A BLACK-ROBED FIGURE,
ESCORTED BY OFFICERS AND WITNESSES AND THE MINISTER, PASSING FOR
A MOMENT FROM ONE PART OF THE BUILDING TO ANOTHER—THE SCAFFOLD
WAS NOT IN SIGHT. YET, WHEN THEY GOT THAT GLIMPSE A YELL OF DELIGHT
RESOUNDED THROUGH ALL THE CITY. THE POIGNANCY OF THAT INCIDENT,
NOT TO SPEAK OF ITS HIDEOUS AND REPULSIVE IMPLICATIONS, MADE AN
IMPRESSION ON OUR MINDS THAT CAN NEVER FADE. SURELY IT WAS FAR
BETTER THAT THE SOLEMN AND AWFUL JUDGMENT OF THE LAW SHOULD
BE EXECUTED AS IN THIS CASE, IN SILENCE AND DIGNITY.

Richmond Religious Herald, 30 November 1911

Well before the 1886 Christmas holidays, the *Richmond Dispatch* and other papers again carried daily front-page articles about Thomas Cluverius. In June of 1885, the local hustings court had convicted the prisoner of Lillian Madison's murder, and in recent months, the Virginia Supreme Court rendered a four-to-one decision against his appeal. Would the governor commute his sentence of death, these papers now asked? Doubtful. Would Cluverius confess? Hard to say. What did the jurors now feel about his impending execution? Nine thought he should hang, and three were not so sure, wrote the *Dispatch*.

The papers reviewed the trial, witnesses, and evidence and retold the story of the crime over and again. A last-minute twist entered the case as well. Cluverius stated that he had been with another woman the night of the murder; honor forbade him from revealing her identity and forcing her forward into publicity and shame in order to save his life. The story was discounted. Yet, 299 Richmonders—2,713 Virginians overall—wrote to the governor or signed petitions asking for clemency in his case. These petitioners cited the fallibility of circumstantial evidence—the same argument employed by the one Supreme Court of Virginia justice who believed the conviction should be overturned. These petitions also brought up a recent change in law that they thought might have affected Cluverius's case: Virginia now allowed accused criminals to testify on their own behalf.[1] By late December 1886, the fascination with the Cluverius case was coming to a boil once more.

On 14 January 1887, virtually the entire issue of the *Dispatch* recapitulated the case, described the state of the last-minute appeals to the governor, and painted the scene at the newly erected gallows inside the jail walls.[2] On the eastern end of the long and narrow jail yard, an eight-foot square platform rose eleven feet above the dirt and sawdust. The pine scaffold supported a crossbeam of black walnut, from which dangled a bright rope of woven multicolored silk. Built in 1828, the jail was situated at one of the lowest points in the city, in the valley of the Shockoe creek between Broad and Marshall Streets downtown. Buildings and hillsides rose to the east and west, and by nine o'clock hundreds of the curious collected in the neighborhood. By midday, the streets, hills, and houses were covered with thousands of people. The execution of Cluverius was to be a private affair; as of 1879, Virginia law limited spectators to necessary attendants and twelve respectable witnesses. But the location of the jail made the event perforce a public one. In addition, Sergeant Smith allowed up to three hundred people to enter the jail yard with passes either forged or illegally distributed. The sergeant was later fined fifty dollars for contempt of court in violating the judge's direct order that no more than twelve be admitted into the jail yard. He defended himself by saying they sneaked in and that he could not risk a riot by expelling them.[3] Prominent in this crowd were reporters; one recalled standing at the railing of the scaffold, not six feet from the trap door.[4] Estimates of the crowd inside and outside the jail walls ranged widely, but each was in the thousands.

Students at the Medical School of Virginia perched on their rooftop on a hill to the northwest, using a telescope and binoculars to get a better view. A photographer, forced to leave the jail yard after taking pictures of the empty scaffold,[5] found a secondary perch on a housetop one block away. Homeowners in the area sold space at their windows and on their roofs, some of which were dangerously crowded. Jail alley was packed with people from end to end, despite the fact that a wall blocked their view; they apparently hoped to find their way into the yard. Others perched on hillsides or in tree branches, and a few even climbed to the tops of telegraph poles with the help of spurs on their heels. The superintendent of the fire alarm department suggested that all the fire bells in the city be rung at the conclusion of the execution so that everyone would know the ordeal had ended. The mayor vetoed this idea. Others called the jail—telephones were just beginning to come into general use. Despite the few Richmonders yet owning Alexander Graham Bell's invention, the jail's single telephone rang more than a hundred times in the hours around midday.

Pushing through the crowds were young boys selling not just the city's newspapers full of Cluverius material, but even a book penned by the convicted man himself. Sold for fifty cents and titled *Cluverius: My Life, Trial, and Conviction*, it told the story of his ill-starred career and supported the idea that Lillian Madison had committed suicide. Its profits went to his aunt, who had paid for his prestigious team of lawyers. For months, rumors had circulated that he might confess, rumors that gained particular credence after it was learned that he was at work writing this volume. All such speculation was in vain—the book only repeated his claims of innocence. But perhaps he would tell all on the gallows in the face of eternity.

The night before, according to the papers, Cluverius had appeared agitated for one of the first times since his arrest. William Hatcher, the local minister who spoke with him regularly, asked him if he had anything more to say. He declined. Frank Cunningham, a local government employee known as "the sweetest tenor in the city," came to the jail at Cluverius's request to sing hymns. In general, it was admitted, the convicted man bore up well, even in this last evening.

The next morning, he remained courteous to his jailers and was stoic in the face of the strain. After eating a hearty breakfast of steak, potatoes, eggs, and coffee, Cluverius was joined by Reverend Hatcher and others as they awaited the governor's final reply to his lawyers. Shortly after noon, they received the word that the governor would not intervene. Said Hatcher: The prisoner's "knees trembled and almost smote one another. That was the terrible moment for him." One last time, Cluverius was left alone with the minister, who asked him if there was anything he should say to the public. Again, Cluverius declined, and he dressed in the new suit provided by his brother.[6] Finally, his arms were bound in front of him, and he was escorted for the last time out of his cell.

A few moments before one o'clock, bustling around the jail door and a cheer from the hillsides turned the crowd assembled in the jail yard toward the emerging convict. Every head was bared as Cluverius walked under guard through the throng to his doom. Cluverius walked past the hundreds in the jail yard, in view of many of the thousands outside the walls. Bracketed by guards, he mounted the fifteen steps at the back of the scaffold, and Sergeant Smith read the court order for his death. Smith then turned to ask Cluverius if he had anything he wished to say.

The crowd was silent; this was the denouement. After months of wondering, months of trying to convince each other of his guilt, of piecing evidence together and wrestling with troubling doubts, this was the time he would confess if ever he would. After all, seventeen years before at such a moment, James Jeter Phillips made a full confession of killing his wife in cold blood. Now Cluverius had the chance to erase all the doubts, to ease the consciences of Richmonders who still wondered if he did it.

"Do you have anything to say?"

"No, sir," he quietly replied, shaking his head.

Reverend Hatcher gave a brief prayer and then addressed the crowd, saying that the prisoner had requested him to say that he bears no ill will toward any on earth. The minister then left the jail yard, not wanting to witness the conclusion of the spectacle. Overwrought and "pale as a sheet," Hatcher walked to a friend's house to compose himself and to prepare an "interview" with himself that would be devoured by everyone in the city when it appeared in the next morning's *Richmond Dispatch*.[7]

The deputies draped a black hood over Cluverius's head then fixed the bright silken rope around his neck. His legs were tied together, and the officials descended from the scaffold. A few seconds later, at 1:09 p.m., the trap door swung out from below him. After ten minutes, his feet dangling just an inch above the ground (the silk having stretched under his weight), Thomas Judson Cluverius was declared dead, and he was cut

184

down twenty minutes later. At this moment, the undertaker arrived in a wagon carrying a coffin, and the jail yard gates opened for his admittance. In a final demonstration of the macabre interest in the scene, it was only through the "liberal use of their clubs" that the police could push the surging crowd back into jail alley and close the gates again.

The papers described in detail the body dangling from the rope—the strange and disturbing gurgling sounds, the frantic twitching of limbs, the rope cutting deeply into the folds of his neck. Despite much interest, the body was put into the coffin without removing the hood, "so there was no opportunity given any one at the jail to see his face."

In the following days, the papers continued to write on the case, describing Cluverius's jail cell and its contents, wondering if anything he left behind included a confession. To no avail: he never confessed, and his last statements as given to Reverend Hatcher and as printed in his book maintained his innocence and asserted the probability that Lillian Madison had killed herself. No more surprises would be in store; no alternative story lines were possible. Frustration remained, but the dynamism, the liminality, the fuel for the story were now gone.

The extent to which Richmonders longed for a confession and the sort of closure it would bring became evident in the wake of the hanging. Charles Wallace wrote in his diary: "The public suspense is over. The poor wretch Cluverius was hanged. He made no statement when asked by the Sergeant if he had anything to say. Simply and feebly his reply was 'no sir.' The people have been maddened by the unsatisfactory ending of this tragedy—a few think him guiltless of Lillian's blood—others think the direct evidence given in court upon his trial did not warrant his conviction—but the larger portion think that evidence satisfactory and when joined to the normal evidence conclusive."[8]

The day after the execution, the *Richmond Dispatch* consoled its still-anxious readership: "The public may rest assured that the Governor had *more* information than any man living concerning this case. He was satisfied—indeed, almost *knew*—that the man was guilty. He never expected a confession."[9] A few days later, the *Dispatch* ran a long story listing six reasons why Cluverius *must* have been guilty, an article that implies much doubt remaining on the subject.[10] The *State* was even more bald, titling an editorial on the day following the execution: "Was he Guilty or Innocent?"

■

In some ways, this final moment encapsulates all of the interest in the cultural event: the focus on the murderer's body, the tenacious hope for assurance and confession, and the interest in violence and in the sharp edges between life and death, innocence and guilt. In another sense, it describes a different object: the action not of the murderer or the law or the populace itself, but rather the action of the state, its punishing institutions, and the cultural frame made for them. The history of executions shows sweeping change over the course of this period but in more than one direction. Like the images and the narratives of murder investigated in previous chapters, these final moments show dramatic changes over time. From virtual carnivals of death, capital punishment in Virginia—and the rest of the nation— moved into a cloistered execution chamber.

The failed attempt to make the Cluverius hanging private underscores the pressures both for and against this change. A strong countertrend threatened this project to civilize capital punishment and perhaps served as the goad prompting repeated attempts by the legislature to make executions private. The cultural treatment of executions grew in volume and in detail throughout the nineteenth century. Already macabre stories in the early 1800s, the narratives of executions in the postbellum period were far more grandiose in scale, filled with gore, vivid descriptions, even illustrations. In that sense, the "public suspense" was anything but over.

This closing moment in the Cluverius case also highlights the dramatic difference between Euro-American and African American social dramas. The most sensational crime stories in the black community had no definitive, cathartic ending at all. Focused as they were on innocence rather than guilt, they ended with prisoners freed and with celebrations but not with culprits receiving their just punishment. The gallows had been cheated, but the villain—Virginia injustice—remained. In their endings, black and white crime sensations demonstrate still further the distance between the two communities on the issues of crime and justice.

Capital punishment is a meaningful issue in the history of the nation as a whole, but it is particularly important in the history of the South. The most violent region of the country by any measure and the one with the most executions as well as lynching victims, the American South followed the national trends in capital punishment only in a general sense. Virginia and the rest of the South retained officially mandated and sanctioned public executions much longer than the rest of the nation, and the transition to privacy in executions was gradual. Among other things, this meant that the gruesome era of lynchings overlapped in most southern states with the last generation of southerners to witness legally sanctioned public executions. The movement away from public executions, therefore, took place in an entirely different climate—racial as well as penal—than that of the North.

This context gives a distinctly southern slant to the debate over public execution. This study of executions in the era of lynching makes it clear that it is not merely that the South was later in prohibiting public executions; the South had, in fact, a very different experience with the issue.

■

THE GALLOWS PUBLIC AND PRIVATE

In the nineteenth century, capital punishment in Virginia changed in two distinct ways at the same time. On the one hand, the gallows moved from fields and open spaces filled with crowds to enclosed spaces. This was a surprisingly slow process, evolving over the course of several generations. On the other hand, the narratives and reports of executions grew dramatically in size and detail. The story of capital punishment in this era is largely the tension between these two themes—a growing desire on the part of some to civilize the process versus a continuing desire among others to see and read about the moment when life meets death, when a convict pays for his crime.

A glance at the history of capital punishment over the long term demonstrates the extent to which both of these themes evolved. Colonial hangings were public affairs, fully accepted as the norm and as appropriate. One Virginian who objected to capital punishment in 1789 wrote to a friend that that he felt "censured for singularity" by the majority for expressing his dislike of public hangings.[11]

The first shift in Virginia's handling of capital punishment—as with the rest of the nation—occurred in the wake of the Revolution and had nothing to do with either the privacy or the publicity of executions. Eighteenth-century British law, the basis for colonial justice, was heavily weighted toward capital and corporal punishments.[12] In the years after independence, each state revised its laws to provide more enlightened and measured punishments for misbehavior. In 1796, Virginia completely rewrote its criminal code, providing death as a penalty for only one offense: murder in the first degree.[13] Although in the years ahead treason and, in certain circumstances, arson would join murder as capital offenses, the trend in Virginia and the rest of the nation was striking—dozens of possible capital crimes were diminished during the 1790s to a spare few. Imprisonment in penitentiaries became the standard for a new, rational criminal justice system.

That said, Virginia and other slave states held onto less enlightened punishments for their slave populations. Imprisonment, of course, could be little punishment for a population not allowed liberties as a matter of course. The new standards of Virginia justice for its white population, then, stood alongside a code that provided for death (or, as often occurred, sale and transportation out of the state) for any slave convicted of a felony as well as for repeated smaller offenses. In addition, even free African Americans faced a slightly different criminal code in antebellum Virginia—death could be imposed for rape or for assaulting whites, not a possible penalty for white offenders.[14]

The first transformation of capital punishment in America was simply an enlightenment effort to curb the excess of its use, and in Virginia and the rest of the South that meant its use against white offenders. Executions remained spectacles performed in the open for several more generations, persisting well into the nineteenth century in the nation as a whole and past midcentury in the South. In 1845, capital punishment was legal in every state in the union, and in 1910 only five states (all northern) had banned the death penalty altogether. The earliest call for privacy in executions was in Pennsylvania in the 1820s, with that state and most of the northeast eliminating public hangings by 1840.[15] Virginia and the rest of the southern states were slower in moving toward privacy, a trend that embodies a differing perspective on the utility of public executions. Even so, a number of southern states, including Virginia, promoted private executions by the 1850s and 1860s, although they typically did not require them for another generation.

Reports of executions in the antebellum period regularly gave attendance estimates, which were, as a rule, in the thousands. Typical was the choice of a field outside the city or town in which the culprit was jailed, clearly a location designed to accommodate large crowds. The 1827 execution of three pirate murderers in Richmond occurred in an open valley—"like a spacious amphitheater" in the words of one newspaper writer—outside the penitentiary. In this instance, the theater of the event was amplified by a long march through the city toward the gallows site. The prisoners were placed upon their coffins in the back of a wagon and paraded under heavy guard through the length of the city from the jail on the eastern side to the penitentiary on the west. As many as seven thousand watched from the surrounding slopes as the condemned men prayed, the ministers spoke, and the penitent and confessed criminals fell to their doom.[16]

By 1850, the legislature and Virginia editors discussed and debated the issue of private versus public execution, but many Virginians continued to believe that the "instructive lessons" of public executions had "a beneficial

188   influence upon the moral feelings [of the community at large], and a re-

straining tendency in regard to the commission of crime."[17] This was the traditional view, held nationwide up to the last generation, and retained for another generation among most whites in the South.

As important as the fact that antebellum executions remained public, the stories of them in the press became increasingly elaborate in the nineteenth century. In Virginia, the sketchy early newspaper coverage served as the seed of later developments in the coverage of executions. Colonial-era papers paid just as scant attention to executions as they did to the crimes and trials that preceded them. Complete coverage of a double execution in 1752 Virginia, for instance, was merely: "George Kerr and Henry Southworth, condemned for murder at the General Court in October, were executed on Friday last."[18]

Press coverage of executions expanded greatly in the nineteenth century. On 1 June 1821, Manuel Garcia and Jose Castillano were executed in a field outside Norfolk for killing their compatriot Peter Lagoardette. Several thousand were reportedly in attendance, and every movement of the two before their deaths was detailed in the pamphlet on the case. This slender volume describes their ascent onto the gallows, the minister's brief oration, their "insensibility" to these wise words, and the drop of the trap door.[19] The *Richmond Enquirer* gave a similar but brief version of this scene, mentioning but not elaborating on each step of the process.[20]

Within the secular coverage given crime and executions in Virginia, religion, confession, and the state of the soul were important enough to mention but in passing rather than as the focus of published reports of the cases. Unlike those in the early Puritan New England tradition, the sermon from the gallows in the Garcia and Castillano case in no way served as the centerpiece of the pamphlet of this crime. It was, in fact, a mere paragraph at the end of a forty-page, trial-centered narrative and a fleeting mention in the newspapers.[21]

Executions were public in Virginia even on the eve of the Civil War, but this rowdy, public spectacle of hanging moderated over the course of several decades in the mid-nineteenth century. After 1855, Virginia began an awkward and gradual transition toward privacy in executions that would last for more than a generation. In that year, a Virginia statute directed that executions take place in the privacy of a jail yard if one was available but left to the judge's discretion the selection of an alternative site.[22] This was, in essence, a suggestion rather than a legal mandate. Indeed, in several cases in the late 1860s, Virginia judges specifically ordered public executions.[23]

When Jeter Phillips was executed in the Henrico County jail yard[24] on

22 July 1870, a crowd of thousands gathered, hoping to obtain entry for the event. The sergeant in charge of the site did not allow everyone inside the jail walls, but neither did he limit the number to the "twelve respectable citizens" the law suggested. No firm numbers exist, but all accounts describe a throng, one claiming it was dense enough that the jailer had to push Phillips through it. A much larger crowd gathered outside, pressing on the gates and hindering anyone with the signed tickets for admittance from coming in. On several occasions, the crowd verged on disorder as they attempted to press by the police; in fact, at one point, the *Dispatch* mentioned—as with the Cluverius case seventeen years later—that the police were called upon to use their clubs to keep the crowds back.[25] This hanging was certainly more private than if it had taken place in a field outside the city but not through any waning public interest in the spectacle.

Even more than with antebellum executions, the press coverage of the Jeter Phillips hanging was elaborate and detailed. Both the *Whig* and the *Dispatch* devoted most of their front pages to the story. A confession, written by Phillips and read by a minister, not only admitted his horrible deed; it also spoke of rumors that were false and complemented the lawyers, police, jurors, and governor for giving him the punishment he deserved.[26]

Surpassing antebellum narratives of the gallows, this moment of the fall of the trap door was described in minute detail. So were all of the particulars leading up to the event: the construction of the scaffold and the height of the drop, the prisoner's last night in jail and how he slept, the walk to the gallows, the tears on the sheriff's face as he read the order to execute Phillips, and the confessed murderer wracked with sobs as he embraced his minister. To the extent that the writers were able, they presented a vivid and detailed portrait of the moment when justice was served on a confessed, repentant murderer, even describing his body in its death throes:

> the drop fell and struck heavily against a sand bag placed on the side of the scaffold with that horrid noise peculiar to the gallows, and James Jeter Phillips was hanging in mid air. For five or ten seconds his body swayed to and fro, and there was no perceptible movement. Soon he commenced the most violent contortions. His legs were drawn up suddenly and were kicking through the air, and his arms were drawn up in a most violent manner. His right arm drew his left almost clear around his body; his right seemed in the attempt to get into his pocket, and his elbows rested high up in his back. These convulsions lasted for about three minutes, when they partially ceased. The muscular contortions

continued for about eight minutes, after which no movement was discerned, and the presumption was that Jeter Phillips was no more.[27]

Exhibiting the detailed and gruesome descriptions that reformers would specifically target in the coming years, the coverage of the Phillips hanging, like that of Cluverius seventeen years later, brought the spectacle to life as much as words could allow.[28] In this way, the Phillips execution was very public indeed. Fewer spectators were able to see the event itself, though not for want of trying. But with newspapers gearing their fare increasingly to a mass audience, their extensive coverage of the hanging brought the event to the attention of a broad range of the population.

If the scaffold was the harrowing instrument of capital punishment in the era of legal public executions, it was also a stage, with its actors raised above the surrounding spectators. Ministers took the opportunity to pray and even preach to the crowd, and Jeter Phillips's confession was not merely reported by the papers the next day; it was performed before the assembled audience. The presence of a crowd, the unavoidable fact of an audience to the proceedings, colored and framed the event, making it dramatic in a literal as well as a figurative sense. Reports of other nineteenth-century executions offer evidence of a panoply of theatrical behaviors—from grandstanding oratory on the part of the condemned or his minister to a sort of participatory response from the crowds (wishing the doomed man well or upbraiding him)—which could be found in the mixed-class audiences of the theaters of the day. Often the reports of hangings mention the amount of time spent on speeches, which could be considerable. A central part of the experience of public execution in the mid-nineteenth century, something that carried over into the pseudo-private execution of Jeter Phillips, was this communication between the scaffold and the assembled crowds.[29]

The Phillips execution demonstrated the combined influence of changing statutes and continued public fascination. As many spectators entered the jail yards as the sergeant allowed, and many more congregated outside the walls. Given the peculiar opportunities presented by the Shockoe valley jail yard, the 1885 Cluverius hanging was witnessed by perhaps as many as the antebellum executions, proving the persistence of fascination with these moments. But they did so in the face of the new rules to restrict just such spectatorship.

Mandated by the government, the experience of capital punishment was changing in the late nineteenth century. Laws barred crowds and photographers from the execution sites, which after 1879 were *required* to be walled enclosures, preferably jail yards.[30] The fine imposed on Sergeant Smith in the Cluverius execution underscores the commonwealth's attempt to alter the tradition of capital punishment as spectacle.

Privacy laws gradually eliminated the crowds in attendance, but executions continued to receive more and more ink in the press, and not only local executions like the hangings of Phillips and Cluverius. The *Richmond Dispatch* devoted nearly its entire front page to the 1890 death of William Kimmler in New York, the first electrocution in the nation. It discussed the crime, the chair, the New York law, and a history of previous modes of capital punishment. This issue even included an engraving representing the prisoner in the chair. This amounted to a veritable spectacle of death itself, despite the fact that the crime and execution were hundreds of miles away in another state.[31] The general growth in print media and sensationalism in the period clearly included an expanded coverage of executions.

If public executions were illegal in Virginia after 1879, it is nevertheless impossible to state precisely when the last one took place. This difficulty is due to the fact that until 1908 every county in the state had control of executions within their jurisdiction, and official practice was erratic before that date. If a county did not already have a suitable jail yard, it would be both expensive and perhaps unpopular to erect a temporary enclosure, and apparently many localities decided to ignore this law. One hanging in 1883 took place on a scaffold a hundred feet from the jailhouse (not in a yard) and was witnessed by a "vast number of spectators." Another that same year occurred inside the Henrico County jail yard, but in front of "hundreds of people."[32] Clearly these were public executions in direct violation of the law, but the newspapers treated the occurrence as commonplace, hardly worth mentioning. But other execution reports in the 1880s clearly state that they were private according to the law's definition, with only witnesses, attendants, and reporters present.[33] In this way, the experience of the Phillips and Cluverius executions accurately represents how uneven was the introduction of privacy in Virginia.

■

THE CHAIR

If the nineteenth century witnessed a slow and uneven movement toward reform in capital punishment, the early twentieth century saw the fulfillment of reformers' hopes in Virginia. When Samuel McCue was hanged in Charlottesville for the 1905 murder of his wife, the authorities not only built the gallows inside the jail yard, they added a wooden barrier to the top of the jail walls to prevent a view from the windows of adjacent buildings. In addition, the local authorities tricked the public, who believed the execution to be at the traditional time of midday, by executing McCue early in the morning before any crowds had gathered.

The interest in the execution had not abated—hundreds had applied to enter the jail yard, and thousands were expected to arrive there later in the morning. What had changed over the course of the nineteenth century was the state's belief in the efficacy of publicity regarding executions. In 1827, the *Richmond Enquirer* applauded the effort of all involved in a public execution of three murderers, finding "much to commend and nothing to censure" in the "imposing" and "melancholy" (not to mention *public*) scene.[34] This despite two of the three ropes breaking at the first attempt. But after the 1905 McCue hanging, private though it was, the *Richmond Times-Dispatch* called for still more reforms—the abolition of all local hangings in favor of executions at the state penitentiary in Richmond. Citing the stress and strain on local communities, the effect on the young, and the awakening of a "morbid and unhealthy interest" in spectacles of death, the newspaper advised the centralization of the state's capital punishment in its fortress of law enforcement on Spring Street in Richmond.[35]

Within three years of the hanging of McCue, a new statute satisfied this call, mandating that all executions in the state take place at the penitentiary. Before this time, city or county sheriffs administered capital punishment, making executions an unprofessional undertaking. Starting with New England states in the 1860s, states began to centralize the instruments of capital punishment in their state penitentiaries. In true Progressive Era form, most states centralized and professionalized capital punishment between 1890 and 1915; Virginia was squarely in the midst of this change.

Virginia similarly followed the trends in the nation regarding its method of execution. Virginia became the fifth state to adopt electrocution, considered instantaneous and therefore more humane than hanging. Beginning on 13 October 1908 and continuing to 1995, Virginia executed all of its death row inmates by electrocution in the state penitentiary.[36]

If Virginia's actions were squarely within the national norms, its debate over the issue was not. Both proponents and opponents of this bill to centralize executions argued in terms of humanitarianism, efficiency, and professionalism but also in terms of race—another clear indication of how important was the racial divide in any discussion of crime in the South. Some legislators argued that local hangings were a "time honored custom" and that Virginia would be out of step with the rest of the South if it adopted this centralized plan for electrocution. What was the benefit of this custom? Among them: "Local hangings served to impress the negroes, and in this way to prevent more of the 'unmentionable crimes.'"[37]

Others obviously disagreed, and the legislation passed in 1908. But the argument of the proponents likewise leaned on racial logic. Counties would be spared the expense and anxiety of confining and executing convicts, argued some, and "the minds of the young and sensitive are spared the horrible impressions which is necessarily produced by more or less public executions in small places." But they also raised an argument about the effects of private electrocution's "swift, quiet, and mysterious" nature:

> With the negro, who constitutes so large a proportion of the criminal population of all Southern States, this argument is undeniably important. The *Times Dispatch* has long contended that the publicity, the excitement and the general hurrah-and-holiday air attending the old-time hanging were a positive allurement to the negro. His strong theatrical sense reveled in the final melodrama in which he was the conspicuous central figure. The electric execution wholly does away with that. The time set for turning on the death current is unannounced, the public is rigorously eluded, and the whole affair is conducted with secrecy and mystery, well calculated to inspire terror in the heart of the superstitious African.[38]

Just so was progressivism in the South a marriage of humanitarian reform, professionalism, and overt racism. The entire field of crime and punishment in the South was overburdened with concerns of race.

The 1908 law made executions more private than ever before and in more than one way. Not only would criminals meet their end in a single, centralized location, but it would occur in the bowels of the building, hidden away. In place of a raised platform before an audience, electrocution took place in a buried, enclosed room, insulating the process from any public interest. Further, the legislation prohibited the publication of details of the electrocutions, although no penalties were stipulated for violation. For the first time, this law attempted to curb more than the number of spectators themselves, regulating even the circulation of information about the execution.[39]

Commensurate with this new secrecy, comparatively little remained of the spectacular in the coverage of Henry Clay Beattie's execution. On 24 November 1911, Beattie died in the death chamber of the state penitentiary in Richmond before twelve witnesses and a handful of guards and attendants. Conspicuous in their absence in the room were members of the press.

No crowd gathered in the rain outside the penitentiary that day except for twenty-five expectant but disappointed reporters.

Compared to the theater of antebellum gallows, twentieth-century executions were circumscribed in every way. Both McCue and Beattie confessed but without anything of the theater of confession from the stage of the gallows.[40] In addition, no photographs or images—which had been so pervasive during the rest of the Beattie case—appeared in regard to his last moments, much less in regard to the execution itself. In fact, some evidence points to a comparative shortage of information altogether about the execution. The *Richmond Evening Journal*, for instance, wrote that he went to the electric chair "bravely or at least with an outward show of fortitude so far as can be ascertained." Later they wrote that the execution was not unusual, "aside from the absurd secrecy which marked everything in connection with it."[41]

Even so, the narratives and reports of this execution remained quite multivalent. Richmond newspapers showed only mild reticence to print whatever they could discover about the process as well as to evoke the grisly event by other means. With good reason, perhaps, for despite the official desire to keep the execution private, the public very much wanted to be party to it. Thousands reportedly wrote to the penitentiary superintendent to ask for admittance to the Beattie electrocution.[42] Both the *Times-Dispatch* and the *Evening Journal* printed brief outlines of the process: when the witnesses entered the chamber, how long before the current was turned on, when he was declared dead, and that nothing unusual occurred in this case. In addition, the *Times-Dispatch* reported that "there was, of course, no way to prevent those who witnessed the execution as witnesses from relating the details of the gruesome scene, and information was easy of access throughout the day from this source." While the *Times-Dispatch* refrained from printing these easily accessible stories of the execution, it said that other papers were openly violating the law. Its editors expected the general assembly to revise the statute to provide for penalties against newspapers violating the ban on publishing particulars of electrocutions.[43] Indeed, the *Washington Post* printed a version of the electrocution in great detail, listing the witnesses present, the final moments in the death chamber, Beattie's continued calmness, and the application of the current three separate times.[44]

Other Richmond papers found ways around the regulations without expressly describing Beattie's death. The *Evening Journal*, for instance, reprinted portions of a report by Charles V. Carrington, surgeon of the

Virginia Penitentiary, on the effectiveness of the previous electrocutions in the state, each of which he witnessed. First, Carrington wrote, witnesses assembled around an "innocent-looking" oak chair on a rubber mat. The prisoner received a prayer, followed by the recitation of the order for execution. Then he was led to the chair and in approximately sixty seconds was readied for the procedure. Straps and buckles confined the prisoner, and attendants attached electrodes to his head and right leg. The current was then switched on for sixty seconds and varied in intensity over that time, starting at maximum (2200 volts) and returning to that position twice more during the course of the minute of electrocution. Carrington continued by describing the effects on the prisoner's body:

> After the current has been cut off, the heart action for a few seconds is tumultuous, churning violently. This most quickly slows off, and in a few more seconds the subject is pronounced dead. He died from shock, paralysis of the respiratory centers and of the heart.
>
> There have been post-mortem findings in which the right side of the heart has been ruptured, owing to the violent contractions of the heart muscle, but under our State law, the surgeon is not permitted to perform any post-mortem.
>
> The temperature of the body is enormously elevated after electrocution, sometimes reading 115 degrees. Rigor mortis sets in unusually early.
>
> You can see from the above account what a swift performance an electrocution is, and I can assure you that it is one of the most solemn, awe-inspiring acts any one can take part in. I have witnessed thirty odd during two years, and the last one was just as fearful in its solemnity as the first one. I hope and believe that the solemn judicial inflicting of the death penalty by electrocution in place of the more or less spectacular hanging, will have a powerful deterrent effect on the criminal classes.[45]

Although this excerpt is itself sensational, the proponents of electrocution, Charles Carrington among them, consistently described the process as "solemn," "awe-inspiring," and yielding "nothing of the spectacular."[46]

In this era of industrial revolution, Americans had not merely a faith in technological progress, but an awe for the majesty of man's accomplishments in bending the forces of nature to human purposes. Steel-girded skyscrapers were rising to the heavens, motion pictures were showing scenes from far away, the Wright brothers had recently taken flight, and Thomas Edison had captured lightning itself in what might be the archetype of the technological sublime: the electric dynamo. Electricity was bringing light itself unto the darkness, and to many it seemed as if the potential benefits of electricity to civilization could hardly be measured. Amazed by the splash of lights at world's fairs and exhibitions, Americans were ready to believe that electricity could work miracles. What could be better than eliminating the pain, suffering, and spectacle of capital punishment by the application of an instantaneous charge of galvanic force?[47]

If this was the standard frame given the process in 1911, it was not created seamlessly. The first criminal executed by electricity was William Kimmler in New York in 1890. That execution was described as "bungling" and "brutal," reminding witnesses of the Inquisition, and making them physically ill.[48] The *Richmond Dispatch* editors were so shaken by these reports that they doubted that another electrocution would ever be allowed. The execution of Kimmler spurred an investigation in New York, not to mention an ongoing debate in national and local periodicals over the use of electricity in capital punishment. This sort of response to the process gives a different, ironic rationale for the privacy mandated in Virginia electrocutions: not merely to preserve the solemnity of the act, but also because of the horrifying spectacle of this putatively more civilized punishment.

Over the years after Kimmler, the horror of the electric chair subsided as later attempts were more successful. Death by electrocution was certainly faster than by hanging, the chief justification for its claim to be more humane. An electric shock, boosters argued, would work so fast that "the brain has absolutely no time to appreciate a sense of pain."[49] But any descriptions of the effects of electrocution were at least as chilling as the scene at the gallows. Of course, the Richmond papers in 1911 were perfectly capable of dissembling in an effort to have it both ways: the *Journal* for instance, printed Carrington's sensational and horrifying description at the same time repeating how solemn and respectable it was.[50]

Despite the gruesome nature of electrocution, this progression in the administration of punishment fits neatly into the "civilizing process" investigated by a number of twentieth-century historians and social thinkers.[51] Punishment moved from public to private, from corporal to institutional. In capital punishment, this meant a move from carnivals of death to more restrained semipublic hangings to completely hidden electrocution. The study of the civilizing process provides meaningful insights into powerful individuals and institutions—the plans, goals, and rhetoric of the middle and upper classes and reformers—and their effects on society.

One consequence of this change was the loss of the theater of spectacle at the gallows. Cluverius said to Dr. Hatcher that he wanted "to avoid everything sensational at my execution," meaning that he wanted to avoid this theater, the drama of sermons, audience, confession, oratory, and performance.[52] Neither McCue nor Beattie was faced with this question of how to avoid or satisfy the public desire for sensation, for executions were different events in the early twentieth century than they had been even a generation before.

Of all the changes in criminal justice in this period, the shift from public executions to private electrocutions was the most obvious: written into the law, creating an entirely different sort of event in the antebellum period and the Progressive Era. The gradual evolution of laws and practices from the mid-nineteenth to the early twentieth century demonstrates the civilizing of society that so many scholars have explored.

Laws and practices were civilized, perhaps, but there was no related civilizing process in the era's cultural history.[53] Instead of moving toward civility, orderliness, and decorum, stories of executions in the press moved in the opposite direction. Unlike state government attempts to mold society into a more civilized shape, the mass media were much more inclined to give the public what they wanted. Throughout the nineteenth century, the stories of capital punishment became ever more elaborate, detailed, thorough, and gruesome. From brief notices in the colonial era, execution coverage grew to several columns in the antebellum period. By the late nineteenth century—the very moment when Virginia and the rest of the South attempted to remove executions from public view—newspapers gave hangings front-page coverage, complete with descriptions of the body's writhing last moments. The minutiae of the crimes were narrated over and again, the blows, angles of fire, graphic details of all sorts sifted and discussed. The crowds still came in 1870, 1887, and 1905, and the state had to use clubs and tricks to keep them away. The public had to be "rigorously eluded," to employ the phrase of a contemporary editor.[54] In 1911, thousands wanted to join the few allowed to descend with Beattie to the death chamber.

The laws were tightening on public shows of state violence, but that is only one of a variety of responses modern society made to acts of violence. Squeezing out around every obstacle that officials erected around capital punishment in the late nineteenth century was a wealth of graphic material on executions printed in the press. This amounted to a sort of macabre dance between popular culture and the law. The gradual steps toward privacy created a growing demand for the particulars printed in the press. In turn, the growing coverage in the mass media provoked the distaste of some reformers, inspiring them to use their influence to tighten the laws excluding the public from the site of execution. This process of negotiation between the public and the authorities demonstrates the various pushes and pulls that culminated in a difficult and extended transition from public to private *and* from brief reports of executions to virtual carnivals of death in print.

Even after this avenue of sensationalism was curbed in 1908, the cultural exploration of murder cases in general remained flush with carnal and prurient material. This cultural treatment was not merely an effort to illuminate social problems, and it was not a part of any civilizing process. Instead it was a wallow in minutiae on crime and violence. And this sort of material was not diminishing in the face of a civilizing society; it was growing. Quickly. If the middle and upper classes were succeeding in using the tools of the state to make criminal punishment more civilized, private, and solemn, they were, at the same moment, also failing utterly to similarly mold American culture.

In the South, this tug-of-war between civility and carnivals of death occurred in a particularly halting and conflicted manner. The desire for enlightened laws for whites was shackled to a much more violent and corporal vision of justice for Virginia's African American population. Why was the state and the wider region in step with the nation's changes in capital punishment in general but so out of step with the national norm regarding the prohibition of public execution? Because southern white lawmakers viewed the law as an instrument of conditioning the black population as well as an instrument of justice. The South's racial ideology had a strong impact on its criminal codes; after all, "the negro recognizes nothing but force." From such a perspective, African Americans' supposed fear of the gallows or, alternately, of the mysterious action of the electric chair, seemed to many whites as important as any niceties of reform or civility. For both sides of the discussion in Virginia, race was bound up with the issue of capital punishment.

■

EXECUTIONS AND LYNCHING

Both the persistence of public executions and the prevalence of lynching describe a southern white culture more comfortable than the rest of the nation with public displays of vengeance. Lynching scholars traditionally mark the 1890s as the high point for lynching, citing statistics that decline over the next thirty years.[55] But several recent state studies demonstrate that Reconstruction included still more lynching, relegating the 1890s to a momentary rise amidst the overall decline of lynching.[56] Whichever view prevails, it is important to note that these are precisely the decades in which southern state legislatures sequestered legal executions away from the interested public. Of the fourteen states most prone to lynching (those in the former Confederacy plus Kentucky, Missouri, and Oklahoma), eleven enacted legislation against public executions between 1879 and the early 1890s. Two of the remaining three states already had legislation, but these laws merely promoted rather than required privacy in executions.[57] In other words, virtually the entire South had state-sanctioned public executions as living memory in the 1890s and as contemporary events in the 1860s and 1870s.[58] The correlation is even more stark when looking at the three states with the most lynchings: Mississippi, Georgia, and Texas. Together these deep South states accounted for 40 percent of all southern lynchings; they are also among the last to strictly prohibit public executions.[59]

This correlation between lynching and public executions is particularly illuminating in terms of the sensationalism that could surround lynching: the sometimes crowded and even celebratory nature of lynching spectacles.[60] To the modern eye, the festive atmosphere conveyed by some lynching reports and images seems nearly inexplicable, a special variety of evil. Not only did whites practice a horrible wrong on the black population, but at times they exulted in doing so. The historical context of state-sanctioned public hangings gives insight into this particular aspect of these horrors: how southern white society could confront the spectacle of hanging in a mood of complaisance, acceptance, and even celebration. Such support was precisely what the state had asked of them just a few years before.

Far from a horror, southern states were actively telling their populations that it was a positive good to watch miscreants die by the rope in this era of lynching. This message was living memory in the 1890s and 1900s and was the commonsense for the entire South in 1870. Perhaps more important, this philosophy was clearly more engrained in the wider populace than in the state, which had to deploy not just jailhouse walls, but also trickery and policemen's clubs to keep hundreds or thousands of potential spectators away from executions.

At the very least, lynch mobs inherited a past from the common public memory of the theater of the gallows. Lynching and public, state-sponsored executions shared an assumption—held by the nation earlier in the century and by the region in the mid-nineteenth century—that viewing a vengeance spectacle could benefit society. Both attracted crowds to witness the death of a supposed miscreant, who in both cases were disproportionately African American. Both could include theatrical elements, including speeches, sermons, and call and response from the audience. Both might be followed by a desire, at least, to obtain a grisly memento from the event—a piece of the rope that hanged Cluverius perhaps or a photograph or even a knuckle of Sam Hose. Supporters of each would claim the event was a festival enforcing law and order, strengthening the community and policing the outer boundaries of decency. Detractors of each would claim that it was a festival of gore and disorder or even a crime in itself.[61] And, crucially, both occurred in the South concurrently. Just seven years before the gruesome and highly publicized lynching of Sam Hose, for instance, a Georgia resident might have witnessed the public hanging of a convicted criminal—sanctioned as an orderly practice of the state's power of capital punishment.[62]

In fact, evidence suggests that officially sanctioned capital punishment of blacks in the South was "even more" public than it was for whites. Philip Schwarz found a number of cases from early Virginia history in which black slaves were not only executed publicly and in gruesome ways, but portions of their bodies were left on display as a warning to others.[63] Throughout the slavery era, state laws allowed more physical punishments and included several more capital crimes for African Americans than did the criminal codes regulating white society. After the Civil War, Virginia retained the whipping post for petty crime, a punishment used chiefly as a humiliating public penalty for black thieves.[64] One of the last official public executions on record in Virginia was of a black man in Richmond, Albert Tyler in 1869, the judge in the case apparently wanting his execution to be a warning to the black community.[65] In this as in other instances, the white press emphasized the color of the crowd; whites commonly assumed that African Americans were particularly drawn to the terrible display and theater of the gallows.[66] How differently did whites in the South view execution for blacks? Some states that had previously privatized executions *reintroduced* public executions for rape in the early twentieth century, apparently as a response to a perceived racial threat.[67]

In fact, blacks were overrepresented in Virginia's capital cases just as they were overrepresented in lynching statistics. Virginia executed one hundred criminals between 1908 and 1920. Of that number 87 percent were African Americans, despite the fact that they made up less than 40 percent of the state's population. It is a commonplace to emphasize that lynching victims were African American (in fact, precisely 87.7 percent of lynching victims between 1882 and 1930 were African American). Just as lynching victims were almost always black, Virginia's executed convicts in the early twentieth century also were almost always black. This further blurs the distinction between extralegal lynchings and the legal but prejudicial system of jurisprudence in the era of Jim Crow.[68]

In this era, many whites came to the same conclusion as the Richmond editor who wrote that "the negro recognizes nothing but force. He is but a child in this respect, or worse—a beast. He has no reason, so sense of right, no knowledge of law, or anything else, in sufficient quantity to guide and restrain him."[69] From this fundamentally prejudiced perspective, couched in an era when public hangings were the accepted and state-sanctioned norm, lynching appears no less horrifying, but neither was it without a chilling historical precedent.

■

CHEATING THE GALLOWS

The stories of white sensations ended with the scene at the gallows; many African American crimes culminated in this same scene, although hanging a black man was seldom considered a sensation. Virginia executed black criminals with a frequency that made the gallows a commonplace. Further, the most interesting and important cases in the black community were stories of black innocence, where the defendants, with the help of the community, successfully cheated the gallows and Virginia's prejudicial legal apparatus. Instead of a festival of death, these African American narratives of justice ended with a celebration of life. In their manner of endings, white and black social dramas of violence and crime again emphasize dramatic differences.

The celebrated Lunenburg murder case included the execution of Solomon Marable, the man who accused and then recanted his incrimination of Mary Abernathy and Pokey Barnes. The *Richmond Planet* covered the hanging as it did everything else in the Lunenburg case, in vivid detail and with images. Four consecutive issues of the *Planet* headlined the execution on the front page, complete with a narrative of his last night, his refusal to speak to a Catholic priest, his dying declaration that David Thompson, a white man, was the murderer, the series of events leading up to his fall from the gallows, and the conflict over what would happen to the dead man's body.[70] These prominent stories also included several halftone photographs taken of Marable earlier in jail and a series of engravings, drawn by editor Mitchell himself, of the hanging and the disposition of the body in the dissecting room at the Medical College of Virginia. Mitchell even published a halftone image of Marable's prostrate body taken moments after the execution, easily the most gruesome halftone printed in Richmond in this era.

This coverage of the Marable execution was comparable to the Thomas Cluverius coverage a decade before—thorough, sensational, and rich with

detail. In illustrations, the Marable coverage was actually much more elaborate than that of Cluverius, including six halftones and eleven engravings in
these four issues. This provides further evidence of the rapidity of the visual
changes in newspapers at this historical moment. The tone of the *Planet*'s
coverage was ambiguous: the hanging was called a tragedy, particularly in
light of Marable's wife and children, but none of the stories framed him as
innocent or the hanging as unjust. Central to the coverage was Marable's
accusation that David Thompson was the killer. For the *Planet*, Marable
committed a crime by assisting the murderer, but the worse offense was
that the real, white culprit was allowed to go free.

The extensive coverage of the Marable hanging was exceptional but not
unique. In 1912, a young black woman, Virginia Christian, was accused of
stealing jewelry. In an argument over this charge, Christian suffocated her
accuser, a white woman named Ida Belote. She was tried, convicted of first-
degree murder, and sentenced to death. Christian confessed to the crime
but claimed it was not premeditated but rather the accidental effect of the
fight between the two women. That would be manslaughter or second-
degree murder rather than a capital offense. Women were rarely executed
in Virginia, and her electrocution received a good deal of press from Richmond's white papers, the *Planet*, and other African American papers across
the nation.[71]

The Marable and Christian executions became prominent stories in the
black community because each was invested with a sense that an injustice
was being done. In general, however, the execution of African Americans in
Virginia did not create such a splash in the press, white or black. Virtually
every Virginia hanging, legal or extralegal and whatever the race, received
print in Richmond's white papers but briefly: a half or full column of a
single issue describing in succinct terms the scene, the crowd, the fall, and
confession if there was one.[72] The *Richmond Planet* printed nothing on
the vast majority of blacks hanged in the commonwealth. If they deserved
conviction for first-degree murder, the *Planet* chose not to focus on their
misdeeds or their penalty. An execution became more relevant to the paper
if there were cause to object: if the prisoner appeared innocent or deserved a
lesser penalty or if the crowds or courts mistreated him or her. For instance,
editor Mitchell believed Virginia Christian deserved clemency from the
governor due to the fact that she was a woman and there appeared to be
mitigating circumstances. Doc Bacon, another convicted murderer in 1903,
was widely thought to be innocent, and therefore his hanging received
notice by the *Planet*.[73] Otherwise, Richmond's black newspaper rarely even
mentioned executions of black criminals.

The greatest sensations of crime and justice for the black community did not end with the gallows at all. In this nadir of African American history, innocent African American freed from prison were the noteworthy events deserving of sensational coverage. Such narratives of black innocence culminated not in a cathartic moment of vengeance at the end of a rope; instead they ended in congratulations sounded from the pulpit of a church.

In May of 1896, Pokey Barnes suddenly found herself a free woman after almost a year facing a capital charge in the Lunenburg murder case. Within a month, editor Mitchell published "Pokey's Own Story," a tale of her life and her imprisonment that filled more than a quarter of the *Planet*'s pages. When the state finally freed Mary Abernathy in September of that year, she was brought directly to Richmond on the train and was regularly in the company of editor Mitchell. Both Barnes and Abernathy were interviewed, posed for photographs, and received many "ovations" from Richmonders. In October, the two traveled to several churches in Richmond, Petersburg, and elsewhere, telling their story and thanking the black community for the support that saved their lives. During these celebrations, Abernathy described "with feeling" "the arrest, the forced march of twenty-five miles dodging from the lynchers," while Barnes's "statement about gazing at her own grave aroused the audience to a great pitch of excitement."[74] These testimonials were set in a wider context of communal activity: others performed musical pieces, and several ministers, not to mention John Mitchell himself, would expound on the occasion.

This sort of communal celebration of justice fit into the cultural norms of the black community. Any hero of the race might receive such honors in the halls of African American churches at this time. Isaac Jenkins, who lived to tell of being (almost) lynched in 1893, similarly toured Richmond's black churches telling his story, showing his wounds, and asking for financial help.[75] A northern black man who broke the rules for segregated seating at a local theater during the 1886 national Knights of Labor convention in Richmond was likewise honored by the local community.[76]

In the twentieth century, however, stories of black innocence became more rare, as the *Planet* and the black middle class turned from their forceful stand against injustice toward a focus on self-sufficiency. In 1914, when a white jury acquitted John Clements of attacking a young white woman, editor Mitchell applauded the victory in an even tone. The *Planet* made no mention of any celebration, speeches, or fund-raising. Again the emotional response of the 1890s had faded to a more distanced observation by the 1910s. Clements was free, the black community was glad, but they were no longer on a crusade.[77]

Black Richmond, like its white counterpart, might revel in the gruesome and sensational aspects of the scene at the gallows. But the more sensational stories in the African American community, where innocence faced the test of a prejudiced judicial system and won, ended on an entirely different note. In a sense, these stories had no clear ending at all. The real culprit, Virginia injustice, was never vanquished; it was only cheated, this time, of its prey.

EPILOGUE

MASS CULTURE'S SEARCH FOR DISORDER

THE LAW HAS BEEN SATISFIED. CLUVERIUS HAS
PAID ITS FULL PENALTY, BUT IT IS FERVENTLY HOPED
THAT NEVER AGAIN IN RICHMOND WILL ANY MAN BE
CONVICTED IN OBEDIENCE TO PUBLIC CLAMOR, OR ONE
EXECUTED AGAINST WHOM THE DEATH SENTENCE
HAD VIRTUALLY BEEN PRONOUNCED BEFORE A
JURYMAN TOOK HIS SEAT IN THE JURY BOX.

Richmond Daily Times, 15 January 1887

After the discovery of Lillian Madison's body in the Richmond reservoir in March of 1885, thousands came to look at the yet-unidentified corpse as it lay in the nearby almshouse. A few days later, she was laid to rest in Oakwood cemetery, her unmarked grave strewn with flowers and an occasional poem, which local newspapers obligingly reprinted. After his execution, the body of Thomas Cluverius was returned to his family, who sent it by train to King and Queen County to be buried in a family plot. Again, the site was unmarked, in this case because the family did not want the morbid and curious to disturb the grave.[1]

Nineteenth-century American society was fascinated with criminals: their acts but also their bodies, their expressions, gait, manner, visage, and images of them appearing in print. This interest in the physiognomy of the criminal continued after the executions, both in the popular mind and in scientific circles. Criminal executions provided one of the few sources of bodies for scientific and medical research. In 1827, the corpses of three pirate-murderers executed outside Richmond's penitentiary walls were exhumed and electrically stimulated to test whether bodies could be revived by "galvanism."[2] Likewise, the body of Charles Guiteau, the assassin of President James Garfield in 1881, was retained by military authorities, who kept his skeleton at an army museum.[3] The body of Solomon Marable, executed for the 1895 Lunenburg murder case, was delivered to the Medical College of Virginia before editor John Mitchell could muster enough influence to convince authorities to ship him back to his relatives in North Carolina for burial. Other corpses were simply snatched from the grave by relic seekers or medical schools in search of bodies for their studies. Helen Jewett, murdered in New York City in 1836, was buried, but local medical students quickly dug her up again. It is said that her "elegant" skeleton could be found displayed in the College of Physicians and Surgeons in New York.[4]

This scientific interest is not surprising in the era of phrenology and physiognomy, particularly given the scientific and medical opportunities presented by the acquisition of any human body. But the wider public interest in observing the dead bodies and the experiments performed on them is more macabre. Related to the interest in souvenirs from lynchings—including ears, fingers, toes, and clothing along with pieces of the rope—this public fascination with corpses never received official sanction. The public was barred from viewing the articulated skeleton of Guiteau assembled at the Army Medical Museum, and "great care was taken to see that none of 208 the bones were carried off by relic-seekers."[5] The hood masking Thomas

Cluverius's face was kept in place when he was lowered from the gallows and not removed for the crowd to see his corpse, as some apparently hoped. Also anticipated by some was a public viewing of his dissection, an event they believed, wrongly, to be mandated by law.[6] In the following days, a judged barred a local man from displaying—to paying customers—the lovely silken rope from the Cluverius execution; he was likewise prevented from selling pieces of it as souvenirs. Similarly, the remaining belongings left in Cluverius's jail cell went not to interested observers, but to his family. The Richmond police received daily requests for any available "relics," particularly leaves from the geranium that he cultivated while in jail.[7]

At the turn of the century, laws promoting the privacy of executions likewise left no room for public interest in corpses. The Beattie family interred Henry's body in Maury cemetery, near their home, before sunrise the second day after his execution. No one but the assistants and witnesses saw his body on the day of execution, and no one but morticians and the family saw it afterward. Oddly, he is buried next to his wife-victim, Louise, and the couple share a common ornate headstone with the words "Beyond the River."[8] The police estimated that 15,000 curious and silent spectators visited the cemetery later on the day he was buried, a number larger than the total population of south Richmond and enough to create a Sunday afternoon traffic jam and to necessitate extra cars on the trolley line into the neighborhood. Police officers patrolled the grave site around the clock for a number of days. The public showed its continued interest, but just as the execution itself had been private, so was this epilogue to the murder.[9]

The bodies were laid to rest, but the stories of these murders were not. With each sensation, Richmonders tried to come to closure, to find a moral to the story, a final solution to solve the disturbing crimes. Editor Mitchell could be firm in his conclusions at the end of each sensation of black innocence: crime occurs regardless of race, blacks were treated unfairly in Virginia courts, and the true villain in African American sensations was the system of justice itself, this time cheated of its prey. In that way, stories of sensational crime in the black community ended definitively but with little reassurance for the future.

In the wake of each execution in Richmond's postbellum white sensations, newspapers and most bystanders were similarly forceful in their conclusions: murder was brutal, murderers should be punished with death, and Virginia's judicial system successfully did its job. This conclusion grew stronger over the years. The many delays in Jeter Phillips's 1867 case did not yield itself to much self-congratulation, but the efficiency of the Virginia judiciary became a central element of the closing moments of later cases. Before the Civil War, sensations lacked these reflective epilogues altogether.

Both the Beattie and Cluverius cases ended with long stories titled "What the Editors Say" or "Response from the National Press" or "Virginia Justice," excerpting paragraphs like the following from the national press: "In the Beattie case, Virginia has set an example in the process of the law which would well be followed by other states of the South. Under ordinary circumstances, a wealthy defendant accused by circumstantial evidence would have secured the advantage of delays and technicalities. But the Virginia court showed that it was made of better stuff."[10] Often the papers specifically praised the judge, lawyers, detectives, police force, and/or the public as well.[11] Even John Mitchell in the *Richmond Planet* praised the action of the governor and the courts for their work to "check crime" in the Beattie case, adding that it proved that "crime is not confined to any one race or to the ignorant and the vicious."[12]

If such successful resolutions to cases were truly commonplace, they would not foment so much congratulation. Often, reflections on such good work were phrased overtly in terms of the incompetence of the past. The editor of the *Religious Herald* wrote in 1911: "In sheer diabolism the murder [by Henry Beattie] lacked nothing. Of provocation to the deed or of mitigating circumstances, the evidence disclosed absolutely nothing. Yet profound and widespread astonishment is expressed—mixed with admiration—at the steady march of justice in such a case!"[13] "Recent decisions" have been dealt with well, continued the editor, clearly indicating the continuing perception of a questionable past for Virginia's courts.

Part of what gave these sensational trials such power was their ambiguity, their many-sidedness. But in the wake of the execution, few wanted to probe any loose ends or dwell on the ambiguity that made the cases so rich. Charles Wallace, the Richmond merchant who had seemed so merciful and considerate of Cluverius during his trial (writing often of his pity for the man and his hope that he was innocent), became vitriolic in his diary at the time of Cluverius's execution:

> The man died as he lived a consummate hypocrite and liar. His whole life was a lie. His last act or one of his last acts was to write a book of lies and thus to make money for his Aunt by a sale of his infamy. No more awful scoundrel can [have] lived than Cluverius. He seemed to be what he was not, a Christian and gentleman. It is this seeming like the gold plate upon coin that passes with the ignorant world for genuine

metal. So you seem to be, so you seem to pray, so you seem to abstain from vicious excess. So you hide from curious eyes your manifold sins. You will pass masked into the church and into society as an exemplary Christian and citizen.

He had the head of a fiend and the smile of an angel. He was eaten up with lust. . . . He was so brutal and so cruel as to embrace the unsuspecting Lillian thrice . . . the day he killed her at the reservoir. If he did not kill her at the reservoir he knows who did kill her there, and he is the only person . . . who could possibly have a wicked motive for having her killed. [C]ircumstances sometimes lie, or rather we misinterpret the truth. But the direct and indirect evidence of Cluverius' guilt is so strong as to be little short of certainty.[14]

So, too, did newspapers emphasize the assurance of guilt, the effectiveness of the police, the speed of the trial, and the justice of the punishment. In hindsight, however, all of this assurance underscores their continuing anxiety, their longing for answers.

With the bodies buried and the stories fading from the community's attention, each of these cases became a part of the historical record. And like the body snatchers before them, many have proven eager to dig up the body of evidence under consideration in this study. First, observers famous enough to write memoirs mentioned the cases they were involved in. Lawyer Henry Robinson Pollard and journalist Herbert T. Ezekiel each recorded important moments from their lives, including the Cluverius case, since it was, in Pollard's words, "the most notable of all the criminal cases in which I took part."[15] In addition, Cluverius's minister, William Hatcher, wrote about the case in his memoir, and his son referred to it again in a biography of his father.[16] Newspapers and local magazines occasionally turned back to the stories, first through the obituaries of various principal actors in the dramas and, later, when other sensational cases arose, leading newspaper writers to conjure up previous criminal spectacles for comparison. Amateur historians also revisited the cases, usually leaning on the pamphlet literature in particular.[17] Similarly, local historians often include a few paragraphs on such cases to spice up their own stories and to give a flavor of what was happening in popular culture and the courts in the era.[18]

But these retellings were necessarily brief and simplified, skeletal remains of the rich stories they once had been. They tended to be brief abstracts of the crime containing several adjectives of horror, a gesture to the tremendous interest shown by the public, and then they moved on. Like physiognomists, the refashioners of these criminal narratives necessarily reduced the cases to thin stereotypes. In May of 1885, as Cluverius stood trial, Richmonders asked each other about the little boy who delivered the torn note, the old man who escorted Lillian into the hotel, and the watch key; they discussed the evidence of suicide, of Cluverius's character, his bearing, and his alibi. They also spoke to each other about their own responses and about the crowds, vengeance, charity, security, morality, and social standing. They looked at the prisoner, his engravings, his book, and the melodramatic frame given the story. This was a rich concoction of issues and questions. At the turn of the twenty-first century, more than one hundred years after the death of Cluverius, the surviving understanding of this crime has dried into a thin, if still compelling, question. It is the one everybody aware of the case has asked me: "Do you think Cluverius did it?"

■

An illustration of crime or a criminal signified something different in 1850 than in 1910. An execution meant something different in the era of public hangings than in the era of private electrocutions. A newspaper communicated a different style of news, a reporter performed a different job, and the police held themselves to new and higher standards. A sensation in 1850 was a fundamentally distinct cultural event compared to one in the 1910s, and there were no Virginia sensations at all in the 1750s or before. With the growing dominance of mass culture, America itself had become sensationalized, changing in the process the nature of violent crime stories.

In the South, these changes paralleled in most ways the national developments in the press, the culture, policing, and sensationalism. From the antebellum period onward, Richmond's sensations in the white community unfolded in ways similar to those in the urban North. In the use of new technologies, the adoption of new reporting, policing, and editorial standards, and in the ever growing volume of print, the South was in keeping with the modernizing influences affecting the rest of the nation.

Most of the South's distinctive features in terms of sensationalism were most clear in the nineteenth century and became less pronounced over time. The starkly divergent early history of crime sensationalism between Virginia and New England can best be explained by the exceptional hold the Puritans had on New England printers along with their prodigious output. From the perspective of the South's experience, execution sermons appear less as a precursor to a national literature on crime than a fascinating northeastern eccentricity. Similarly, Richmond's experience fails to find a dramatic turning point in regard to sensationalism in either the penny press in the middle of the nineteenth century or the yellow press at its end.

Rather, they both were pieces of a more gradual evolution in the nature of Richmond's society and culture, with every generation experiencing more detailed, elaborate, and prurient narratives of the murders in their midst. The 1846 Hoyt-Myers trial attracted more press attention than any before, but it pales before the carnival of print on the 1867 Phillips case. In turn, the Phillips case looks paltry in comparison to the Cluverius murder just eighteen years later, and the 1911 Beattie case dwarfs them all. Throughout the nineteenth century, Richmond's editors were more reticent than their northern counterparts to sully women's reputations. By the early twentieth, few issues were left off the pages of the Richmond press, including disreputable women and even some sexual content.

How else was the South distinctive in regard to crime, culture, and sensation? It persisted in executing criminals in public decades later than the rest of the country, in part because of race. The whites in power assumed that the publicity of public punishment was helpful in cowing black aggression, and when southern legislatures debated the issue, race was a part of their deliberations. The South also persisted in treating blacks differently in the judicial process at every level, making black convictions the norm and black acquittals the sensational story in the African American community. And, of course, lynching. In addition, the white press downplayed black crime and black sensations: what can be sensational about confirming white assumptions about black aggression and inherent criminality? African Americans traversed an utterly different cultural, policing, and legal terrain in this era compared to whites either in the South or nationally.

If the South experienced most of the same developments as the rest of the nation, it did so in its own way, putting the pieces together with distinct attention to the gender and racial norms of the region. This study of the South and sensationalism throws a raking light across the scholarship of crime and culture developed in the North. In this light, several central concerns of those scholars—Puritan execution sermons and the penny press chief among them—stand out as particularly unrepresentative of the experience of the South. It also shows the South paralleling some other developments but at a different pace and with different emphases, such as in the region's hesitancy to renounce public executions and its persistent concern about protecting the respectability of womanhood. On issues of race, the South simply charts a separate course in sensations unconnected to themes developed in the scholarship on other regions.

In turn, this study approaches the history of violence in the South from a different perspective as well. If it emphasizes how appropriate it is that most scholarship has focused on racialized violence, it also shows how much concern white southerners expressed in white crimes, sensationalizing them more than any other. The gendered nature of these stories is particularly striking: the relationship between violence, womanhood, and sensationalism is central to the region's cultural history and is worthy of more study. If most studies of southern violence emphasize how the region is exceptional, this one offers a caution: it is only in some particular regards that the South experienced the rising tide of mass culture's sensationalism in ways different from the rest of the country.

Throughout the South and the nation, the police, legislators, and middle-class reformers undertook increasingly elaborate efforts to create order in the new urban landscape; at the same time, mass culture engaged in its own "search for disorder" in this era. By 1911, Richmond, the South, and the nation had embraced a modern sensibility, and reformers had effectively limited not only the viewing of executions, but also the press writing about them. But from beginning to end, the narratives of murder stories in the early twentieth century were more carnal, detailed, and gruesome than those of the Victorian era. The Progressive Era had a streak of bloodlust in it, not only in terms of lynching in the South and the big-stick diplomacy of Teddy Roosevelt, but also in the prurient longing to explore the salacious details of stories of murder and betrayal.

The Beattie murder coverage concerned blood spots on Midlothian Turnpike, Louise's body and her wounds, sexually transmitted diseases, prostitution, fast young men, images of all those associated with the case, and columns and columns of ink describing everything possibly connected to the murder. There were longer discussions of the evidence—the wounds and blows and blood—in the papers, more papers discussing them, and new technologies to pass this information along more accurately and loudly, halftones and all.

The development of the halftone at the turn of the century lends a metaphor for these broader changes in American culture. Engraving was a medium of stark blacks and whites, images carved one at a time by craftsmen; they were rare and often fictive. Just so, sensational crimes often found their nineteenth-century cultural treatment in newspapers and pamphlets to be stark melodramatic stories of fiends and angels, narratives developed more erratically by individual editors and authors. The stories, like the engravings, were more rare, and when they were developed, they tended to characterize not only the exterior reality, but also the internal, more meaningful struggle between darkness and light.

214 In contrast, halftones were mechanical, mass-produced, objective rep-

resentations of outward appearances rendered in shades of gray. After the turn of the century, mass-produced, detailed, objective representations of violent crime in prose as well as image presented a story not so stark, told with more "shades of gray." Sensations themselves became halftones in the late nineteenth and early twentieth centuries: ever present, visual, geared to a broad audience, and presented as a "straight" view of the world.

On the day of Thomas Cluverius's execution in 1887, the two sons of Richmond merchant Charles Wallace responded to the imminent event in divergent ways. In this difference, the two boys embodied the two poles of this cultural transition. "This is the day appointed for Cluverius to hang," wrote the father in his diary. "Jeff got a 'permit' from the Sergeant to sketch the scaffold, prisoner, etc." Like mass culture itself—allowing more access to the details of crime than ever before—Jeff wanted to get close to the action, to see what could be seen. But the other son felt it was too much to bear: "Charlie asked his mother not to wake him up until after the execution be over. Such is the difference of tone between my two sons."[19] Responding more emotionally to the hanging, perhaps like a character in a melodrama might have, Charlie did not even want to be awake for the horror of it.

Just so did Richmond's culture respond to sensational stories of violent crime with different "tones." It never renounced melodrama, but it was moving in the direction of young Jeff Wallace and mass culture's enthusiasm for seeing what can be seen. And year by year, Americans in the twentieth century saw more than ever before.

■

By the way, I *do* believe Cluverius did it.

NOTES

INTRODUCTION

1. Details re-created from Lysander Rose testimony, 13 May 1885, transcript, *Commonwealth v. Cluverius*, 1:20–33, Meredith Family Papers, Virginia Historical Society (VHS), Richmond. Headlines at the beginning are from the *Richmond Whig*, 21 March 1885. The formal citation for this case is *Cluverius v. Commonwealth*, 81 Va. 787 (1886).

2. William H. Taylor testimony, 13 May 1885, transcript, *Commonwealth v. Cluverius*, 1:131–81.

3. Joseph H. Dodson testimony, 20 May 1885, transcript, *Commonwealth v. Cluverius*, 2:874–78.

4. *Richmond Dispatch*, 16 March 1885. Events of the first week of this crime sensation are taken from the *Richmond Dispatch* and *Richmond Whig*, 14–20 March 1885.

5. *Richmond Dispatch*, 15 March 1885.

6. Ibid.

7. Harry Calligan Diary, 1883–1885, 15, 19 March, 4, 5, 8 June 1885, Valentine Museum, Richmond. This diary has since been published: Gregg D. Kimball, "The Diary of Harry Calligan: Coming of Age in Industrial Manchester," *Journal of the Chesterfield Historical Society* 3 (1997): 2–58.

8. *Annual Report of the Chief of Police to the Mayor of Richmond* (Richmond: various local printers, 1874–1915). This series of reports, bound with other reports to and from the mayor, can be found at the Richmond Public Library. Although such statistics from this era are notoriously suspect, they can at least render a general estimate of the frequency of violent crimes.

9. *Richmond Dispatch*, 15, 27 September, 5, 6 October 1877 for the Bennett murder; *Richmond Dispatch*, 17, 18 March, 7, 16, 18 April 1879 for Baccigalupo.

10. I borrow "social drama" from Victor Turner. See his "Social Dramas and Stories about Them," in *From Ritual to Theatre: The Human Seriousness of Play* (New York: Performing Arts Journal Publications, 1982), 61–88.

11. *Frank Leslie's Illustrated Weekly*, 6 June 1885, 253, 255; *National Police Gazette*, 18 April 1885, 4, 6.

12. Pamphlets: George A. Booker, *The Virginia Tragedy: Trial and Conviction of Thomas J. Cluverius for the Murder of Lillian Madison* (Richmond: Johns and Goolsby, 1885); Thomas J. Cluverius, *Cluverius: My Life, Trial, and Conviction* (Richmond: Andrews, Baptist and Clemmitt, 1887). Melodramatic fiction: Phillip Leigh, *Lillian's Marriage and Murder: Cluverius Did Not Kill Her; The Sequel Told* (Richmond: Patrick Keenan, 1887); "Old Man Bruce, the Richmond Detective, or 'Piping' the Reservoir Mystery," vol. 3, no. 304, of

the *Old Cap. Collier Library* (11 June 1888), a weekly series issued by Munro's Publishing House of New York. Poem: [A Richmond Lady,] *Cousin Tommie* (Richmond: C. F. Johnston, 1885). Memoirs: William E. Hatcher, *Along the Trail of Friendly Years* (New York: Fleming Revell Co., 1910); Henry Robinson Pollard, *Memoirs and Sketches of the Life of Henry Robinson Pollard* (Richmond: Lewis Printing Co., 1923), 191-98; Herbert T. Ezekiel, *Recollections of a Virginia Newspaperman* (Richmond: H. T. Ezekiel, 1920), 40-46.

13. Charles Montriou Wallace Diary, 13 May 1885, 9, 15 January 1887, Manuscripts Division, Perkins Library, Duke University, Durham, N.C.

14. Charles Meredith, prosecuting attorney, received dozens of letters, which are collected in the Meredith Family Papers. Meredith also collected articles on the case in a scrapbook. Another Richmonder who pasted newspaper articles on the Cluverius case into his scrapbook was J. P. Burke, Burke Family Papers, VHS. Another diary briefly mentioning the case was that of Frederick Alexander Gaines, 15 January 1887, VHS.

15. *Religious Herald*, 30 April 1885.

16. *Richmond Dispatch*, 12 February 1887; the *Whig*, 8 June 1885. Several papers mention the celebrity of the witnesses: *New York Times*, 22 March 1885; *Religious Herald*, 30 April 1885. One acquaintance of Madison's in Richmond was so beset by callers with questions that this young woman felt compelled to move temporarily from her house. The *Whig*, 31 March 1885.

17. First quotation: Wallace Diary, 27 May 1885; second quotation: the *State*, 28 March 1885.

18. The three best are Fitzhugh Brundage, *Lynching in the New South: Georgia and Virginia, 1880-1930* (Urbana: University of Illinois Press, 1993); Stewart E. Tolnay and E. M. Beck, *A Festival of Violence: An Analysis of Southern Lynchings, 1882-1930* (Urbana: University of Illinois, 1995); and George Wright, *Racial Violence in Kentucky, 1865-1940: Lynchings, Mob Rule, and "Legal Lynchings"* (Baton Rouge: Louisiana State University Press, 1990).

19. Bertram Wyatt-Brown, *Southern Honor: Ethics and Behavior in the Old South* (New York: Oxford University Press, 1982); Edward Ayers, *Vengeance and Justice: Crime and Punishment in the Nineteenth-Century American South* (New York: Oxford University Press, 1984); Joel Williamson, *The Crucible of Race: Black-White Relations in the American South since Emancipation* (New York: Oxford University Press, 1984).

20. Suzanne Lebsock, *A Murder in Virginia: Southern Justice on Trial* (New York: Norton, 2003); Ann Field Alexander, "'Like an Evil Wind': The Roanoke Riot of 1893 and the Lynching of Thomas Smith," *Virginia Magazine of History and Biography* 100 (April 1992): 173-206; Jane Dailey, "Deference and Violence in the Postbellum Urban South: Manners and Massacres in Danville, Virginia," *Journal of Southern History* 63 (1997): 553-90; Deborah A. Lee and Warren R. Hofstra, "Race, Memory, and the Death of Robert Berkeley: 'A

Murder . . . of . . . Horrible and Savage Barbarity,'" *Journal of Southern History* 65 (1999):41–76; William A. Link, "The Jordan Hatcher Case: Politics and 'A Spirit of Insubordination' in Antebellum Virginia," *Journal of Southern History* 64 (1998): 615–48; Richard F. Hamm, *Murder, Honor, and Law: Four Virginia Homicides from Reconstruction to the Great Depression* (Charlottesville: University of Virginia Press, 2003); Glenda E. Gilmore, *Gender and Jim Crow: Women and the Politics of White Supremacy in North Carolina, 1896–1920* (Chapel Hill: University of North Carolina Press, 1996); Laura F. Edwards, *Gendered Strife and Confusion: The Political Culture of Reconstruction* (Urbana: University of Illinois Press, 1997).

21. In this very rich vein of scholarship, the best overview—in fact, the best overview of the entire field of the social history of crime—is Roger Lane's *Murder in America: A History* (Columbus: Ohio State University Press, 1997). See also Eric Monkonnen "A Disorderly People? Urban Order in the Nineteenth and Twentieth Centuries," *Journal of American History* 68 (1981): 539–59; Ted Gurr, "Historical Trends in Violent Crime: A Critical Review of the Research," in *Crime and Justice: An Annual Review of Research*, vol. 3, ed. Michael Tonry and Norval Morris (Chicago: University of Chicago Press, 1981), 295–353.

22. David Johnson, *Policing the Urban Underworld* (Philadelphia: Temple University Press, 1979); Eric Monkonnen, *The Police in Urban America* (New York: Cambridge University Press, 1981); Robert Fogelson, *Big City Police* (Cambridge, Mass.: Harvard University Press, 1977); Roger Lane, *Policing the City: Boston, 1822–1885* (New York: Atheneum, 1971); and John C. Schneider, *Detroit and the Problem of Order, 1830–80: A Geography of Crime, Riot, and Policing* (Lincoln: University of Nebraska Press, 1980).

23. David Rothman, *Discovery of the Asylum: Social Order and Disorder in the New Republic* (Boston: Little, Brown and Co., 1971); William J. Bowers, *Legal Homicide: Death as Punishment in America, 1864–1982* (Boston: Northeastern University Press, 1984). A cultural history of punishment in this era is Louis Masur, *Rites of Execution: Capital Punishment and the Transformation of American Culture, 1776–1865* (New York: Oxford University Press, 1989).

24. Virginius Dabney, *Richmond: The Story of a City*, rev. ed. (Charlottesville: University of Virginia Press, 1990), 238. An earlier local history treats the Cluverius case much more thoroughly, if only reiterating the narrative: W. Asbury Christian, *Richmond: Her Past and Present* (Richmond: L. H. Jenkins, 1912), 390–94. Two recent histories of Richmond either mention the case only in a single sentence, as in Michael B. Chesson's *Richmond after the War, 1865–1890* (Richmond: Virginia State Library, 1981), 187, or not at all, as in Marie Tyler-McGraw's *At the Falls: Richmond, Virginia, and Its People* (Chapel Hill: University of North Carolina Press, 1994).

25. Daniel A. Cohen, *Pillars of Salt, Monuments of Grace: New England Crime Literature and the Origins of American Popular Culture, 1674–1860* (New York:

Oxford University Press, 1993); Karen Halttunen, *Murder Most Foul: The Killer and the American Gothic Imagination* (Cambridge, Mass.: Harvard University Press, 1998). In a related development, historians of literature have turned from their interest in New England transcendentalism to take a closer look at the undercurrents of nineteenth-century popular culture that lie "beneath the American Renaissance": sentimental literature ("scribbling women"), Gothic fiction, minstrelsy, burlesque, and ephemeral story papers and dime novels. On this, see David S. Reynolds, *Beneath the American Renaissance: The Subversive Imagination in the Age of Emerson and Melville* (Cambridge, Mass.: Harvard University Press, 1988); Cathy N. Davidson, *Revolution and the Word: The Rise of the Novel in America* (New York: Oxford University Press, 1986); Robert C. Toll, *Blacking Up: The Minstrel Show in Nineteenth-Century America* (New York: Oxford University Press, 1974); Peter Brooks, *The Melodramatic Imagination: Balzac, Henry James, Melodrama, and the Mode of Excess* (New Haven, Conn.: Yale University Press, 1976); Robert C. Allen, *Horrible Prettiness: Burlesque and American Culture* (Chapel Hill: University of North Carolina Press, 1991); Michael Denning, *Mechanic Accents: Dime Novels and Working-Class Culture* (New York: Verso, 1987).

26. Andie Tucher, *Froth and Scum: Truth, Beauty, Goodness, and the Ax Murder in America's First Mass Medium* (Chapel Hill: University of North Carolina Press, 1994); and David Ray Papke, *Framing the Criminal: Crime, Cultural Work, and the Loss of Critical Perspective, 1830–1900* (Hamden, Conn.: Archon Books, 1987), both center on this transition in journalism and its connections to crime. Both Cohen, *Pillars of Salt*, and Halttunen, *Murder Most Foul*, also discuss this transition. See also Michael Schudson, *Discovering the News: A Social History of American Newspapers* (New York: Basic Books, 1978); and Dan Schiller, *Objectivity and the News: The Public and the Rise of Commercial Journalism* (Philadelphia: University of Pennsylvania Press, 1981).

27. The two best case studies to date are Lebsock, *Murder in Virginia*, and Patricia Cline Cohen, *The Murder of Helen Jewett: The Life and Death of a Prostitute in Nineteenth-Century New York* (New York: Alfred Knopf, 1998). Lebsock's book concerns the Lunenburg case discussed in chapter 4. A recent volume collects a series of discrete murder case studies throughout American history: Robert Asher, Lawrence B. Goodheart, and Alan Rogers, eds., *Murder on Trial: 1620–2002* (Albany: State University of New York Press, 2005). See also Amy Gilman Srebnick, *The Mysterious Death of Mary Rogers: Sex and Culture in Nineteenth-Century New York* (New York: Oxford University Press, 1995); J. Anthony Lukas, *Big Trouble* (New York: Touchstone, 1997); Gerald McFarland, *The "Counterfeit" Man: The True Story of the Boorn-Colvin Murder* (New York: Pantheon, 1990); and Charles Rosenberg, *The Trial of the Assassin Guiteau: Psychiatry and the Law in the Gilded Age* (Chicago: University of Chicago Press, 1968).

28. Cohen, *Pillars of Salt*, and Halttunen, *Murder Most Foul*. See also Daniel E. Williams, "Rogues, Rascals, and Scoundrels: the Underworld Literature of Early America" *American Studies* 24 (1983): 5–19.

29. A number of very good studies stress these changes, centering their evaluations on the largest metropolitan dailies. This focus on the biggest and the first, however, appears to overstate the importance of each of these transitions in the wider field of American journalism. See Tucher, *Froth and Scum*; Schudson, *Discovering the News*; Frank Luther Mott, *American Journalism, a History: 1690–1960*, 3rd ed. (New York: Macmillan Co., 1962); Michael Emery, Edwin Emery, and Nancy Roberts, *The Press and America: An Interpretive History of the Mass Media*, 9th ed. (Boston: Allyn and Bacon, 2000); and Schiller *Objectivity and the News*.

30. U.S. Census Bureau, *Thirteenth U.S. Census, 1910*, vol. 1: *Population* (Washington, D.C.: U.S. Government Printing Office, 1913), 82–83.

31. In the legal context, "a story is an elegant symbolic framework in which a large amount of information can be organized, compared, tested, and interpreted to yield a clear judgment about disputed versions of an action. . . . Structural characteristics of stories alert jurors to such things as the sufficiency of the evidence, the consistency of an interpretation with the entire body of evidence, the importance of any particular discrepancy, and the degree of doubt attached to an interpretation." W. Lance Bennett, "Rhetorical Transformation of Evidence in Criminal Trials: Creating Grounds for Legal Judgment," *Quarterly Journal of Speech* 65 (1979): 311.

One scholar has recently gone so far as to argue that popular trials (not all trials) are best understood not in legal terms, but as a genre of public discourse. Robert Hariman, "Performing the Laws: Popular Trials and Social Knowledge," in *Popular Trials: Rhetoric, Mass Media, and the Law*, ed. Robert Hariman (Tuscaloosa: University of Alabama Press, 1990), 17–30. A confluence of literary and legal scholarship has recently produced a burgeoning collection of works parsing the significance of legal rhetoric and storytelling, particularly in the context of popular trials. See Peter Brooks and Paul Gewirtz, eds., *Law's Stories: Narrative and Rhetoric in the Law* (New Haven, Conn.: Yale University Press, 1996). For an excellent article on the stories of John Brown's trial, see Robert A. Ferguson, "Story and Transcription in the Trial of John Brown," *Yale Journal of Law and Humanities* 6 (1994): 37–73.

32. Aletha C. Huston, Edward Donnerstein, Halford Fairchild, Norma D. Feshbach, Phyllis A. Katz, John P. Murray, Eli A. Rubinstein, Brian L. Wilcox, and Diana M. Zuckerman, *Big World, Small Screen: The Role of Television in American Society* (Lincoln: University of Nebraska Press, 1992), 54.

33. *Richmond Whig and Public Advertiser*, semiweekly edition, 28 October 1846.

34. *Century Magazine*, May 1911, 46.

CHAPTER 1

1. Alexander Purdie and John Dixon, *Virginia Gazette*, 18 July 1766. For a full treatment of this case and its political context, see Carl Bridenbaugh, "Violence and Virtue in Virginia, 1766; or, The Importance of the Trivial," *Proceedings of the Massachusetts Historical Society* 76 (1964): 3–29.

2. In addition to the divisions sparked by the Stamp Act crisis, the respected and lately deceased Speaker of the House of Burgesses was recently revealed to have misused colonial funds to benefit friends and colleagues. See Bridenbaugh, "Violence and Virtue."

3. Purdie and Dixon, *Virginia Gazette*, 17 October 1766. The articles on this case appear between 20 June and 30 October 1766, in Purdie and Dixon's *Virginia Gazette*.

4. These numbers are from Charles Evans, *American Bibliography*, vol. 1: *1639–1729* (New York: Peter Smith, 1941), 443–46. The dates for first printers in the thirteen colonies are: Massachusetts (1639), Pennsylvania (1685), New York (1693), Connecticut (1709), Maryland (1726), Rhode Island (1727), Virginia (1730), South Carolina (1732), North Carolina (1751), New Jersey (1755), New Hampshire (1756), Delaware (1761), and Georgia (1762). Virginia reportedly had in 1682 a printer who attempted to print the laws of the colony but was prevented from doing so. See Evans, *American Bibliography*, 56.

5. Quoted in William Waller Hening, *Statutes at Large of Virginia*, vol. 2 (New York: Bartow, 1823), 517.

6. Parks's early work included an eclectic mix of books, including a number of volumes of colonial statutes as well as a widely used guide for colonial county officials (the first of its kind in the colonies); he also printed an appreciation of the governor who allowed him to set up shop and the colonies' first cookbook. Parks, *Typographia, an Ode on Printing* (Williamsburg: William Parks, 1730); E. Smith, *The Compleat Housewife* . . . (Williamsburg: William Parks, 1742); George Webb, *The Office and Authority of a Justice of the Peace* . . . (Williamsburg: William Parks, 1736).

William Clayton-Torrence evaluated the entire output of Virginia's presses in his *A Trial Bibliography of Colonial Virginia* (Richmond: Davis Bottom, 1908 and 1910). Of the 177 printed works he evaluated, 93 were for the government (53 percent), 28 were newspapers (16 percent; this is counting the newspaper for an entire year as one document. Arguably, this work—performed every week—deserves a larger place on the balance sheet of colonial printing.), 24 were almanacs (14 percent), which were the most popular (and least expensive) printed items in colonial Virginia, 18 were religious works (10 percent), and 14 were miscellaneous works not of a religious nature (8 percent).

The first newspaper in the colonies was established in Boston in 1704; the first in the South was the *South Carolina Gazette* in 1732, making the *Virginia Gazette* the South's second newspaper.

7. William Parks died in 1750, at which time William Hunter, Parks's apprentice,

took over until his own death in 1761, whereupon another apprentice, James Royle, followed suit until 1766. John Tebbel, *The Creation of an Industry, 1630–1865*, vol. 1 of *A History of Book Publishing in the United States* (New York: R. R. Bowker, 1972), 121–23.

8. Quoted in Stephen Botein, "'Meer Mechanics' and an Open Press: The Business and Political Strategies of Colonial American Printers," *Perspectives in American History* 9 (1975): 168.

9. *The Vain Prodigal Life, and Tragical Penitent Death of Thomas Hellier . . .* (London: Sam. Crouch, 1680). This brief murder story in verse is difficult to interpret. One could argue that London is simply the printing center for all the colonies and that this should be considered the first Virginia crime narrative. But I see the linkages as more tenuous than this, considering it more a London narrative taking Virginia as its setting. A 1702 parody in verse, for example ("The Loyal Address of the Clergy of Virginia" [Williamsburg: Printed for Fr. Maggot, at the sign of the Hickory Tree, in Queen St., 1702.]), claims Virginia origins as well but appears to be a broadside published in London and for obscure political goals. At any rate, the Hellier narrative was not produced in the colonies, and it is unclear whether it ever circulated there.

The second Virginia crime publication is likewise difficult to place. The eight-page poem was published in Stockbridge, Massachusetts: John Leland, *A True Account of How Mathew Womble . . .* (Stockbridge: Richard Lee, 1793).

10. This analysis comes from my own reading of a scattered selection of issues of the *Gazette*. It is also mirrored in the evaluation given Virginia's early national papers by Lester J. Cappon in his *Virginia Newspapers, 1821–1935: A Bibliography with Historical Introduction and Notes* (New York: D. Appleton-Century Co., 1936), 3. The 18 August 1738 issue of the *Virginia Gazette* was typical: this small format, two-column, four-page issue consisted of a half-page letter from Europe (usually from London or Paris but, in this issue, from Belgrade), more than two pages of letters and official documents from London, and a half page each of advertisements and local governmental and shipping news.

Others studying colonial papers render similar verdicts: The *Pennsylvania Gazette*, for instance, cleaved to the model of the *London Gazette* in printing official pronouncements, foreign news, news from England, then London, then advertisements. Proportionately, almost 60 percent of the *Pennsylvania Gazette* comprised items on the military and diplomacy; sensational material (accident, fire, crime, punishment) took up merely 11 percent of the space. See Charles E. Clark and Charles Wetherell, "The Measure of Maturity: The *Pennsylvania Gazette*, 1728–1765," *William and Mary Quarterly*, 3rd ser., 46 (1989): 279–303, esp. 283, 292.

11. *Virginia Gazette*, 24 January 1777.

12. Ibid., 6 May 1737.

13. Rooted in the prodigious output of New England printers, the well-developed

scholarship on early northern crime and culture describes a seventeenth-century genre of execution sermons that changed its nature over the course of two centuries. This is a rich and meaningful narrative of cultural change convincingly argued by a number of scholars. See Daniel A. Cohen, *Pillars of Salt, Monuments of Grace: New England Crime Literature and the Origins of American Popular Culture, 1674–1860* (New York: Oxford University Press, 1993); Karen Halttunen, *Murder Most Foul: The Killer and the American Gothic Imagination* (Cambridge, Mass.: Harvard University Press, 1998); Daniel E. Williams, "Rogues, Rascals, and Scoundrels: The Underworld Literature of Early America," *American Studies* 24 (1983): 5–19.

Before 1729, fully 70 percent of colonial printers, publishers, and book-sellers worked in the New England states. As late as the 1730s and 1740s, they produced more than one-half of all colonial imprints, a majority of which was religious in nature. Evans, *American Bibliography*.

14. Examples of execution sermons and related genres from England and Germany can be found in Daniel Cohen, "Blood Will Out: Sensationalism, Horror, and the Roots of American Crime Literature," in *Mortal Remains: Death in Early America*, ed. Nancy Isenberg and Andrew Burstein (Philadelphia: University of Pennsylvania Press, 2003), 31–55; Joy Wiltenburg, "True Crime: The Origins of Modern Sensationalism," *American Historical Review* 109 (December 2004): 1377–1404.

The closest approximation of an execution sermon in Virginia was a reprint from England in one edition of the *Virginia Gazette*: a one-page exploration of the last moments of a British forger, William Smith, in 1751. This article included a letter asking for clemency as well as another letter and accompanying ode published in jail before he was hanged. Smith is very penitent in these letters and in the poem, and so it appears he had learned a good lesson on the cost of sins as he prepared "to launch into the irremeable Gulph of Eternity." *Virginia Gazette*, 31 January 1751. The previous issue of the *Gazette* (24 January) also devotes most of its first page to the story of a crime, the "gentleman highwayman," but does not include a confession. Both of these issues were quite out of keeping with the norms of the *Virginia Gazette*, and both appeared in the first month of William Hunter's tenure as publisher of the paper. Perhaps these reprints from London were readily available "filler" for a harried printer trying to work out how to accomplish all that he had to. Or perhaps he used this interesting material as a means of building a readership as he tried to get the business back off the ground. Whatever his motives, late January 1751 looks very different from any other moment in the eighteenth-century *Virginia Gazette*.

15. I have found no examples of an execution sermon from Pennsylvania, but there are several extant pamphlets that include confessions and various warnings to others. See, for example: *The Narrative of William Sweeting* (Philadelphia: Daniel Lawrence, 1792); *An Account of the Robberies Committed by John Mor-*

rison (Philadelphia: [Anthony Armbruster?], 1751); and *The Last Words and Dying Confession of the Three Pirates Who Were Executed This Day (May 9th, 1800)* (Philadelphia: Folwell's Press, 1800). Many Pennsylvania pamphlets make either no mention or only fleeting mention of religion, sin, God, or the lessons to be learned from the crimes, focusing instead on describing the crimes or, particularly, leading the reader through the trial. For the general norms in Pennsylvania printing, see Tebbel, *Creation of an Industry*, 83–117, and Clark and Wetherell, "Measure of Maturity."

16. Cohen, *Pillars of Salt*, 184. In the eighteenth and early nineteenth centuries, New England execution sermons and last speeches were gradually replaced by a host of new cultural forms: broadsides, ballads, trial reports, and increasing newspaper coverage. This secular treatment was much more akin to what could be found in other parts of the country. In this way, what several scholars have described as a "new," secular form of exploring crime in New England can best be interpreted as the region slowly joining the cultural trend of the rest of British North America. In this, crime and culture follow a similar trend to that found by Jack Green (*Pursuits of Happiness: The Social Development of Early Modern British Colonies and the Formation of American Culture* [Chapel Hill: University of North Carolina Press, 1988]) in that New England's cultural development looks less like the birth of American culture and more like a utopian religious aberration from the colonial norms. While Daniel Cohen certainly does not use these terms, he nicely contextualizes the development as a Puritan New England phenomenon, emphasizing the "almost exclusively *regional* character of the execution sermon . . . no gallows sermons were published in North America during the seventeenth century outside New England, and only a very few appeared elsewhere in America during the eighteenth century." Cohen, "Blood Will Out," 51.

   New England newspapers—born in 1704 when the Puritan elites were already loosening their grip on the region—were never so focused on crime. Papers occasionally covered piracy and counterfeiting, finds Cohen, but "most devoted little more than an occasional stray paragraph to offenses like theft, burglary, robbery, rape, and murder." Cohen, *Pillars of Salt*, 15.

17. William Byrd of Westover had the most famous (and largest) early Virginia library, and of those volumes bibliographers have been able to locate, only two were published in the colonies, both in Williamsburg. Similarly, Thomas Teackle's much smaller seventeenth-century library consisted entirely of books published in Europe. Given that most Virginians could not have accumulated such libraries, there is little reason to believe that smaller libraries included more books from colonial printers than did those of these two planters. Edwin Wolf, "The Dispersal of the Library of William Byrd of Westover," *Proceedings of the American Antiquarian Society* 68 (1958): 20–106; Jon Butler, "Thomas Teackle's 333 Books: A Great Library on Virginia's Eastern Shore, 1697," *William and Mary Quarterly* 49 (1992): 449–91.

18. Books were shipped from London along with other finished goods. General merchants would have a few books on hand—almanacs, Bibles, and a few others—that locals would purchase along with other goods from England. Richard D. Brown, *Knowledge Is Power: The Diffusion of Information in Early America, 1700–1865* (New York: Oxford University Press, 1989), 44. In the coming decades, newspapers began to circulate from colony to colony—two murderers, in fact, were caught in Pennsylvania due to an article reprinted from the *Virginia Gazette*. The 21 October 1737 edition included the confession of one of the four murderers, who named the other parties. His confession was reprinted in Philadelphia newspapers, resulting in the capture of two of the others. Fairfax Harrison, "The Colonial Post Office in Virginia," *William and Mary Quarterly*, 2nd ser., 4 (1924): 73–92. Virginians felt content with their connections with Britain; many thought that if there were a postal system connecting them to the North that southerners would not use it much anyway.

19. Surviving records of William Hunter and James Royle from the 1750s and 1760s showed them exchanging books with printers in Pennsylvania, Maryland, and North Carolina, although most of their trade was with Britain. No trade was recorded with New England printers. Cynthia Stiverson and Gregory Stiverson, "The Colonial Retail Book Trade: Availability and Affordability of Reading Material in Mid-Eighteenth-Century Virginia," in *Printing and Society in Early America*, ed. William Joyce (Worcester, Mass.: American Antiquarian Society, 1983), 132–73. Their unpublished report of this work is even more detailed: Stiverson and Stiverson, "Books Both Useful and Entertaining: A Study of Book Purchases and Reading Habits of Virginians in the Mid-Eighteenth Century" (Williamsburg: Williamsburg Foundation, 1977).

20. The original law allowing for a newspaper in Virginia stipulated that it would be called the "Virginia Gazette," so there were a half-dozen newspapers of this title in the last half of the eighteenth century.

21. Susan B. Carter, ed., *Historical Statistics of the United States: Earliest Times to the Present; Millennial Edition*, vol. 1: *Population* (New York: Cambridge University Press, 2006), 26, 113, 359. Newspaper growth is from Charles Evans, *American Bibliography*, vol. 9: *1793–4* (New York: Peter Smith, 1941).

22. Cynthia Kierner, *Scandal at Bizarre: Rumor and Reputation in Jefferson's America* (New York: Palgrave, 2004), 40–42, 77–81.

23. Ibid.

24. There are a number of copies of these letters in archives, but the most widely available copies are reprinted in William Cabell Bruce's *John Randolph of Roanoke*, vol. 2 (New York: Octagon Books, 1970), 274–95; quotations are from pages 276, 278, 280, 283, 285. Nancy believed that "John Randolph of Roanoke" was a pretentious title to give himself, and in her letter the title was always inside of quotation marks.

25. These letters circulated but haltingly; this is a peculiar cultural phenomenon in

which a number of different editions of the letters are now in archives but with a variety of cautions that they not be circulated. The catalog of the Virginia Historical Society (VHS) nicely captures the rumor mill in its description of one of these publications: "Copies made by an unidentified person from copies made by Frederick Johnston from copies made by Judge Fleming Saunders from the originals." John Randolph correspondence with Ann Cary (Randolph) Morris, 1814-15, handwritten, VHS (there are two handwritten copies, one written into a blank book, the other prefaced with "the personal, private property of C. W. Throckmorton"); "Ardent Correspondence between John Randolph and Ann Cary (Randolph) Morris, 1814-15," typescript, VHS; *Correspondence between John Randolph of Roanoke and Mrs. Gouverneur Morris* (s.l.: s.n., 18??) (this copy has printed on it: "This must, in no event, be allowed out of the family"); *Spicy Correspondence between John Randolph of Roanoke and His Cousin Nancy* (Lynchburg: J. P. Bell, 1888).

26. Frank Luther Mott, *American Journalism, a History: 1690-1960*, 3rd ed. (New York: Macmillan Co., 1962), 48-59; quotation from 51.

27. Evans, *American Bibliography*, vol. 9, and Roger P. Bristol, *Supplement to Charles Evans' American Bibliography* (Charlottesville: University of Virginia Press, 1970). The religious pieces included sermons and other tracts, but chiefly they were the published minutes from the yearly conferences of a variety of Protestant denominations, principally the Baptists. In the wake of the disestablishment of the Anglican faith as Virginia's official religion, other faiths demonstrated a flurry of activity, and the minutes of each local district meeting of Baptists found its way into print, as did several statewide meetings for a variety of denominations in the 1790s.

In 1793, the Virginia press printed 64 publications, of which 19 (30 percent) were governmental, 18 (28 percent) were religious in nature, 17 (27 percent) were almanacs and newspapers, 10 (16 percent) were miscellaneous and/or difficult to categorize from their titles. The Virginia press had come a long way from publishing 2 items in 1733 and 3 in 1743, but it still accounted for only about 3.6 percent of the nation's printed matter in 1793. It was growing but remained an adjunct to the larger publishing centers of London, Boston, New York, and Philadelphia.

28. Douglas Egerton, *Gabriel's Rebellion: The Virginia Slave Conspiracies of 1800 and 1802* (Chapel Hill: University of North Carolina Press, 1993).

29. *Virginia Argus*, 14 October 1800. Some issues are missing and perhaps contain further stories on the insurrection. The missing ones are 19, 23, 26, and 30 September and 10 October. The entry from the issue before (7 October 1800) simply read: "The noted Gabriel received his trial yesterday—he will be executed at the gallows of this city, this day." An earlier entry (16 September 1800) read: "On Friday were executed in this city, pursuant to sentence, five of the negroes concerned in the late atrocious conspiracy and insurrection;

and yesterday, five others concerned in the same business. Several others are under sentence for Thursday next. 'Tis most devoutly to be wished, that these examples may deter all future attempts of this diabolical nature."

All other coverage of this conspiracy—in extant issues—was in the form of letters: one containing political accusations in this contentious election year (3 October 1800—a Jeffersonian responding to Federalist claims that the insurrection started with a Jeffersonian ally), others defending a local white man's reputation (also in the 3 October 1800 edition), and one from a man attending the trials of the accused insurrectionists (14 October 1800). This last piece is the most engaged treatment.

30. *Norfolk Herald*, 27 September 1800. This is an odd use of "imprimatur" if that is what the letter writer intended, for he clearly seems to mean not a "license to print," but its opposite, a ban. Like the Richmond papers, the *Norfolk Herald* also published the governor's proclamations, along with brief paragraphs discussing in general Richmond's fears, the apprehension of Gabriel, and the masses of trials, convictions, and executions. The *Herald* also published two substantial articles about the insurrection—both letters from observers relating the discovery of the planned rebellion and the trials of those accused. These letters discuss the recruitment of participants, the meetings to plan their actions, and the goals of gaining weapons in Richmond's armories and of bringing the blacks in the rest of the state and the South to their banner. Unlike in either of the Richmond papers, this coverage, though just as brief, at least rendered a clear perspective on the nature of the insurrection.

31. *Norfolk Herald*, 27 September and 18 October 1800. Coverage in all three newspapers begins on 16 September (two weeks after the discovery of the insurrection). The *Norfolk Herald* published 4½ columns of material in nine separate editions over five weeks. The *Richmond Examiner* published seven columns of material in nine separate editions over 4½ weeks (although, there was so much repetition in this paper that it really amounted to only four stories of three columns length of distinct information). The *Virginia Argus* published five columns of material in four issues over four weeks, although five issues are missing for this span of the *Argus*.

32. "Horrid Murder! Abel Clemmons Murdered His Wife and Eight Children," Special Collections Department, Alderman Library, University of Virginia, Charlottesville. This is the first unless we consider the first one to have been the 1793 broadside in defense of Richard Randolph's honor.

33. *Cruel Murder!! A True Account of the Life and Character of Abel Clemmens, Who Was Executed at Morgantown, Virginia, on Monday, the 30th of June, 1806, for the Murder of His Wife and Eight Children* (Morgantown: J. Campbell, n.d. [1806]; reprinted in Philadelphia: James O'Hara, 1806).

34. *Virginia Argus*, 4 May 1816.

35. A Member of the Bar of Nottoway County (A.B.S.), *Report of the Trials of Capt. Thomas Wells, before the County Court of Nottoway, sitting as an Examining*

Court, at the August Term, 1816—Charged with Feloniously and Maliciously Shooting with Intent to Kill Peter Randolph, Esq., Judge of the 5th Circuit, and Col. Wm. C. Greenhill (Petersburg: Marvel W. Dunnavant, 1816). The anonymous author assures readers that he was not paid by either party and that he gives the "testimony in full, without expressing any opinion as to the legality or illegality of its admission. The public must judge for themselves." It is difficult to evaluate this claim of objectivity from two hundred years later.

36. Of the major Richmond Newspapers, the *Compiler* began in 1813 as a daily (which typically meant six days a week, no issue being printed on the Sabbath), the *Whig* went to daily production in 1828, the *Enquirer* in 1844. Most papers also put out semiweekly or weekly editions for their rural readers. Cappon, *Virginia Newspapers, 1821–1935,* 164–195.

37. For more on early literacy, I recommend Cathy N. Davidson, *Revolution and the Word: The Rise of the Novel in America* (New York: Oxford University Press, 1986), and Ronald Zboray, *A Fictive People: Antebellum Economic Development and the American Reading Public* (New York: Oxford University Press, 1993).

38. Cohen, *Pillars of Salt,* 31.

39. *An Account of the Apprehension, Trial, Conviction, and Condemnation of Manuel Philip Garcia and Jose Demas Garcia Castillano* (Norfolk: C. Hall, 1821).

40. *Richmond Enquirer,* 27 and 30 March, 3, 6, 17, and 27 April, and 5 June 1821.

41. *A Brief Sketch of the Occurrences on Board the Brig Crawford, on her Voyage from Matanzas to New York; Together with An Account of the Trial of the Three Spaniards, Jose Hilario Casares, Felix Barbeito, and Jose Morando* (Richmond: Samuel Shepherd, 1827); *Richmond Enquirer* 13, 17, 20, and 24 July 1827.

42. Scholars working on the North have likewise found that it was during this era that pamphlets began to center on the trial process. Cohen, *Pillars of Salt,* 26–32, 167–246; Halttunen, *Murder Most Foul,* 91–134. One early Virginia pamphlet started with a sermon before engaging in a more trial-centered narrative: Gabriel Nourse, *Narrative of the Life, Trial, Confession, Sentence of Death, and Execution of Ebenezer W. Cox* . . . (Winchester: Samuel H. Davis, 1830).

43. Marvin Davis Evans, "The Richmond Press on the Eve of the Civil War," *John P. Branch Historical Papers of Randolph Macon College* 1 (January 1951): 9–15.

44. Editor of the *Courier and Compiler*; quoted in Cappon, *Virginia Newspapers, 1821–1935,* 4.

45. For more on this duel, see Barbara J. Griffin, ed. "Thomas Ritchie and the Code Duello," *Virginia Magazine of History and Biography* 92 (1984): 71–95, and *A Full Report, Embracing All the Evidence and Arguments in the Case of the Commonwealth of Virginia vs. Thomas Ritchie, Jr.* . . . (New York: Burgess, Stringer and Co., 1846).

46. Kenneth Greenberg, ed. *The Confessions of Nat Turner and Related Documents* (Boston: Bedford/St. Martin, 1996).

47. *The Confessions of Nat Turner, Leader of the Late Insurrection in Southampton, Va.* (Baltimore, Md.: T. R. Gray, 1831). In fact, its coverage of the execution is an extraordinarily generic single paragraph, not even giving the time but rather the range of times that the judge had decreed—between the hours of ten and two. There is also a three-paragraph treatment of his trial at the end of the document, the purpose of which appears to be to lend credence to the validity of the *Confessions* by including Turner saying "I have made a full confession to Mr. Gray, and have nothing more to say."

48. This passage is about halfway through the confessions. The most widely accessible version would be Greenberg, *Confessions of Nat Turner*, 50.

49. The judge in Turner's trial asked him if he had anything to say, and the prisoner stated that "he had nothing but what he had before said." Presumably this refers to his statements as printed in the papers and in this volume.

50. Greenburg, *Confessions of Nat Turner*, 103.

51. The only other Turner pamphlet is a very brief, bland narrative of the butcheries that takes a hard turn in the last four pages to become an antislavery tract. In fact, it links reports of insurrections in Maryland, Delaware, North Carolina, and St. Domingo with Nat Turner's to create a mélange of slavery's potential violence. Samuel Warner, *Authentic and impartial narrative of the tragical scene: Which was witnessed in Southampton County (Virginia) on Monday the 22d of August last, when fifty-five of its inhabitants (mostly women and children) were inhumanly massacred by the blacks! Communicated by those who were eye witnesses of the bloody scene, and confirmed by the confessions of several of the blacks while under sentence of death* (New York: Warner and West, 1831). At the same time, a northern paper, the *Albany Evening Journal* (1 September 1831), published an article looking back to review the earlier Gabriel's rebellion from a similar vantage of how slavery breeds violence. The *Richmond Enquirer* then took them to task (21 October 1831), reprinting a number of their claims and contrasting them to the trial records and original newspaper coverage to show how mistaken their story was by both romanticizing Gabriel and misrepresenting almost every fact in the case.

52. *Richmond Enquirer*, 30 August 1831. At another point (4 September 1831), the editor reports hearing "so much, and so many errors about the events in Southampton, that it is some satisfaction to us to lay before our readers the following account, in the truth of which every reliance may be placed."

53. Ibid., 26 August and 8 November 1831.

54. Ibid., 26 and 30 August 1831; emphasis in original. Some reports even contradicted others in the same issue. One letter, for instance, reported the capture of the leader of the insurrection, necessitating the insertion of a parenthetical note by the editor: "It seems from Gen. Eppes' last dispatch" (also printed in

that edition) "that the writer is mistaken in supposing the principal leader has been apprehended." (*Richmond Enquirer*, 30 August 1831).

55. *Richmond Enquirer*, 4 September 1831; emphasis in original. Similarly brief lists of the condemned appear in other issues: 12 and 23 September 1831.

56. Ibid., 12 November 1831. Execution notices, one paragraph each, are from Norfolk and Petersburg papers, respectively: 18 and 22 November 1831.

57. Those published elsewhere are: *A Full Report, Embracing All the Evidence and Arguments in the Case of the Commonwealth of Virginia vs. Thomas Ritchie, Jr.* (New York: Burgess, Stringer, and Co., 1846); *An Authenticated Report of the Trial of Myers and Others, for the Murder of Dudley Marvin Hoyt* . . . (New York: Richards and Co., 1846); *The Letters and Correspondence of Mrs. Virginia Myers, (which have never before been published or even read in Court,) to Dudley Marvin Hoyt* . . . (Philadelphia: n.p., 1847).

58. *Richmond Enquirer*, 16 and 18 July 1846, for notices of the discovery of the murder; late September 1848, for the trial of Epes; the brief notice of the execution, copied from the *Petersburg Republican*, ran in the 27 December 1848 edition. See also the pamphlet on the murder: J. M. H. Brunet, *Trial of William Dandridge Epes, for the Murder of Francis Adolphus Muir* (Petersburg: J. M. H. Brunet, 1849).

59. *Richmond Whig*, 27 October 1846.

60. *Richmond Whig and Public Advertiser*, semiweekly edition, 28 October 1846. During the preliminary trial (13 and 16 October), in contrast, the *Whig* had published a number of trial reports. For more on the culture of acquitting husbands who killed their wives' lovers, see Hendrik Hartog, "Lawyering, Husbands' Rights, and 'the Unwritten Law' in Nineteenth-Century America," *Journal of American History* 84 (June 1997): 67–96.

61. *Richmond Enquirer*, 27 October 1846.

62. Ibid., 9 November 1846; coverage of the case runs from 29 September–27 October 1846. The fullest coverage appears on 14 October, and, sadly, the editions of 15 and 16 October are absent from the extant microfilm. This paper's front page, along with most of pages three and four, are full of notices and advertisements. News of any sort received little coverage, and political news (along with reports from the developing Mexican War) predominated. Coverage of crime sensations, then, was at least a secondary concern to these editors.

63. *Philadelphia Public Ledger and Daily Transcript*, 22 October 1846. For further pointed sarcasm, see also 5, 24, and 29 October and 2 November 1846.

64. *Richmond Enquirer*, 9 November 1846. The Myers-Hoyt case is, in fact, a nice adjunct to the theme of regionalism and murder cases in Richard F. Hamm's *Murder, Honor, and Law: Four Virginia Homicides from Reconstruction to the Great Depression* (Charlottesville: University of Virginia Press, 2003).

65. In fact, the *Richmond Enquirer* declined to publish Myers's letter, which is the

only difference in the letter-printing strategies of the two Richmond papers. See the discussion that follows.

66. *Richmond Whig*, 15 October 1846; *Richmond Enquirer*, 14 October 1846.

67. *An Authenticated Report of the Trial of Myers and Others*, 39. It remains unclear whether this would be pregnancy or venereal disease, but it seems certain that this refers to something gynecological.

68. *Richmond Enquirer*, 14 October 1846.

69. *Richmond Whig*, 15 October 1846. The previous day, the *Whig* had written that it was not the delicate nature of the letters but fiscal considerations that had made them hesitant to publish them: "we deem it unnecessary to publish on account of their irrelevancy at this stage of the trial, and because their exceeding voluminousness would be a tax on our columns not justified by their interest." The *Enquirer* did not ruminate on their choices of letters but in the 13 October edition did mention a practical reason for their not being published the day before: "The length of the interesting Mexican news precludes us from publishing the letters, &c."

70. *Richmond Enquirer*, 14 and 17 June 1836.

71. Ibid., 26 and 29 March 1850; 2, 5, and 9 April 1850. *Richmond Semi-Weekly Examiner*, 26 and 29 March 1850; 2, 5, and 9 April 1850. See also 7, 11, and 21 December 1849; 3 and 6 September 1850. After the verdict was announced, the *Examiner* continued its coverage by finishing off the publication of closing arguments and by giving various opinions of the press on the verdict.

72. Elvira A. Bruce to Charles Bruce, 6, 20, and 30 October 1846, Elvira A. (Cabell) Henry Bruce Collection, VHS.

73. James A. Cowardin, one of the owners of the *Dispatch*, had attempted to devote the *Times and Compiler* to commercial matters and local news and away from politics beginning in 1838, but that attempt failed within five years. It is unclear what brought that mass-oriented paper down, although the partisan divisions in advertising in addition to the panic of 1837 could explain its demise. The *Dispatch* gained a large circulation rather early due to its low price, but it took many years to build an advertising base, since other papers held their partisan advertisers rigidly in line. See the obituary for James Cowardin, *Richmond Dispatch*, 22 November 1882, as well as a later reflection on the paper's evolution, 2 July 1895.

74. David Ray Papke, *Framing the Criminal: Crime, Cultural Work, and the Loss of Critical Perspective, 1830–1900* (Hamden, Conn.: Archon Books, 1987), 25.

75. Andie Tucher, *Froth and Scum: Truth, Beauty, Goodness, and the Ax Murder in America's First Mass Medium* (Chapel Hill: University of North Carolina Press, 1994), 46–61. This is the perspective of most historians of this era, and my research confirms it. It contradicts much of Dan Schiller's *Objectivity and the News: The Public and the Rise of Commercial Journalism* (Philadelphia: University of Pennsylvania Press, 1981), however, which argues that the penny press in this era fostered the rise of objectivity as a goal for journalists. I find

little evidence of this either in my own research or, frankly, in the equivocal and thin evidence he provides.

76. Jane and John Williams killed the entire Winston family on 19 July 1852. Coverage in the *Dispatch* ran from 20 July to 28 October. Thirteen stories ran in those three months, far above the average for such cases previously, yet something like one-tenth the number that the Phillips case would elicit fifteen years later.

77. *Awful Disclosures! or Narrative and Confession of Henry Delter, the Murderer of His Five Wives* (Richmond: Barclay and Co., 1851); William Murdock, *Trial, Conviction, and Confession of Mary B. Thorn* (Norfolk: William C. Murdock, 1854). A reworked version of the Thorn pamphlet, with the dates of the crime changed, appeared the next year, published by Thomas Braden of Norfolk. Another such pamphlet is *The Authentic Confessions of William Masterson* (Philadelphia/Richmond: M. L. Barclay, 1854). Based in Philadelphia (but sometimes, like here, claiming other places of publication), the Barclay company printed dozens if not hundreds of fictional pamphlets in this period. For a discussion of antebellum fictional works centering on female criminals like Mary Thorn, see Dawn Keetley's "Victim and Victimizer: Female Fiends and Unease over Marriage in Antebellum Sensational Fiction," *American Quarterly* 51 (1999): 344–84. For a discussion of the Barclay company, see Thomas M. McDade, "Lurid Literature of the Last Century: The Publications of E. E. Barclay," *Pennsylvania Magazine of History and Biography* 80 (1956): 452–64. See also William Wadsworth, *The Murderer's Cave; or, The Punishment of Wickedness* (Boston: N. Coverly, 1818).

78. This is the central argument of Andie Tucher's *Froth and Scum*. It is also predicated upon the reading revolution of the nineteenth century outlined in Davidson, *Revolution and the Word*, 55–79. See also Tebbel, *Creation of an Industry*, 240–51, and Halttunen, *Murder Most Foul*, 69–73.

79. The *Southern Opinion* (1867–69) was an important innovation in the press of Virginia, but it was not the commonwealth's first illustrated weekly. The *Southern Illustrated News*, sporting a single engraving on the cover of each eight-page issue, was published in Richmond during the Civil War (1862–65). In this, Virginia is in keeping with national trends. The first major illustrated weeklies were *Frank Leslie's Illustrated Newspaper* (1855) and *Harper's Weekly* (1857), although the *National Police Gazette* began publishing a decade earlier and in its first years included a single image on the front page of each issue.

80. Carter, *Historical Statistics of the United States*, 26, 113, 359. Richmond's growth, from 3,761 in 1790 to 16,060 in 1830 to 37,910 in 1860, also outpaced national growth in population by a good margin. The national population grew almost sixfold as the North's development and immigration outstripped Virginia's, displacing it from its position as the most populous state (up to 1810) to the fifth most populous by 1860. Without much European immigration and with the ending of the international slave trade, Virginia's population grew

mostly by natural increase, lessened substantially by a continuous movement of people, free and slave, to the west and southwest. From 1790 to 1860, the state's population grew by an average of 9 percent each decade. This is compared to 35 percent each decade for the nation as a whole and 40 percent each decade for Richmond.

81. *Richmond Dispatch*, 2 July 1895.

82. This first batch of stories in the *Richmond Dispatch* on the Phillips case ran between 1 and 29 March 1867.

83. J. Wall Turner, *The Drinker's Farm Tragedy: Trial and Conviction of James Jeter Phillips for the Murder of His Wife* (Richmond: V. L. Fore, 1868).

84. *Richmond Dispatch*, 20–29 October 1868. The case before the court of appeals, of course, would have been a repeat of the testimony already given, twice in this case, before lower courts. In my reading of nineteenth-century trial coverage, appeals cases were always treated more briefly in the papers.

85. *Richmond Dispatch*, 26 March 1869.

86. *Southern Opinion*, 17 October 1868.

87. Ibid., 5, 12, 19, and 26 September 1868.

88. Ibid., 12 September and 17 and 24 October 1868. As other scholars have found, such embellishments were rather common in the mid-nineteenth-century press and certainly would not be out of keeping with the character of editor Pollard. According to this tale, after receiving a sentence of death in his second trial during the summer of 1868, Jeter Phillips persuaded his jailer to allow him to stop at a lowly saloon (and brothel, though reports do not imply he had a rendezvous there) called the "Lone Cottage" on his way back to his cell. After he returned to jail, he wrote a number of letters to the women in this house of ill repute, saying, among other things, that he "missed seeing their sweet faces."

89. *Southern Opinion*, 16 January and 13 and 27 March 1869.

90. Quoted in the *Richmond Enquirer*, among others, 19–20 June 1867.

91. In fact, it is difficult to pinpoint exactly when lawyers began to argue that the press perverted the judicial system. Karen Halttunen writes (*Murder Most Foul*, 72) that as early as 1821 "attorneys were routinely claiming the impossibility of their clients' receiving a fair trial because of the advance publicity," but this seems a bit early. In fact her citation for this claim lists pamphlets from 1821, 1833, 1845, and 1855, opening the question as to whether 1821 should stand as the best date for this development to be considered routine. In contrast, Patricia Cline Cohen argues that lawyers in the 1836 trial of Richard Robinson for the murder of Helen Jewett were "simply unaccustomed to factoring in press coverage, especially since the penny press with its pretrial coverage was a new force in public life." Instead, they simply ignored the issue entirely: "Attempts at managing, or 'spinning' the new lay in the future." Cohen, *The Murder of Helen Jewett: The Life and Death of a Prostitute in Nineteenth-Century New York* (New York: Alfred Knopf, 1998), 281.

CHAPTER 2

1. Quoted in Eldridge B. Hatcher, *William E. Hatcher: A Biography* (Richmond: W. C. Hill Printing Co., 1915), 243; the *State*, 28 March 1885.
2. The *Whig*, 31 March 1885; R. P. Dillard testimony, 25 May 1885, transcript, *Commonwealth v. Cluverius*, 4:1518, Meredith Family Papers, Virginia Historical Society (VHS), Richmond. Hereafter, testimony from this trial will be cited simply as "transcript" followed by the volume and page numbers.
3. The city had torn down the old city hall and courts building in 1874, and the new one (now known as the "old city hall") would not open until 1894. In the interim, the city government, including the hustings court, operated from a welter of makeshift offices downtown.
4. U.S. Census, Tenth Census, 1880, manuscript, Enumeration District 40, pp. 22–23, King William County, Virginia; John Walker testimony, 15 May 1885, transcript, 1:390.
5. Charles Madison to Jane Tunstall, 11 August 1881, Aylett Family Papers, VHS.
6. U.S. Census, Tenth Census, 1880, manuscript, Enumeration District 36, p. 44, King and Queen County, Virginia.
7. Madison to Tunstall; Jane Tunstall saw the Madisons as uncouth dirt farmers, being particularly offended by the gossiping of Lucy Madison, Lillian's mother. The Madisons, in turn, saw Tunstall as an overbearing, haughty meddler. In one letter, Charles Madison took offense because Tunstall had not visited his home and had made arrangements for Lillian's schooling without first consulting him. He even termed the treatment of his wife as "persecution" and wrote that he heard Tunstall was ready to "spit in his face" if she saw him again. Lucy Madison accused Tunstall in 1881 of writing to her "like I was a heathen" and of misinterpreting everything she had said and written in the past three years.
8. Mrs. Tunstall to Charles Madison, [August 1881]; Lucy Madison to Jane Tunstall, 25 May 1881; M. A. C. [Mary A. Cluverius] to Lucy Madison, 8 February, n.y. [probably 1881], Aylett Family Papers. Other relatives of Tunstall likewise saw her as a difficult woman who was willing to throw her weight around. Mary Cluverius, who lived with Tunstall for a few years in the 1870s, wrote that "she has ordered us out of her house a thousand times" and was currently angry with them and not coming down to meals.
9. This wider conflict concerned accusations against Tunstall's sister for maiming a young black girl shortly after the Civil War. Tunstall must have (willfully) forgotten this incident, and when the Madisons refreshed her memory, she was horrified by their bad taste. Jane Tunstall testimony, 26 May 1885, transcript, 4:1638–1709; Charles J. Madison testimony, 21 May 1885, transcript, 3:1147–79. In 1866, a sister of Jane Tunstall's, Ann Abrahams, was accused of taking a hot iron and badly burning a young black girl who worked for her. This young girl, previously Abrahams's slave, was severely injured, and the

"Yankees" took note of the ghastly case and made it into a famous instance of southern white mistreatment of freedpersons. The episode resurfaced in the early 1880s when Lillian's father received a copy of a New York paper detailing the matter, probably *Harper's Weekly* (28 July 1866), which contained a brief letter from Richmond describing the case and a drawing taken from a photo of the marks on the girl's back. The *Richmond Dispatch* covers the Abrahams case on 31 July 1866; the *New York Daily Tribune* has an extensive article complete with courtroom testimony on 25 July 1866. Madison testimony, 1175–76. According to Tunstall, the Madisons were simply insulting her sister by bringing up the trial. From the perspective of the Madisons, they simply verified what was already common knowledge; they claimed that the issue only arose after Tunstall herself had raised it during a visit. This became a very heated issue between the sides of the family: one letter admits that the Abrahams matter was "the cause of all the fuss." It was surely the subject of repeated references of having "something we need to talk about in person" between Tunstall and Lucy. M. A. C. to Lucy Madison, 8 February, n.y. [1881?]; Lucy Madison to Jane Tunstall, 25 May 1881, Aylett Family Papers.

10. M. A. C. to Lucy Madison, 8 February, n.y. [1881?].

11. B. W. Cluverius to Lucy Madison, 9 August 1881, Aylett Family Papers. In this letter, the father of the accused murderer adds to the evidence of a family breach by saying that "if you scold [Lillian] for staying after we kept her [from going], I nor none of my family shall ever come to see you again." He clearly believed that the Madisons would assume Lillian simply disobeyed their instructions, perhaps a common occurrence.

12. Tunstall testimony, 1642.

13. Letters corroborate Tunstall's testimony that Lillian frequently found clandestine means of seeing her banned relations, meeting them at a nearby sawmill, for instance, or simply in the woods or on the road. Likewise they found means to correspond outside the medium of the regular post. Tunstall would enclose a letter to Lillian in one to her aunt, who would then hand deliver it. Similarly, Lillian would send her letters to an old woman living nearby who would then take them to Tunstall. Ibid., 1652–53.

14. Madison testimony, 1154–55.

15. William Edwards testimony, 28 May 1885, transcript, 5:1939–45. Edwards was present at the resolution of the Biggs affair. The four men corresponding with Lillian were: Biggs, Lallie Prince, Willie Pointer, and a Mr. Shinault. According to both Edwards and Charles Madison, one of the Shinault letters included a suggestion that they meet in Richmond, although Lillian's father denied that the letter said she would never return. Madison testimony, 1160–68.

16. Madison testimony, 1155, 1160.

17. Lillian Madison to Jane Tunstall, 21 [no month] [1881], Richmond Hustings Court Records, June 1885, Library of Virginia (LVA), Richmond. This is not

dated, but Jane Tunstall identified it as a letter she received in 1881. Its references and context are in keeping with their correspondence that remains from that year.

18. Tunstall testimony, 1638–1709; Jane Tunstall to Charles Madison, [August 1881], Aylett Family Papers.

19. Walker testimony, 374–78.

20. Charles Madison to John P. Walker, 8 October 1884, Aylett Family Papers.

21. Madison testimony, 1168.

22. Tunstall testimony, 1638–1709. Although this letter was written on 16 November 1884, Tunstall was describing a letter she had seen or heard of, written at an unspecified earlier time. The Charles Madison letter, therefore, could reflect on the same moment of violence. Her swollen face might, then, refer to his own beating of his daughter.

23. Madison to Walker; emphasis in original.

24. Madison testimony, 1160–61.

25. *Richmond Dispatch*, 5 January 1887; Margaret Dickinson testimony, 19 May 1885, transcript, 2:758.

26. George Wright testimony, 20 May 1885, transcript, 2:953–59.

27. Charles Montriou Wallace Diary, 10 and 14 May 1885, Manuscripts Division, Perkins Library, Duke University, Durham, N.C.

28. Ibid., 5 June 1885.

29. Ibid., 15 January 1887.

30. U.S. Census, Seventh Census, 1850, manuscript, p. 94, Gloucester County, Virginia; U.S. Census, Eighth Census, 1860, manuscript, p. 574, King William County, Virginia; U.S. Census, Tenth Census, 1880, manuscript, Enumeration District 36, p. 48, King and Queen County, Virginia; Thomas J. Cluverius, *Cluverius: My Life, Trial and Conviction* (Richmond: Andrews, Baptist and Clemmitt, 1887), 11–13.

31. Cluverius, *My Life*, 11–13; Tunstall testimony, 1638–1709.

32. *Catalogue of Richmond College, Session 1880–81* (Richmond: Wm. Ellis Jones, 1881) and similar editions for 1882 and 1883, Virginia Baptist Historical Society, University of Richmond; Cluverius, *My Life*, 13–20.

33. Dr. J. E. Courtney testimony, 28 May 1885, transcript, 5:1952–64; Rev. H. H. Harris testimony, 27 May 1885, transcript, 4:1929–30.

34. Mary Curtis testimony, 21 May 1885, transcript, 3:1115–37.

35. John B. Yarrington testimony, 27 May 1885, transcript, 4:1886–87; Courtney testimony, 1952–64; Dr. W. C. Barker testimony, 26 May 1885, transcript, 4:1778–80; and others.

36. Walker testimony, 380–96.

37. Claggett B. Jones testimony, 15 May 1885, transcript, 1:512–14; A. W. Archer testimony, 15 May 1885, transcript, 1:515–36; Henrietta Winbush testimony, 15 May 1885, transcript, 1:537–62.

38. Madison testimony, 1168.

39. Ibid., 1170.

40. Nolie Bray statement, transcript, 5:1802.

41. *Richmond Whig*, 21 March 1885. In fact, the full title, in four alliterative, exclamatory lines, was: "Mystery of the Morgue! Revelations of the Reservoir! A New Colleen Bawn! Murder of Fannie Lillian Madison!"

42. Dion Boucicault, *The Colleen Bawn; or, The Brides of Garryowen* (London: Thomas Hailes Lacy, 1865); there were various other printings during the 1860s.

43. Boucicault, *Colleen Bawn*, 43, 46.

44. Peter Brooks, *The Melodramatic Imagination: Balzac, Henry James, Melodrama, and the Mode of Excess* (New Haven, Conn.: Yale University Press, 1995), 41. Brooks offers the best study of this genre. Also useful is Robert B. Heilman's *Tragedy and Melodrama: Versions of Experience* (Seattle: University of Washington Press, 1968).

45. Cathy N. Davidson, *The Revolution and the Word: The Rise of the Novel in America* (New York: Oxford University Press, 1986), 110–50; Susanna Rowson, *Charlotte Temple; and Lucy Temple*, ed. Ann Douglas (New York: Penguin, 1991).

46. Davidson, *Revolution and the Word*, 110–50; Amy Gilman Srebnick's *The Mysterious Death of Mary Rogers: Sex and Culture in Nineteenth-Century New York* (New York: Oxford University Press, 1995), 109–57. Joseph Holt Ingraham, Charles Burdett, and Ned Buntline also produced fictional accounts of the Mary Rogers murder.

47. *Richmond Dispatch*, 31 May 1885 and 15 January 1887.

48. "How I Became a Murderer," *Richmond Standard*, 24 July 1880; "The Detective's Story," *Southern Opinion*, 28 December 1867; "A Murderer's Story," *Richmond Planet*, 14 June 1902.

49. *Richmond Dispatch*, 24 April 1885.

50. This parallels one of the most fascinating discoveries in Patricia Cline Cohen's study of the 1836 murder of Helen Jewett: how the victim herself manipulated her clients by providing them with a sentimental tale of her own fall from virtue into prostitution. Cohen argues than many of the romantic stories of Jewett's life related by the press were of her own creation, founded as they were in the fantasies that she so deftly created for her male companions. In fact, one of Jewett's aliases was "Helen Mar," the heroine of an early-nineteenth-century historical romance. Cohen, *The Murder of Helen Jewett: The Life and Death of a Prostitute in Nineteenth-Century New York* (New York: Alfred A. Knopf, 1998), 43.

51. Davidson, *Revolution and the Word*, 146.

52. Other examples of the press and public turning a crime story in different directions in the nineteenth century can be found in Karen Halttunen's *Murder Most Foul: The Killer and the American Gothic Imagination* (Cambridge,

Mass.: Harvard University Press, 1998) and Srebnick's *Mysterious Death of Mary Rogers*.

53. Walker testimony, 374–473; Tunstall testimony, 1638–1709; Madison testimony, 1160–64.

54. Halttunen, *Murder Most Foul*, 183–86.

55. Walker testimony, 374–473.

56. An alternative explanation might be that they never saw the evidence developed above: most of the letters between family members are currently a part of the Aylett Family Papers, and William Roane Aylett was one of the two prosecuting attorneys in the Cluverius case. At the time, none of these were introduced as evidence in court, nor were they ever printed in the local press. The prosecution clearly knew of the Madison family troubles and this epistolary evidence of it, but did they share this with the defense or hide it from them? Even if they did not have these letters, the defense would surely have known of at least much of this material from the Cluverius and Tunstall families.

57. The statement of Emmet Williams is transcribed into the Cluverius trial transcript (5:2172), and that of Carey Madison is likewise in the transcript (5:2037). Wrangling between the lawyers over the introduction of Carey Madison's letters takes place the day before (5:1931–39). Her flirtation with these men was possibly an attempt to attract a husband once she realized she was pregnant. Nothing definitive points in that direction, however, and no one at the time publicly drew such an inference.

58. W. W. Crump, quoted in John D. Lawson, *American State Trials*, vol. 17 (St. Louis: Thomas Law Books, 1935), 444–45.

59. Lawson, *American State Trials*, 486.

60. "On the Delaware," *Commonwealth v. Cluverius*, Richmond Hustings Court Records, June 1885. Several witnesses were called to verify different aspects of this weekend, but the chief one was John Walker himself. Walker testimony, 374–473.

61. Walker testimony, 374–473.

62. N. W. Ayer and Sons, *Newspaper Annual* (Philadelphia: Ayer and Sons, 1885), 124–25.

63. The most detailed coverage of it said simply that it was "as vile a production as ever befouled any language." Unsigned editorial, *Virginia Law Journal* 9 (August 1885): 508.

64. *Richmond Dispatch*, 19 March 1885.

65. Ibid., 31 March 1885.

66. Ibid., 8 May 1885.

67. Ibid., 20 March 1885.

68. This style of rendering the horrors of the reservoir's neighborhood is repeated on 31 March, when the *Dispatch* printed an account of the "Night on the Small-Pox Hospital Grounds."

69. Ibid., 14 January 1887.

70. Wallace Diary, 14 May 1885; G. W. ("a woman") to Colonel Aylett, 2 June 1885, Aylett Family Papers.

71. J. Wall Turner, *The Drinker's Farm Tragedy: Trial and Conviction of James Jeter Phillips for the Murder of His Wife* (Richmond: V. L. Fore, 1868), 4, 29.

72. *Daily Enquirer and Examiner*, 19 November 1867.

73. *Daily Enquirer and Sentinel*, 19 June 1867.

74. Phillips was first tried in the county court of Henrico in July of 1867. He was before the Henrico Circuit Court in October and November of 1867, a proceeding that ended in a hung jury. He was retried by that court in June and July of 1868 and was convicted of first-degree murder.

75. For more on the development of a nineteenth-century interest in death and bodies, see Karen Halttunen, "The Pornography of Violence," in *Murder Most Foul*, 60–90. I feel that Halttunen might overplay this voyeuristic interest in the specifics of bodily violence and death, but it is nevertheless an important component of the popular literature of the time.

76. *Daily Enquirer and Sentinel*, 25 June 1867.

77. Judge Christian's sentence quoted in the *Daily Enquirer and Examiner*, 11 July 1868.

78. David Ray Papke, *Framing the Criminal: Crime, Cultural Work, and the Loss of Critical Perspective, 1830–1900* (Hamden, Conn.: Archon Books, 1987); Andie Tucher, *Froth and Scum: Truth, Beauty, Goodness, and the Ax Murder in America's First Mass Medium* (Chapel Hill: University of North Carolina Press, 1994), 62. Amy Srebnick devoted much of *The Mysterious Death of Mary Rogers* to the numerous and various ways that Rogers and her death were typecast by newspapers and later by novelists.

79. Daniel Cohen, *Pillars of Salt, Monuments of Grace: New England Crime Literature and the Origins of American Popular Culture, 1674–1860* (New York: Oxford University Press, 1993), 167–246; quotation, 198. In "The Beautiful Female Murder Victim: Literary Genres and Courtship Practices in the Origins of a Cultural Motif, 1590–1850," *Journal of Social History* 31 (1997): 277–306, Cohen takes this argument further, connecting broad social changes in courtship to the sentimental novel and to the development of a stereotype in the literature of true crime. Karen Halttunen (*Murder Most Foul*, 47–48) has employed different terms—the gothic imagination rather than legal romanticism, for instance—but comes to similar conclusions regarding the relationship between true crime and the literary tastes of the era.

80. Cohen, *Murder of Helen Jewett*, 19–89, 312–18. In fact, the most vilified people connected to the case were Rosina Townsend (Jewett's madam) and prostitutes in general. Richard Robinson was not only acquitted; he was cheered for the fact.

81. Halttunen, *Murder Most Foul*, 172–207; quotation, 184.

82. Wallace Diary, 28 May 1885.

83. Curtis testimony, 1115–37. Curtis was a little confused on the dates, something the defense attempted to exploit. She said she had been away from her father's home ("on the town") for three years, making her start in prostitution in 1882, when Cluverius would have still been in law school. But when asked for a date, she very definitively stated that it was in 1883 that she left her father's home. Perhaps Cluverius visited her while on trips to Richmond from the county, or perhaps Curtis was mistaken, and it was in 1882 that she entertained him, while he was in school.

84. W. W. Crump, quoted in *Richmond Dispatch*, 4 June 1885.

85. Handwriting analysis was in its infancy at this point, but the Cluverius trial included several witnesses that the prosecution argued were experts in distinguishing handwriting, including one member of a brokerage firm and another bank clerk. Both argued that the poem and several letters were written by the same person as other writings known to be in Cluverius's hand. W. R. Quarles testimony, 18 May 1885, transcript, 2:622–38; James D. Craig testimony, 18 May 1885, transcript, 2:639–69. Other witnesses who had lived with Madison in Bath County also were asked about her handwriting, but the judge later struck their testimony because he did not consider them expert witnesses. This broached a long debate over the nature of this type of evidence and the requirements for such expertise. See transcript, 2:674–746, 807–15, and 821–40.

86. William T. Martin testimony, 20 May 1885, transcript, 2:960–79; Curtis testimony, 1115–37; William Tucker testimony, 22 May 1885, transcript, 3:1274–92; Thomas E. Stratton testimony, 22 May 1885, transcript, 3:1311–36.

87. Charles Meredith, closing argument, transcript, *Commonwealth v. Cluverius*, 72–74, Meredith Family Papers, Virginia Historical Society (VHS), Richmond.

88. Ibid., 112–14.

89. *Daily Enquirer and Sentinel*, 14 June 1867.

90. *Southern Opinion*, 5 September 1868. And when the evidence in the case was heard, Pollard continued, "it was the most convincing ever offered, and the entire community pronounced him 'guilty.'" Judge Christian's sentence of death, "the most sublimely beautiful that ever fell from mortal lips," according to Pollard, was filled with ideals "which blanche[d] every cheek and moisten[ed] every eye in that trembling crowd."

91. Testimony of George Turner quoted in *Richmond Dispatch*, 21 June 1867.

92. John S. Wise, *The Lion's Skin: A Historical Novel and a Novel of History* (New York: Doubleday, Page, and Co., 1905), 178.

93. *Southern Opinion*, 13 March 1869.

94. Phillip Leigh, *Lillian's Marriage and Murder: Cluverius Did Not Kill Her; The Sequel Told* (Richmond: Patrick Keenan, 1887).

95. "Old Man Bruce, the Richmond Detective; or, 'Piping' the Reservoir Mystery," vol. 3, no. 304, of the *Old Cap. Collier Library* (11 June 1888), a weekly series published by Munro's Publishing House of New York.

96. W. C. Elam, "Murder Most Foul," *Lippincott's Magazine of Literature, Science, and Education*, November 1869, 503–9. In the real case, James Jeter Phillips was nursed by (Virginian) Mary Pitts, married her, and killed her; Indiana Turner was a local woman reportedly involved with Jeter at the time of the murder.

Another version of the Phillips murder appeared in thinly veiled form in *The Lion's Skin*, a novel by a local lawyer. This "historical novel and novel of history" chiefly concerned other matters, but several pages outlined the Phillips murder, keeping quite close to the facts of the case. Yet the author allowed himself to invent a fictive and melodramatic scene that emphasized the upstanding nature of the accused murderer. According to this version, Phillips was kneeling at his bedside saying nightly prayers at the moment the sheriff broke in and charged him with the murder of his wife. Said the young lawyer/hero of the story: Jeter "had been an excellent soldier and was regarded as an unusually gentle, exemplary, religious young man." Wise, *The Lion's Skin*, 175–79, 185. Jeter was actually arrested while walking across a field to go to work. But on the whole, the novel presents the series of events about as accurately as the local papers did.

97. Robert A. Ferguson, "Story and Transcription in the Trial of John Brown," *Yale Journal of Law and Humanities* 6 (1994): 37–73.

98. *American Publisher's Circular and Literary Gazette*, 29 December 1855, 262–63; quoted in John Tebbel, *The Creation of an Industry, 1630–1865*, vol. 1 of *A History of Book Publishing in the United States* (New York: R. R. Bowker, 1972), 224.

99. Harry Calligan Diary, 6 January 1885, Valentine Museum, Richmond; reprinted in Gregg D. Kimball, ed., "The Diary of Harry Calligan: Coming of Age in Industrial Manchester," *Journal of the Chesterfield Historical Society* 3 (1997): 30.

100. [A Richmond Lady,] *Cousin Tommie* (Richmond: C. F. Johnston, 1885). Richmonders left other poems on Lillian's grave, and some were published in the newspapers and in a pamphlet on the case. *Richmond Dispatch*, 12 May 1885; George Booker, *The Virginia Tragedy: Trial and Conviction of Thomas J. Cluverius* (Richmond: Johns and Goolsby, 1885), 37, 84–85, 92–93.

101. Brooks, *Melodramatic Imagination*, 24.

102. Victor Turner, *From Ritual to Theatre: The Human Seriousness of Play* (New York: Performing Arts Journal Publications, 1982), 10. See also his *The Ritual Process: Structure and Anti-Structure* (London: Routledge and Kegan Paul, 1969).

103. "Memorial of Judge W. W. Crump," *Virginia Law Register* 2 (1897): 915–17; Paul B. Barringer, James Mercer Garnett, and Rosewell Page, *The University of Virginia: It's History, Influence, Equipment, and Characteristics* . . . (New York: Lewis Publishing Co., 1904), 2:241–42; *Virginia Biography*, vol. 4 of *History of Virginia* (Chicago: American Historical Society, 1924), 231–32;

H. R. Pollard, "William Roane Aylett," *Virginia Law Register* 6 (1920): 570–72; H. M. Smith Jr., "Henry Robinson Pollard," *Virginia State Bar Association Reports* 36 (1924): 114.

104. Meredith closing argument, 73, 48.

105. Booker, *Virginia Tragedy*, 148. One letter to Meredith asks for copies of the speeches of the prosecution to be sent to Alexandria, where the correspondent and others would like to read them in their entirety. J. T. Sherwood to C. V. Meredith, 16 June 1885, Meredith Family Papers.

106. H. C. Underhill, *A Treatise on the Law of Criminal Evidence* (Indianapolis, Ind.: Bowen-Merrill, 1898), 8. Sensations tend to have a certain sort of mystery: tantalizingly close to having enough evidence to be certain of the culprit's guilt but without complete assurance. A complete mystery foreshortens the possibility of sensation. For example, a German peddler, Sammox Rosdeitcher, was murdered by someone using a hatchet in the countryside north of Richmond in 1890. Four different people were arrested for killing "Mox," but the thin evidence available did not prove a connection to any of them; ultimately, the murder went unsolved and the story dropped out of the papers. The mystery of Mox's death generated intense interest and concomitant newspaper coverage: the *Dispatch* printed five times the number of stories on Rosdeitcher's murder than it did for the more straightforward Baccigalupo attack mentioned in the introduction. The mystery was gripping, but the evidence was too weak to keep this story and the investigation moving forward. *Richmond Dispatch*, 29 July–11 October 1890.

107. The early history of Anglo-American theories of circumstantial evidence can be found in Barbara J. Shapiro, *"Beyond Reasonable Doubt" and "Probable Cause": Historical Perspectives on the Anglo-American Law of Evidence* (Berkeley: University of California Press, 1991), esp. 200–246.

108. S. March Phillips, *A Treatise on the Law of Evidence* (New York: Banks, Gould, and Co., 1849), 440–41.

109. Francis Wharton, *A Treatise on the Law of Evidence in Criminal Issues*, 8th ed. (Philadelphia: Kay and Brother, 1880), 26–27.

110. Wallace Diary, 27 May 1887.

111. Rufus Ayers, William R. Aylett, and Charles V. Meredith, "Brief for the State," in *In the Supreme Court of Appeals of Virginia, Richmond: T. J. Cluverius v. the Commonwealth: Brief for the State* (Richmond: n.p., 1886), 3; emphasis in original.

112. *Richmond Dispatch*, 29 January 1867. See also, "Proved Innocent Too Late—Circumstantial Evidence," *Richmond Dispatch*, 1 August 1868.

113. "A Strange History—Colorado Miner's Mystery," *Richmond Dispatch*, 3 January 1886; "Circumstantial Evidence," ibid., 1 April 1885.

114. Richmond Police Benevolent Association, "History of the Richmond Police Department" (Richmond: J. L. Hill Printing Co., 1901); see also, *Illustrated Richmond Police and Fire Department Directory* ([Richmond]: John T. West,

1896), 7–13; Louis Bernard Cei, "Law Enforcement in Richmond: A History of Police-Community Relations, 1737–1974" (Ph.D. diss., Florida State University, 1975), 1–59.

115. The chief of police argued that the force had a duty to go wherever citizens assembled but admitted that officers were "very severely criticized" by the public at large "for doing duty at places of amusement," meaning saloons. John Poe Jr., "Annual Report of the Chief of Police to Mayor W. C. Carrington," 1 January 1887; printed in the *Annual Message of the Mayor of Richmond* (Richmond: Everett Waddey, 1887), 5. See the *Richmond Dispatch*, 26 June 1878, for a list of offenses that garnered dismissal; for an example of a dismissal due to an officer beating a man, 2 June 1874. During the Cluverius murder trial, William S. Courtney testified that police officers Nowlan and Tomlinson inappropriately furnished whiskey to him while they discussed his knowledge of the case. William S. Courtney testimony, 27 May 1885, transcript, 5:1875–76.

116. John Poe Jr., "Annual Report of the Chief of Police to Mayor W. C. Carrington," 1 January 1885; printed in the *Annual Message of the Mayor of Richmond* (Richmond: Walthall and Bowles, 1885), 1.

117. John Poe Jr., "Annual Report of the Chief of Police to Mayor A. M. Keiley," 31 January 1875; printed in the *Fifth Annual Message of the Mayor of Richmond* (Richmond: James E. Goode, 1875), 302.

118. *Richmond Whig*, 30 Sept. 1888. Similarly, in his 1875 assessment of the city, Mayor Keiley explained that the large number of arrests that year was "due to the culpable facility with which some magistrates issue warrants, oftentimes confounding felonies with misdemeanors, and still more frequently using processes without justification." Keiley, *Fifth Annual Message of the Mayor of Richmond*, x.

119. Demonstrating the depths of the reputation held by detectives, the commonwealth's attorney in one case against Wren asked "what chance does even a tramp stand at night in the hands of Jack Wren?" A particularly vocal spectator applauded this sentiment and was pursued by officers out of the courtroom (he was not caught). *Richmond Dispatch*, 4 June 1879.

120. These fees for successful return of stolen property were ended in 1879. *Richmond Dispatch*, 8 November 1879.

121. One Richmond editorial pointed to the renowned Vidocq and other European detectives: "the most successful and distinguished thief-takers have invariable [*sic*] been distinguished graduates of all the schools in the university of crime." *Richmond Enquirer and Examiner*, 8 July 1868.

122. *Richmond Enquirer*, 14 February 1871.

123. Calloway Brown, "Revision of Our Criminal Laws," *Virginia Law Register* 5 (January 1900): 579.

124. *Richmond Dispatch*, 18 March 1873.

125. See, for instance, the *Richmond Dispatch*, 22 October 1893.

126. A man accused of rape was found guilty of attempted rape, despite the fact that the evidence clearly supported actual rape rather than an attempt. Richard H. Tebbs to Editor, "The Weatherholtz Case, Again—The Downs Case Contra," *Virginia Law Register* 2 (March 1897): 870–71. This lenient decision was surely influenced by the fact that the woman was "notorious" and black and that the accused was white.

127. "The Miscarriage of Justice in Weatherholtz's Case," *Virginia Law Register* 2 (January 1897): 697–700; W. B. Kegley to Editor, "The Weatherholtz Case," *Virginia Law Register* 2 (February 1897): 787–89. This reticence to convict in capital cases such as these prompted the Virginia legislature to introduce the possibility of lesser sentences than death for first-degree murder. In 1914, the general assembly changed the wording of the law to read: "Murder in the first degree shall be punished with death, or by confinement in the Penitentiary for life or for any term not less than twenty years." *The Code of Virginia, 1919,* vol. 2 (Richmond: Davis Bottom, 1919), 1790.

128. Philip Lybrook to Henley Lybrook, 22 April 1842, Lybrook Family Letters, Special Collections, University of Virginia Library, Charlottesville.

129. *Richmond Religious Herald*, 30 April 1885.

130. Wallace Diary, 13 May 1885.

131. Hatcher, *William E. Hatcher*, 246.

132. Prosecuting attorney Meredith likened Cluverius to Judas Iscariot and Benedict Arnold. In turn, Henry Pollard, one of Cluverius's defense attorneys, alluded to Jesus in his closing arguments. *Richmond Dispatch*, 3–4 June 1885. John Brown famously appropriated the words of Jesus in his attempt to turn himself into a martyr after the Harpers Ferry debacle; see Ferguson, "Story and Transcription in the Trial of John Brown," 61.

CHAPTER 3

1. These details come from the *Richmond Times-Dispatch*, 19 July 1911.

2. *A Full and Complete History of the Great Beattie Case; Most Highly Sensational Tragedy of the Century* (Baltimore, Md.: Phoenix Publishing Co., 1911), 9–10. Hereafter, this will be cited as *Great Beattie Case*.

3. Gertrude Stein, "Picasso," in *Gertrude Stein on Picasso*, ed. Edward Burns (New York: Liveright, 1970), 30.

4. *New York Evening Post* editorial reprinted in the *Richmond Times-Dispatch*, 28 November 1911. A longer reprint of this editorial appears in the *Nation*, 30 November 1911, 514–15.

5. Charles Merz, "Bigger and Better Murders," *Harper's Monthly Magazine*, August 1927, 341.

6. Manchester and Richmond merged in 1910, and the area was then identified simply as south Richmond.

7. U.S. Census, Thirteenth Census, 1910, manuscript, Enumeration District 56, visitation 55, Richmond, Virginia.

8. In fact, Beattie Sr. listed his business as dry goods in the 1900 census and as a department store in 1910.

9. Henry C. Beattie Sr. testimony, 31 May 1911, transcript, *Commonwealth v. Henry Clay Beattie Jr.*, 17:1020, Chesterfield County Courthouse; U.S. Census, Thirteenth Census, 1910, manuscript, Enumeration District 80, visitation 120, Richmond, Virginia; *Great Beattie Case*, 11–12.

10. Beattie Sr. testimony, 17:997–1000.

11. Henry C. Beattie Jr. testimony, 4 September 1911, transcript, *Commonwealth v. Beattie*, 24:1409; William H. Sampson testimony, 2 September 1911, transcript, *Commonwealth v. Beattie*, 20½:1219–44c and 21:1245–78. While both Henry and his friend William Sampson stated that they lived a "fast" or "dissipated" life, very little in this case clearly defines what that means at this time and to these young men. Implied was a congeries of youthful and disreputable pastimes: joyriding in cars, sporting events of several sorts, drinking, and engaging prostitutes. But rarely were any of these events specifically and unequivocally tied to Beattie, except in the case of Beulah Binford, discussed below. One exception was this passage in the Beattie testimony in which he was asked if he used Beulah to "gratify [his] passions" and Beattie answered "Well, she was one of them." Beattie Jr. testimony.

12. Jessie E. Binford testimony, 28 August 1911, transcript, *Commonwealth v. Beattie*, 8:490–98; Beattie Jr. testimony, 24:1401–60; quote, 1409; Beulah Binford testimony, transcript, *Proceedings of Coroner's Inquiry upon the Death of Mrs. Louise Owen Beattie*, 21–22 July 1911, 103–20, Chesterfield County Courthouse.

13. Jessie Binford testimony, 8:498–506; Sampson testimony, 20½:1221; Beattie Jr. testimony, 24:1401–24; Beulah Binford testimony. She soon moved to a house of prostitution in Danville, Virginia, and then began living with a local baseball player there, taking his name. The baby was first raised by Binford relatives, but Beulah's mother placed more pressure on Beattie, threatening to expose him, and so Henry arranged for his adoption by a local childless couple. Soon, Binford moved with her new beau to Danville, Illinois, and by February 1911, migrated yet again to live with her mother in Norfolk, Virginia. The papers later reported that this baby had died before his first birthday, and Beattie was forced by further threats of exposure into paying for the child's burial.

14. *Richmond Dispatch*, 25 August 1910. Everyone in the family testified that they kissed good-bye; for example, Douglas B. Beattie testimony, 1 September 1911, transcript, *Commonwealth v. Beattie*, 18:1047, and (a cousin) Frederick R. Beattie testimony, 2 September 1911, transcript, *Commonwealth v. Beattie*, 21:1245–1309. Friends of Louise testifying to their good marriage are in sequence in the transcript (20:1175–79).

15. Beulah Binford testimony, 113–15; Sampson testimony, 20½:1223–26; Henri-

etta Pitman testimony, 28 August 1911, transcript, *Commonwealth v. Beattie,* 8:508–18.

16. Beulah Binford testimony, 111; May Stuart testimony, 24 August 1911, transcript, *Commonwealth v. Beattie,* 2:82–87; H. C. Beattie to Mrs. R. T. Fisher, 14 July 1911, *Commonwealth v. Beattie,* Chesterfield County Courthouse.

17. Mrs. Robert V. Owen testimony, 28 August 1911, transcript, *Commonwealth v. Beattie,* 7:469–74; E. W. Farley (pharmacist) testimony, 29 August 1911, transcript, *Commonwealth v. Beattie,* 11:701; Dr. A. G. Franklin testimony, transcript, 28 August 1911, *Commonwealth v. Beattie,* 8:480–88; Dr. Herbert Mann testimony, 5 September 1911, transcript, *Commonwealth v. Beattie,* 27:1720–26.

18. *Great Beattie Case,* 40.

19. *Wilmington (Del.) Evening Journal,* 15 August 1911.

20. Only twice did brief passages, one-third of a page each, mention her life before the fateful evening of July eighteenth. One touched on her wedding day the summer before; the other, her unhappiness in marriage and how she contemplated divorce. *Great Beattie Case,* 29, 40.

21. *Richmond Times-Dispatch,* 24 July 1911. The "Death of Louise Beattie" section of this chapter, in fact, bears witness to this focus: of its twelve paragraphs, two treat the couple together, one focuses on Louise, and nine concentrate on Henry, Beulah, or his trial. The evidence that remains for the historian is clearly skewed away from the victim and toward the accused, just as in nineteenth-century cases.

22. *Richmond Times-Dispatch,* 9 September 1911. This passage became exception No. 15 in the appeal of the Beattie lawyers to overturn his conviction.

23. Ibid. Another article the following day mirrors some of these ideas, calling Beattie an "anachronism, a thing unique among mankind, a reversion to a type of a thousand years ago. . . . Like an amoeba, he moves a hand or a foot when touched, but not a heart, for there he lacks. He seems about as richly endowed with nerves and human feeling as a jelly fish."

24. *Richmond Religious Herald,* 27 July 1911.

25. Adon Yoder, "Who Killed Louise Beattie," *Idea,* 26 August 1911, 5, 8, 11.

26. *Harper's Monthly Magazine,* October 1913, 796.

27. *Southern Opinion,* 17, 24 October 1869.

28. *Richmond Times-Dispatch* (editorial), 12 August 1911; photo series: 8 August 1911.

29. *News Leader,* 25 July 1911; *New York Times,* 7 October 1911.

30. *Religious Herald,* 24 August 1911. The two papers mentioned in the last line of the editorial would represent to the audience of 1911 the extremes of the yellow, sensational press.

31. Ibid., 30 April 1885.

32. *Richmond Times-Dispatch,* 29 August 1911.

33. *Richmond Evening Journal*, 28 August 1911, extra no. 4. Their extra no. 5 for this day contained more of the testimony of Mrs. Owen as well as a doctor's report of Beattie's venereal disease. Accused of sending obscene matter through the mail, the *Journal* had to defend itself in U.S. district court. The judge of that court finally quashed the case, agreeing with the defense that they should not be prosecuted for printing testimony given in an open court of law. *United States v. Journal Co., Inc.*, 197 F. 415 (5 June 1912).

34. *Great Beattie Case*, 40.

35. *Richmond Times-Dispatch*, 5 September 1911; Beattie Jr. testimony, 1409. The actual testimony is considerably more forthright: "Q—You had carnal knowledge of a child under fourteen years of age, for nearly a whole year—which would be rape under the law—and yet you were not able to break loose from her? A—I could have broken; there was nothing to break loose from; I was going with her—I didn't see any reason why I should not; she represented herself to be much older—in fact, she looked older to everybody, and no one in the world would have taken her to be a girl of thirteen years—with the reputation she had. Q—She had enough influence over you to make you commit rape under the law, for eleven months. A—I did not know I was committing rape. Q—Don't you know that to have carnal knowledge of a girl, even with her consent, under fourteen years old, you could be electrocuted for it? A—I say I didn't know she was under fourteen."

36. *Richmond Times-Dispatch*, 8 September 1911. The *New York Times* (8 February 1907) also noted that "there were women in the courtroom" during Evelyn Nesbit Thaw's recitation of her "relations" with Stanford White—telling the story that inspired her husband to kill White in 1906. In this case, both the *New York Times* and the *Richmond Times-Dispatch* employed euphemism when discussing White drugging and raping Evelyn. Her head pounded, things went black, and she woke in a bed surrounded by mirrors, screaming. Very vivid and prurient but without the actual words "rape" or "sex." The *Times* employed both an overall report of the day's testimony and several pages of testimony; the *Times-Dispatch* employed a summary of the testimony for this case of great interest but which also occurred hundreds of miles away.

37. In a peculiarly one-sided defense of the privacy needs of Victorian elites, Rochelle Gurstein argues that the turn of the century saw the beginning of a modern craze of publicity and the concomitant breakdown of privacy in America: "the moderns of a century ago succeeded in discrediting their Victorian forebears and in opening the public sphere to matters previously believed to be private and therefore unfit for public display." Gurstein, *The Repeal of Reticence: A History of America's Cultural and Legal Struggles over Free Speech, Obscenity, Sexual Liberation, and Modern Art* (New York: Hill and Wang, 1996), 6. I believe it was a more gradual process than she admits, emerging over the course of several generations in the nineteenth and early twentieth centuries, and I am

not as fatalistic about the consequences of that development. But the change in American culture is clear—the press and public were willing to discuss much in the early twentieth century that would have been shameful two generations before; they became desensitized to the shocking. One delight in Gurstein's polemical book is the prodigious and wonderful bounty of genteel critics of modern mores that she presents.

38. *Nation*, 30 November 1911, 514-15.

39. "The Cause of the Beattie Murder—May Stuart's Testimony the Clue—Points to the Real Guilty Party," *Idea*, 5 August 1911, 5-7.

40. "Three Recent Murders Chargeable to the Police Board," *Idea*, 7 October 1911, 12. Yoder went far enough in his claims against Richmond institutions to provoke an angry response. His accusations against powerful Richmonders prompted a series of lawsuits for libel, at least one of which Yoder won. After being jailed more than once and after facing litigation for years—both of which predictably confirmed Yoder's belief in the corruption among the city's powerful—he was forced from the Richmond newspaper scene in 1911.

41. *Great Beattie Case*, 9.

42. *Religious Herald*, 17 August 1911.

43. Ibid., 30 November 1911; Carl Snyder, "The Encouragement to Kill!" *Collier's*, 25 November 1911, 15-17. In fact, *Collier's* itself makes this connection to the Beattie case and other recent murders.

44. This sort of coverage can be found in any of the Richmond papers during the course of the trial, 22 August–9 September 1911.

45. Quotation from Silas Bent, "The Art of Ballyhoo," *Harper's Monthly Magazine*, September 1927, 487. Statistics: Roger Lane, *Murder in America: A History* (Columbus: Ohio State University Press, 1997), 181-88; Eric H. Monkkonen, "A Disorderly People? Urban Order in the Nineteenth and Twentieth Centuries," *Journal of American History* 68 (1981): 539-59. According to Lane, the murder rate in Philadelphia fell from the antebellum period to the turn of the century by almost one-third, and this trend is comparable to that in both the United States and the rest of the industrializing world. Note that this measures murder *rates* (homicides per 1,000 population); with a quickly growing population, the strict number of crimes *did* go up in this period, as one must expect.

46. Donald B. Dodd, comp., *Historical Statistics of the States of the United States, Two Centuries of the Census, 1790-1990* (Westport, Conn: Greenwood Press, 1993), 457-58.

47. Per capita GNP (in terms of constant, 1958 dollars) for the nation rose from $531 in 1870 to $1,229 in 1910. U.S. Census Bureau, *Historical Statistics of the United States, Colonial Times to 1970, Pt. 1* (Washington: U.S. Government Printing Office, 1975), 224.

48. *Eighth U.S. Census 1860*, vol. 3: *Manufacturing* (Washington, D.C.: U.S.

Government Printing Office, 1865), 617; *Thirteenth U.S. Census, 1910*, vol. 9: *Manufacturing* (Washington, D.C.: U.S. Government Printing Office, 1913), 1278.

49. U.S. Census Bureau, *Historical Statistics of the United States*, 382.

50. U.S. Census Bureau, *Tenth U.S. Census, 1880*, vol. 1: *Population* (Washington, D.C.: U.S. Government Printing Office, 1883), 919; U.S. Census Bureau, *Thirteenth U.S. Census*, vol. 1: *Population*, 1203–4, 1239. Figures for Richmond and Virginia literacy are not available for 1870 or before. Statistics on the number of newspapers per capita follows this trend in literacy. In 1900, the South as a whole had 1.6 daily papers of at least 7,500 circulation per million population, whereas the ratio for the northeast was 6.5 per million population. The ratio for the nation as a whole was 4.0 per million. Delos F. Wilcox, "The American Newspaper: A Study in Social Psychology," *Annals of the American Academy of Political and Social Sciences* 16 (July 1900): 73.

51. *Religious Herald*, 14 September 1911. For a national view of journalism and murder cases in this era, see George Alger, "Sensational Journalism and the Law," *Atlantic Monthly*, February 1903, 145–51.

52. *Richmond Dispatch*, 2 July 1895. The article proudly discusses the growth of the press machinery and how the paper's new machine can print multiple pages as fast as 20,000 in an hour.

53. Charles Merz, "The American Press: A Summary of the Changes in a Quarter-Century," *Century Magazine*, November 1926, 103–10. In addition, the number of dailies and weeklies being published as well as the size of their circulations expanded enormously in this period, far outpacing population growth. In 1860, the nation could boast of 387 daily papers with a combined circulation of a little less than 1.5 million; by 1909, 2,600 dailies were reaching something more than 24 million readers. U.S. Census Bureau, *Historical Statistics of the United States*, 810. Due to consolidations, 1909 marks the high point for the number of dailies. In the next manufacturing census (1914), twenty fewer dailies were publishing, and the decline in gross numbers continued through most of the century.

54. Phillips: 127 stories in 867 days of printing (or 0.15 per day); Cluverius: 172 stories in 576 days of printing (or 0.3 per day); Beattie: 203 stories in 153 days (or 1.33 per day).

55. By the 1880s, reporting tended more toward descriptive and even verbose narrations of developments. Whereas approximately one-third of the *Dispatch* articles on the Phillips case were brief, one-paragraph updates, only about one-ninth of the Cluverius coverage fits into that category: 40 of 127 *Richmond Dispatch* articles for Phillips were of this minimalist variety—a short paragraph or less; for Cluverius, 20 of 172. Similarly, the Phillips case prompted the *Dispatch* to devote all of its front page to the story only once, whereas the paper carried such extensive coverage four times during the Cluverius sensation. *Richmond Dispatch*, 23 July 1870 for full-page Phillips coverage; for Cluverius coverage:

31 March, 7 May 1885, 14, 15 January 1887. The Beattie case never filled the front page of the *Richmond Times-Dispatch*, however. Due to changes in style, the case often dominated the first page, but other stories appeared as well. Instead, the stories from the front page jumped to the inside, sometimes filling the majority of several additional pages.

56. An average of 5.4 articles in the *Richmond Times-Dispatch* covering 2.6 pages appeared each day of the Beattie trial compared to 1 article of 0.6 pages each day of the Cluverius trial. Cluverius: 28 articles covering 17.2 pages, roughly, over the course of 27 days (6 May to 5 June, 1885); Beattie: 102 articles covering 49.5 pages, roughly, over the course of 19 days (22 August to 9 September 1911). Interestingly, the burgeoning coverage did not merely rise along with the size of newspapers; it actually outpaced that growth. The 1885 trial of Cluverius occupied nearly 16 percent of the printed space in the *Richmond Dispatch*, whereas during the Beattie trial, 17 percent of the much larger *Richmond Times-Dispatch* dealt with the sensation.

Such coverage, of course, would vary with each individual murder sensation and each paper consulted, and the McCue case does not confirm this trend. Instead of verbatim testimony and thorough treatments of the arguments, as in the Beattie case, the coverage by the *Times-Dispatch* of the 1904 trial of Samuel McCue (the former mayor of Charlottesville accused of murdering his wife), like that of the Cluverius case before it, consisted of daily summaries. The coverage of the McCue case was greater than the coverage of the Cluverius case, the paper printing more than twice the number of articles per day as in the Cluverius case (0.64 per day or 86 articles per 135 days of printing), and the summaries were marginally longer (0.8 pages each day of the trial). But given the quadrupling of the page length of the newspaper at the turn of the century, the percentage of printed space devoted to the McCue trial was only 5 percent. This case, unlike either of the others, did not take place in Richmond or the surrounding counties but rather much further to the west. Distance clearly diminishes the immediacy of any sensation. *Richmond Times-Dispatch*, 18 October–6 November 1904.

The complex events known as the Hillsville tragedy likewise demonstrate a growing trend. In the multiple trials of the Allen gang for shooting up a courthouse in Hillsville, Virginia, dozens of articles appeared in the press over the course of more than a year, starting on 15 March 1912. This event is particularly difficult to compare to the other crimes under consideration here, for it involved multiple deaths, manhunts, and trials. Despite also occurring a hundred miles to the west of Richmond, the Allen case fostered a tremendous amount of interest, in this case due less to the mystery involved (there were dozens of witnesses) than to the thrilling manhunt and the horror of the killings. For more on the history of the Allen case, particularly its ties to local politics, see Randal L. Hall, "A Courtroom Massacre: Politics and Public Sentiment in Progressive-Era Virginia," *Journal of Southern History* 70 (May 2004): 249–92.

57. Bent, "Art of Ballyhoo," 493. A thoughtful reflection on the relationship between murder and newspapers can be found in Charles E. Grinnell's "Modern Murder Trials and Newspapers," *Atlantic Monthly*, November 1901, 662–73.

58. For Lizzie Borden: *Boston Globe*, 5–21 June 1893. Early editions filled as many as four, five, and six pages of the paper with the case, and late-day editions added more stories from the first half of the day's trial. For Harry Thaw: *New York World*, 24 January–13 April 1907.

59. Before the Civil War, the average length of a pamphlet was 53 pages; in the later period, pamphlets were twice as long: 110 pages in the late nineteenth century, 167 pages in the twentieth century. This phenomenal growth is actually deceptive given the changes in printing due to the growing availability of cheap paper in the late nineteenth century: longer pamphlets do not necessarily imply more information, since print density per page decreased by almost one-half.

One scholar of crime pamphlets, David Ray Papke, has argued that the genre of crime pamphlets diminished after 1860 into a diffuse and pale shadow of its heyday in the early nineteenth century. Papke, *Framing the Criminal: Crime, Cultural Work, and the Loss of Critical Perspective, 1830–1900* (Hamden, Conn: Archon Books, 1987), 30–31. This appears to be a rather odd passage in Papke's book, for he strongly argues that crime pamphlets "passed from the scene" in the second half of the nineteenth century, but he then proceeds to mention a number of interesting counterexamples: pamphlets on Charles Guiteau, Lizzie Borden, the Molly Maguires, the Haymarket rioters as well as several lesser-known murderers. It appears that Papke dismisses these because they fit less easily into his typology of crime—the frames of "rogue" and "fiend"—rather than because they actually demonstrate the genre passing from the scene. The evidence from Virginia supports continuity in publications; what changes is the nature of those publications.

What follows is a complete a list of Virginia crime publications up to the Progressive Era, listed by date of publication, that I have found. If readers know of others, I would be very eager to learn of them: *The Vain, Prodigal Life, and Tragical Penitent Death of Thomas Hellier* (London: Sam. Couch, 1680); John Leland, *A True Account, How Mathew Womble Murdered His Wife (Who was Pregnant) and His Four Sons, on June the 19th, 1784* (Stockbridge, Mass.: Richard Lee, 1793); St. George Tucker, "To the Public," broadside, 5 May 1793, Tucker-Coleman Papers, Swim Library, College of William and Mary, Williamsburg; "Horrid Murder! Abel Clemmons Murdered His Wife and Eight Children," broadside, 1805, Clarksburg, Special Collections Department, Alderman Library, University of Virginia, Charlottesville; *Cruel Murder!! A True Account of the Life and Character of Abel Clemmens, Who Was Executed at Morgantown, Virginia, on Monday, the 30th of June, 1806, for the Murder of His Wife and Eight Children* (Morgantown: J. Campbell; reprinted in Philadelphia: James O'Hara, 1806); A Member of the Bar of Nottoway County (A.B.S.), *Report of the Trials of Capt. Thomas Wells, before the County*

Court of Nottoway, Sitting as an Examining Court, at the August Term, 1816 — N
Charged with Feloniously and Maliciously Shooting with Intent to Kill Peter O
Randolph, Esq., Judge of the 5th Circuit, and Col. Wm. C. Greenhill (Petersburg: T
Marvel W. Dunnavant, 1816); Francis S. O'Reilly, *The Evidence in the Case of* O
Commonwealth against Francis S. O'Reilly for Stabbing James Madison Pleas- T
ants (Richmond: Franklin Press, 1819); *An Account of the Apprehension, Trial,* O
Conviction, and Condemnation of Manuel Philip Garcia and Jose Demas Garcia P
Castillano (Norfolk: C. Hall, 1821); *The Interesting Trial of William F. Hooe,* A
for the Murder of William Simpson . . . to which Is Added, His Confession, and G
an Account of His Execution, which took place on June 30th, 1826 (New York: E
Joseph M'Cleland, 1826); *A Brief Sketch of the Occurrences on Board the Brig* 99
Crawford, on Her Voyage from Matanzas to New York; Together with an Account
of the Trial of the Three Spaniards, Jose Hilario Casares, Felix Barbeito, and Jose
Morando (Richmond: Samuel Shepherd, 1827); Gabriel Nourse, *Narrative of*
the Life, Trial, Confession, Sentence of Death, and Execution of Ebenezer W. Cox,
Who was Executed at Charlestown, Jefferson County, Va. August 27th, 1830, for
the Murder of Col. Th. B. Dunn, United States Superintendent at Harpers-Ferry,
January 29th 1830: To which Is Now Added the Appeal of Daniel Stipes, One of
the Parties Accused: Likewise a Melancholy Account of the Murder of Thos. Grif-
fin Thornton, Late Sheriff of Caroline County, Va. Perpetrated by Charles Young;
with the Astounding Providential Incidences which Led to the Conviction of the
Assassin: The Whole Interspersed with Such Moral and Religious Reflections as
Are Calculated, Not to Familiarize the Reader with Scenes of Blood, but, Like
a Friendly Landsman in View of a Coasting Mariner, to Raise above the Rocks
the Warning Beacon (Winchester: Samuel H. Davis, 1830); *The Confessions*
of Nat Turner, Leader of the Late Insurrection in Southampton, Va. (Baltimore,
Md.: T. R. Gray, 1831); Samuel Warner, *Authentic and impartial narrative of*
the tragical scene: Which was witnessed in Southampton County (Virginia) on
Monday the 22d of August last, when fifty-five of its inhabitants (mostly women
and children) were inhumanly massacred by the blacks! Communicated by those
who were eye witnesses of the bloody scene, and confirmed by the confessions of
several of the blacks while under sentence of death (New York: Warner and West,
1831); *A Full Report, Embracing All the Evidence and Arguments in the Case*
of the Commonwealth of Virginia vs. Thomas Ritchie, Jr. (New York: Burgess,
Stringer, and Co., 1846); [Editor of the *Richmond Southern*], *An Authenti-*
cated Report of the Trial of Myers and Others for the Murder of Dudley Marvin
Hoyt (New York: Richards and Co., 1846); *The Letters and Correspondence of*
Mrs. Virginia Myers (which have never before been published or even read in
Court) to Dudley Marvin Hoyt (Philadelphia: n.p., 1847); J. M. H. Brunet,
Trial of William Dandridge Epes, for the Murder of Francis Adolphus Muir
(Petersburg: J. M. H. Brunet, 1849); *Particulars of the Dreadful Tragedy in*
Richmond on the Morning of the 19th July 1852: Being a Full Account of the
Awful Murder of the Winston Family (Richmond: John D. Hammersley, 1852); 253

The Trial of James H. Johnson ([Virginia]: n.p., 1859); *The Evidence in the Case of Commonwealth vs. Vincent Witcher, et. al.* (Lynchburg: Virginia Job Office, 1860); J. Wall Turner, *The Drinker's Farm Tragedy: Trial and Conviction of James Jeter Phillips, for the Murder of His Wife* (Richmond: J. Wall Turner, 1868); *An Account of the Curtis Homicide and Trials of John E. Poindexter* (Richmond: Dispatch Steam Printing House, 1879); Eugene Grissom, "Report of the Trial of James Thomas DeJarnette for Homicide at Danville, Virginia," *North Carolina Medical Journal* 7 (1881): 319–66; George A. Booker, *The Virginia Tragedy: Trial and Conviction of Thomas J. Cluverius* (Richmond: Johns and Goolsby, 1885); *In the Supreme Court of Appeals of Virginia, Richmond: T. J. Cluverius vs. Commonwealth* (Richmond: n.p., 1885); Thomas J. Cluverius, *Cluverius: My Life, Trial, and Conviction* (Richmond: Andrews, Baptist, and Clemmitt, 1887); John T. Clark, *Was Rev. J. R. Moffett Murdered?: Clark v. Commonwealth*, D. M. 43 Z, from the Corporation Court of the City of Danville (Richmond: Taylor and Dalton, 1893); Evan R. Chesterman and Joe F. Geisinger, *History of the McCue Case* (Richmond: Williams Printing Co., 1904); James H. Lindsay and John S. Patton, *The McCue Murder* (Charlottesville: Progress Printing Co., 1904); J. Bunyan Jones, *History of the Case of the Commonwealth of Virginia v. Samuel Hardy* (Norfolk: Hampton Roads Paper Co., 1910); *Great Beattie Case*; J. J. Reynolds, *The Allen Gang* (Baltimore, Md.: I. and M. Ottenheimer, 1912); Edgar James, *The Allen Outlaws* (Baltimore, Md.: Phoenix Publishing Co., 1912); Samuel S. Hurt, *"Gentlemen, I Ain't a-Goin'": The Hillsville Tragedy* (Roanoke: Stone Print and Manufacturing Co., 1913); Edwin Chancellor Payne, *The Hillsville Tragedy: Complete Story of the Allen Clan* (Chicago: M. A. Donohue and Co., 1913).

The following are fictional crime pamphlets purporting to concern Virginia: William Wadsworth, *The Murderer's Cave; or, The Punishment of Wickedness* (Boston: N. Coverly, 1818); *Awful Disclosures! or Narrative and Confession of Henry Delter, the Murderer of His Five Wives* (Richmond: Barclay and Co., 1851); William Murdock, *Trial, Conviction, and Confession of Mary B. Thorn* (Norfolk: William C. Murdock, 1854); *The Authentic Confessions of William Masterson* (Philadelphia/Richmond: M. L. Barclay, 1854); William C. Elam, "Murder Most Foul," *Lippincott's Magazine of Literature, Science, and Education*, November 1869, 503–9; *"Cousin Tommy!": A Parody by a Richmond Lady* (Richmond: C. F. Johnson, Publisher, 1885); Phillip Leigh, *Lillian's Marriage and Murder: "Cluverius Did Not Kill Her"; The Sequel Told* (Richmond: Patrick Keenen, Printer, 1887); "Old Man Bruce, the Richmond Detective; or, 'Piping' the Reservoir Mystery," vol. 3, no. 304, of the *Old Cap. Collier Library* (11 June 1888), a weekly series put out by Munro's Publishing House of New York.

60. Michael Schudson, *Discovering the News: A Social History of American Newspapers* (New York: Basic Books, 1978), 57–60.

61. S. N. D. North, *History and Present Conditions of the Newspaper and Periodical Press of the United States* (Washington, D.C.: U.S. Government Printing

Office, 1884), 110; printed in vol. 8 of the *Tenth U.S. Census, 1880*; Wilcox, "American Newspaper," 73.

62. The *Richmond Whig*, party organ of the Readjusters and then Republicans, failed in 1888.

63. Eugene Harter, *Boilerplating America: The Hidden Newspaper* (Lanham, Md.: University Press of America, 1990); Brooke Fisher, "The Newspaper Industry," *Atlantic Monthly*, June 1902, 745-53.

64. This national interest was in stark contrast to nineteenth-century reporting. The Jeter Phillips murder of 1867 was never mentioned in the *New York Times*. The Cluverius case of 1885 received more extensive treatment—thirty-seven articles over the two-year span that the case was before the public (fourteen times on the front page but no editorials). It is important to note the increasing size of the *New York Times*, which grew from an eight-page paper (daily and Sundays) in 1870 to eight pages daily with a twelve- to sixteen-page Sunday edition by 1885. By 1911, the *Times* had grown to an eighteen- to twenty-two-page daily and a Sunday edition made up of eight *sections*, each of which was as large as the entire paper in 1870.

National magazines likewise discussed the Beattie case as much or more than any previous Virginia sensation. The *Nation*, 30 November 1911 and 11 January 1912, and *Collier's*, 25 November 1911, discussed or at least referenced the Beattie murder in articles and editorials on the press or crime. Cluverius was mentioned in a few periodicals in passing (*Frank Leslie's Illustrated Weekly*, 9 May and 6 June 1885; *National Police Gazette*, 18 April 1885, 4, 6), but the Phillips case was not, except in a fictional short story (see chapter 2).

65. *New York Times*, 4 September 1911.

66. *Richmond Times-Dispatch*, 31 August 1911.

67. Merz, "American Press," 103-10.

68. Michael Schudson, "Question Authority: A History of the News Interview," *The Power of News* (Cambridge, Mass.: Harvard University Press, 1995), 72-93; quote, 74. In 1875, Mark Twain wrote a humorous short piece about a reporter attempting to explain to his interviewee what an interview was: "It is all the rage now," he says, "to interview any man who has become notorious." Samuel Clemmens, "An Encounter with an Interviewer," in *Lotos Leaves*, ed. W. F. Gill (Boston: W. F. Gill, 1875); reprinted in Walter Blair, ed., *Selected Shorter Writings of Mark Twain* (Boston: Houghton Mifflin, 1962), 131-34.

69. Hugh Dalziel Duncan, *Culture and Democracy* (Totowa, N.J.: Bedminster Press, 1965), 53; quoted in Schudson, *Discovering the News*, 85.

70. Ray Stannard Baker, *American Chronicle* (New York: Charles Scribners Sons, 1945), 183-84.

71. Similarly, no Virginia crime pamphlet published before the Civil War included the name of the author; the closest they came were "by the editor of the Richmond Standard" or "by a member of the bar." In the twentieth century, nearly all crime paperbacks listed an author, and the two 1904 McCue murder

pamphlets were each written by reporters from Virginia newspapers. Evan R. Chesterman and Joe F. Geisinger, *History of the McCue Case* (Richmond: Williams Printing Co., 1904); James H. Lindsay and John S. Patton, *The McCue Murder* (Charlottesville: Progress Printing Co., 1904).

72. Dix is interviewed and reprinted, respectively, in the *Richmond Times-Dispatch*, 29 and 30 July 1911. Another article on the out-of-town press, accompanied by a photo, appeared on 31 August 1911.

73. Michael Schudson, "What Is a Reporter?" *Power of News*, 94-110.

74. Michael Emery, Edwin Emery, and Nancy Roberts, *The Press and America: An Interpretive History of the Mass Media*, 9th ed. (Boston: Allyn and Bacon, 2000), 183.

75. For a contemporary view of the role of the Associated Press in shaping the news, see "The Problem of the Associated Press," *Atlantic Monthly*, July 1914, 132-37. A Richmond reporter emphasized the impact of telegraphy's speed in the age of extra editions and daily deadlines when he wrote that his articles "were mostly written in the Courtroom of Culpepper Courthouse, while the trial of the Strother brothers was in progress and were filed for the wire without editing and in most instances a page at a time. When the verdict came in, the Richmond papers had their issues on the streets less than five minutes after Culpepper knew the fate of the accused." Evan Rayland Chesterman, Scrapbook vol. 13, VHS.

76. Quotation: Dorothy Ross, "Modernist Social Science in the Land of the New/Old," in Dorothy Ross, ed. *Modernist Impulses in the Human Sciences, 1870-1930* (Baltimore, Md.: Johns Hopkins University Press, 1994), 171; Robert H. Wiebe, *The Search for Order, 1877-1920* (New York: Hill and Wang, 1967); Dorothy Ross, *The Origins of American Social Science* (New York: Cambridge University Press, 1991), 143-300; Peter Novick, *That Noble Dream: The "Objectivity Question" and the American Historical Profession* (New York: Cambridge University Press, 1988), 1-108. These fields introduced national professional associations in 1884, 1885, 1903, and 1905, respectively.

77. See, for example, John Idler, "How Richmond Is Housed," the *Survey*, 11 April 1914, 54-55; Gustavus Adolphus Weber, *Report on Housing and Living Conditions in the Neglected Sections of Richmond* (Richmond: Whittet and Shepperson, 1913); and the YWCA "Know Your City" survey, 1911, Cabell Library, Special Collections, Virginia Commonwealth University, Richmond.

78. Leonard D. Savitz, "Introduction," in Gina Lombroso-Ferrero, *Cesare Lombroso's Criminal Man*, repr. ed. (Montclair, N.J.: Patterson Smith, 1972), v-xx; quotation from Lombroso, 6-7. For a summary of Lombroso's criminology in the context of competing philosophies, see David A. Jones, "Positivism after the Rise of Science," in *History of Criminology: A Philosophical Perspective* (New York: Greenwood Press, 1986), 81-132.

79. *Nation*, 11 January 1912, 29.

80. Piers Beirne, *Inventing Criminology: Essays on the Rise of Homo Criminalis*

(Albany: State University of New York Press, 1993), 143–85; David A. Jones, *History of Criminology: A Philosophical Perspective* (New York: Greenwood Press, 1986), 185–88.

81. Clarence S. Darrow, "Realism in Literature and Art," the *Arena*, December 1893, 98–113; edited and reprinted in Neil Harris, *The Land of Contrasts, 1880–1901* (New York: George Braziller, 1970), 279–88; quote, 286.

82. The two best and most recent works on the broad impact of realism in American life are Miles Orvell, *The Real Thing: Imitation and Authenticity in American Culture, 1880–1940* (Chapel Hill: University of North Carolina Press, 1989), and David E. Shi's *Facing Facts: Realism in American Thought and Culture, 1850–1920* (New York: Oxford University Press, 1995). See also: Amy Kaplan, *The Social Construction of American Realism* (Chicago: University of Chicago Press, 1988): 1–14; Eric J. Sundquist, "Introduction: The Country of the Blue," in *American Realism: New Essays*, ed. Eric J. Sundquist (Baltimore, Md.: Johns Hopkins University Press, 1982), 3–24; René Wellek, "The Concept of Realism in Literary Scholarship," in *Concepts of Criticism* (New Haven, Conn.: Yale University Press, 1963): 222–55.

83. Theodore Dreiser, *Sister Carrie* (New York: Doubleday, Page, 1900). According to literary critic René Wellek, any distinction between realism and naturalism was blurred at best at the time. With this in mind, I treat the two as closely related movements. Wellek, "Realism in Literary Scholarship," 233.

84. Shi, *Facing Facts*; Sundquist, "Introduction," 19; Wellek, "Realism in Literary Scholarship," 240–41.

85. Similarly, Samuel McCue was arrested for the murder of his wife in September 1904 and was convicted and executed for the crime within five months. The Allen clan, accused of shooting up a courtroom in western Virginia in 1912, were all charged, arraigned, and all appeals were heard within the space of a year and a half.

86. All of these innovations in Richmond are reported in the *Annual Report of the Chief of Police to the Mayor* for the years 1899 to 1913. For improvements in policing in general in this period, see Simon A. Cole, *Suspect Identities: A History of Fingerprinting and Criminal Identification* (Cambridge, Mass.: Harvard University Press, 2001), and Lane, *Murder in America*, 146–213.

87. Quotation: John F. Kasson, *Amusing the Million: Coney Island of the Turn-of-the-Century* (New York: Hill and Wang, 1978), 6.

88. Karol L. Kelley, *Models for the Multitudes: Social Values in the American Popular Novel, 1850–1920* (New York: Greenwood Press, 1987), 107–35; Herbert F. Smith, *The Popular American Novel, 1865–1920* (Boston: Twayne Publishers, 1980), 28; James D. Hart, *The Popular Book: A History of America's Literary Taste* (New York: Oxford University Press, 1950).

89. Kelley, *Models for the Multitudes*, 107–35; Gail Bederman, *Manliness and Civilization: A Cultural History of Gender and Race in the United States, 1880–1917* (Chicago: University of Chicago press, 1995), particularly 10–20, 217–32;

John F. Kasson, *Houdini, Tarzan, and the Perfect Man: The White Male Body and the Challenge of Modernity in America* (New York: Hill and Wang, 2001), 157–218.

90. Quoted in Willard G. Bleyer, *Main Currents in the History of American Journalism* (Boston: Houghton Mifflin, 1927), 328, 357–64. Named for the comic strip "The Yellow Kid" so prominent at this time, this was a brand of brash journalism turned toward the sensual, lurid, and sensational, including screaming headlines and self-promotional stunts.

91. The antics of both Pulitzer's *World* and Hearst's *Journal* as they competed for sensational coverage of the Spanish-American War became benchmarks in the history of press extravagance. The yellow press also engaged in occasional stunts, like sending reporter Nellie Bly on a trip around the world to beat Jules Verne's fictional record (by eight days), and fakery, such as claims of finding "Real American Monsters and Dragons." Emery, Emery, and Roberts, *Press and America*, 176–198.

92. Harry Kollatz Jr., "'Send the Rascals to the Tall Timber': Adon Yoder," *Virginia Cavalcade* 46 (Summer 1996): 34–47.

93. Emery, Emery, and Roberts, *Press in America*, 192, 204; Frank Luther Mott, *American Journalism, a History: 1690–1960*, 3rd ed. (New York: Macmillan Co., 1962), 539–41. As with both the prominence of violence narratives in Puritan publishing and the importance of the penny press, this yellow journalism seems from the perspective of Virginia's history to be overemphasized in the scholarship of the press. I suspect that the journalistic norm in this period, as with the dawn of the penny press, was less a radical break with the past than it was a series of innovations and a shift of emphasis—change more moderate and gradual than most histories of the press allow.

94. Most histories of journalism choose a representative paper to embody each of these movements, often the *New York Times* to demonstrate the rationalization of news reporting and the *New York World* to represent the sensational yellow journalism of the period. For instance, see Schudson, *Discovering the News*, 88–120. The scholarship of the press regularly has placed New York at its center, which leads, I believe, to a misunderstanding of the dynamics of change in the medium across the nation as a whole, exaggerating the impact of both the penny press of the 1830s and the yellow press at the turn of the century. Much of the history of journalism irrationally characterizes the nineteenth century as a more erratic era, with the press swinging between the poles of political reporting and mass scandal sheets. A more reasoned analysis for the nation as a whole would emphasize the gradual elaboration of a number of mainstream innovations in technology and style: reporting, entertaining features, sports, interviews, crime, and so on.

95. This mix of professional and salacious, of dispassionate and sensational, can be found throughout much of American culture at this time, including advertising and the clinical discussions of sex and other bodily functions. See, respec-

tively, Jackson Lears, *Fables of Abundance: A Cultural History of Advertising in America* (New York: Basic Books, 1994), 137–61, and Gurstein, *Repeal of Reticence*.

96. *Century Magazine*, May 1911, 46.

97. *Outlook*, 2 February 1907, 276.

98. Merz, "Bigger and Better Murders," 341.

99. Binford was not alone in this effort. A few years earlier, Evelyn Nesbit Thaw—famous as a witness in the trial of her husband in 1907 for murdering her former lover, the respected architect Stanford White—returned to show business (having been a performer before her marriage), spending several decades in the theater, vaudeville, and other venues. See Paul Baker, *Stanny: The Gilded Life of Stanford White* (New York: Free Press, 1989), 317–400.

100. *New York Times*, 10 and 12 October and 25 November 1911; *Richmond Times-Dispatch*, 8 September 1911. The last mention in the press of Beulah Binford comes just a few months later, when she was living with the family of the theatrical producer who had signed her. She had changed her name and reportedly was attempting to begin a new life.

CHAPTER 4

1. These events can be found in any of the Richmond papers in June and July of 1895. "*Barnes v. Commonwealth*," Records and Briefs of the Supreme Court of Appeals of Virginia 68 (1895): 121.

2. Suzanne Lebsock, *A Murder in Virginia: Southern Justice on Trial* (New York: Norton, 2003), 59.

3. The historical scholarship generally mentions the Lunenburg case rarely and in passing. But Suzanne Lebsock's recent book—*Murder in Virginia*—explores the case in depth and quite well. For more on John Mitchell's wider career, see Ann Field Alexander, *Race Man: The Rise and Fall of the "Fighting Editor," John Mitchell Jr.* (Charlottesville: University of Virginia Press, 2002). This chapter was substantially complete before either of these volumes appeared, and while it is consonant with both, it investigates Mitchell's changing perspective on crime and sensation in greater depth than either book.

4. Interestingly for this study, Mitchell's first column for the *Globe* described the public hanging of a black woman for killing her husband. See Alexander, *Race Man*, 24.

5. *Colored American Magazine*, March 1902, 295–98.

6. The *Richmond Planet* began publishing in 1883, but only a handful of issues survive from the 1880s. A full run of the paper begins in 1890.

7. J. H. Derbyshire to M. C. Cardozo, 16 July 1895, and Derbyshire to Col. H. C. Jones, 16 July 1895, Correspondence of C. T. O'Ferrall, Executive Papers, Library of Virginia (LVA), Richmond. See also, "*Barnes v. Commonwealth*," Records and Briefs, 121–30; *Journal of the Senate of the Commonwealth of Virginia, 1895* (Richmond: J. H. O'Bannon, 1895), 115–21. The steps taken by the

militia are recorded also in the *Report of the Adjutant-General of the State of Virginia* (Richmond: J. H. O'Bannon, 1895), 64–67.

8. *Richmond Times*, 17 July 1895.

9. Ann Field Alexander, "'Like an Evil Wind:' The Roanoke Riot of 1893 and the Lynching of Thomas Smith," *Virginia Magazine of History and Biography* 100 (1992): 173–206. Members of the militia in Lunenburg were approached concerning the possibility of releasing the prisoners to them, supposedly to extract a confession and discover where the missing money was. *Richmond Times*, 23 July 1885.

10. In fact, there were 1,540 extralegal hangings in the 1890s, 1,108 of which were of blacks. During the first decade of the 1900s, there were 895 lynchings (796 involving blacks), and in the 1910s the numbers dropped further, to 621 (565 involving blacks). Margaret Werner Cahalan, *Historical Corrections Statistics of the United States, 1850–1984* (U.S. Department of Justice, Bureau of Justice Statistics, 1986), 11. Lynching statistics are notoriously incomplete, but these numbers, based on Tuskegee Institute's yearly tabulations of lynching, at least give us a general sense of the scope of the practice.

11. W. Fitzhugh Brundage, *Lynching in the New South: Georgia and Virginia, 1880–1930* (Urbana: University of Illinois Press, 1993), 263. In contrast, a deep South state like Georgia had 116 lynchings in the 1890s, falling to 99 and rising again to 137 in the following two decades before a dramatic decline in the 1920s (to 41).

12. The fourth defendant, Mary Barnes, mother of Pokey, was with Mr. Pollard in his fields at the time of the murder. She could not be charged with first-degree murder, and the prosecuting attorneys indicted her for conspiring before the fact, a second-degree murder charge. She was found guilty and sentenced to ten years in prison.

13. *Richmond Times*, 13 July 1895.

14. "*Barnes v. Commonwealth*," *Records and Briefs*, 118; *Richmond Times* and *Richmond Dispatch*, 16 July 1895.

15. "*Barnes v. Commonwealth*," *Reports of Cases in the Supreme Court of Appeals of Virginia* 92 (1895): 803.

16. Observers frequently emphasized that the only evidence against the women was Marable's accusation, a point driven home in the governor's review of the case against Mary Barnes, Pokey's mother. The "several conflicting and contradictory statements" of Marable constituted the "only testimony against her." Charles O'Ferrall, "Communication from the Governor of Virginia Transmitting List of Pardons," Senate Document No. 4, *Journal of the Senate of the Commonwealth of Virginia* (Richmond: R. H. O'Bannon, 1897), 4.

17. *Journal of the Senate of the Commonwealth of Virginia, 1895*, 117.

18. Reported in the *Richmond Dispatch*, 13 July 1895, and in the *Richmond Planet*, 20 July 1895.

19. *Richmond Times*, 16 and 17 July 1895

20. "Affidavit of F. W. Cunningham," in "*Barnes v. Commonwealth*," *Records and Briefs*, 131-33. Also reported in the *Richmond Dispatch*, 20 July 1895 and the *Richmond Planet*, 27 July 1895. David Thompson was never seriously pursued as a suspect—he had an alibi. As for the money, none of it was ever recovered, except for the two twenties held by Marable.

21. *Richmond Dispatch*, 23 July 1895. The *Dispatch* was not alone in assuming nothing would be done for these defendants. Some of the evidence in the case was lost at this time, apparently because no one believed the items would ever be needed again. See Lebsock, *Murder in Virginia*, 249-51.

22. Affidavits of several militiamen can be found in "*Barnes v. Commonwealth*," *Records and Briefs*, 131-37. In addition, some white editorial writers reported their belief in the prisoners' innocence, though they could also be ambivalent on this issue; see, for instance, the *Richmond Dispatch*, 23 July 1895.

23. *Richmond Planet*, 2 January 1897.

24. Ibid., 28 December 1895.

25. "*Barnes v. Commonwealth*," *Reports of Cases*, 807. For the report on the decision, see *Richmond Times*, 13 December 1895. Rather than an ominous sign, ordering a new trial "on technical grounds" was actually the norm for the Virginia supreme court. Samuel Pincus demonstrates that the court generally decided cases on procedural rules and, less frequently, ordered new trials due to a lack of evidence for the charge. In this thorough study, Pincus finds that the commonwealth's highest court, in notable contrast to its lower courts, was remarkably evenhanded toward blacks, reversing judgments even in interracial crimes and violations of antimiscegenation statutes, two hot-button issues for white Virginians. Samuel Norman Pincus, "The Virginia Supreme Court, Blacks, and the Law, 1870-1902" (Ph.D. diss., University of Virginia, 1978).

26. *Richmond Planet*, 18 April 1896.

27. *Richmond Times*, 20 August 1895.

28. Ibid., 26 April 1896. The delay might simply have been practical—they started to deliberate late on a Saturday evening and reconvened on Monday. They discussed the case on Sunday but did not cast ballots until they reconvened on Monday morning.

29. *Richmond Planet*, 2 May 1896.

30. *Richmond Dispatch*, 13 May 1867.

31. A very similar rock battle occurred in 1896 with the attempted arrest of a young black girl for fighting the police. *Richmond Dispatch*, 13 October 1896. Other "riots" over police arrests were reported in the *Dispatch* of 26 June 1878, 3 August 1887, 16 January 1889, and 9 May 1867, the last case followed up on 27 May. On justice and African American activism during Reconstruction, see William A. Blair, "Justice versus Law and Order: The Battles over the Reconstruction of Virginia's Minor Judiciary, 1865-1870," *Virginia Magazine of History and Biography* 103 (1995): 157-80, particularly 173-76.

32. The clearest expression of this comes from the work of Howard Rabinowitz; see

in particular, "The Conflict between Blacks and the Police in the Urban South," in *Race, Ethnicity, and Urbanization: Selected Essays* (Columbia: University of Missouri Press, 1994), 167–80, and his chapter "Justice" in Rabinowitz, *Race Relations in the Urban South* (New York: Oxford University Press, 1978), 31–60. See also the latter half of Edward Ayers, *Vengeance and Justice: Crime and Punishment in the Nineteenth-Century American South* (New York: Oxford University Press, 1984). For a different explanation from the urban North, see Roger Lane, *Roots of Violence in Black Philadelphia, 1860–1900* (Cambridge, Mass.: Harvard University Press, 1986). Lane finds no convincing evidence of institutional racism in Philadelphia's policing and court systems. He explains racial disparities in crime and incarceration by pointing to the very different place of blacks in the modern, industrial, urban order: African Americans, in essence were forced to remain in a premodern role, and their crime rates reflect that place. In contrast, in the South, racism was more overt.

33. *Richmond Planet*, 18 October 1890. Other southern black papers made similar complaints. For one instance, see Eugene J. Watts, "The Police in Atlanta, 1890–1905," *Journal of Southern History* 39 (1973): 172.

34. A. M. Keiley, *Fourth Annual Message of the Mayor of Richmond* (Richmond: Evening News Steam Presses, 1874), xiv.

35. *The Code of Virginia, 1849* (Richmond: William F. Ritchie, 1849), 723, 753–54. Other antebellum codes duplicate these distinctions. See Philip J. Schwarz, *Twice Condemned: Slaves and the Criminal Laws of Virginia, 1705–1865* (Baton Rouge: Louisiana State University Press, 1888), and his *Slave Laws in Virginia* (Athens: University of Georgia Press, 1996).

36. *Acts of the General Assembly of Virginia, passed in 1865–6* (Richmond: Allegre and Goode, 1866), 90.

37. *Richmond Dispatch*, noting black members of jury: 11 February 1883; the "novel sight" of an all-black jury in Manchester, Virginia: 7 July 1879.

38. George Campbell, *White and Black: The Outcome of a Visit to the United States* (London: Chatto and Windus, 1879), 300–301.

39. *Richmond Dispatch*, 7 July 1901. One Alabama judge went so far as to say that blacks had no place even observing trials. Speaking to the black onlookers, he said: "Now, you Negroes go home and stay there or you will get into trouble. This is a white man's country and a white man's court and you Negroes must keep to your places." Quoted in the *Richmond Planet*, 7 August 1897.

40. *Strauder v. West Virginia*, 100 U.S. 303 (1880); *ex parte Virginia*, 100 U.S. 339 (1880).

41. *Virginia v. Rives*, 100 U.S. 313 (1880).

42. Not until the 1930s did the U.S. Supreme Court amend this ruling on race and jury selection. See Abraham L. Davis and Barbara Luck Graham, *The Supreme Court, Race, and Civil Rights* (Thousand Oaks, Calif.: Sage Publications, 1995), 18–25.

43. *Richmond Planet*, 27 July 1889 and 28 January 1899. See also 7 January 1911,

when Mitchell again clearly pointed toward lower courts and juries as the problem: "as a rule, [miscarriage of justice] is in the cases of magistrates and juries. Southern judges higher up have always been disposed to accord justice in keeping with the State laws." This follows closely the findings of Blair ("Justice versus Law and Order") for Reconstruction.

44. *Richmond Planet*, 20 July 1895; *Richmond Dispatch*, 13–21 July 1895; Lebsock, *Murder in Virginia*, 72, 85, 94, 210, 241.

45. *Richmond Planet*, 16 September 1899; for another parallel among dozens: 21 November 1896. One study of Georgia convicts found that blacks were sentenced to terms twice as long as those of whites. See Leon F. Litwack, *Trouble in Mind: Black Southerners in the Age of Jim Crow* (New York: Vintage, 1999), 252.

46. *Richmond Planet*, 8 July 1899. See also "Can Get Justice Here!" 1 November 1902. For a consideration of capital punishment and race in this era, see chapter 6.

47. *Richmond Times*, 6 May 1896.

48. Lebsock, *Murder in Virginia*, 262–63.

49. *Richmond Times*, 6 May 1896.

50. O'Ferrall, "Communication from the Governor of Virginia," 4–5. See also *Richmond Planet*, 2 January 1897.

51. Henry Vance Davis, "The Black Press: From Mission to Commercialism, 1827–1927" (Ph.D. diss., University of Michigan, 1990), 173.

52. To give two examples literally among dozens: *Richmond Planet*, 29 September 1894 and 21 November 1896.

53. The first sensational treatment—"Women Innocent"—was on 27 July, a month after the *Planet* first reported the crime, six weeks after it took place. The first mention of the crime at all was an editorial simply arguing that the courtroom was the place to decide such a case and that no mob should be allowed to preempt such justice. *Richmond Planet*, 29 June 1895.

In contrast to the *Planet*'s sensational treatment, Richmond's white papers were ambivalent about the case. The *Richmond Dispatch*, the city's largest daily, remained cautious, raising a number of questions about the strength of the case against the women but also persistently emphasizing that the judge and jury "would hardly have found the women guilty upon Solomon's unsupported testimony" (23 July 1895). The *Dispatch* believed that the full trial record would show more corroborative testimony than brief press reports from the trials implied. The *Richmond Times* was more critical, clearly arguing that Marable was unconvincing, that his testimony was all that convicted the women, and that justice demanded a new trial.

54. Because the *Planet* was a weekly, this averages exactly 1.5 articles or editorials for every issue in these eighteen months. Some articles and editorials were short, but others, especially those reporting trial developments, could be as long as two full pages of the four-page *Planet*. For comparison, the *Richmond*

Dispatch covered the case almost daily during the various trials and appeals, but these were, in general, short reports of the progress of the case. Between the discovery of the crime in June 1895 and Pokey Barnes's release eleven months later, the (daily) *Dispatch* printed eighty-two stories and editorials, a number comparable to the (weekly) *Planet* for that period. Regular editorials on the possibilities of the innocence of the Lunenburg women in the first few months of the *Dispatch*'s coverage ended in September 1895; thereafter, it covered this case strictly through reports, generally quite short ones. The *Richmond Dispatch* reported on each of the surprising turns in the story: the state supreme court demanding new trials (13 December 1885), the nolle prosequi against Pokey (6 May 1886), Mary's (second) conviction remanded to the lower court (3 September 1886), and Mary attaining her freedom (22 September 1886). But the paper published not a single editorial about any of these developments, and the last two turns in Mary's story each merited only a single, half-column article. The white response to this story of justice to blacks was therefore notably muted: the papers recorded what happened, but the matter was quickly dropped.

55. One of the prominent stories in the early months of this sensation was simply a list of all contributors, with the headline "Lunenburg Case—Shall We Save the Women?" See *Richmond Planet*, August–September 1895. On the NAACP's later efforts to publicize particularly disturbing cases of injustice and to fund legal teams to appeal convictions, see Mark Robert Schneider, *"We Return Fighting": The Civil Rights Movement in the Jazz Age* (Boston: Northeastern University Press, 2002).

56. *Richmond Planet*, 27 July 1895; 18 April and 2 May 1896.

57. Ibid., 27 July 1895, 16 May 1896.

58. Mitchell played this role to the hilt. On more than one occasion he wrote of his own sacrifices in service of the goal of freeing these innocents: "All of our means are at the disposal of these poor creatures, and should the public fail in any wise to heed their appeals, we shall spend our money and mortgage or sell our possessions until we are reduced to the level of a beggar with only our abilities and past friendships to reimburse us for the loss we have sustained." *Richmond Planet*, 2 May 1896. The limit of John Mitchell's self-congratulation was perhaps reached when he printed a song written in his honor: "Let Us Rally 'Round John Mitchell," sung to the tune of "Hold the Fort," 21 September 1895.

59. *Richmond Planet*, 17 October 1896, 2 January 1897.

60. *Richmond Dispatch*, 18 July 1893.

61. Another example of this sort of innocent-sensation is the case of Simon Walker, accused of killing a man in 1889 and sentenced to hang. At the last moment, the governor commuted Walker's sentence to a jail term, due in part to efforts of the black community. No copies of the *Planet* exist for 1889, but Mitchell

refers to this case in a self-congratulatory article at the end of the Lunenburg case, 24 October 1896.

62. "There should be no more cowards among the negroes of the South, but that they would fight it out there with the ballot, or if necessary, with the bullet," said John Mitchell in a meeting of the Afro-American Press Association in Philadelphia in 1892. *Richmond State*, 28 September 1892.

63. *Richmond Planet*, 26 February 1898.

64. Ibid., 8 February 1890.

65. Ibid., 26 February 1898.

66. New York *Freeman*, 29 May 1886; narrated in Ann Field Alexander, *Race Man*, 42. No copies of the *Planet* exist from this time, but this northern black paper carried a treatment of the story, and many biographical sources reference it. The lynching occurred in Charlotte County, but the threat came from a town just across the Prince Edward County line, leading several scholars to say that these events occurred there (for instance, Brundage, *Lynching in the New South*, 165). But Mitchell himself wrote that it was Charlotte County, and other biographical works from the 1890s as well as the original notice of the lynching in the *Richmond Dispatch* (7 May 1886) concur. See his "Shall the Wheels of Race Agitation Be Stopped?" *Colored American Magazine* 5 (1902): 386.

67. *Richmond Planet*, 27 August 1892; see also a similar story that appeared on 31 July 1897.

68. Ibid., 2 June 1894.

69. The *Planet* took a similar tone in several other instances. When a black man south of Lynchburg was shot three times, he was nonetheless able to beat off his attackers—who numbered fourteen—and make his escape into the dark woods about his house. The story's emphasis was not on the crimes with which he was charged, the gruesome details of his wounds, or even injustice. Instead the article centered on his will and effort. The first headline (of six) neatly summed up the central focus of the article: "Whipped Them All." *Richmond Planet*, 12 June 1897. See also stories on 15 January 1893 and 31 July 1897.

70. *Richmond Planet*, 13 July 1895. A similar article, "A Colored Man's Deadly Aim," appeared a few years later, 12 April 1902.

71. Lawrence W. Levine, *Black Culture and Black Consciousness: Afro-American Folk Thought from Slavery to Freedom* (New York: Oxford University Press, 1977), 410–11; John W. Roberts, "'You Done Me Wrong': The Badman as Outlaw Hero," in *Trickster to Badman: The Black Folk Hero in Slavery and Freedom* (Philadelphia: University of Pennsylvania Press, 1989), 171–219. Roberts argues convincingly that the realities facing blacks in the postemancipation period made possible such "bad men" becoming outlaw folk heroes to many in the black community.

72. *Richmond Planet*, 15 January 1893.

73. Ibid., 2 February 1895.

74. I. Garland Penn, *Afro-American Press and Its Editors* (1891; repr. ed., New York: Arno Press, 1969), 183–87; *New York World*, 22 February, 1887; quoted in Penn, *Afro-American Press*, 183, and in William J. Simmons, *Men of Mark: Eminent, Progressive, and Rising* (1887; repr. ed., New York: Arno Press, 1968), 320; see 314–21. This reputation grew even more in 1898 when he became one of the nation's most outspoken critics of the treatment of blacks in the military during the Spanish-American War, coining the cry "No Officers, No Fight!" See Alexander, *Race Man*, 89-101. See also: *Colored American Magazine*, March 1902, 295–98.

75. *Plessy v. Ferguson*, 163 U.S. 537 (1896).

76. *Richmond Planet*, 16 May 1914; *Richmond Times-Dispatch*, 20 June 1914. For further analysis of race and rape in this era, see Linda Lundquist Dorr, *White Women, Rape, and the Power of Race in Virginia, 1900-1960* (Chapel Hill: University of North Carolina Press, 2004).

77. *Richmond Times-Dispatch*, 24 June 1914.

78. Ibid., 30–31 October 1914.

79. *Richmond Planet*, 7 November 1914.

80. In part, this difference might be explained by the fact that so many in the white community voiced their belief in his innocence: several of the newspapers, for example, and one of the Henrico magistrates who first heard the case. But the Lunenburg and Jenkins cases also had found many whites in support of the "obvious" innocence of the accused.

81. For Clements editorials: *Richmond Planet*, 16 and 23 May, 27 June, 4 July, and 7 November 1914.

82. *Richmond Planet*, 27 June 1914.

83. At various moments in the case, the *Planet* reprinted stories from all three of the most prominent Richmond dailies: the *Times-Dispatch*, the *Evening Journal*, and especially the *News Leader*. I can find only two stories that might have originated with the *Planet* (16 May and 31 October 1914), and even these might be reprints. The Clements case circulated in the press between 12 May and 7 November 1914.

84. *Richmond Planet*, 4 July 1914.

85. Ibid., 7 November 1914.

86. *Cleveland Gazette*, 24 July 1903; *Little Rock Reporter*; quoted in the *Planet*, 15 October 1904. Alexander also reports that the *Gazette* editorialized that the *Planet* "has not shown its old time vigor." Reprinted in the *Planet*, 31 January 1903. Alexander, *Race Man*, 118.

87. The literature is rich with sources tracing this movement, beginning with C. Vann Woodward's *The Strange Career of Jim Crow* (New York: Oxford University Press, 1955). See also Edward Ayers, *The Promise of the New South: Life after Reconstruction* (New York: Oxford University Press, 1992), particularly the chapter "The Turning of the Tide," 283–309; and Litwack, *Trouble in*

Mind, particularly 217–79. In Virginia, the constitutional convention of 1901 added poll taxes and literacy restrictions to voting. Further laws segregating public transportation took effect in 1904 and 1906 and are discussed below. In addition, Richmond passed an ordinance (and Virginia passed a law the next year) favoring residential segregation by race in 1911, an effort that faced legal challenges for decades. Overt racial segregation in residences was declared unconstitutional, but the commonwealth responded simply by passing more subtle efforts. *Acts and Joint Resolutions of the General Assembly of the State of Virginia, 1912* (Richmond: Davis Bottom, 1912), 330. See also, Christopher Silver, *Twentieth-Century Richmond: Planning, Politics, and Race* (Knoxville: University of Tennessee Press, 1984), 109–13.

88. *Richmond Planet*, 10 October 1908.

89. Ibid., 7 March 1908. This reading of the *Richmond Planet*'s changed tone at the turn of the century is a view shared by Ann Field Alexander, Mitchell's biographer. She ascribes this to both being dispirited after a series of defeats and the rising prominence of other business concerns taking more of his time and energy. Other black editors, such as Calvin Chase of the Washington, D.C., *Bee*, made a similar shift from ambivalence or opposition to B. T. Washington to supporting him in this historical moment. In the case of Chase, Washington began to offer his paper financial support; I have found no evidence of such a connection with John Mitchell. See David Howard-Pitney, "Calvin Chase's Washington *Bee* and Black Middle-Class Ideology, 1882–1900," *Journalism Quarterly* 63 (1986): 89–97.

90. *Richmond Planet*, 10 October 1908.

91. Alexander, *Race Man*, 117–19; Fitzhugh Brundage, "'To Howl Loudly': John Mitchell Jr. and His Campaign against Lynching in Virginia," *Canadian Review of American Studies* 22 (1991): 335–36.

92. *Richmond Planet*, 6 March 1897. Mitchell was a delegate to Republican state and national conventions, joined other southern blacks on unproductive missions to President Benjamin Harrison to discuss southern injustice, and served on the Richmond City Council from 1888 to 1896. Much of Ann Field Alexander's *Race Man* involves Mitchell's political education, particularly 73–119 and 131–42. After Mitchell's electoral defeat, it would be a half century before another black person served on the Richmond City Council.

93. *Richmond Planet*, 29 December 1906. This Brownsville episode sent wide ripples throughout the southern black community. If the most famous—and studied—race riot in the period occurred in Atlanta in 1906, this Brownsville conflict and the ensuing action taken against the soldiers is perhaps the most deserving of further scholarly attention. For his part, Mitchell voiced his displeasure of Roosevelt's "monumental blunder" on the front pages and editorials from November 1906 into 1907 and occasionally beyond. Booker T. Washington wrote to then-Secretary of War William Howard Taft that "I have never in all my experience with the race, experienced a time when the entire people

NOTES TO PAGES 133–34

have the feeling that they have now in regard to the administration." Booker T. Washington to William Howard Taft, 20 November 1906, in Louis R. Harlan, ed. *The Booker T. Washington Papers*, vol. 9: *1906–8* (Urbana: University of Illinois Press, 1972), 141.

94. *Acts and Joint Resolutions Passed by the General Assembly of the State of Virginia during the Extra Session of 1902-3-4* (Richmond: J. H. O'Bannon, 1902 [*sic*]), 990. At the same time, there was a considerable loss of revenue for black public schools—an issue of concern to the entire black community. Like many other states in the South, Virginia at the turn of the century began to allow local tax dollars to be spent as the localities saw fit just so long as schools were in session for at least four months of the year. Within ten years, the average annual amount spent on white children was nearly double that spent on black children. This was yet another loss to the black community. See Alexander, *Race Man*, 111–14.

95. *Acts and Joint Resolutions Passed by the General Assembly of the State of Virginia during the Extra Session of 1906* (Richmond: Davis Bottom, 1906), 92. It is difficult to gauge how widespread this boycott was: the white papers ignored it, other than making early declarations of its failure. The *Planet* continued to speak of a vast majority of streetcar patrons continuing to walk as late as October 1904. It seems probable that initial enthusiasm waned over the course of months. Not only was that the pattern for similar conflicts in other locales, but the coverage of the boycott in the *Planet* dwindled as well. In one sense, however, the effort was a success: the drop in fares due to the boycott contributed to the bankruptcy of the streetcar company that year. See August Meier and Elliott Rudwick, "Negro Boycotts of Segregated Streetcars in Virginia, 1904-1907," *Virginia Magazine of History and Biography* 81 (1973): 479–87. For an analysis of the wider issue of streetcars, corporate policies, and segregation in the South, see Walter E. Campbell, "The Corporate Hand in an Urban Jim Crow Journey" (Ph.D. diss., University of North Carolina, Chapel Hill, 1991).

96. David S. Cecelski and Timothy B. Tyson, eds., *Democracy Betrayed: The Wilmington Race Riot of 1898 and Its Aftermath* (Chapel Hill: University of North Carolina Press, 1998). For the Atlanta riot, see Dominic J. Capeci Jr. and Jack C. Knight, "Reckoning with Violence: W. E. B. Du Bois and the 1906 Atlanta Race Riot," *Journal of Southern History* 62 (1996): 727–66; Joel Williamson, *The Crucible of Race: Black/White Relations in the American South since Emancipation* (New York: Oxford University Press, 1984), 180–223; and, Charles Crowe, "Racial Massacre in Atlanta, September 22, 1906," *Journal of Negro History* 54 (1969): 150–73.

97. See Kevin Gaines, *Uplifting the Race: Black Leadership, Politics, and Culture in the Twentieth Century* (Chapel Hill: University of North Carolina Press, 1996).

98. *New York Times*, 17 September 1904, and *Richmond Planet*, 1 October 1904.

99. *Richmond Planet*, 30 April 1904.

100. For more on the success stories in the midst of segregation, see James D. Watkinson, "William Washington Browne and the True Reformers of Richmond, Virginia," *Virginia Magazine of History and Biography* 97 (1989): 375–98; Elsa Barkley Brown, "Womanist Consciousness: Maggie Lena Walker and the Independent Order of St. Luke," *Signs* 14 (1988): 610–34; W. P. Burrell, "History of the Business of Colored Richmond," *Voice of the Negro* 1 (1904): 317–22. The experience and significance of these black "aristocrats" can be found in Willard B. Gatewood, *Aristocrats of Color: The Black Elite, 1880–1920* (Bloomington: Indiana University Press, 1990).

101. *Richmond Planet*, 27 August 1904, 6 August 1910.

102. Ibid., 6 August 1910.

103. Ibid., 1 June 1907. See also 23 March 1907, 19 September 1914, and the sarcastically titled "Spasm of Virtue," 18 August 1906, on a North Carolina prison sentence for a lyncher. He also lashed back in a series of editorials responding to Thomas Nelson Page's racist assertions in the national press. Page, a famous Virginia literary figure and informal spokesman on southern matters, calmly promoted the white supremacist view of Reconstruction and the present "Negro problem." Mitchell, writing to a much more circumscribed audience, challenged his assumptions. See *McClure's Magazine* and the *Richmond Planet*, March–May 1904 and again in March 1907.

104. *Richmond Planet*, 4 May 1907, 15 July 1911, 18 October 1913.

105. Reading through the issues in January, May, and September of 1897 and 1913, I tallied all stories centered on the courts, crime, police, lynching, or any related issue. I chose the months at random and decided on these years simply to avoid years that I knew included crime sensations (such as 1895–96 with the Lunenburg case or 1915 with the killing of a prominent black family man, Armisted Walker). In the fourteen issues published in these months of 1897, the *Planet* printed forty-five brief articles (one paragraph to half a column), twenty editorials, and seventeen long stories (over half a column—most were more than a column). The fourteen issues analyzed in 1913 (I added the first issue of February to make this sample also comprise fourteen issues) included forty-eight short articles but only six editorials and six long stories.

Lynchings, a major concern to Mitchell and the *Planet*, declined in the opening decades of the twentieth century. This was particularly true in Virginia, although editor Mitchell always published on lynchings from throughout the nation. But lynchings of blacks continued to average more than seven every month of the decade of the 1900s. Added to this was the regular eruption of racial violence in the form of race riots, discussed below. Particularly given the changes in Mitchell's style of coverage of crime and justice overall, the sharp drop in gross numbers of stories on violence indicates much more than a simple reflection of changes in lynching.

106. I inventoried the same months and years as for the *Planet*, yielding in the

Cleveland Gazette of 1897: twenty-seven short articles, two long ones and six editorials. In 1913, this fell to eighteen short articles, one long story, and four editorials. In both years, the *Gazette* was four pages in length.

107. I could not attempt a similar comparison of years for the *New York Age* because extant copies of it for the 1890s are few and scattered. In a 1913 sample, however, the *Age* included slightly more—particularly in the longer stories—than the other papers I inventoried: nine short articles on crime and violence, six longer ones, and nine editorials.

108. Arthur Johnson and Ronald M. Johnson, "Away from Accommodation: Radical Editors and Protest Journalism, 1900–1910," *Journal of Negro History* 62 (October 1977): 325–38; David Domke, "The Black Press in the 'Nadir' of African Americans," *Journalism History* 20 (1994): 131–38; Gunner Myrdal, *An American Dilemma: The Negro Problem and Modern Democracy* (1944; repr., New York: Harper and Row, 1962), 913–14.

109. Jesse Duke was run out of Alabama, but he moved to another southern state, Arkansas, and continued to publish a series of newspapers, although it is unclear how outspoken he remained. Manly and Wells moved north. Allen W. Jones, "The Black Press in the 'New South': Jesse C. Duke's Struggle for Justice and Equality," *Journal of Negro History* 64 (1979): 215–28; Capeci and Knight, "Reckoning with Violence"; Louis R. Harlan, "Booker T. Washington and the *Voice of the Negro*, 1904–1907," *Journal of Southern History* 45 (1979): 45–62; Cecelski and Tyson, *Democracy Betrayed*; Alfreda M. Duster, ed., *Crusade for Justice: The Autobiography of Ida B. Wells* (Chicago: University of Chicago Press, 1970), 47–59. Soon, Eugene N. Bryant would be another editor forced to flee ahead of a mob. See Neil R. McMillen, *Dark Journey: Black Mississippians in the Age of Jim Crow* (Urbana: University of Illinois Press, 1989), 176.

110. In the months inventoried in 1897, the *Savannah Tribune* ran thirty-four short stories on crime, five long ones, and five editorials. In 1913, the totals fell to ten short stories on crime, one long one, and three editorials.

111. By the 1910s, the *Planet* included a piece of syndicated fiction in every issue, and recurring columns ("The Dairy," "Farm and Garden") also were probably syndicated, though it is unclear what syndicates marketed to African American papers in this era. This is an important missing chapter in the history of the African American press, for it is possible that substantial portions of putatively black papers in this era were written by white syndicates. Although the *Planet* apparently did not, other African American papers subscribed to boilerplate services (subscribers received precast stories and features that they could place wherever they wanted as they typeset their issues). Several of the same stories—with identical typefaces, line spacing, titles, and accompanying images, can be found in the *Cleveland Gazette* and the *Savannah Tribune*. See, for instance, "Afro-American Cullings" (a regular feature of both) and "In Defense of Miss Annie Smoot" in their editions of 25 January 1913. On

syndication in general (but not African American newspapers) see Richard A. Schwarzlose, *The Nation's Newsbrokers*, 2 vols. (Evanston, Ill.: Northwestern University Press, 1990). The literature on boilerplate is extremely thin; see Eugene Harter, *Boilerplating America: The Hidden Newspaper* (New York: University Press of America, 1991).

112. Davis, "Black Press." This is the central thrust of Davis's dissertation. He divides 1827 to 1927 into a number of periods and takes a generous sampling of the black press in each period, using a space-allocation analysis to discern changes in emphasis in the papers. News and advertising were the largest categories in each period, but in antebellum papers, six of the eight categories filled at least 10 percent of the space, whereas in the twentieth century, news and advertising accounted for 35 percent and 30 percent of the space, respectively. This amounts to a growth of 17 percent in news and ads at the expense of "expression categories."

113. *Richmond Planet*, 16 March 1907.

114. Ibid., 20 June 1914. Another example would be an editorial on 1 November 1913: "A Miscarriage of Justice" concerned comparisons between white and black penalties for theft. A strongly worded title, but the article was ambivalent, largely concerned with praising the white police justice who gave a white criminal a jail sentence instead of simply a fine (the thief appealed and in a jury trial received only a fine). Davis ("The Black Press," 276–84) uses a less-than-convincing case as his central example in this section, but he nevertheless develops an important argument concerning how commercialism led to the general toning down of the content of black papers in this era.

115. *Richmond Planet*, 18 February 1905.

116. Ibid., 2 December 1911. The coverage of the Beattie murder in the *Planet* started on 29 July 1911 and continued in most issues through November. Some stories were listed as coming from the *Times Dispatch* or, more rarely, from the *News Leader* or *Evening Journal*. But most were not attributed, and it is only by looking at the *Planet* in conjunction with the *Times-Dispatch* that it becomes evident that every story is reprinted word-for-word from the white papers of the city.

117. *Richmond Planet*, 16 January 1909. Here again, Davis, in his "The Black Press," finds a trend among African American papers in this era toward chastising the missteps of those of their own race, particularly those of the lower class.

118. *Richmond Planet*, 16 January 1909.

119. Ibid., 28 August 1915. Mitchell criticized other blacks for more than criminal wrongdoing: "The white folks are not our worst enemies. They wish us to succeed and advise us to support each other. It is the envious jealous hearted people of our own color that handicap us and retard our progress." Ibid., 24 May 1913.

120. Ibid., 7 March 1908.

121. Cecelski and Tyson, *Democracy Betrayed*; Capeci and Knight, "Reckoning

with Violence"; Brooks Miles Barnes, "The Onancock Race Riot of 1907," *Virginia Magazine of History and Biography* 92 (1984): 336–51. See also the *Richmond Planet*, 17 and 24 August 1907 and occasionally thereafter for the next year. For an earlier (1883) riot in Danville, Virginia, see Jane Dailey, "Deference and Violence in the Postbellum Urban South: Manners and Massacres in Danville, Virginia," *Journal of Southern History* 63 (1997): 553–90.

122. A prominent exception to this trend is W. E. B. Du Bois, who responded to the 1906 Atlanta riot and the persistent repression of southern blacks with a turn toward Marxism and a more vocal opposition to Jim Crow, albeit—and importantly—in the context of a move to the North. See Capeci and Knight, "Reckoning with Violence."

123. *Richmond Planet*, 16 January 1909.

124. Ibid., 4 July 1914.

125. Booker T. Washington, in Louis R. Harlan, ed., *The Booker T. Washington Papers*, vol. 1: *The Autobiographical Writings* (Urbana: University of Illinois Press, 1972), 153.

126. The defeatism model is complicated also by the fact that militancy, which has been so highly valued in the wake of the civil rights successes of the mid-twentieth century, paid few dividends as events unfolded in the late-nineteenth-century South. As bold and forceful as were Mitchell and other southern editors, they did not significantly slow the quickening current of disfranchisement, Jim Crow, and racial violence. Mitchell helped to save individuals like Isaac Jenkins and the Lunenburg women, but his efforts and those of the wider black community failed to alter in a meaningful way the broader racial prejudice facing African Americans.

This is an unresolved issue among historians of the period: whites were clearly to blame for the worsening conditions facing blacks in the South under Jim Crow, but how should African Americans have responded? After all, what *is* strength of character in the face of what can only be called systematic and violent repression? Booker T. Washington's vision of racial harmony has not fared well in such evaluations. For example, in *Uplifting the Race*, Kevin Gaines characterizes the self-help effort of the era's black middle class as false consciousness, internalizing the racist notions of whites and distancing elites from the black rabble in a misguided attempt to avoid the prejudice meted out to poor blacks. From this perspective, John Mitchell was cowed by the power of whites, turning against his own in order to win some measure of approval from the white establishment. He was in denial about the fact that the mere display of respectability and prosperity could mark a black man in the South as "uppity." Gaines and others frame this uplift effort as a failure, pointing to the rising tide of racism as proof. Evidence for this perspective can certainly be found in Mitchell's writings.

But is there any indication that militancy paid better dividends to the black communities of the South at this moment? Mitchell's vocal activism in the

1890s certainly did not, and the flight of assertive editors like Jesse Duke, Alex Manly, Max Barber, Ida B. Wells, and Eugene Bryant to the North also militates against this idea. More aggressive stands might simply have resulted in more retaliatory violence.

Gaines goes so far as to say that Booker T. Washington helped to make popular racism respectable (58), though the wider book is notably more complex and nuanced on this issue. Indeed, well-to-do blacks were often targets of violence because of their prosperity. Observers at the time noted this; in fact, the *Voice of the Negro* (1 [1904]: 514–16) chastised John Mitchell personally for seeming to forget this. Ann Alexander likewise demonstrates how Mitchell's successes in the business world simply drew more attention, opposition, and white regulatory oversight. "It is absolutely essential," admitted Mitchell in 1915 in what looks like a repudiation of the accommodation philosophy, "to have political rights and to exercise them in order to protect property." See *Race Man*, 170–84; quotation, 177.

But this logic against accommodation and the uplift ideology is not firm, for it does not take into consideration the extraordinary repression that was the context of the era. It remains unexplained what actions blacks could have taken to mitigate the damage caused by southern white intimidation, violence, and prejudice. Caught in a Catch-22 situation, southern African Americans listened ever more closely to the alluring stories of economic and political possibilities in the North and the West as the twentieth century progressed.

Historians long for a positive end to this story of repression. Many find it in moments of activism that they can frame as seeds that come to flower in the later civil rights movement. The *Crisis* and the *Defender*, published in the North, give evidence of this militancy, but some historians seek such evidence in the more exhausted soil of the South as well. Even Leon Litwack's nuanced and lyrical *Trouble in Mind* ends with the hopefully titled chapter "Crossroads," detailing the active and forceful lives of outlaw Robert Charles, boxing champion Jack Johnson, and editor and antilynching advocate Ida B. Wells, among others. But John Mitchell's path suggests that this ending is a deceptively hopeful reading of this historical moment in terms of those who remained in the South. After all, Robert Charles was killed, Ida B. Wells fled the South, and Jack Johnson fled the United States altogether. Under the extraordinary pressures of white supremacy, southern black militancy metamorphosed into something quite distinct from the activism we so admire: a strong-willed but nonconfrontational uplift effort. Perhaps it would be more fitting to reverse the last two chapters in *Trouble in Mind*, exchanging "Crossroads" for the more somber "Enduring" as a more apt ending of a book that does not reach the more substantive crossroads of the Great Migration lying just ahead.

127. Ralph Ellison, *Invisible Man* (New York: Vintage, 1980), 16.

128. *Richmond Planet*, 8 June 1901.

129. Quoted in Alexander, *Race Man*, 155. Arguably, Mitchell was correct on this

point—the later civil rights movement rested on the foundation of economic gains made in southern black communities in the twentieth century, particularly advances made during World War II and the postwar boom. Blacks in Richmond simply did not have the means to sustain a boycott of the streetcars in 1904. Blacks in Montgomery sustained their boycott for a year, due in part to the twentieth-century proliferation of cars and the ability of blacks to purchase them.

130. *Colored American Magazine* 5 (1902): 386–91.

131. Mitchell's later years were difficult. Due to the post–World War I recession, adamant white oversight, and his own questionable business practices, his bank failed in 1922, and he narrowly avoided a term in the penitentiary. He continued to publish the *Planet*, but blacks in Richmond in the 1920s were as likely to read the city's white papers or the competing black weekly, the *St. Luke's Herald*. He left little in the way of a legacy—while Maggie Walker and Giles Jackson both had Richmond buildings named for them, Mitchell has been largely forgotten until recently. For these later years, see Alexander, *Race Man*, 185–209.

CHAPTER 5

1. Charles H. Sweeney testimony, 25 May 1885, transcript, *Commonwealth v. Cluverius* 4:1590–97, Meredith Family Papers, Virginia Historical Society, Richmond.

2. Charles Montriou Wallace Diary, 14 and 15 May 1885, Manuscripts Division, Perkins Library, Duke University, Durham, N.C.

3. Thomas J. Cluverius, *Cluverius: My Life, Trial, and Conviction* (Richmond: Andrews, Baptist and Clement, 1887), 43–44.

4. William M. Ivins Jr., *Prints and Visual Communication* (Cambridge, Mass.: Harvard University Press, 1953); Estelle Jussim, *Visual Communication and the Graphic Arts: Photographic Technologies in the Nineteenth Century* (New York: R. R. Bowker Co., 1974); Neil Harris, "Iconography and Intellectual History: The Halftone Effect," in *Cultural Excursions: Marketing Appetites and Cultural Tastes in Modern America*, ed. Neil Harris (Chicago: University of Chicago Press, 1990), 304–17; Miles Orvell's *The Real Thing: Imitation and Authenticity in American Culture, 1880–1940* (Chapel Hill: University of North Carolina Press, 1989) is a fascinating and rich discussion of the changes in American culture, including two chapters on photography. But he evaluates the era's changes along a different axis, for he is focused on the aesthetics of art photography rather than on photojournalism.

5. James W. Carey, "Walter Benjamin, Marshall McLuhan, and the Emergence of Visual Society," *Prospects* 11 (1986): 29–38.

6. David Ray Papke, *Framing the Criminal: Crime, Cultural Work, and the Loss of Critical Perspective, 1830–1900* (Hamden, Conn.: Archon Books, 1987), 21.

For an example of a pamphlet title page with both the coffin and the hanging figure, see *The Life and Dying Confession of James Hamilton* (Albany: n.p., 1819).

7. Such images can be found on page 4 of most issues of the *Gazette*. None of these stock images in the *Gazette* related to crimes of violence.

8. *Richmond Dispatch*, 10 March 1860.

9. It is in this sense of developing particularized, detailed stories that Cathy N. Davidson (*The Revolution and the Word: The Rise of the Novel in America* [New York: Oxford University Press, 1986]) and Karen Halttunen (*Murder Most Foul: The Killer and the American Gothic Imagination* [Cambridge, Mass.: Harvard University Press, 1998]) can describe early-nineteenth-century sentimental novels and crime stories as "realistic" despite their rampant use of melodramatic and sentimental imagery and techniques.

10. *Trial of William Dandridge Epes for the Murder of Francis Adolphus Muir* (Petersburg: J. M. H. Brunet, 1849).

11. Quote from *Richmond Dispatch*, 10 March 1860.

12. Charles A. Dana, "The Making of a Newspaper Man," in *The Art of Newspaper Making: Three Lectures* (New York D. Appleton and Co., 1895), 95–96.

13. Examples of these phrases abound. For reprinted examples, see Daniel Cohen, *Pillars of Salt, Monuments of Grace: New England Crime Literature and the Origins of American Popular Culture, 1674–1860* (New York: Oxford University Press, 1993), 236, and Patricia Cline Cohen, *The Murder of Helen Jewett: The Life and Death of a Prostitute in Nineteenth-Century New York* (New York: Alfred A. Knopf, 1998), 255, 307.

14. Other studies of crime and culture echo this characterization of illustration in this era, although none pursue this line of thought very far. See, for example, Papke, *Framing the Criminal*, 21–25, and Andie Tucher, *Froth and Scum: Truth, Beauty, Goodness, and the Ax Murder in America's First Mass Medium* (Chapel Hill: University of North Carolina Press, 1994), 28, 152, 156–58. Karen Halttunen's *Murder Most Foul* provides a wealth of examples of this simplistic and stereotyped style, and she argues for a general trend in pamphlets toward characterizing the criminal as a "monster" distinguishable from the norm. However, she does not emphasize the connection between this trend and images, and she discusses illustration itself only in passing. Patricia Cline Cohen (*Murder of Helen Jewett*) and Amy Gilman Srebnick (*The Death of Mary Rogers: Sex and Culture in Nineteenth-Century New York* [New York: Oxford University Press, 1995]) each provide other examples of antebellum engravings but similarly do not pursue this avenue of investigation. This is not meant as a criticism of any of these works; they were simply pursuing other historical prey.

15. *An Account of the Apprehension, Trial, Conviction, and Condemnation of Manuel Philip Garcia and Jose Demas Garcia Castillano* (Norfolk: C. Hall, 1821).

16. For examples of this presentation of dispassionate images as early as the 1830s and 1840s, see Cohen, *Pillars of Salt*, 228, 232–33, 236; and the two images facing page 33 of Karen Halttunen, *Murder Most Foul*.

17. *Trial of Richard P. Robinson* . . . (New York: n.p., 1836). A reproduction of this image can be found in Tucher, *Froth and Scum*, 29.

18. *The Confession of the Awful and Bloody Transaction in the Life of Charles Wallace* (New Orleans: E. E. Barclay and Co., 1851). This image is reprinted in Srebnick, *Mysterious Death of Mary Rogers*, 70.

19. Srebnick, *Mysterious Death of Mary Rogers*, 135.

20. Halttunen includes twenty-nine images from antebellum pamphlets, thirteen of which illustrate the necessarily fictive re-creations of the moment of action, the other sixteen being portraits, diagrams, and the scene of the crime or the trial. While it is hard to say how representative this sample is for the entire genre of crime pamphlets, these images demonstrate the variety of sorts of engravings, only a few of which appear dispassionate. Images from earlier English and German pamphlets have an even greater tendency to caricature the action of the murder scene. See Daniel Cohen, "Blood Will Out: Sensationalism, Horror, and the Roots of American Crime Literature," in *Mortal Remains: Death in Early America*, ed. Nancy Isenberg and Andrew Burstein (Philadelphia: University of Pennsylvania Press, 2003), 31–55; Joy Wiltenburg, "True Crime: The Origins of Modern Sensationalism," *American Historical Review* 109 (December 2004): 1377–1404.

21. *National Police Gazette*, 13 December 1845, 129. For a close treatment of this case, see Cohen, *Pillars of Salt*, 195–246.

22. Francis John Martin Jr., "The Image of Black People in American Illustration from 1825 to 1925" (Ph.D. diss., University of California, Los Angeles, 1986), 136. For colonial and early national period images of blacks, see Barbara E. Lacey, "Visual Images of Blacks in Early American Imprints," *William and Mary Quarterly* 53 (January 1996): 137–80.

23. Marcus Aurelius Root, *The Camera and the Pencil, or the Heliographic Art* (1864; repr. ed., Pawlet, Vt.: Helios, 1971), 44. For more on the history of phrenology, see Charles Colbert, *A Measure of Perfection: Phrenology and the Fine Arts in America* (Chapel Hill: University of North Carolina Press, 1997); Roger Cooter, *The Cultural Meaning of Popular Science: Phrenology and the Organization of Consent in Nineteenth-Century Britain* (New York: Cambridge University Press, 1984); David de Giustino, *Conquest of Mind: Phrenology and Victorian Social Thought* (Totowa, N.J.: Rowman and Littlefield, 1975). For a related development, see Mike Hawkins, *Social Darwinism in European and American Thought, 1860–1945: Nature as Model and Nature as Threat* (New York: Cambridge University Press, 1997).

24. Peter Brooks, *The Melodramatic Imagination: Balzac, Henry James, Melodrama, and the Mode of Excess* (New Haven, Conn.: Yale University Press, 1976), 24–55.

25. E. K. Hough, "Expressing Character in Photographic Pictures," *American Journal of Photography* 1 (15 December 1858): 212–13; quoted in Alan Trachtenberg, *Reading American Photographs: Images as History, Mathew Brady to Walker Evans* (New York: Hill and Wang, 1989), 40.

26. J. Wall Turner, *The Drinker's Farm Tragedy: Trial and Conviction of James Jeter Phillips for the Murder of His Wife* (Richmond: V. L. Fore, 1868). This image is a second-generation engraving, taken from one that appeared in the *Southern Opinion* on 2 May 1868. This secondary engraver altered the picture to make it even more ghastly than the original. The two images share the disturbing, cavernous eyes and a generally villainous look, but the original image has a closed mouth rather than this peculiar grimace. Note the similarities to the engraving of a man whose "cruelty almost exceeded belief" in figure 10.

27. Root, *Camera and Pencil*, 43–44.

28. *Southern Opinion*, 2 May 1868.

29. *Richmond Enquirer and Sentinel*, 14 June 1867.

30. For the early history of the daguerreotype, see Richard Rudisill, *Mirror Image: The Influence of the Daguerreotype on American Society* (Albuquerque: University of New Mexico Press, 1971), and John Wood, ed., *America and the Daguerreotype* (Iowa City: University of Iowa Press, 1991). In the same year, 1839, William Henry Fox Talbot invented another form of photography, the calotype, which was superior in many ways—particularly by allowing for reproducible prints—but was much less popular than Daguerre's invention. Particularly problematic were Talbot's patent restrictions on the process, which prevented the broad adoption of the calotype.

31. The collodion process was a great improvement in photography, combining the detail of the daguerreotype with the reproducibility of Talbot's calotype, but it was a very cumbersome process. As its name implies, the wet-plate process involved the use of a liquid emulsion (collodion) on a glass negative and required processing both immediately before and immediately after exposure. In essence this meant that a photographer had to carry not only a camera and glass negatives, but also a complete darkroom if he ventured forth from his studio. The stereograph and tintype arose in the 1850s and 1860s from the collodion process. They each show how photography continued to grow in popularity and in the range of its uses; by 1860, it had spilled out of the parlor and upscale galleries into the whimsical, the inexpensive, and the novelty corners of American culture. For a more thorough history of early photography, see Beaumont Newhall, *The History of Photography from 1839 to the Present* (New York: Museum of Modern Art, 1982), 30; Michael L. Carlebach, *The Origins of Photojournalism in America* (Washington, D.C.: Smithsonian Institution Press, 1992), 13–22.

32. William Ivins saw the medium as the undistorted visual representation of nature itself, as a medium without syntax and therefore as a revolution in the graphic arts and in visual representation generally. See his *Prints and Visual*

Communication. Scholars in the late twentieth century continued to see photography as revolutionary but in a more complicated context, complete with the panoply of subjectivities attendant to any form of communication. See, for example, Jussim, *Visual Communication and the Graphic Arts*; Trachtenberg, *Reading American Photographs*; and Jennifer Green-Lewis, *Framing the Victorians: Photography and the Culture of Realism* (Ithaca, N.Y.: Cornell University Press, 1996). Miles Orvell includes two particularly helpful chapters on the changing aesthetics of photography in *Real Thing*, 73–102, 198–239.

33. A very nice discussion of Galton can be found in Alan Sekula's "The Body and the Archive," *October* 39 (Winter 1986): 40–55.

34. Professor S. F. B. Morse, in a speech before the annual supper of the National Academy of Design, 24 April 1840; quoted in Root, *Camera and the Pencil*, 391; emphasis in original. Root's subtitle, "The Heliographic Art," emphasizes this nineteenth-century belief that photographs were "sun paintings" rather than man-made artifacts.

35. Carlebach, *Origins of Photojournalism*, 150–51. Most important of the early reproduction techniques was photo-lithography, based on the repulsion of ink by oil—not a process adaptable to the fast-moving rollers of newspaper presses.

36. These developments are more fully discussed in Michael Emery, Edwin Emery, and Nancy Roberts, *The Press and America: An Interpretive History of the Mass Media*, 9th ed. (Boston: Allyn and Bacon, 2000), 94–96, 116–17; and Michael Schudson, *Discovering the News: A Social History of American Newspapers* (New York: Basic Books, 1978), 31–35.

37. That artistic barriers existed is made clear by the fact that the technology to print halftone photographs was available by 1890 but was first used by a daily paper in 1897. Many factors might have influenced this delay, which remains something of a mystery in the literature: simple inertia, satisfaction with the quality of engravings, questions about the quality of halftones, competing designs making owners reticent to invest, and opposition from engravers. See R. Smith Schuneman, "Art or Photography: A Question for Newspaper Editors of the 1890s," *Journalism Quarterly* 42 (1965): 43–52.

38. Engravings from other sensations in this era, such as the famous Lizzie Borden case in 1893, have a similar appearance. *Boston Globe*, 4–21 June 1893. The *Globe* printed 126 engravings in its early editions during these 2½ weeks. Almost every engraving was of the style found in figures 1–3. In fact, this method endures well past the adoption of the halftone for communicating certain kinds of hypothetical information that photographs cannot capture. For instance, later murder sensations, like the Leo Frank case, include engraved diagrams showing the murder scene (a factory) with the path taken by the murderer drawn in. See the *Atlanta Constitution* or the *Atlanta Journal* between 28 July and 27 August 1913.

39. S. N. D. North, *History and Present Conditions of the Newspaper and Periodi-*

cal Press of the United States (Washington, D.C.: U.S. Government Printing Office, 1884), 125–26; printed in vol. 8 of the *Tenth U.S. Census, 1880.*

40. Henry Peach Robinson, "Illustration," *Photo-American* 6 (June 1895): 228–29.

41. Carlebach, *Origins of Photojournalism,* 150–55; Newhall, *History of Photography,* 123–24.

42. Writing about a rather primitive engraving of the jury posing on the stairs of the state capitol, a local merchant, Charles Montriou Wallace, emphasized the uneven development of engravings—and the persistence of ethnic stereotypes—when he noted the accuracy of acquaintances pictured: "Dispatch pictures the jury—old Lee's face good, Lowenstein's poor. Lee looks more like a jew than jew Lowenstein." Wallace Diary, 22 May 1885.

43. Carlebach, *Origins of Photojournalism,* 160–65; Emery, Emery, and Roberts, *Press and America,* 188–90.

44. Frederick Ives, *Autobiography of an Amateur Inventor* (Philadelphia: Innes and Sons, 1928 [privately printed]), 54. The use of the halftone migrated from book and periodical publishing in the early 1890s to weekly papers and finally to daily newspapers, becoming the dominant form of illustration in the opening years of the twentieth century.

45. Henry Vance Davis, "The Black Press: From Mission to Commercialism" (Ph.D. diss., University of Michigan, 1990), 165–68, 194–95.

46. Martin, "Image of Black People."

47. *Richmond Planet,* June 1895 to January 1897. The *Planet* introduced halftones in 1894 (29 December is the earliest example I can find). Richmond's dailies introduced them before 1901 (*Richmond News,* already in evidence on 5 January 1901; I have not found any earlier examples), in 1901 (*Richmond Times,* by 1 September), and in 1902 (*Richmond Dispatch,* by 20 July).

48. Since the images are scattered through twenty-two months of the paper, I cannot be sure I have found every image associated with the Cluverius case. I know thirty were printed; I am sure the number did not exceed forty.

49. The increase was just as dramatic when comparing the high point of the sensations, the trials. During the Beattie trial, the paper averaged six halftones a day (107 photographs between 22 August and 9 September 1911, an eighteen-day trial) compared to an average of 0.7 engravings a day when Cluverius stood trial in 1885 (twenty engravings in twenty-seven days of publishing between 6 May and 5 June, Monday through Saturday). And, of course, zero images of any sort were used during the 1867 Phillips trial.

50. For a listing of all extant Virginia crime pamphlets, see note 59 of chapter 3. Focusing on some of the most famous nineteenth-century murder cases nationally, antebellum pamphlets averaged just over two images, a number that rose to six as early as the 1870s and even higher in the coming years. In an evaluation of the copious collection of the American Antiquarian Society: four of

the most sensationalized cases of the antebellum era—the murders of Helen Jewett (1836), Samuel Adams (1841), Maria Bickford (1845), and Dr. George Parkman (1849)—fostered nineteen different pamphlets between them, each averaging 2.2 engravings. The murder of Albert Richardson in 1870 and the 1872 divorce scandal of Henry Ward Beecher (admittedly a different sensation but sensational nonetheless) fostered eight pamphlets, with an average of 5.6 images.

51. *Richmond Times-Dispatch*, 12 August 1911.

52. *New York World*, 24 January–13 April 1907.

53. *Atlanta Constitution*, 28 July–26 August 1913. For comparison, the *Atlanta Journal* published similar numbers in covering the Leo Frank case: twenty-nine engravings and eighty-six halftones during the trial.

54. For a discussion of "straight" photography, see Newhall, *History of Photography*. To compare with another Virginia case, the *Richmond Times-Dispatch* printed twenty-eight halftones in its five months of coverage of the Samuel McCue case (6 September 1904–14 February 1905). This was almost as many images as in the earlier Cluverius case, despite the fact that the McCue crime did not take place in Richmond but in Charlottesville, seventy miles to the west.

55. *Chicago Herald and Examiner*, 21 July–11 September 1924. For evaluations of their features, see 1, 4, 7, and 9 June and 28 July 1924. Paula Fass has evaluated and reproduced one set of these images, though I would argue that she overstates their prominence in the crime's coverage by saying that images in the Leopold and Loeb case "often" included physiological analysis; see her "Making and Remaking an Event: The Leopold and Loeb Case in American Culture," *Journal of American History* 80 (1993): 919–51, esp. 925 and 935.

56. Warren Susman, "'Personality' and the Making of Twentieth-Century Culture," in *New Directions in American Intellectual History*, ed. John Higham and Paul Conkin (Baltimore, Md.: Johns Hopkins University Press, 1979), 212–26. For more on this change, see chapter 3.

57. *Richmond Times-Dispatch*, 10 September 1911.

58. Ibid., 7 August 1911.

59. Halttunen, *Murder Most Foul*, 167.

60. Grace Elizabeth Hale, *Making Whiteness: The Culture of Segregation in the South, 1890–1940* (New York: Pantheon Books, 1998). For a host of graphic images of lynching, see James Allen, *Without Sanctuary: Lynching Photography in America* (Santa Fe, N.M.: Twin Palms, 2000). These images are very disturbing, yet it is quite difficult to determine precisely their place in the culture of the South. Were they hidden, a violent pornography circulating around the South but in limited numbers and more subcultural than an accepted part of normal southern culture? They are such shocking images that historians might be inclined to overstate their cultural role: of the thousands of lynchings that

took place in this era, we have dozens—not thousands—of extant images. On the other hand, they are horrifying, fascinating, and telling cultural artifacts: too complex a subject to adequately address here.

61. Jussim, *Visual Communication*, 289.

62. Ivins, *Prints and Visual Communication*, 134.

63. David E. Shi, *Facing Facts: Realism in American Thought and Culture, 1850–1920* (New York: Oxford University Press, 1995), 96–97; Eric J. Sundquist, *American Realism: New Essays* (Baltimore, Md.: Johns Hopkins University Press, 1982), 18–19.

64. Roland Barthes, *Camera Lucida: Reflections on Photography*, trans. Richard Howard (New York: Hill and Wang, 1981), 5.

65. *New York Times*, 8, 9, 10, and 12 September and 13 October 1911; *Richmond Times-Dispatch*, 8 September 1911. The Binford movie, like the Jack Johnson–Jim Jeffries interracial boxing match films of 1910, fostered early conflicts over motion picture censorship in localities across the nation. As with photography, the authenticity of motion pictures made many subjects disturbing to some viewers. For the conflict in Durham, North Carolina, over the screening of Beulah Binford's film, for example, see the *Raleigh News and Observer*, 22 October and 1 November 1911.

66. At least one variety show was barred from showing slides illustrating the Beattie case. *Richmond Times-Dispatch*, 2 September 1911.

CHAPTER 6

1. Petitions to the governor, documents submitted to the governor, 9–31 Dec. 1886, Secretary of the Commonwealth, Executive Papers, 1866–1962, record group 13, box 77, Library of Virginia, Richmond. This new statute, passed in January 1886, allowed accused felons to testify for the first time. Cluverius's defense lawyers argued that he would have taken advantage of this possibility if it had existed at the time of his trial.

2. Unless otherwise noted, this re-creation of the scene at the gallows comes from a compilation of stories printed in the *Richmond Dispatch*, 15 January 1887; the *Richmond Daily Times*, 15 January 1887; and the *Richmond State*, 14 January 1887.

3. *Richmond Dispatch*, 15 February 1887.

4. Herbert T. Ezekiel, *Recollections of a Virginia Newspaperman* (Richmond: H. T. Ezekiel, 1920), 43.

5. This photographer came close to taking pictures of the hanging from the jail yard itself. The judge of the hustings court, which was in charge of the execution, learned from the *Dispatch* on the day of the execution that a photographer would attend. The judge wrote to Sergeant Smith to remind him to obey the law in regard to who could view an execution and specifically barred the photographer from being there. Sergeant Smith received the letter two hours

before the hanging and expelled the photographer but did not reduce the crowd down to the "twelve respectable citizens" the law allowed. *Richmond Dispatch*, 15 February 1887.

6. Eldridge B. Hatcher, *William E. Hatcher: A Biography* (Richmond: W. C. Hill Printing Co., 1915), 247–49. This last meeting with Rev. Hatcher was not so fully reported in the newspapers of the time but comes instead from Hatcher's son.

7. Ibid., 251–52.

8. Charles Montriou Wallace Diary, 14 Jan. 1887, Manuscripts Division, Perkins Library, Duke University, Durham, N.C.

9. *Richmond Dispatch*, 15 January 1887. On this day, the *Dispatch* devoted, for the second day in a row, the entire front page, and part of the second, to the story. The header for this series of articles comprised eighteen separate titles; in the era before huge banner headlines, this was about as sensational as newspapers could get.

10. *Richmond Dispatch*, 15 January 1887; emphasis in original; ten reasons guilty: 18 January 1887.

11. Jos. Herndon to the Rev. M. R. Stevenson, 11 Jan. 1789, Herndon Family Papers, Special Collections, University of Virginia Library, Charlottesville.

12. Before 1796, Virginia criminal law closely followed that of England, which advocated corporal punishments and hanging for a wide variety of offenses, violent and otherwise. In the words of William Blackstone: in English law, capital punishment was "inflicted (perhaps inattentively) by a multitude of successive independent statutes, upon crimes very different in their natures. [N]o less than a hundred and sixty [felonies] have been declared worthy of instant death." William Blackstone, *Commentaries on the Laws of England* (Boston: T. B. Wait and Sons, 1818), 4:18. The harsh British law was mitigated in part by legal measures like the benefit of clergy—a plea, generally accepted, by which a first offender could have his sentence commuted. To Americans, such measures were simply further proof of the erratic, illogical, and corrupt nature of their legal inheritance—Virginia was quick to outlaw the plea of benefit of clergy.

13. Samuel Shepherd, *Statutes at Large of Virginia* (Richmond: Samuel Shepherd, 1835), 2:5. For an overview of the changes in Virginia's criminal code at this time, see Kathryn Preyer, "Crime, the Criminal Law, and Reform in Post-Revolutionary Virginia," *Law and History Review* 1 (1993): 53–85.

14. *The Code of Virginia, 1849* (Richmond: William F. Ritchie, 1849), 753–54. For Virginia slave laws, see Philip Schwarz, *Twice Condemned: Slaves and the Criminal Laws of Virginia, 1705–1865* (Baton Rouge: Louisiana State University Press, 1988) and his *Slave Laws in Virginia* (Athens: University of Georgia Press, 1996).

15. John D. Bessler, *Death in the Dark: Midnight Executions in America* (Boston: Northeastern University Press, 1997), 40–45; Louis P. Masur, *Rites of Execu-*

tion: Capital Punishment and the Transformation of American Culture, 1776–1865 (New York: Oxford University Press, 1989), 93–116. Stuart Banner's *The Death Penalty: An American History* (Cambridge, Mass.: Harvard University Press, 2002) also has a chapter on this transition, but he misses a number of the subtleties of the change, misrepresenting some legislation as the first privatization laws in several states, for instance, and generally making the transition in the South later. He mentions the transition for North Carolina, Oklahoma, Florida, and Texas, for instance, as occurring between 1909 and 1923 when each of these states had enacted privacy laws between 1868 and 1887. Banner's overall arguments hold, however, and Masur's treatment is fine, if skewed to the experience of the North (and particularly to Pennsylvania).

16. *Richmond Enquirer*, 21 August 1827. This report stresses the macabre as it relates how two of the three ropes broke during the first attempt, forcing another. For a pamphlet on the trial of the three pirates, see *A Brief Sketch of the Occurrences on Board the Brig Crawford, on Her Voyage from Matanzas to New York; Together with an Account of the Trial of the Three Spaniards, Jose Hilario Casares, Felix Barbeito, and Jose Morando* (Richmond: Samuel Shepherd, 1827).

17. *Richmond Dispatch*, 11 September 1852. This editorial on capital punishment appeared the day after the public execution of a slave for murdering her owners. The legislature had recently debated making hangings private but decided against making any change. The editor was emphatic: "it is impossible for any human being to be made worse, or to be encouraged in the commission of crime, by witnessing such an awful sight." Yet the phrasing implies that this issue had become a question demanding an adamant rebuttal.

18. *Virginia Gazette*, 27 December 1752. For a brief view of punishments in the early colonial period, see Bradley Chapin, *Criminal Justice in Colonial America, 1606–1660* (Athens: University of Georgia Press, 1983), 50–58. For more on regional difference and the execution sermon, see chapter 1.

19. *An Account of the Apprehension, Trial, Conviction, and Condemnation of Manuel Philip Garcia and Jose Demas Garcia Castillano* (Norfolk: C. Hall, 1821).

20. *Richmond Enquirer*, 5 June 1821.

21. *An Account of the Apprehension*, 39–40.

22. *Acts of the General Assembly of Virginia, passed in 1855-6* (Richmond: William F. Ritchie, 1856), 36–37. The text reads: "whenever sentence of death is to be executed, if the convict be in jail, around or adjoining which there is a yard of sufficient size enclosed by a wall, such sentence shall be executed within such enclosed yard, unless the court, by which such sentence was pronounced, direct otherwise." In addition, the new law also stipulated who should attend: attorneys, "twelve respectable citizens," ministers, officers. Both restrictions, however, left loopholes: the court could order a public execution, and the officer in charge could invite as many "guard[s] and assistants as [he] shall see fit." 283

The vague nature of this first act is in keeping with norms for the nation. Most northern states enacted such legislation in the 1830s and 1840s, and most similarly emphasized placing the scaffold inside jail walls but left to the discretion of local authorities how many spectators would be allowed in. The earliest private executions were typically private only in name. See Masur, *Rites of Execution*, 93–116.

23. Albert Tyler's judge believed that the entire community needed to see him pay for his crime—thousands obliged him by attending. See *Richmond Dispatch*, 1 April 1869 (sentenced); 31 May 1869 (hanged).

24. This jail was in Richmond but not in the bottom of the Shockoe valley, and it did not, therefore, provide the vantage points from surrounding hills available at the Cluverius execution.

25. *Richmond Dispatch*, 23 July 1870; *Richmond Whig*, 23 July 1870.

26. *Richmond Whig*, 23 July 1870.

27. *Richmond Dispatch*, 23 July 1870.

28. Similar vivid coverage—although shorter in length—can be found in the execution of Garcia and Castillano in 1821 or in the pirate hangings of 1827.

29. For instance, *Richmond Dispatch*, 31 May 1869.

30. *Acts and Joint Resolutions Passed by the General Assembly of the State of Virginia during the Session of 1878–79* (Richmond: R. E. Frayser, 1879), 380. The text reads: "it shall not be lawful hereafter in this state to execute the death penalty on any condemned criminal in a public manner, but only in the presence of such officers of the law as may be necessary to see that the sentence of the court is properly carried into effect." The parallel passage in the 1887 *Code of Virginia* emphasized this change, beginning forcefully: "in no case shall sentence of death be executed in a public manner." If a walled yard was not already available, the officer in charge was ordered to erect a temporary barrier to spectators. *The Code of Virginia, 1887* (Richmond: James E. Goode, 1887), 949–50.

31. *Richmond Dispatch*, 7 Aug. 1890. The papers also continued to print extensively on local executions, of course. For an example in the 1890s, see coverage of the execution of Philip Norman Nicholas in the *Dispatch*, 21, 25, and 26 July 1895.

32. Ibid., 23 June and 15 September 1883.

33. For example, see ibid., 20 December 1879, 6 November 1880, or 12 January 1884.

34. *Richmond Enquirer*, 21 August 1827.

35. *Richmond Times-Dispatch*, 11 February 1905.

36. As of January 1995, condemned felons could choose between electrocution and lethal injection. In this, Virginia's history is again in line with the rest of the nation. By 2002, only one state, Nebraska, had electrocution as its only method of capital punishment. All other states that continue to use the death penalty either have a choice of methods or have moved to lethal injection.

37. *Richmond Times-Dispatch*, 6 March 1908.

38. Ibid., 14 October 1908.

39. *Acts and Joint Resolutions Passed by the General Assembly of the State of Virginia during the Session of 1908* (Richmond: Davis Bottom, 1908), 684–86. The text reads: "the superintendent of the State penitentiary is directed to provide a permanent death chamber, which shall have all the necessary appliances for the proper execution of felons by electrocution." On reporting the executions, the act stated: "No newspaper or person shall print or publish the details of the execution of criminals under this act. Only the fact that the criminal was executed shall be printed or published." This is again in keeping with national trends. New York first enacted such a gag rule in 1889, and a number of states followed suit in the next generation. See Bessler, *Death in the Dark*, 47–67.

40. These were pragmatic confessions: short, barely religious, to the point, and printed in newspapers rather than spoken before a gallows audience. Samuel McCue left a message that was a single sentence mediated through his ministers: "Mr. J. S. McCue this morning stated in our presence and requested us to make public that he did not wish to leave this world with suspicion resting on any human being other than himself; that he alone is responsible for the deed, impelled to it by an evil power beyond his control, and that he recognizes the sentence as just." *Richmond Times-Dispatch*, 11 February 1905. Similarly, Henry Beattie admitted his guilt in three brief sentences: "I, Henry Clay Beattie, Jr., desirous of standing right before God and man, do on this the 23rd day of November, 1911, confess my guilt of the crime charged against me. Much that was published concerning the details was not true, but the awful fact, without the harrowing circumstances, remains. For this action, I am truly sorry, and believing that I am at peace with God, and am soon to pass into His presence, this statement is made." Ibid., 25 November 1911.

41. *Richmond Evening Journal*, 24 November 1911, extra no. 5.

42. *Richmond Times-Dispatch*, 25 November 1911.

43. Ibid.; *Richmond Evening Journal*, 24 November 1911.

44. *Washington Post*, 25 November 1911. The standard procedure was to vary the current a number of times; the *Post* or its witness probably misinterpreted this as three separate shocks.

45. *Richmond Evening Journal*, 24 November 1911, extra no. 2. This article was taken from Charles V. Carrington, "The History of Electrocution in the State of Virginia," *Virginia Medical Semi-Monthly*, 25 November 1910; also published separately in Richmond by Williams Printing Co., 1910.

46. This perspective can be found in newspaper reports (for instance, the report of the first Virginia electrocution, *Richmond Times-Dispatch*, 14 October 1908), in Carrington's "History of Electrocution," and in his yearly reports as surgeon at the penitentiary. *Annual Report of the Board of Directors of the Virginia Penitentiary* (Richmond: Davis Bottom, 1908 and 1909).

47. For more on the electric chair and the technological sublime, see Jürgen

Martschukat, "'The Art of Killing by Electricity': The Sublime and the Electric Chair," *Journal of American History* 89 (2002): 901–21.

48. *Richmond Dispatch*, 7 August 1890.

49. New York State Commission on Capital Punishment, *Report of the Commission to Investigate and Report the Most Humane and Practical Method of Carrying into Effect the Sentence of Death in Capital Cases* (Albany: Argus Co., 1888); quoted in Martschukat, "Art of Killing," 915.

50. Other articles were similarly calculated to awaken the senses to the experience. Perhaps the most overt of these is the how-does-it-feel? story, such as "Hanging—The Sensation of Being Strung Up by the Neck," *Richmond Dispatch*, 17 July 1887; or "The Effects of Hanging on a Convicted Felon," *Richmond Dispatch* 7 March 1885; or "How Electrocution Feels," *Literary Digest* 10 (1894):166. Oddly, the article on the experience of being hanged included the subtitle "Murderer Baker says the gallows is not particularly unpleasant." A similar story can be found in the *Southern Opinion* (10 October 1868), where the editor attempts to give a "truthful account" of a hanging, as opposed to the newspapers "describ[ing] the execution in the usual terms."

51. Norbert Elias, *The Civilizing Process* (Oxford: Blackwell Publishers, 2000). Most prominent in the analysis of the "civilizing" of institutions of punishment is Michel Foucault. See his *Discipline and Punish: The Birth of the Prison* (New York: Vintage, 1979) as well as other works. For work specifically on the history of the civilizing of punishment in the United States, see David J. Rothman, *The Discovery of the Asylum: Social Order and Disorder in the New Republic* (Boston: Little, Brown, and Co., 1971) and *Conscience and Convenience: The Asylum and Its Alternatives in Progressive America* (Boston: Little, Brown, and Co., 1980).

52. Hatcher, *William E. Hatcher*, 246.

53. There are a number of problems with Foucault's treatment of punishment, from his false—but riveting—contrast between the brutal torture and quartering of an attempted regicide, on the one hand, and the later institutionalization in penitentiaries, on the other hand (they are apples and oranges), to his sweeping claims that cause historians to cry out in pain at the horror of his lack of specific sources and context. Nevertheless, his broad argument about the changing nature of modern institutions is compelling, engrossing, and—despite its faults—convincing at least in general terms.

The problem with this perspective on the civilizing process in general—and Foucault's particular approach to capital punishment—is that it describes a project, a goal of reformers and thinkers. In that way it is one-sided, missing most issues of interest to this study. Foucault's is a study of elites, institutions, and reformist rhetoric rather than a more multifaceted history of a culture or of cultural change. He did not turn his attention to the spectators and the popularity of and public fascination with the violence of public torture in the premodern era, for instance. How did the populace experience the gruesome dismemberment of the regicide that Foucault graphically uses to start *Discipline and Punish*? Did they cower before the authority of the monarch, or did they revel in the carnival of death, experiencing it in ways the monarch would never have anticipated or approved of? Instead of exploring these issues, Foucault assumes the success of the institutions in power, emphasizing the role of this public torture in cementing ties between royal power and the subservient populace. Similarly, Foucault neglected the range of ways in which the public consumed images and stories of violence and punishment in the modern era of "normalized" bodies and civilizing institutions.

Simply put, official institutions *did* change as Foucault argued, and this study of Virginia law adds further evidence of this evolution. But at the same time, much more was changing in the wider culture, much of it working in the opposite direction. A very different and conflicted story emerges when viewed from the perspective of popular culture.

Although it is true that none of these nineteenth-century accused murderers were drawn and quartered, the public remained fascinated with violence, including the violence applied to the criminal's body—its effect, its look, what happened. And that is aside from considering the rising prominence of lynching in this period. This interest was not simply some vestigial remnant from an earlier era; it was dynamically growing in American culture. The mass culture of the time increasingly focused on stories of violence, and the twentieth century would be saturated with stories of gore and brutality—fiction and nonfiction, written and on film. There was a civilizing process, but there was also a brutalizing process in American culture. Those studying the civilizing process generally miss this second phenomenon and thereby misrepresent the direction taken in modern cultural history.

54. *Richmond Times-Dispatch*, 14 October 1908.

55. It is difficult to delimit exactly what makes lynching different from simple murder; statistics therefore vary widely and are almost always incomplete. Strictly rigorous and dependable numbers on lynchings have yet to be published for most states. The most venerated historical data begin after the end of Reconstruction: 1882 for Tuskegee Institute's yearly count of lynching and 1889 for the NAACP's *Thirty Years of Lynching* (New York: NAACP, 1919). Most scholars studying lynching have either begun with these data sets or follow them by adopting a beginning date in the 1880s. See Stewart E. Tolnay and E. M. Beck, *A Festival of Violence: An Analysis of Southern Lynchings, 1882–1930* (Urbana: University of Illinois, 1995); James Elbert Cutler, *Lynch-Law: An Investigation into the History of Lynching in the United States* (New York: Longman, Green, and Co., 1905); and Walter White, *Rope and Faggot* (New York: Knopf, 1929).

56. Three state studies demonstrate this trend; no published work shows more lynchings in the 1890s than during Reconstruction. If one were to factor in population growth, the prevalence of lynching in the Reconstruction era would

be that much more exaggerated. In terms of overall numbers, Kentucky had 15 percent more lynchings during Reconstruction than in the 1890s (117 lynchings between 1866 and 1875 as compared to 99 lynchings between 1889 and 1898); Louisiana, 33 percent more (230 lynchings between 1867 and 1876 as compared to 153 between 1891 and 1900); and central Texas, 100 percent more (57 Lynchings between 1866 and 1875 as compared to 29 between 1889 and 1898). The same data sets (and years) yield similar proportions when restricting consideration to lynchings of African Americans: Kentucky had 21 percent more lynchings of blacks during Reconstruction (87 compared to 69), Louisiana had 28 percent more (165 compared to 118), and central Texas had many fewer but still 13 percent more lynchings of blacks in Reconstruction than in the 1890s (24 compared to 21). With each, I measured and compared ten-year spans from Reconstruction and the 1890s, choosing the dates to maximize the number of lynchings in each to be sure to capture the high point. George Wright, *Racial Violence in Kentucky, 1865-1940: Lynchings, Mob Rule, and "Legal Lynchings"* (Baton Rouge: Louisiana State University Press, 1990), 307-19; Giles Vandal, *Rethinking Southern Violence: Homicides in Post-Civil War Louisiana, 1866-1884* (Columbus: Ohio State University Press, 2000), 94; Michael Pfeifer, *Rough Justice: Lynching and American Society, 1874-1947* (Urbana: University of Illinois Press, 2006), 165-72; William D. Carrigan, *The Making of a Lynching Culture: Violence and Vigilantism in Central Texas, 1836-1916* (Urbana: University of Illinois Press, 2004), 275-87.

There are justifications for this compartmentalization of eras of southern racial violence, particularly given that during Reconstruction much of the violence was actually overt political terrorism in service of the overthrow of Republican governments. That is a different dynamic than white majorities later violently repressing African American minorities. The best articulation of this distinction is in Fitzhugh Brundage, *Lynching in the New South: Georgia and Virginia, 1880-1930* (Urbana: University of Illinois Press, 1993), 7. Christopher Waldrep also explores this distinction, arguing that Reconstruction "outrages" were considered (by some at least) to be against the public and the public good; in essence the KKK *aspired* to become lynchers, those expressing the will of the community through their violence, but they failed to do so. In the lynching era, lynchers succeeded in convincing the wider public that they expressed the will of the community. See his *The Many Faces of Judge Lynch: Extralegal Violence and Punishment in America* (New York: Palgrave, 2002), 68; and Carrigan, *Making of a Lynching Culture*, 132-61.

There are other mysteries in the lynching statistics that beg for further study. For instance, why do Oklahoma, Missouri, and Florida—with the smallest African American communities in the South—have disproportionately high numbers of lynchings, ranking first, fifth, and second, respectively, in lynchings per one thousand blacks? (Texas and Arkansas are not far behind in this comparison.) Why does South Carolina, with the largest proportion of African

Americans in its population, have relatively few lynchings (ranking tenth), while Mississippi, Georgia, and Louisiana—the next three in the proportion of blacks in their populations—rank first, second, and fourth, respectively, in the highest number of lynchings? Virginia, for its part, has the lowest number of lynchings overall and the lowest when compared to the size of its black population. All of these comparisons employ the lynching numbers from the NAACP (1889–1919) and the 1890 census population data from Susan B. Carter, ed., *Historical Statistics of the United States, Earliest Times to the Present*, vol. 1: *Population* (New York: Cambridge University Press, 2006), 180–379.

57. Because each state charted its own course and worded its legislation in different ways, this issue is difficult to boil down. Several states (true of the North as well) first legislated privacy where convenient, that is, where jail walls were available. Later, they amended these laws to require privacy. Nine states enacted legislation that unequivocally prohibited public executions in this era: Alabama and Virginia (1879), Kentucky (1880), Louisiana (1884), Arkansas, Missouri, and Oklahoma (1887), Tennessee (1889), and Georgia (1893). A tenth, South Carolina, enacted a law in 1878 with a loophole—"if the same [within an enclosure] can there take place in such manner"—but deleted that phrase by 1894. (Despite poring over every year's *Acts of the Legislature*, I have been unable to pinpoint the exact year of this deletion.) Three of these states had longstanding laws on the books suggesting (but not requiring) that executions be private: Alabama (1840), Virginia (1855), and Georgia (1859).

North Carolina (1868) and Texas (1879) each promoted privacy but did not strictly require it, including the phrases "as much removed from public view as the means within his control will allow" and "where there is a jail in the county so constructed that a gallows can be erected therein," respectively. The state with the most lynchings, Mississippi, was the first in the South to ban public executions (1839), but in 1850, the state changed the wording to be a suggestion: in an enclosed yard "unless the board of supervisors . . . for good cause shall designate some other place." These suggestions persisted until the early twentieth century, when each state centralized executions under state rather than local control: North Carolina (1909), Mississippi (1916), and Texas (1923).

Acts Passed at the Annual Session of the General Assembly of the State of Alabama (Tuscaloosa: Hale and Phelan,1840), 150; *Acts of the General Assembly of Alabama* (Montgomery: Barrett and Brown, 1879), 45; *Acts Passed at the 1887 Session of the General Assembly of the State of Arkansas* (Little Rock: Woodruff and Pew, 1887), 29; *Code of the State of Georgia* (Atlanta: John H. Seals, 1861), 889–90; *Acts and Resolutions of the General Assembly of the State of Georgia, 1893* (Atlanta: George W. Harrison, 1894), 41–42; *Acts of the General Assembly of the Commonwealth of Kentucky, vol. 1* (Frankfort: E. H. Porter, 1880), 60–61; *Acts Passed by the General Assembly of the State of Louisiana* (Baton Rouge: Leon Jastremski, 1884), 102; *Laws of the State of Mississippi* (Jackson:

Printed for the State, 1839), 110; *Laws of the State of Mississippi* (Jackson: Fall and Marshall,1850), 105–6; *Laws of Missouri* (Jefferson City: Tribune Printing Co., 1887), 169; *Laws and Resolutions Passed by the General Assembly of the State of North Carolina* (Raleigh: N. Paige, 1868), 34; *Revisal of 1908 of North Carolina*, vol. 2 (Charleston, S.C.: Walker, Evans, and Cogswell Co., 1908), 3, 283–84; *Statutes of Oklahoma, 1890* (Guthrie: State Capital Printing Co., 1891), 1010; *Acts and Joint Resolutions of the General Assembly of the State of South Carolina* (Columbia: Calvo and Patton, 1878), 381; *Revised Statutes of South Carolina, vol. 2* (Columbia: Charles A. Calvo, 1894), 447; *Acts of the State of Tennessee* (Nashville: Marshall and Bruce, 1889), 85; *Penal Code of State of Texas* (Galveston: A. H. Belo and Co., 1879), 98–99; *Acts of Virginia* (1855–6), 36–37; *Acts of Virginia* (1878–9), 380.

58. Florida is the exception, and even Florida was only a few years earlier, banning public executions in 1868. *Acts and Resolutions Adopted by the Legislature of Florida* (Tallahassee: Tallahassee Sentinel, 1868), 110–11.

59. Mississippi (1916) and Texas (1923) were the last two southern states to strictly prohibit public executions. Georgia passed legislation earlier (1893), but that still makes it one of the last to do so. *Laws of the State of Mississippi, 1916* (Memphis: E. H. Clare and Bro., 1916), 330; *General Laws of the State of Texas* (Austin: A. C. Baldwin and Sons, 1923), 111; *Acts of Georgia* (1893), 41–42.

60. This is another side of lynching that requires more systematic study. Some lynch mobs were small groups of men operating in secret while other lynchings were well publicized, led by prominent members of the community, and included photographers, picnics, and other horrifying adjuncts. It is unclear which predominated and whether there were regional and/or chronological differences in the nature of lynching. The best study to date on this issue is Brundage, *Lynching in the New South*. He finds that something over 60 percent of the lynchings in these two states were perpetrated by groups of fewer than fifty men acting more or less in secret and/or without ritual. Between 30 percent and 40 percent of lynchings were "mass" lynchings, often accompanied by torture, performed within the theater of the gallows on display at public executions.

61. For more on how lynchings could also be public spectacles, see Grace Elizabeth Hale, *Making Whiteness: The Culture of Segregation in the South, 1890–1940* (New York: Pantheon, 1998), 199–239.

62. Georgia abolished public executions in 1893; Sam Hose was lynched in 1899. On the lynching of Sam Hose, see Leon F. Litwack, *Trouble in Mind: Black Southerners in the Age of Jim Crow* (New York: Vintage, 1998), 280–83, and Hale, *Making Whiteness*, 209–15.

63. Philip J. Schwarz, *Slave Laws in Virginia* (Athens: University of Georgia Press, 1996), 69. Schwarz has found seventeen sentences against slaves in which either the head or the quartered body was to be displayed after hanging. I have found no evidence of whites treated in like manner. See also Paul W.

Keve, *The History of Corrections in Virginia* (Charlottesville: University Press of Virginia, 1986), 12–13.

64. Virginia banned the whipping post, reintroduced it in the 1870s, and finally prohibited the practice under the reforming Readjuster administration in 1882. Discussions among whites of its benefits in restraining misbehavior by blacks and proposals to again reintroduce it persisted for another generation. *New York Times*, 1 May 1882; William A. Blair, "Justice versus Law and Order: Battles over the Reconstruction of Virginia's Minor Judiciary, 1865–1870," *Virginia Magazine of History and Biography* 103 (1995): 170–71.

65. *Richmond Dispatch*, 1 April and 31 May 1869. Tyler's execution was as theatrical as any that had come before. He rode in a wagon from the Richmond city jail to the gallows erected on a hill outside of town. A crowd numbering more than three thousand spoke with him along the way, and when the procession arrived, Tyler gave a speech as if he were a minister himself, followed by hymns and another minister's words.

66. A similar spectacle can be found in the 1852 execution of John Williams, a slave accused of poisoning a white family. Many theatrical elements were here, but Williams was disappointed in his attempts to address the crowd. The authorities, believing such a speech could incite disorder, allowed him only to announce his continuing claim of innocence. *Richmond Dispatch*, 23 October 1852, and *Particulars of the Dreadful Tragedy in Richmond* (Richmond: John D. Hammersley, 1852), 39–40.

67. Arkansas and Kentucky both reintroduced public execution for rape. See *Acts and Resolutions of the General Assembly of the State of Arkansas* (1901), 105 (they eliminated public execution for this crime again in 1905), and *Acts of the General Assembly of the Commonwealth of Kentucky* (Frankfort: State Journal Co., 1920), 693–94.

68. Statistics on capital punishment become dependable once a state centralized its procedures, which means 1908 for Virginia. Data are from William J. Bowers, *Legal Homicide: Death as Punishment in America, 1864–1982* (Boston: Northeastern University Press, 1984), 514–16. For comparison, the proportion of executed convicts who were black in North Carolina in this era was almost identical to that in Virginia. Kentucky's proportion (taken from Wright, *Racial Violence in Kentucky*, 325–28) was lower—60 percent—for the period 1872 to 1920, but Kentucky's black population was much smaller (14 percent in 1890) than either Virginia's (38 percent) or North Carolina's (35 percent).

Others have made another argument linking capital punishment with lynching: that lynching declines after the 1890s in part due to the more effective "legal lynchings" of the ordinary operation of southern jurisprudence. See, for example, Wright, *Racial Violence in Kentucky*, and James W. Clarke, "Without Fear or Shame: Lynching, Capital Punishment, and the Subculture of Violence in the American South," *British Journal of Political Science* 28 (1998): 285. See also Neil McMillen, *Dark Journey: Black Mississippians in the Age of Jim Crow*

(Urbana: University of Illinois Press, 1989), 197–253, for a close evaluation of both legal and extralegal treatment of blacks in Mississippi.

69. "The Negro Knows No Law," *Southern Opinion*, 14 March 1868.

70. *Richmond Dispatch*, 11, 18, and 25 July and 1 August 1896. Marable was executed on 3 July. His widow had been promised the return of his body for burial, even though Virginia law allowed the bodies of prisoners to be used for medical education. At first, the corpse was taken to Richmond to the medical college. Once again, Mitchell found a crusade to rally the community around, and he was arrested briefly for interfering with the business of the medical college. Ultimately, Mitchell was not penalized, and Marable's body was released to his widow. This was yet another small victory for Mitchell.

71. *Richmond Planet*, 13 July and 24 and 31 August 1912. The stories ran through the spring and summer of 1912. Darryn Eroll Moten, "'A Gruesome Warning to Black Girls': The August 16, 1912, Execution of Virginia Christian" (Ph.D. diss., University of Iowa, 1997).

72. For example, the executions of John and Jane Williams in 1852: *Richmond Dispatch*, 11 September and 23 October 1852; Aleck Gardner in 1870: *Richmond Dispatch*, 12 February 1870; Doc Bacon in 1903: *Richmond Times-Dispatch*, 4 October 1903.

73. Virginia Christian: *Richmond Planet*, 13 July and 24 August 1912; Doc Bacon: 3 October 1903.

74. *Richmond Planet*, 17 October 1896.

75. Ibid., 9 June 1894.

76. See Peter Rachleff, *Black Labor in the South: Richmond Virginia, 1865–1890* (Philadelphia: Temple University Press, 1984), and Michael Trotti, "Charting Richmond's Fun: The Changing Shape of Commercial Amusements in Richmond, Virginia, 1880–1920" (M.A. thesis, University of North Carolina, 1993).

77. *Richmond Planet*, 7 November 1914.

EPILOGUE

1. *Richmond Dispatch*, 16 January 1887.

2. *Richmond Enquirer*, 21 August 1827. Forty years later, a famous Philadelphia murderer, Anton Probst, was likewise the subject of an experiment to determine the effects of electricity on muscular action. In addition, a powerful lens was focused on his eyes "to verify the truth of the theory that upon the retina of the eye of one who dies a sudden death is imprinted, as by photography, the image of the last object upon which it rests." See William B. Mann, *Trial of Anton Probst* (Philadelphia: T. B. Peterson and Brothers, 1866), 120.

3. *Richmond Dispatch*, 1 July 1882.

4. Patricia Cline Cohen, *The Murder of Helen Jewett: The Life and Death of a Prostitute in Nineteenth-Century New York* (New York: Alfred A. Knopf, 1998), 250.

5. *Richmond Dispatch*, 27 December 1883. Even with this "great care," hundreds each day in the early 1880s reportedly asked to see the skeleton or the belongings of Guiteau and were disappointed.

6. *Richmond Daily Times*, 15 January 1887. The autopsy of Guiteau prompted reports throughout the national press as well, in part due to a dispute among the doctors who performed it. See the *Richmond Dispatch*, 7 July 1882.

7. *Richmond Dispatch*, 12 February 1887. "Souvenirs still in demand" is the subtitle of this article printed a month after the execution.

8. The Beattie plot includes Henry's mother, who died in 1901—some say from heartache over the deaths of her twin daughters in 1898 and 1900—as well as his father, grandfather, and others. The Owens and Beattie families were close before the murder, and Louise was buried in the Beattie plot before her husband was arrested.

9. *Richmond Times-Dispatch*, 27 November 1911. As for the five-month-old Beattie baby orphaned by his mother's murder and father's execution, he was adopted by his maternal grandparents, renamed for his mother—L. Wellford Owen—and grew up in Pennsylvania. He married and settled in upstate New York and at his death in 1996 he had two children, five grandchildren, and one great-grandchild. U.S. Census, Fourteenth Census, 1920, manuscript, Enumeration District 127, Dauphin County, Pennsylvania; *Albany Times-Union*, 4 June 1996.

10. Quoted in the *Richmond Times-Dispatch*, 18 November 1911.

11. See, for instance, the *Richmond Times-Dispatch*, 9 September 1911.

12. *Richmond Planet*, 2 December 1911.

13. *Religious Herald*, 30 November 1911.

14. Charles Montriou Wallace Diary, 15 Jan. 1887, Manuscripts Division, Perkins Library, Duke University, Durham, N.C. Ellipses represent a tear in the diary's page; it is unclear whether any words are missing.

15. Henry Robinson Pollard, *Memoirs and Sketches of the Life of Henry Robinson Pollard* (Richmond: Lewis Printing Co., 1923), 191–98; Herbert T. Ezekiel, *Recollections of a Virginia Newspaperman* (Richmond: H. T. Ezekiel, 1920), 40–46.

16. William E. Hatcher, *Along the Trail of Friendly Years* (New York: Fleming Revell Co., 1910); Eldridge B. Hatcher, *William E. Hatcher: A Biography* (Richmond: W. C. Hill Printing Co., 1915), 240–52.

17. An interesting exception to this rule is the obituary of Henry Beattie's father, who died in 1917. The notice referred to his family, his wife, and his businesses, framing him as an important figure in the history of Manchester and Richmond, but did not mention the murder, probably in compassionate deference to his standing and importance to the area. See *Richmond Times-Dispatch*, 18 July 1917.

The most notable and deft of the efforts of local historians is Harry Kollatz Jr., "The Great Beattie Murder Case," *Richmond Magazine*, April 1998,

38–45. See also, G. Watson James Jr., "The Jeter Phillips Case or the Drinker's Farm Tragedy," *Virginia Trooper*, March–July 1954; G. Watson James Jr., "Excerpts from 'Cluverius, My Life, Trial, and Conviction,'" *Virginia Trooper*, September–October 1952; Ben Pope, "The Beattie Case," *Virginia Record*, June–August 1955; and Ben Pope, "The Cluverius Case," *Virginia Record*, January 1956.

18. Many histories of Richmond include something on the Cluverius case; several mention Phillips and Beattie as well. See especially W. Asbury Christian, *Richmond: Her Past and Present* (Richmond: L. H. Jenkins, 1912), 295–98 (Phillips), 391–94 (Cluverius), and 532–35 (Beattie); and Virginius Dabney, *Richmond: The Story of a City*, rev. ed. (Charlottesville: University of Virginia Press, 1990), 238 (Cluverius). Jay Robert Nash, ed., *Encyclopedia of World Crime* (Wilmette, Ill.: CrimeBooks, 1990), is particularly uneven, with several errors, though it does mention Beattie (1:292–93), Cluverius (1:734–35), and Phillips (3:2,459). The Cluverius transcript was also edited to join a collection of state trials from throughout the nation: John D. Lawson, *American State Trials*, vol. 17 (St. Louis: Thomas Law Book Co., 1936), 379–506.

19. Wallace Diary, 14 Jan. 1887.

INDEX